WEIRD CANADA

BATHROOM READERS' INSTITUTE
ASHLAND, OREGON

WEIRD CANADA

By the
Bathroom Readers'
Institute

OUR "REGULAR" READERS RAVE!

"I love Uncle John's books so much I quoted one of them in my Master's thesis."

—Meg B.

"The best thing to pleasantly pass the time doing what nature intended? Read *Uncle John's*, of course!"

—Brian H.

"*Uncle John's Bathroom Reader* keeps me on the edge of my seat!"

—Jeremy C.

"I've been a fan of *Uncle John's Bathroom Readers* for years. I now have a whole bookshelf in my bathroom."

—Bandia A.

"It's better than chocolate. It's better than pudding. I daresay it's better than chocolate pudding."

—Josh W.

"I've been a member in 'good sitting' since the beginning. It's been my Christmas present to myself for the past 25 years!"

—Matt C.

"Everything I know I learned from Uncle John."

—Michelle W.

"Reading *Uncle John's Bathroom Reader* sure beats reading the back of the hairspray can or counting the tiles on the floor!"

—Jackie P.

UNCLE JOHN'S WEIRD CANADA
BATHROOM READER®

Produced by Print Matters, Inc. (www.printmattersinc.com) and the Bathroom Readers' Institute

For information, write:
The Bathroom Readers' Institute,
P.O. Box 1117,
Ashland, OR 97520
www.bathroomreader.com
Cover design by XXXX
ISBN-13: 978-1-60710-891-7 / ISBN-10: 1-60710-891-7

Library of Congress Cataloging-in-Publication Data

Uncle John's bathroom reader weird Canada.
pages cm
ISBN 978-1-60710-891-7 (pbk.)
1. Canada—Humor. 2. Curiosities and wonders—Canada.
PN6231.C19U53 2013
818'.607—dc23

2013014047

Printed in the United States of America
First Printing
1 2 3 4 5 6 7 8 17 16 15 14 13

THANK YOU!

The Bathroom Readers' Institute sincerely thanks the people whose advice and assistance made this book possible.

Gordon Javna
Brian Boone
Jay Newman
Don Rauf
Thom Little
Trina Janssen
Andy Taray
Christy Taray
Jack Feerick
Megan Todd
Jon Cummings
Will Harris
Brandon Hartley
Eleanor Pierce
Dave Lifton
Michael Conover
Kim Griswell
Michael Centore
Michael Troy
Ken Mondschein

Kelly Tomkies
Ann Morrill
Michael Cramer
Celia Seupel
Carol Ersepke
Devanand Madhukar
Jack Mingo
Melinda Allman
Aaron Guzman
Blake Mitchum
"Baron von" Rothschild
David "Archie" Andrews
Raincoast Books
Pete MacDougall
Sandy Cooper
Paddy Laidley
Jamie Broadhurst
Terry Fox
Robin Sparkles
Thomas Crapper

CONTENTS

Because the BRI understands your reading needs, we've divided the contents by subject.

MOUTHING OFF

SHOOTS AND SCORES

ACT NATURALLY

IN THE NEWS

STAGE & SCREEN

SPOOKY STUFF

LAW & ORDER

IT'S JUST POLITICS

CREATURE FEATURES

PEOPLE ARE STRANGE

HISTORICALLY ODD

GE-ODD-GRAPHY

COME TO CANADA

CANADIANA

WATCH YOUR LANGUAGE

IT'S A BLUNDERFUL LIFE

THAT'S DEATH!

FORGOTTEN HISTORY

POT-POURRI

CANUCK, CANUCK, WHO'S THERE?

Uncle John loves Canada! We always make sure to include something about the Great White North in every single one of our books.

But our Canadian readers kept asking for more— "we want an *entire* book, a full, gigantic, Nunavut-sized *Uncle John's Bathroom Reader* all about Canada!" they begged. "Belive us, plenty of great stuff goes down up here." Our readers are a discerning bunch, conneisseurs of fun facts, terrific trivia, and unbelievable esoterica. We couldn't do just *any* book about Canada, and fill it with hockey statistics, Mountie jokes, and photos of Anne Murray. Uncle John just couldn't do that. And it's because Uncle John knows a secret about Canada.

Canada is a *really weird* place.

Behold: *Uncle John's Bathroom Reader Weird Canada*. A whopping 400 pages chockful of every odd, nutty, crazy, preposterous, silly—and even scary—person, place, or thing, that's ever been associated with Canada. Ghosts in the Yukon? It's here. The refusal to adhere to the standards of time in Newfoundland? It's in *Uncle John's Weird Canada*. And so are stories about…

• Creatures, real and *possibly* real, like Sasquatch, the Ogopogo monster, and the Grolar Bear

• The world's smallest library, and the world's largest pierogi

• The only-in-Canada fad of "bed-pushing"

• The man with a window in his stomach

• A ghost-hunting agency in Vancouver that finds the things you can't see, and a bookstore in Toronto full of the books that *they* don't want you to read

• How the government's push for "Canadian content" led to the worst TV show in world history, and the funniest duo in sketch comedy history

• Weird stuff you never knew about Canadian mainstays, such as Wayne Gretzky, Bryan Adams, Neil Young, Guy Lafleuer, Joni Mitchell, and the Barenaked Ladies

• Funny thoughts on Canada—and what it means to be Canadian —from singular Canadian minds like Stephen Leacock, Will Ferguson, and Douglas Coupland

• More alien encounters, haunted hotels, and unexplained noises than you can shake a (hockey) stick at

And of course, you'll find the usual dose of weird news, strange people, odd animals, goofy places, and refreshing tales of unlikely success and spectacular failure that you'll always find in one of those regular old states-centric *Bathroom Readers*.

In short, there's something for everyone in Canada, from Canada, or who just plain loves Canada, whether you're a Slurpee-slurper in Winnipeg or stand-up Sasquatch from Saskatchewan. Welcome to *Weird Canada*—but we don't have to tell you that—you probably already live there.

Enjoy reading...and chimo!
(And a hearty hello from Chimo–that's him down there.)

–Uncle John and the BRI staff

CLAM EYES ALL AROUND!

Canadians' preternatural prowess with porter extends to mixed libations–that is, the pioneering of the beer cocktail.

CAMEL PISS

Ingredients: Canadian beer + tequila, dark rum, ouzo, anise liqueur, and Mountain Dew.

Details: We assume this gets its name from its yellow color and strength. Some say real camel piss can cure baldness. Can this drink do the same?

CANADIAN CAR BOMB

Ingredients: Canadian beer + Canadian whisky.

Details: Made with all Canadian ingredients, this potent elixir will tide you over during the ride to the next party.

CLAM EYE

Ingredients: Canadian beer, Clamato, celery salt, Tabasco and Worcestershire sauces.

Details: With a Clamato as a featured ingredient, this cocktail brings to mind the Caesar—Canada's version of the Bloody Mary but with clamato juice.

FLAMING ENGINEER

Ingredients: Canadian beer, Amaretto Canadian whisky, and orange juice.

Details: For relief from their rigorous academic load, the engineering students at Ryerson University in Toronto designed this special drink.

PORCH CLIMBER

Ingredients: Canadian beer, frozen pink lemonade, vodka, and Canadian whisky.

Details: This drink also goes by the name porch crawler. This robust mix will have you either crawling or climbing back onto the porch. Some say it should be prepared in a large cooler. The pink lemonade version noted here has also been dubbed the "Pink Panty Dropper."

A version made with Sprite is called "Skip and Go Naked."

Hudson's Bay Company's charter required visiting royalty to receive two elk heads and two beaver pelts.

WEIRD CANADIANS

Where does that "quirky Canuck" stereotype come from, anyway? Might have something to do with all these quirky Canucks.

"You look at the floor and see the floor. I look at the floor and see molecules."

–Dan Aykroyd

"I decorated my house like a medieval gothic castle. Chandeliers and red velvet curtains. My bedroom is pink and black, my bathroom is totally Hello Kitty. I have a massive pink couch and a big antique gold cross."

–Avril Lavigne

"Babies have big heads and big eyes, and tiny little bodies with tiny little arms and legs. So did the aliens at Roswell! I rest my case."

–William Shatner

"At one point, I was perceived as only being angry, but now I'm being perceived as angry, peaceful, and spiritual."

–Alanis Morissette

"What would happen if you melted? You know, you never really hear this talked about much, but spontaneous combustion? It exists!"

–Keanu Reeves

"The rockets and the satellites, the spaceships that we're creating now, we're pollinating the universe."

–Neil Young

"My child was not only carried by me, but by the universe."

–Celine Dion

"I have my cards read every time I pass a tarot-reader booth. I'd be so embarrassed to have one of those 900 numbers appear on my phone bill, because I don't know how I would explain it to my manager. It would almost be like saying, 'Okay, I'm white trash.'"

–Jennifer Tilly

"To me, the sky is an infinite movie. I never get tired of looking at what's happening up there."

–k. d. lang

"Everything that happens to me is very cosmic."

–Tommy Chong

"I'm king of the world!"

–James Cameron

A Dairy Queen in Toronto made the largest ice cream cake— 10.13 tons (22,333 pounds).

HEADS OFF!

If you lose your way here, you just may lose your head.

VALLEY OF THE (HEADLESS) DOLLS

Accessible only by air, water, or overland travel from the town of Tungsten in the Northwest Territories, the Nahanni Valley spreads out over 250 acres of unspoiled nature in far north above the 60th parallel. Because hot springs and sulfur geysers keep the valley warmer than the surrounding areas by about 30°, a mist shrouds the valley year-round.

STRUCK IT RICH? NOPE

The region of the South Nahanni River specifically carries the eerie nickname of the Valley of the Headless Men, which started at the turn of the 20th century in 1908. In 1906, two brothers—Willie and Frank McLeod—set off through the valley to make their fortune in Klondike, where the gold rush was in full swing. For two years, nothing was heard about the brothers. Those who knew the duo thought they must have struck it rich finding gold. But in 1908, an expedition through the valley discovered two bodies that turned out to be the McLeod brothers—and they were both headless.

Sure, two decapitated fortune seekers is creepy, but it's not enough to give an entire region such a macabre nickname. In 1917, a Swiss prospector named Martin Jorgenson was found lying dead next to his burned cabin. Again, the head was missing. Much later in 1945, a miner from Ontario was found in the valley, dead in his sleeping bag. Once again, his head was nowhere to be found.

WHO'S TAKING ALL THOSE HEADS?

So with four tales of unexplained decapitation and 44 reported disappearances, the Nahanni also gained the name "Valley of the Headless Men."

There have been many theories on the decapitations and disappearances. Some blame hostile natives; others say it could be the work of the Waheela—a wolf-like cryptid reported to live in the Nahanni Valley or possibly prehistoric bear-dogs that have somehow survived in the wilderness. Some even suspect a murderous . . .Sasquatch.

St. Paul, Alberta, has an official UFO landing welcome pad.

EERIE EARFULS

Canada is a noisy place, from the mournful call of the loon to the chilling call of the vampire wolf-beasts.

THE HOWL OF THE ROUGAROU?

In French culture, a *rougarou* or *loup garou* is a human with the head of a dog or wolf— or basically, a werewolf or *lycanthrope*. When French settlers came to Quebec in the 17th century, they brought along the myth of the loup garou.

There are various ways that one might become this monstrous wolf beast. One story says that if you merely talk to a loup garou, you will be cursed to become the creature yourself for a period of 101 days.

Others say that you have to be bitten by a rougarou to become one. Another legend holds that the rougarou are men who have been cursed for not going to church or for shirking other responsibilities. Going to confession can sometimes cure them. One story says a loup garou is a man possessed by the devil and that pricking his skin and drawing blood can return his humanity. Some First Nations tribes have their own legends of the loup garou. The Ojibwa have the rugaru, for instance. The French certainly spread the myth. Windigo (a human who is enchanted and compelled to eat humans) is a local version of the werewolf.

CALL OF THE WILD

Bizarre and mysterious sounds have been spooking many across the country. In a forest in Conklin, Alberta, in 2012, an eerie roar was captured on videotape. Just a few days later, a similar roar was recorded in The Pas, Manitoba, more than 1,000 kilometers (620 miles) away.

The loud noise seems to come from the sky—it swells and recedes. Dogs become scared and bark incessantly. Oddly enough, similar sounds were recorded in Denmark and Sweden at the same time. Search on YouTube to find recordings of the unearthly din. Could it be the unworldly whir of an alien spacecraft? Take a listen for yourself and decide.

The Mi'kmaq people of the Maritimes believe Glooscap was the first human...

THE COOLEST HOTEL

Come to the Hotel Glace in Quebec...and just chill.

SANGFROID SAVOIR FAIRE

There are several ice hotels in the frozen climes of Scandinavia, but Hotel de Glace is the only one in North America. Not only is Hotel de Glace constructed entirely out of ice, but it is also erected annually from scratch. Every year, a new design is chosen, so the hotel is never quite the same.

Just 10 minutes outside of Quebec City, the frozen fortress consists of about 15,000 tons of snow and 500,000 tons of ice. About 60 workers take a month to ready the hotel for its January opening. Metal frames are used to mold and shape the ice and snow, and when the elements are securely frozen in place the supports are removed. Architects adhere to traditional building safety standards.

WARM ON THE INSIDE

The hotel has about 85 bedrooms. (The bathrooms are heated and in a separate structure called the Celsius Pavillion.) The four-foot-thick ice walls offer some insulation, and the bed frames are entirely made of ice. Visitors sleep warmly in deer pelts and Arctic sleeping bags on top of a real mattress that protects from the chilly, ice-block bed frame. Still, the rooms are a bit brisk with temperatures below freezing—they average between −5 and −2.7°C, or 23 and 27°F.

While a few rooms have fireplaces, outdoor spas and saunas help warm guests in time for bed. The hotel's décor goes above and beyond your average igloo's—archways, columns, sculpture, and a dazzling ice chandelier all decorate the hotel. Colored lights reflect off the snow and produce an otherworldly atmosphere.

There's a bar as well—made all of ice, of course, including the seats, which are covered in caribou skins so you don't freeze your tush. The cocktail glasses themselves are also made of ice, and cold cuts are served on ice plates. All the cold may give you an irresistible urge to be close to another human. If you want to get married, an ice chapel for Nordic-style weddings is available. There's also a nightclub and movie theater in the hotel. For a different type of fun, guests zip down the grand 18-meter (60-foot) ice slide. But by the end of May, the entire hotel has usually melted into the St. Lawrence River.

...He was created out of a bolt of lightening in the sand.

ICE WORMS

In a world of extremes, the small survive.

LIVING UP TO THEIR NAME

Ice worms, very small worms that live on glaciers on the western slopes of the Canadian Rocky Mountains, live up to their name in more ways than one. First, of course is their habitat of choice: ice. They thrive in the ice, using pollen and algae they find there as food. But like ice, they actually melt and die when the temperatures reach about 40 degrees Fahrenheit (No they don't say "What a world, what a world," but they're probably thinking it.)

Fortunately for ice worms, they live in places where they can burrow deep into glaciers to stay cold when the sun is out, and they resurface to eat when the sun goes down, keeping them from the melting point.

COLORFUL AS WELL AS PLENTIFUL

Most ice worms appear dark brown or black in color, but some people have seen them in other colors as well, like red, blue, or white. These colors make them look like very tiny (they're only about 2 centimeters or about three-quarters of an inch long) pieces of thread on the ice. As long as they're able to stay cold, they can live up to ten years, which may be why they can multiply profusely. In fact, they outnumber humans by an astounding amount. According to scientists performing work for the North Cascades Glacier Climate Project (NCGCP) on the Suiattle Glacier of Glacier Peak, there was an estimated mean density of ice worms on the glacier at 2600 ice worms per square meter. Since the overall glacial area of the peak is 2.7 square kilometers, that means there were over 7 billion ice worms on Suiattle Glacier, more than Earth's entire human population.

THEY MAY BE SMALL, BUT THEY'RE STILL INSPIRING

The English poet, Robert William Service, discovered the ice worms while he was living in Canada and wrote a couple of poems mentioning them. He is credited for making them famous, but they gained more widespread exposure when the writers of the TV show *The X-Files* created an episode of the series that included them. In it, their own version of parasitic ice worms burrowed deep inside a human host's brain and made that person want to kill.

UNCOMMON FIXTURES WON'T HOLD FAST

These convoluted Canadian carts are fun but a bit draining.

THE WORLD'S CLEANEST SPORT

During the last weekend in July in Nanaimo, British Columbia, seafaring folk slap outboard motors on bathtubs and race a 58-kilometer (36-mile) course across the harbor. These aren't your average bathtubs, however. They're tricked out and streamlined to glide across the waters at speeds of around 50 kilometers (30 miles) per hour.

ULTIMATE BODY SHOP

Contestants construct their competitive racing tubs by taking old bathtubs and building hulls around them of aluminum, fiberglass, and other materials. Many tubbers make a vessel out of fiberglass by using a bathtub as a model mold. Tubbers can win for speed, but prizes also go to best overall children's theme, best theme, and zaniest decorations. The race began during the city of Nanaimo's centennial in 1967, when 200 tubbers inaugurated the event. Because of the race, Nanaimo is sometimes known as the hub, pub, and tub city.

HIGH-SPEED TOILET

Here's a story Uncle John can really get behind. Canadian stuntwoman Jolene Van Vugt, 31, holds the record for riding the fastest motorized toilet in the world. In May of 2012, Van Vugt hopped a plane to Sydney, Australia, and climbed aboard a contraption that was essentially a go-kart with a porcelain toilet instead of a seat. "I came out here to jump straight on the toilet," she told reporters. This may have been one of the longest trips to the toilet, but it was well worth it for Van Vugt.

The Canadian pushed her toilet on wheels to a speed of 72.4 kilometers (45 miles) per hour. "I never thought I'd be the fastest toilet rider in the world," she said.

...He administered LSD in experiments at the Weyburn Mental Hospital in the late 1950s.

LOONY LAWS

Believe it or not, these laws are real.

• You may not drag a dead horse down Yonge Street (one of the more infamous streets in Toronto) on a Sunday.

• You may not eat ice cream on Bank Street (the major shopping street in downtown Ottawa) on a Sunday.

• It is illegal to kill a sasquatch in British Columbia.

• A law in Alberta says that it is illegal to use dice to shoot craps. (How else can you play?)

• You may not fill a bathtub with more than 8.9 centimeters (3.5 inches) of water in Etobicoke (a suburb of Toronto). Perhaps this one was passed to help prevent babies from drowning.

• You will be breaking the law in Nova Scotia if you water the lawn while it is raining.

• In Montreal, you are not allowed to wash your car in the street or park your car in a way that blocks your own driveway.

• In Kanata, Ontario, it was illegal to have a clothesline in your backyard. Clothesline bans were put in place in Kanata and other towns because some developers and homeowners thought clotheslines and the poles that support them destroyed the views. The bans were lifted in 2008 to help with energy conservation.

• In Fort Qu'Appelle Quebec, a teen who walks downtown Main Street with his shoes untied could be arrested. Shoes must be tied!

• Throughout Canada, you would be breaking a law if you removed your bandages in public. Was this law passed so people wouldn't be grossed out?

• Officially, you are not allowed to pay in pennies for an item that costs 50 cents.

• You better keep your lawn mowed in London, Ontario. A city by-law states that if the grass in your front yard is longer than 3.8 centimeters (1.5 inches) you can be fined $200.

• An old law from British Columbia states that a bankrupt drunk who gets thrown into jail must be given a bottle of beer by the jailer if he demands it.

Joann Matvichuk began International Yarn Bombing Day in Alberta, Canada, in June, 2011...

JOIN THE PARTY

Conservative? Liberal? Bloc Québécois? Boring!

RHINOCEROS PARTY

One of Canada's most absurd and long-lasting political institutions was the Rhinoceros Party. Founded in 1963 by Quebec separatist Dr. Jacques Ferron, the Rhinoceros Party brought a sense of humor to the Canadian political scene. Among its many proposals have been a repeal of the law of gravity, paving over all of Manitoba, putting the national debt on a Visa card, and moving Toronto and Montreal closer together. The party has said that the rhino is an appropriate symbol for a politician because it is generally slow moving and dim-witted but can move as fast as hell when it senses danger.

Party member Bryan Gold once described his party's platform as "two feet high and made of wood." In a broadcasted appearance, Rhino candidate Michel Rivard said, "I have but two things to say to you: 'Celery' and 'sidewalk.' Thank you, good night."

The Rhinos officially disbanded in 1993. Along the way they offered up as many as 120 candidates, and they managed to finish as high as second in a number of parliamentary elections.

GODZILLA AND SATAN

In 2001, Brian "Godzilla" Salmi revived the party, earning his nickname by wearing a Godzilla suit while campaigning. In 2007, the Rhinos and Godzilla were back in action, announcing a $50 million lawsuit against Canada that contested an election reform law that had stripped the party of official status in 1993. Godzilla, now using the name Dark Clown Lord Satan, filed the suit as Satan v. Her Majesty the Queen. There's a lack of available information regarding the case, but it seems that Salmi did not run for or get elected to office. In the spirit of the Rhino Party, however, we leave you with these inspiring campaign pledges:

- Provide higher education by building taller schools.
- Abolish the environment (because it's too big and too hard to clean).
- Ban Canadian winters.
- Turn Montreal's Ste-Catherine Street into the world's longest bowling alley.
- Mandate three official languages: English, French, and illiteracy.

THE WILD, WILD WIND

A wind that has its own name...should also be a car model.

OFF THE CHINOOK

While winters can be frigid along the eastern Rocky Mountains, warm winds called Chinooks can send temperatures climbing suddenly and dramatically. The Chinooks start as moist weather patterns, originating off the Pacific coast. The breezes cool as they climb the western slopes, but they rapidly heat up as they sink down the eastern mountainsides, sometimes hiking temperatures by 10 degrees in a matter of minutes. Humidity drops as well when the winds barrel in, sometimes by more than 40 percent. The warming winds can make a foot of snow vanish in an hour. In January 1966, the temperature rose 21° in four minutes when a Chinook blew into Pincher Creek, Alberta. On January 11, 1983, temperatures in Calgary shot up 30° Celsius in four hours, from −17° to 13°.

In southwestern Alberta, Chinooks can clock in at 120 kilometers (75 miles) per hour. On November 19, 1962, Lethbridge was blasted by 171 kilometer (106 mile) per hour gusts. While the winds may bring welcome relief from the cold, many say they also bring migraine headaches. The number of migraines often spikes when the Chinooks blow through; locals call them "Chinook headaches."

FULL OF HOT AIR

Mother Nature can take a beating, too. Trees can dehydrate from the warmth. The thermal forces kill foliage and cause wood to split. The white birch cannot live through rapid heat shifts. Evergreen needles can dry out and turn red, causing a phenomenon called red belt. Looking up into the mountain, people may spot a line of red evergreens—these are trees that have lost the life in their needles due to dehydration. The dehydration can trigger forest fires as well. With soil moisture disappearing, the soil can blow away, and melting snows can expose plants and animals before winter has ended. So the winds can have devastating effects on wildlife.

The strong positive charge that is often in the air of the Chinooks can even electrify wire fences. Cattle have been electrocuted from the sudden mysterious electrification. Sounds are also said to be carried great distances along the winds—such as trains that are miles away.

The greatest landside in North American history buried the small town of Frank, Alberta in 1903.

CLOSE ENCOUNTERS MAKE BAD THERAPY

Do you have to be mad to treat a psychopath?

NO ROUND TRIP

In 1968 Elliott Barker, a psychiatrist at the Oak Ridge Hospital for the criminally insane in Penetanguishene, Ontario, thought that he could cure psychopaths. His solution: nude psychotherapy sessions, fueled with LSD, treatments lasting for 11-day stretches. The patients, all male, volunteered to be placed in a windowless, 2.4-by three-meter room called the Total Encounter Capsule. The soundproof room had a sink and toilet and a one-way mirror in the ceiling. The patients were fed through straws in the door. There were no beds—patients had to sleep on a small rug over a foam mat. There was no privacy of any kind. Through being nude, the patients were supposed to be more inclined to reveal their inner selves—the LSD was supposed to ease their communication.

THERAPY CAN BE VERY REVEALING

Dr. Barker procured batches of LSD, as well as the full approval of the Canadian government. With rooms lit 24 hours a day and no clocks or calendars, patients were unable to tell day from night. Confusion, disorientation, and serious confrontations between the men ensued. The psychopaths were encouraged to go to their rawest emotional places by screaming and clawing at the walls and confessing fantasies of forbidden sexual longings. Barker thought these patients were burying their insanity deep beneath a facade of normality. He thought his technique would somehow summon the madness so patients could be "born again" as empathetic human beings.

At first, the results seemed promising. The tough, young prisoners were slowly transforming and seeming to care for each other. Psychopathic murderers were now gentle. Many were declared cured and freed. On average, 60 percent of criminal psychopaths released into the outside world will become repeat offenders. With the patients under Dr. Barker's care, that rate hit 80 percent. The capsule treatment made patients worse.

The Enchanted Forest in Revelestoke, B.C., features over 350 fairy folk figurines.

BEATLE INFESTATION AT THE FAIRMONT

John Lennon and Yoko Ono held a historic bed-in at Montreal's Fairmont Hotel . . . and recorded a lasting anthem of peace there, too.

PAJAMA PARTY

Between March 25 and 31 of 1969, John Lennon and his wife Yoko Ono slipped on their pajamas and held a seven-day "bed-in" for peace at the Amsterdam Hilton. They had just gotten married on March 20, and they knew the world media would give them lots of attention. With America fighting the Vietnam War, the couple staged the event to promote peace. They invited the press in every day from 9 am to 9 pm.

The couple wanted to hold a second bed-in in New York, but John wasn't allowed in the United States at the time because of a conviction for marijuana possession the previous year. They wound up holding the next one in the stately Fairmont Queen Elizabeth Hotel in Montreal for 10 days starting on May 26. They took corner suite rooms 1738, 1740, and 1742.

ALL ACCESS PASS

They made themselves completely available to anyone who wanted to come into their bedroom and ask them questions. They gave a series of interviews, and the couple invited celebrities and other guests to join them including comedian/advocate Dick Gregory, Tommy Smothers, Quebec separatist Jacques Larue-Langlois, Timothy Leary, Toronto Rabbi Abraham Feinberg, musician Petula Clark, members of the Canadian Radha Krishna Temple, and American cartoonist Al Capp.

On June 1, in the hotel affectionately called the Queen E, they recorded "Give Peace a Chance" in their suite's living room. The song was released in July 1969 and reached number 2 in the United Kingdom and number 14 on the Billboard Hot 100 in the United States. Today, the suite's walls display memorabilia composed of press articles, framed gold records, and pictures of John and Yoko.

LET THEM EAT LOBSTER

Lobsters: the original peasant food?

PLUS, THEY'RE HIGH IN B12!

Lobster fishing off the East Coast of Canada is a tradition dating back 150 years. And it's big business—the Lobster Institute at the University of Maine estimates that the lobster industry accounts for more than $4 billion of economic activity in the United States and Canada. In the summer of 2012, a lobster glut sent prices plummeting—hurting lobstermen in both Canada and the United States.

Lobster is often sold as a luxury item in restaurants today, and it's priced higher than most seafood. But it wasn't always that way. Go back 200 years and lobster was the food of poor people. It was considered the meal of indentured servants and lower society. British POWs during the Revolutionary War supposedly revolted over being fed too much lobster. For some, it was seen as the equivalent of eating rats. It was even used to make fertilizer.

ENJOY IT WHILE YOU CAN

Reportedly, folks in the Canadian Maritimes in the early 1800s would bury their lobster shells in the yard rather than suffer the shame of having someone see them toss the lobster carcasses in the trash. But by the mid-19th century, tastes were shifting, and gradually lobster became the elite thing to eat. Poor folks could no longer afford the tasty crustacean.

LOBSTERS IN THE FOUNTAIN OF YOUTH

Scientists believe that lobsters do not age in any traditional sense and could potentially live indefinitely because their organs do not degenerate. It has been suggested that, absent predators, lobsters could live on and on. It takes a lobster six to eight years to reach a market weight of approximately .45 kilograms (1 pound). To put a lobster to sleep, place it on to its back for a few minutes. Some prefer to do this before placing lobster in the boiling water used to cook it. One more fascinating fact: Lobsters have taste organs located in their feet.

...It's one of the world's oldest passenger sternwheelers and on display in Kaslo.

LET'S GO CURLING!

It's chess on ice.

• Only one company in Canada, Canada Curling Stone Co., is authorized to make curling stones. The granite comes from northern Wales.

• In 2001, pigeons caused insulation to fall onto the ice in the Brier—the Canadian men's national finals—causing a significant delay.

• Today, opposing teams take the ice at Biers to the sounds of bagpipes. However, for the first few championships, they entered to the sound of a harmonica.

• The term for a curling tournament, bonspiel, comes from the Gaelic "bonn," for "coin" or "corner," and "spéil," for skate—though the "spiel" may also be a borrowing from the German word for "play."

• Bonspiels are never played for cash but for (sometimes weird) prizes like cars or steaks.

• Famous curler Paul Gowsell was once known as "the rebel of curling." He earned his other nickname "Pizza Paul" when he once ordered a pizza to ice level for his team, which ate it during a match.

• In the 2000s, NBC planned a reality show called *Rockstar Curling* to find the United States's 2010 Vancouver Olympics curling team. Bruce Springsteen and Jon Bon Jovi were discussed as contestants.

• In 1912, the Mayflower Curling Club in Halifax was used as a temporary morgue for victims of the *Titanic* disaster.

• Winnipeg journalist "Cactus" Jack Wells turned down a lucrative play-by-play hockey announcing gig to keep working curling matches.

• The physical demands of sweeping can raise the curler's heart rate to 200 beats per minute.

• Using a "sweep ergometer," or instrumented curling brush, researchers have found that rapid sweeping works best with fast-moving stones by raising the temperature of the ice. For slow-moving stones, the curler can apply more downward pressure and still cover the same spot twice.

WAR PIGS

In 1859, the U.S. and Canada went hog wild and nearly went to war...over a pig.

THE OINK HEARD ROUND THE WORLD

San Juan Island is now part of Washington State and for a while in the 19th century both England and the United States disputed who owned the land. Most of Canada was clearly defined as British, but around San Juan Island, boundaries were ill-defined. On June 15, 1859, a pig belonging to Englishman Charles Griffin of the Hudson's Bay Company made its way into "an enemy territory"—the land of an American settler named Lyman Cutlar. Cutlar shot and killed the pig. The fuse leading to war was lit.

"It was eating my potatoes," said Cutlar, who had already warned Griffin to keep his pig out of his potato patch.

"It is up to you to keep your potatoes out of my pig," Griffin replied.

UP IN ARMS

Griffin reported the incident to British authorities, who threatened to arrest Cutlar. The U.S., however, sent Cutlar military protection in the form of the 9th Infantry. In response, the British sent three warships. Forces and tensions on both sides mounted. About two months after the execution of the pig, American troops numbered 461 and British forces grew to 2,140, and five warships. But by August, no guns had been fired.

In Washington, many were shocked that an international conflict might erupt over the shooting of a pig. President James Buchanan was eager to defuse the situation and sent General Winfield Scott, commanding general of the U.S. Army, to help work out the situation. Through his negotiations, tensions were eased and both sides agreed to hold fire while the issue was worked out.

Although the killing of a pig triggered the problem, the central matter was about who owned San Juan Island. For about 12 years following the incident, this question was debated but not resolved. The British and Americans finally went to a third party to resolve the dispute. On October 21, 1872, Kaiser Wilhelm I of Germany declared the San Juan Islands as American property. Land north of the 49th parallel was Canadian, and to the south it was American. A month later, British troops left the area.

...You can visit. It's overlooking Kootenay Lake in Boswell.

CAR TROUBLE

A Canadian may have invented the car (really!), but Canada can't be blamed for the trouble that it causes!

CHAIN REACTION

In the spirit of the holiday season, in 2012 one drive-through customer at a Winnipeg Tim Hortons paid for the customer behind him. When the next customer pulled up, he appreciated the gesture and paid for the customer behind him. The effect repeated itself until 228 generous folks had bought a coffee for the person behind them. The goodwill was infectious, and the paying-it-forward lasted about three hours. (One Grinch ended it all when he refused to pay for the customer behind him, although his coffee had already been paid for.)

THIS CAR MAY RAISE A FEW EYEBROWS

LaCrosse sounds like a harmless enough name. In fact, it's supposed to have a certain air of class about it, and that's why Buick chose it for its 2003 sedan. Buick also said that the name is inspired by the sport lacrosse, giving it a hint of youthfulness and action.

When Buick was about to launch the LaCrosse in Canada in 2005, the company learned that *la crosse means* "self-love" or masturbation in Quebecois slang. So General Motors renamed the car "Allure" ... in Canada only.

DO NOT HIRE THIS PERSON TO VALET

When Tripta Kaushal pulled into a parking lot (car park) at a gym in 2009, it should have been a very simple job. The spaces were big. She pulled straight in. She was driving slowly. And then as she approached a raised divider between parking spaces, she seemed to hit the gas, jump the low barrier, and send the front of her BMW X5 driving over two cars parked in front of her.

Instead of getting help or leaving a note, Kaushal drove off. What she didn't know is that closed circuit cameras caught her in the act. Police easily identified her and her car from the surveillance footage. An Ontario court judge fined her $500 and put her on six months of probation.

(THIS IS NO) CRAPPY CEREAL

Grape Nuts doesn't have grapes or nuts in it. Fortunately, "Holy Crap" cereal is just a name, too.

MORNING CONSTITUTIONAL

In 2009 Corin Mullins set out to create cereal for her husband, Brian, who suffers from food allergies. With fiber, buckwheat, chia, and various nontraditional ingredients, Corin concocted a gluten-free, vegan, organic cereal that Brian loved. They thought the cereal was so good they decided to sell it locally.

Calling the cereal Hapi Food, the couple sold their first 10 bags at the Sechelt Farmers Market on the Sunshine Coast, British Columbia, in May 2009. When their very first customer said, "Holy crap! This is good cereal," Brian decided to change the name. The renaming turned out to be a marketing stroke of genius. Daily sales shot up 1,000 percent—from 10 to 100 under its new name, Holy Crap.

THE TASTE OF SUCCESS

When they sold their cereal at a kiosk at the Granville Island Market during the 2010 Olympics, media attention built and orders started streaming in. The tipping point came after their appearance on the CBC show *Dragon's Den.* In the show, aspiring entrepreneurs pitch to five multimillionaires with the expertise—and the money—to turn great ideas into incredible fortunes. Although the Mullins were offered a deal, it was never finalized. But the power of publicity paid off. The week after the show aired, their online store generated $1 million.

ASTRONOMICAL POPULARITY

The cereal is now carried in over 2,000 grocery and health stores throughout Canada. It's proven to be a hit with athletes, diabetics, dieters, outdoor enthusiasts, travelers, and people with high blood pressure, severe food allergies, and other food sensitivities. In 2012, Holy Crap cereal rocketed to the International Space Station where Canadian Astronaut Chris Hadfield ate it during his five-month mission.

...It's just .9 meters or about 4 feet wide at the narrowest point.

ATHLETIC IMPERATIVE

From arena to field house, winning is the only thing.

A WORTHY DODGE

The University of Alberta in Edmonton may have an obsession when it comes to dodgeball. In 2011, the school set a record when 2,012 players pelted each other with balls in what was declared the largest dodgeball game in history. But Alberta only wore the crown for a short time.

Seven months later, the University of California, Irvine, had 4,000 players winging balls at each other. UA felt the sting of defeat. On February 3, 2012, in front of representatives from *Guinness World Records*, the school gathered 4,979 students, staff, and alumni to clobber each other in the Butterdome—setting the new world record ...again.

AN UNFORGETTABLE WORKOUT

In January 2008 at about 10 p.m., 17-year-old Matthew Giguere took a break from working out at the fitness center in Tatamagouche to get some fresh air. Giguere, who was visiting from Sorel-Tracy, Quebec, looked out across the bay and spotted what he thought was a brightly lit ship.

He didn't think much about it, beyond that it was cool to see a three-masted ship all lit up at night. He described it as bright white and gold. He tried to get a young woman in the gym to come take a look at the unique sight, but she just continued with her workout. Giguere admired the vessel for a few minutes and went back into the gym to exercise. When he came out later, the ship was gone. When he learned of the ghost ship legend, he realized he had seen the fabled ship.

In the spring of 2012, a real ghost ship drifted off the coast of western Canada. An empty Japanese fishing boat, which had been swept away from a Japanese coastal town during the tsunami of 2011, was spotted bobbing in the waters near the Queen Charlotte Islands. The magnitude 9.0 earthquake off Japan's northeast coast on March 11, 2011, triggered a nearly 23-meter (75-foot) wall of water that flattened waterfront towns, killing 16,000.

A decommissioned DC-13 airplane serves as the world's largest weathervane in Whitehorse, Yukon.

HOCKEY FIGHT IN CANADA

Hockey seems to be the one thing that can transform the normally overly polite Canadian into a frothing, raging beast.

THERE'S ALSO A PUCK

Fighting has become an expected part of hockey. Certain players on hockey teams are assigned to be the "enforcers." This is usually one player per team who is assigned to be the fighter, tough guy, or "goon" who responds to violent play from the opposing team. They are often the most popular players on the teams.

• In the mid-seventies, Bobby Hull of the Winnipeg Jets brawled with Birmingham Bulls Dave Hanson. Hanson got his knuckles caught in Hull's toupee, and it came off in his hand during the melee, enraging the Winnipeg fans.

• In a 2007 game, Ottawa right-winger Chris Neil whacked the Buffalo captain. Drury's forehead hit the ice, and he started bleeding profusely. That sparked a bench-clearing brawl. Even the coaches joined in the ruckus.

• Early in an April 1984 game, the Quebec Nordiques and Montreal Canadiens engaged in a full team against team fight. In the third quarter, *another* fight sent all players to the box. Referees gave 252 penalty minutes and ejected 10 players. Many refer to the night as the Good Friday Massacre.

• On March 5, 2004, the Ottawa Senators battled the Philadelphia Flyers and five consecutive fights broke out in the final minutes of the game. That night an NHL-record 419 penalty minutes were dispensed and 20 players were ejected.

• The only known death directly related to a hockey fight occurred when Don Sanderson of the Whitby Dunlops, a top-tier senior amateur team in Ontario's Major League Hockey, died in January 2009, a month after sustaining a head injury during a brawl.

Pingualuit Crater Lake was formed in the middle of the tundra in Quebec by a meteor.

BEAVER FEVER!

And their butt glands were used for perfume.

LEAVE IT TO BEAVERS

In the 1600s, French Catholics were settling in Canada and hunting beaver for their pelts and for their *castoreum*. Castoreum is a yellowish secretion from the castor scent glands of either a male or female beaver. The beaver releases castoreum from sacs near the anus. The unctuous substance, which carries a pungent odor, combines with urine to mark the beaver's territory. The animals also groom the castoreum into their fur with their feet, making them waterproof. The substance helps keep a beaver's skin dry even when while swimming.

EAU DE ANAL GLAND

The secretion was also used as a main ingredient in perfumes and in medicines. Perfumers described the scent as "wild and bodily," "lustful and passionate." Of course, perfume sellers didn't play up the fact that these stimulating smells were coming directly from a beaver's anal glands. Some trappers would combine the castoreum with cloves, nutmeg, cinnamon, alcohol, and acetylsalicylic acid (aspirin) and sell it as a cure-all. The substance is still used as a fixative in perfumes to reduce evaporation and extend the scent, but it is generally synthetically produced.

TGIF

In the 17th century, the fur trade was still going strong. After taking the fur from the beavers, many trappers didn't waste the meat. But for Catholic trappers and for natives who had converted to Catholicism, beaver was meat, and in the Catholic religion, meat was forbidden to be eaten on Fridays. The Bishop of Quebec pleaded with the higher-ups in the Church to make beaver meat an exception to the rule. Because the rodent was seen as semi-aquatic and a fantastic swimmer, the Church officially declared that the beaver was a fish. The declaration kept the Church from alienating Catholics in Canada who could now eat beaver on Fridays and throughout Lent with a clear conscience.

The world's smallest jail is believed to be in Rodney, Ontario...

BIEBER FEVER!

Fame can make anyone a little nutty, even Canadian teen dream Justin Bieber.

MONKEY BUSINESS

In March 2013, Bieber's pet capuchin monkey, Mally, was held up by German customs officials when Bieber entered the country during his European tour.

Bieber had neglected to bring the necessary health documents for his pet. Mally was cared for by an animal shelter and later was given a home at a German zoo, where she still made her home as *Weird Canada* went to press.

SPEAKING FRANKLY

In Amsterdam Bieber visited the Anne Frank House. Bieber wrote this in the guestbook: "Truly inspiring to be able to come here. Anne was a great girl. Hopefully she would have been a Belieber." (A "Belieber" is, of course, a devoted Justin Bieber fan.)

MASKED MAN

To avoid the paparazzi in 2012, he donned a metallic gold mask in Venice Beach, California. It didn't work. In 2013, while in London, he put on a gas mask. Needless to say, a guy strolling the streets in a gas mask will usually draw attention, not divert it.

URINE TROUBLE

In July 2013 TMZ released video of Bieber peeing in a janitor's mop bucket as he and a posse of obnoxious friends left a New York City night club through the back. The same clip also caught the celebrity inexplicably cursing out a photograph of former U.S. President Bill Clinton.

A few days after, Bieber called the former president and apologized. Mr. Clinton graciously accepted.

...It's only 24.3 square meters (about 270 square feet).

RAISE YOUR TRAYS, AND NO SHAPE-SHIFTING!

Travel can really change a person.

UP IN THE AIR

Imagine you're on a plane from Hong Kong flying to Canada and there's an elderly white male passenger sitting next to you. He's wearing a flat cap, brown cardigan sweater, and wire-rimmed spectacles. He gets up to use the restroom. No big deal. But then he returns to his seat as a young, Asian male. The old man who had been seated next to you is nowhere to be found.

You did notice the young-looking hands of your former seatmate, and now you wonder: Could the young man have transformed?

On October 29, 2010, this exact scenario happened on an Air Canada flight from Hong Kong to Vancouver. Flight staff noticed the transformation and notified authorities on the ground to be ready for an arrest. Upon landing, the passenger was taken off the plane by Border Services Officers. The man then asked for refugee status.

A BAG MR. ROGERS WOULD ENVY

When security questioned the asylum-seeker about wearing a disguise, he initially denied it. Upon searching his bags, however, officers found a peel-off silicon face and neck mask as well as the cap, cardigan, and eyeglasses of the old man. The status of the young refugee is still unknown.

A CASE OF FORSAKEN IDENTITY

Air Canada spokesman Peter Fitzpatrick said that multiple identity checks have to be completed in Hong Kong International Airport for anyone to board a plane, so the disguise that this guy was using must have been quite good. This passenger was able to board using someone else's boarding pass.

It is believed that he somehow swapped boarding passes with another person, but further details have not been revealed. The question remains: Who was that masked old man?

The word "cyberspace" was coined by Canadian writer William Gibson.

FART DOG MAKES GOOD

The genius of the Canadian literary tradition has no parallel.

PASSING GAS

Glenn Murray of Fredericton, N.B., created a hit series with the American William Kotzwinkle centered on a flatulent canine. *Walter the Farting Dog* has proven to be a real knockout. The first book hit stores in 2001, and a decade later close to 1.5 million copies had been sold. Today, there are five titles in the series, including *Walter the Farting Dog Banned from the Beach* and *Walter the Farting Dog Farts Again.* The books have spent many weeks at the top of the *New York Times* bestseller list and have been translated into at least 16 languages.

HIGH FART

If you haven't caught wind of Walter yet, the books are all about a flatulent pooch who always manages to save the day by releasing a stinker. Murray and his writing partner Kotzwinkle have become stars of children's fiction. Kotzwinkle's wife, Elizabeth Gundy, has contributed to many of the plots—she's dubbed Murray and Kotzwinkle's silent but deadly partner.

Those in the book-publishing world put the writing duo in a genre of potty humor for kids that includes the Captain Underpants series and *Zombie Butts from Uranus*. These tomes of children's literature have been wildly popular with kids but have come under criticism by some teachers and parents who view them as overly juvenile and improper. Defenders of these books say that they get kids who never would have picked up a book before into reading.

Murray firmly believes that you have to give children something they want to read about—and what kid can resist a lovable, farting canine? Murray has received fan letters from administrators in a hospital cancer ward thanking him for creating a book that makes kids laugh and takes their mind off their ordeal.

FART-NOMENON

The idea was hatched when Kotzwinkle told Murray about a real 68-kilogram (150-pound) mastiff that had a horrible gas problem due to his diet of beer and doughnuts. The dog released such noxious fumes that it once cleared out everyone in a stationery store.

Along with T-shirts, mugs, and magnets, there is now a cuddly Walter the Farting Dog plush doll that emits three different fart sounds. Could a scratch-n-sniff book be far behind?

Canadian Pacific Railway named a hamlet Hairy Hill for all the buffalo hair they found there.

WRITING A WILL FROM SCRATCH

An unfortunate farmer shows grace under fire.

WHERE THERE'S A WAY, THERE'S A WILL

When Cecil George Harris left his home to work in his fields near Rosetown in Saskatchewan on the morning of June 8, 1948, he bid his wife and two small children goodbye and told them that he'd see them late that night.

WHEN NEUTRAL ISN'T

Just about an hour after leaving, he accidentally left his tractor out of gear while making some repairs. The tractor moved backwards and trapped Harris's left leg underneath a rear wheel. His leg bled profusely, and no one came to find Harris for nine hours. When he did not return home late that night, his wife went to look for him. She found him at about 10:30 p.m. and rushed him to the hospital, where he died.

Harris didn't have an official will. And he was unconscious by the time he was taken to the hospital, so he made no mention of leaving the world a message.

FENDING FOR HIS LIFE

Days after the accident, neighbors examining the scene of the accident noticed a few words scratched into the fender. They read: "In case I die in this mess, I leave all to the wife. Cecil Geo. Harris."

Although his leg was pinned, his hands were free and Harris had used his pocketknife to etch those few words as he lay dying.

The fender was removed from the tractor and submitted to the courts, which determined it to be a legitimate handwritten will. The fender was filed with the registrar of wills as the Last Will and Testament of George Harris at the Surrogate Court in the District of Kerrobert, Canada. In 1996, the fender was turned over to the College of Law at the University of Saskatchewan and put on public display in the library.

The world's longest hockey game was a benefit held in May 2012 in Chestermere, Alberta...

SHOVEL OFF

Some products just aren't meant to be.

THE WORST SHOVEL IN THE WORLD!

To help make the lives of Canadian soldiers easier during World War I, Ena McAdam designed a shovel with a hole in it. The idea sounds about as practical as making a canteen with no bottom, and many look at the shovel now with astonishment. What might the German enemies have thought when they heard they were battling a country that invented a shovel with a hole in it? That Canada hoped to defeat the Germans by making them laugh to death? But the McAdam Shovel was far from a practical joke.

SPREAD THIN

McAdam's shovel had a dual purpose. It could act as both a spade for digging and as a shield. Soldiers could fire through the hole at the enemy and yet be protected by the flat part of the blade. The shovel, of course, had one glaringly obvious flaw. It was very difficult to dig productively using a shovel that had a hole in it. The tool also had a less obvious problem—the blade had to be very thick and heavy to stop gunfire. So the McAdam Shield Shovel gave a soldier a lot of extra weight to lug around.

NETWORKS REALLY HELP

Despite its extra-heavy blade, bullets from almost any German gun could penetrate it. So the shovel really offered zero protection, was impractical for digging, and was tiring to carry around. Still, Ena McAdam was the personal secretary to Sam Hughes, the Canadian minister for the Department of Militia and Defence (1914–16), and Hughes bought into the concept.

In 1914, Hughes ordered 25,000 of the shovels at a cost of $34,000. He distributed the shovels to his theatre commanders for testing. They were all astounded by how impractical they were, and they refused to issue them to their troops. Ultimately, the McAdam Shovel project was buried—production was discontinued and the shovels were sold for scrap for $1,400.

...It lasted 246 hours (over 10 days). The final score: 4,178 to 3,845.

CITY ANIMALS

The loon and wolf may define Canadian animals, but the real stories are in the city.

PACK YOUR TRUNKS

Shu Mei, a resident of Newmarket, Ontario, woke up to an incredibly bad smell one morning in 2007. "I opened the front door and I didn't know what the smell was," Mei told reporters. "But not good. And then I saw it."

What Mei saw might have been left behind by a colossal mutant dog from the neighborhood. While that may seem far-fetched, the truth is even stranger.

CAUGHT IN THE ACT

In reality, an elephant had pulled her own Operation Dumbo Drop and left behind her "calling card." But what was an elephant doing roaming the streets of this peaceful suburban neighborhood? Mei wasn't imagining things. Other neighbors reported peering out their windows in the very early hours of the morning to spy pachyderms munching leaves on a tree and hanging out on the street corner.

Elephants strolling through Newmarket aren't the norm, but the Garden Bros. Circus was in town and the power supply to the electric fence that keeps the elephants penned in was cut off. Someone accidentally tripped over the cord that kept the fence charged. Susie and Bunny, two of three Asian elephants kept by the circus, realized that they could easily break out and take a walk around town.

IT'S RAINING GEESE

On April 22, 1932, the townspeople of Elgin, Manitoba, found a delicious goose dinner dropping from the sky. A flock of Canada geese were flying overhead during an electrical storm. The unfortunate birds ran afoul of some lightning, and 52 of them were electrocuted in midflight. The geese all plummeted into Elgin, where the citizens celebrated. They gathered the geese and served them on dinner tables throughout the town.

In the 1760s, Britain was considering trading Canada for France's Guadeloupe.

CRONENBERGIAN

Toronto-born writer-director David Cronenberg (Scanners, The Fly, Crash) *is an odd duck.*

"We've all got the disease—the disease of being finite. Death is the basis of all horror."

"I identify with parasites."

"Art is somewhat subversive of civilization. And yet at the same time it seems necessary for civilization. You don't get civilization without art."

"A superhero movie, by definition, is a comic book. I think people who are saying *The Dark Knight Rises* is 'supreme cinema art,' I don't think they know what they're talking about. It's still Batman running around in a stupid cape."

"Everybody's a mad scientist, and life is their lab. We're trying to experiment to find a way to live, to solve problems, to fend off madness and chaos."

"I don't think there's anything man wasn't meant to know. There are just some stupid things that people shouldn't do."

"My dentist said to me the other day, 'I've enough problems in my life, so why should I see your films?'"

"Censors tend to do what only psychotics do: They confuse reality with illusion."

"We are at a major epoch in human history, which is that we don't need sex to re-create the race. You can have babies without sex."

"If you embrace the reality of the human body, you embrace mortality, and that is a very difficult thing for anything to do because the self-conscious mind cannot imagine non-existence. It's impossible to do."

"When you're in the muck you can only see muck. If you somehow manage to float above it, you still see the muck but you see it from a different perspective."

"I think I do my best subversiveness by not worrying about whether I'm subversive or not."

"I don't have a moral plan, I'm a Canadian."

The Tanwars from Richmond, B.C., found a 20-inch wide maple leaf in 2011—the biggest in history.

WHALE TALES

People like whales...but do they like us?

DROP OUT, TUNE IN

Ready to rock out to the Big Beluga? Or Twist and Spout? That's what you might expect to hear from a DJ on a radio station dedicated to whale sounds. While ORCA FM didn't air any human voices, in 1998 it became the world's first all-whales-all-the-time radio station. Broadcasting from Vancouver Island, it let listeners hear the sounds of killer whales who live in the nearby Robson Bight ecological whale sanctuary. About 200 killer whales come to summer in Johnstone Strait on the northeast coast of Vancouver Island and enjoy meals of salmon, which are plentiful in this area. They also enjoy their own special spa treatment—rubbing themselves on the pebble beaches. ORCA-FM maintained an underwater microphone, located offshore in about 30 meters (about 98 feet) of water. Those within 15-kilometers (about nine miles) of the sanctuary could tune into the enchanting, mysterious calls of the killer whales.

THE SCENT OF MONEY

Canadian scientists have found a way to synthesize whale waste from fir trees. Why would you want to synthesize whale waste? Good question. A particular type of whale waste that is spewed out of sperm whales is called *ambergris*, and it is a key ingredient in high-end perfumes. In *Moby Dick* (published in 1851), Herman Melville refers to ambergris and its use in perfumes. He described it as "an essence found in the inglorious bowels of a sick whale" that was "largely used in perfumery, in pastiles, precious candles, hair powders, and pomatum [hairdressing oil]." During the time of Charles II in the late 1600s, ambergris was eaten—the king's favorite meal was eggs and ambergris. For decades, ambergris has been called whale vomit—but it's not really vomit. Ambergris is a solid, waxy, flammable substance of a dull grey or blackish color produced in the sperm whale's digestive system. The word comes from the French for "gray amber."

The highest streetcar line in the world runs along the High Level Bridge in Edmonton...

THE "NAKED" TRUTH

Which is to say this is a page of facts about Canada's favorite oddball rock band, the Barenaked Ladies.

• Former member Steven Page is the second-cousin of '90s Canadian reggae-rapper Snow ("Informer").

• Barenaked Ladies are the first Canadian band to have a Ben & Jerry's flavor named in their honour. In May 2009, the company debuted "If I Had 1,000,000 Flavours," a take-off on their song "If I Had a $1000000." It's vanilla and chocolate ice cream, peanut butter cups, chocolate-covered toffee, white chocolate chunks, and chocolate-covered almonds.

• The band's humorous lyrics and stage rapport almost got them a variety show. In 2005, they made a pilot for Fox called *Barenaked Ladies Variety Show.* The network opted not to bring it to a full series.

• The Barenaked Ladies wrote the music for and recorded a musical version of Shakespeare's *As You Like It.* It was produced by the Stratford Festival of Canada in 2005. (Why didn't they write the lyrics? Because the Shakespeare dialogue was pretty good to begin with.)

• In 2013, Ed Robertson wrote a song with Chris Hadfield, a Canadian musician...and astronaut. To promote music education, Robertson performed the song live in the CBC studios, with Hadfield joining in via satellite from the International Space Station.

• It's a tradition to throw Kraft Dinner onstage at their concerts.

• The group as a whole cameoed in Dave Foley's 1997 film *The Wrong Guy* as singing policemen.

• The band first got popular in the U.S. when Canadian actor Jason Priestly got them a gig playing on an episode of his show, *Beverly Hills, 90210.*

• One of the band's biggest hits is "Brian Wilson." It's about the depressive, agoraphobic period of the Beach Boys' singer's life. In 2000, "Brian Wilson" was covered at a series of concerts by...Brian Wilson.

...It is 46 meters (150 feet) high.

THE KIDS IN THE HALL

The sketch comedy show The Kids In The Hall *ran on the CBC from 1988 to 1994. Try to enjoy these standout quotes, even though somebody's "crushing your head" right now.*

"Forgive them, Father, for they know not what they do, for they walk through this life in toe-crampity shoes."

—Scott Thompson (as Jesus)

"I once shot a man just to watch him die, then I got distracted and missed it. Oh, my friends tried to describe it to me, but it just isn't the same."

"All right now, son, I want you to get a good night's rest. And remember, I could murder you while you sleep. It's easy, son, all you have to do is be quiet and willing to do it. And son, I am willing to do it. And, I've got quiet shoes. Good night, son. Sleep well."

"Hi, I'm Kevin McDonald. Or, as you might know me at home, 'the Kid in the Hall we don't like.'"

"I believe the aliens are here to collect decorative spoons."

"The hard thing about being a mass murderer isn't the murdering part. It's the mass part."

"In closing, as you lay there convalescing in your hospital bed, I'm forced to wonder, what were you doing riding your bike on the sidewalk anyway? Side-*WALK*? Maybe sometimes we bring heartache upon ourselves. Signed, the guy that collapsed your trachea."

"So when people say to me 'let sleeping dogs lie,' I say to them, friend, sleeping dogs—they eventually wake up...and chew out the throat of democracy!"

"When I was born, my mother mistook the afterbirth as my twin. And the cuter one, too, apparently, as I was immediately sold to the cleaning woman for a stamp."

"An optimist says, 'The drink is half full.' A pessimist says, 'The drink is half full, but I might have bowel cancer.'"

"I'm a Canadian. It's like an American, but without the gun."

RUSH! RUSH!

Little known facts about Canada's favorite prog-rock power trio.

• Rush once opened for the retro group Sha Na Na. They were booed off stage.

• The inspiration for the eight-minute, epic "By-Tor and the Snow Dog" on *Fly By Night* was the band's road manager's mouthy German shepherd, who would bite anyone who came near. "He's a By-Tor," the manager would say.

• Neal Peart was for many years a devotee of Ayn Rand, who emphasized the individual over society and denounced the poor as parasites. He has since denounced Rand's doctrine of selfishness and called himself a "bleeding-heart libertarian."

• Alex Lifeson was born Aleksandar Živojinović to Serbian parents—his stage name is an almost literal translation of his Serbian name.

• Unlike other bands from the '70s, Rush never trashed hotel rooms. However, Lifeson was tasered, arrested, and had his nose broken in 2003 at the Ritz-Carlton hotel in Naples, Florida. The incident stemmed from what the guitarist called the hotel and sheriff's office's "incredibly discourteous, arrogant, and aggressive behavior." The hotel chain later settled for damages.

• To obtain a better sound, Geddy Lee gave up his onstage amplifiers, preferring to plug directly into the venue's mixing console. The newly freed space on his side of the stage was then filled with random set pieces, including Maytag dryers, chicken rotisseries, and a vending machine.

• Lee is the son of Jewish holocaust survivors from Poland. His name, Geddy, came from when a friend heard his mother's pronunciation of his real name, Gary. He later legally changed his name.

• Bassist Geddy Lee is fishing buddies with another bassist, Les Claypool of Primus. (It's unknown if they go bass fishing.)

NAME THAT AD!

They can't all be Molson's "I am Canadian!" Can you match the advertising slogan with its Canadian brand? (Answers below.)

1. "Ever been to sea, Billy?

2. "It's mainly because of the meat."

3. "The champagne of ginger ales."

4. "We've licked them at the front, you lick them at the back."

5. "Because it fiiiits!"

6. "Where you give like Santa and save like Scrooge."

7. "The before hand lotion."

8. "It is possible."

9. "A good chew and peanuts, too."

10. "Wear a moustache!"

11. "The soap of beautiful women."

12. "Only in Canada? Pity."

13. "Relax. It's just a game."

14. "Makes beef sing."

a) Thrifty Stamps

b) Milk

c) Canadian Tire

d) Eat More

e) Canada Dry

f) HP Sauce

g) Dominion

h) Cap'n Highliner

i) Calay

j) Red Rose Tea

k) Bank of Montreal

l) Canadian Hockey Association

m) Brown's Short Man's Store

n) Trushay

Answers: 1. h), 2. g), 3. e), 4. a), 5. m), 6. c), 7. n), 8. k), 9. d), 10. b), 11. i), 12. j), 13. l), 14. f)

In 2005, Canada became the first country outside of Europe to legalize same-sex marriage.

HAIL CAESAR!

How a mix of clam juice, tomato juice, and vodka became Canada's national cocktail?

THE MAN WITH THE CLAMS

In the States, the Bloody Mary reigns as a favorite hair-of-the-dog hangover "cure." The equivalent in Canada is the Bloody Caesar. Bartender Walter Chell invented the Caesar in 1969 at the Westin Hotel in Calgary. The hotel was opening an Italian restaurant, and the owner asked Chell to create a drink to go with the Mediterranean food. Chell was inspired to make his own mash of tomato juice and clams, which he then combined with vodka, Worcestershire sauce, and Tabasco. Putting clam nectar in a cocktail was certainly a unique twist.

Because he was Italian and the drink was to accompany Italian food, Chell called it the Caesar. Chell said that the name Bloody was added after a British tourist tried the drink and proclaimed it "bloody good." Of course, it *does* bear a similarity to the Bloody Mary.

SOME SAY CLAMATO

Some say that Chell not only invented the cocktail but also created "clamato" juice itself. Shortly after Chell debuted the Bloody Caesar, Mott's introduced Clamato. Chell was never able to claim any financial right to his million-seller idea, but Mott's hired him to promote the product.

The drink is now considered Canada's national cocktail and is served at just about every bar throughout the country. Some Caesar aficionados say that the drink has never made a splash in the States because it can't break the "clam barrier"—the fishy flavor profile just may not suit U.S. taste buds.

MORE CAESAR TRIVIA

- The Toronto Institute of Bartending runs a "Caesar School" at different locations in Canada to train bartenders in how to make variations of the drink.
- Mott's holds an annual "Best Caesar in Town" competition as part of the Prince Edward Island International Shellfish Festival.
- An ultra-Canadian version of this cocktail includes bacon-infused vodka, maple syrup, and a glass rimmed with Tim Hortons coffee rounds.

The world's strongest current is in the Nakwakto Rapids at Slingsby Channel, British Columbia.

THE BEER MILE

Two ways to keep warm in the cold climes of the North Country are vigorous exercise and copious consumption of alcohol. One tradition said to have originated in Kingston, Ontario, combines these two pursuits into a single competitive endeavor.

LAPPING IT UP

Pretty much exactly what it sounds like, the rules of the Beer Mile are simple: contestants must chug one beer for each of four laps around a 400-meter track. The "four beers–four laps" rule is the acknowledged worldwide standard (known as the "Kingston Rules"), though some variations apply. For instance, a popular woman's version of the event involves the chugging of only three beers.

Other commonly agreed-upon rules: beer must be five percent alcohol (or greater); no special modifications may be made to cans (such as poking holes to "shotgun" the beer or using special "wide-mouth" versions); and, perhaps most difficult to stomach, competitors who vomit during the course of a race must run a penalty lap at the end (however, multiple vomitings do not mean multiple laps).

HOPS TO IT

The in-Canada record for the Beer Mile is an astounding 5:09, run by Jim Finlayson of Victoria, B.C., in 2007. Outside of Canada, Josh Harris ran a 5:04 at the 2013 Autumn Classic in Melbourne, Australia. In August 2012, the Beer Mile got an added "professional" boost when American Nick Symmonds, a fifth-place Olympic finisher in the 800-meter race, ran a beer mile in 5:19. His beer of choice for the event: Coors.

The traditional Canadian Beer Mile has expanded to include other examples of "digestive athletics." The Chocolate-Milk Mile demands contestants chug 12 ounces of the beverage for each lap; an Egg-and-Milk Mile substitutes three eggs and 500 milliliters of milk. Rumors abound of die-hard competitors completing the Beer Mile's Holy Grail: "The 24 in 24 in 24" involves chugging 24 beers over 24 miles—all in less than 24 hours. The reputed record for this challenge of the liver and the legs: 14 hours, though the time has not been authenticated.

Visitors to Vancouver's Expo 86 came down with "hiker's rash"...

WEED CANADA

Though Canada is, by and large, more tolerant of recreational marijuana use than other countries, it's still illegal. So don't be stupid, criminals.

HOLY SMOKE

At the Church of the Universe in Hamilton, the parishioners didn't just pass a collection basket—they passed a joint. The sect was founded by Walter Tucker in 1969 and held as its core beliefs that marijuana use is a sacrament. Conflict between the church and local authorities culminated in Tucker being sentenced to a short stint in prison in 2008. Tucker died in 2012, but the Church continues to advocate for the reform of Canadian marijuana laws. The church teaches that ganja is the "Tree of Life" described in the Book of Revelations and that being nude like Adam and Eve brings us closer to God, making them a great deal more fun than most religions.

HEY KIDS!

When Ryan Place opened a business in Esquimalt, B.C., in December 2012, he thought he might follow McDonald's lead and promote it with a mascot. The only problem was that Place's business is the Bong Warehouse, and his mascot was a cuddly, giant, fluffy, blue-colored water pipe named "Bongy" who stands outside the store and invites shoppers to come in and look around. The town council was not so smitten with the cartoonish Bongy. Some council members felt that Bongy was promoting an illegal activity, and that the company is using a character that might appeal to kids. Place disagrees. "People smile when they see him," he defended his creation, though he did not clarify exactly why they were smiling.

HAZY DUTY

Canadian troops fighting in Afghanistan in the 2000s frequently had to contend with Taliban fighters taking cover in the region's dense cannabis groves. Marijuana is a very tough plant and difficult to see through, even with thermal devices, difficult to cut down, and impossible to drive through. Even when the soldiers could get the stuff to burn, it introduced new problems: "A section of soldiers that was downwind from that had some ill effects and decided that was probably not the right course of action," General Rick Hillier, chief of the Canadian defense staff, remarked in 2006.

...their legs broke out due to toxic fumes seeping up from underground.

THE MITCHELL REPORT

There's nothing inherently weird about the distinguished, beloved, and iconic Canadian singer Joni Mitchell. Or is there?

• While Mitchell's mother was pregnant with her, she had the measles, and Mitchell herself contracted polio at age eight. These resulted in what Mitchell called physical "anomalies," that made her unpopular in high school and "tricky knuckles," or weaknesses in her hands that (some have written) compelled her to create the alternate guitar tunings for which she is famous.

• Mitchell wrote "Woodstock," the defining song about the historic 1969 music festival. Except that she wasn't there. She was stuck in New York City, booked to appear on The Dick Cavett Show. Her boyfriend at the time, Graham Nash, described the festival to her. Later Nash remarked that Mitchell captured the experience of Woodstock perfectly; in fact she captured it better than anyone who was actually there.

• She doesn't always get along with other musicians. "Americans have decided to be stupid and shallow since 1980," she told the *Los Angeles Times* in 2010. "Madonna is like Nero; she marks the turning point." And as for her once friend Bob Dylan, she said, "Bob is not authentic at all. He's a plagiarist, and his name and voice are fake. Everything about Bob is a deception."

• According to Mitchell, her pet peeves are the music business ("a cesspool"), celebrity obsession ("people will flick their Bic at anything"), and current music ("appallingly sick, with boring chord movement").

• Mitchell started smoking cigarettes very young, but to this day she denies a link between her smoking and obvious changes in her vocal range and ability. It's her age, she says, that impacts her voice, adding "I have smoked since I was nine so obviously it didn't affect my early work that much." Also a well-respected painter, she further notes that making music was at first a "hobby," a way for her to pay for cigarettes while attending art school.

Anna Haining Bates (1846–1888) was a giantess. The Nova Scotian measured 2.28 m (7' 6") tall.

KILLING HOUDINI

Don't come to Canada if you're a world-famous illusionist.

NO ESCAPE

The master magician was performing in October 1926 at The Princess Theatre in Montreal. Upon the invitation of the dean of the faculty of psychology of McGill University, Houdini came to talk to the students. By most accounts, Houdini was asked by a group of students if he could take a blow to the gut and not feel the pain at all. Houdini said of course, although he usually had to prepare his muscles to take the punch. But one student didn't give him a chance. The student, J. Gordon Whitehead, hauled into the magician without warning. Strong and about six-foot tall, Whitehead delivered some powerful blows. He socked the escape artist about four times, right in the belly, before Houdini asked the student to stop. Houdini appeared to be in great pain but went on to give his performances, despite great discomfort.

LAST EXIT

Leaving Montreal by train shortly after the incident, Houdini arrived in Detroit feeling ill. He continued to give performance there with 104-degree temperature. He went to see a doctor who diagnosed him with acute appendicitis. The doctor removed the appendix the next day. Houdini stayed in the hospital a few days and appeared to be getting better. But Houdini had peritonitis, a potentially lethal inflammation of the tissue that lines the abdomen, and his health then took a sudden turn for the worse. On October 31, 1926, Houdini died at age 52. His last words were, "I am weaker. I guess I have lost the fight." His appendix must have ruptured somewhere between Montreal and Detroit–possibly near St. Thomas, Ontario. For a long time, people suspected that the McGill student's punches were to blame. Ruth Brandon, the author of *The Life and Many Deaths of Harry Houdini*, writes that most now believe that Whitehead's punches could not have caused Houdini's death. The hit could have affected the intestine, but not the appendix. Brandon believes that the magician already had appendicitis before he arrived in Montreal. No charges of wrongdoing were ever brought against Whitehead.

Play ball: The oldest baseball diamond is in London, Ontario, dating to 1877.

A MAN NAMED BLADDER

A small town's name honors a local man who advised helped locate an air base.

THE SCENIC ROUTE

Iqaluit, the largest community of the Nunavut Territory and its capital, owes its establishment to an enterprising man named (sort of) Nakasuk. During World War II, the U. S. Navy was looking for long, flat locations in Canada where it could build a chain of bases that would be used for flights connecting North America to the UK through arctic Canada, Greenland, and Iceland, all part of the DEW line, which stands for Distant Early Warning line, a system of radar stations.

Since Nakasuk knew the area well, he stepped up to help the U.S. military find a location for its base at Iqaluit (also called Frobisher Bay until 1987). The base at Iqaluit wasn't used much by the Americans, but that didn't stop other people, many of them Inuks, from moving to the area after word got around that the base would be there. Nakasuk, who had been raised at a nearby sealing camp near Pangnirtung, is considered Iqaluit's original and founding resident. After advising the U.S. military to establish its base there, Nakasuk never left.

THE LEGACY FORMS

Although no historians theorize why Nakasuk stayed, it could be related to the meaning of Iqaluit's name in the Inuk language: place of many fish. Or perhaps he was confident that the settlement would quickly grow thanks to the military base. Whatever the reason, this founding citizen's name is memorialized in the name of one of Iqaluit's two schools, Nakasuk School. Perhaps the reason no other places in the city bear the founding father's name is that its meaning in Inuktitut is "bladder." It actually took about sixty years from that fateful day Nakasuk chose the location for Iqaluit to become a city. It was officially named a city in 2001, and its population in 2013 was 6,699.

BLACK COMEDY

From 1983 to 2002, humorist Arthur Black hosted Basic Black on CBC Radio, Canada's top place to hear interviews with some of Canada's...well, let's just call them "eccentrics." Here are some of Black's most memorable guests over the years.

• Lydia Hiby—a pet counselor to talks to animals telepathically. Yep, she's a psychic for pets.

• Imre Somogyi—a psychic who can tell your future by reading your feet, toes, and in between (humans only).

• Trevor Weekes, author of the 1983 book Teach Your Chickens to Fly. (Weekes was at least kidding...we think.)

• A woman known only as "Jeannie M.," who is the world's first and foremost maker of taxidermied rats to be used as Christmas tree ornaments.

• Didgeridoos are a distinctly Australian instrument. Not many people in Canada make them, but Paulu Rainbowsong does. He demonstrated to Black how he makes them out of PVC pipe.

• Performance artist Linda Montano. At the time of the interview, she was in the middle of her latest project—she'd tied herself to a man for a year, literally—with a six-foot-long length of rope.

• The important civil servant in charge of a very important office in Gimli, Manitoba: the Skunk Control Officer.

• Judy Williams, who runs Wreck Beach—the Vancouver playland paradise for brave Canadian nudists.

• "Marge the Rancher" of Saskatchewan. She launched the company "Marge's Muffs," which makes "ballmuffs"—winter gear for the exposed scrotums of bulls.

...2,390 kg (5,269 lbs.), set by the Kitchener-Waterloo Hospital Auxiliary in 1993.

HUMOUR US

Who says Canadians aren't funny?

"If Sting retires, will he change his name to Stung?

–Colin Mochrie

"Paul McCartney was in the room with us. At one point he was three feet away from me and all I kept thinking was, *If I run up and kick him in the crotch right now, I'll be the most famous man alive!*"

–Seth Rogen

"When I go to a restaurant I know every girl in there wants to come say hi and be sexually aggressive, but they're all so gripped by shyness they don't even make a move. In some cases the shyness is so severe they won't even look at me."

–Michael Cera

"You know what I do almost every day? I wash. Personal hygiene is part of the package with me."

–Jim Carrey

"What's better than sex? You know when you hold a piss for a really long time and you finally get to go? That's up there."

–Deryck Whibley, Sum41

"When my agent told me I'd been asked to host Canada's Walk of Fame, I was surprised and delighted–surprised I still had an agent, and delighted to be allowed back into Canada."

–Tom Green

"If it ain't broke, you're not trying."

–Red Green

"Singers aren't supposed to have dairy before a show, but we all know I'm a rule breaker."

–Justin Bieber

"I'm capable of living in the moment. I'm especially capable of living in the moment of sitting on my sofa and watching other people's moments."

–Samantha Bee

"They say that if you're afraid of homosexuals, it means that deep down you're actually a homosexual. That worries me because I'm afraid of dogs."

–Norm Macdonald

"Never trust sheep."

–Ryan Stiles

THE SOUND OF THE NORTHERN LIGHTS

The weirdest sounds you'll ever see!

LIGHTS, CORONA, ACTION

One of northern Canada's most beautiful natural phenomena is the Aurora Borealis, commonly known as the Northern Lights. The brilliant effects are caused when explosions on the sun's surface throw particles into the sun's atmosphere, or corona. The *corona* is hot enough (upwards of 2,000,000 °C!) to break these particles down into their base components of protons, electrons, and nuclei. In this process, hydrogen becomes a gas called plasma.

When plasma flows out of the corona through a passage in the sun's magnetic field, it travels through space for approximately 40 hours before entering the earth's thermosphere, approximately 96 to 128 kilometers (60 to 80 miles) above the earth's surface. The earth's magnetic fields "funnel" the plasma into the atmosphere, and the particles of the plasma pull the magnetic field lines together to create the colorful displays.

A ROARING BOREALIS

Strangely, many people claim to hear noises when they see the Northern Lights. Described as "cracking," swishing, or "rustling," reports of such sounds date back centuries and make for vigorous debates among long-time aurora viewers.

The main argument against the existence of such sounds is that the auroras are too far away: it would simply take too long for the sound to travel from the thermosphere to the listener's ears. Additionally, the air between the earth's surface and the upper atmosphere is too thin to carry sounds with such distinct nuances.

One explanation holds that reported sounds are electrical phenomena caused by the aurora. Another states that the "sounds" are actually signals picked up by the human eye and neurologically misconstrued: it seems that in very quiet environments, electrical impulses from the eye are redirected to the part of the brain that processes sound.

...It measured 64 centimeters (just over 2 feet) by 17 centimeters (6.7 inches).

ART BRUTES

The museum scene gets nasty.

BLOODY GOOD

Istvan Kantor gained notoriety in 1988 after being arrested at the Museum of Modern Art in New York City for spraying an X of his own blood on the museum wall between two Picassos. Some drops got on a Picasso, and Kantor was charged with vandalism. "Inevitably some blood will always go on the [other] works," Kantor is quoted as saying. The Blood Campaign started, says Kantor, to fund neoism, his multimedia performance art movement of rebellion, innovation, and experimentation. Said Kantor, "It was all about the idea, how art is serving society."

Though he was banned 1991 from the National Gallery of Canada for a blood "gift" and booted from the Art Gallery of Toronto in 2006 for performing in the nude with computer parts clipped to his privates in front of an Andy Warhol work, Kantor had found support in 1985 in Montreal: after he splattered an X of his blood on the museum wall Musee d'Art Contemporain the director told Kantor if he'd been notified beforehand, he would have scheduled an official performance.

In 2004, the Kantor–amid controversy–won a top prize in the Canadian art world, the $12,000 The Governor General's Award in Media and Video.

TRITE FIGHT

Toronto's multimedia performance artist Jubal Brown won fame in 1996 protesting "oppressively trite and painfully banal" art. Executing his planned Responding to Art triptych, Brown threw up in blue all over Mondrian's Composition in Red, White and Blue at New York City's Museum of Modern Art. The blue was a combination of blue cake icing, blueberry yogurt and blue Jell-O. "I don't hate Mondrian," Brown said to the New York Times reporter. "I picked him because he's such a pristine symbol of Modernism." Six months earlier, the 22-year old art student vomited in red all over Dufy's Harbor at Le Havre at the Art Gallery of Ontario, because it "was just so boring it needed some color." The third piece of the triptych, vomit in yellow, never materialized, perhaps because museum officials were planning to file charges for vandalism.

The most "dislikes" for a Canadian video on YouTube goes to Justin Bieber's "Baby"...

LOUDLY NOTED

The Bank of Canada just can't get it right.

DIRTY, SEXY MONEY

To counter counterfeiting, the Bank of Canada added lots of new images and features to currency redesigned in 2009. But some people thought the $100 bill's DNA strands resembled adult toys, and others thought the transparent "windows" were shaped like a woman's body. Then there was the issue of the National Vimy Memorial. Embedded on the back of their new $20 bill, the picture features two monoliths graced by naked Grecian figures representing truth and justice. Many Canadians complained it was too pornographic. Some who didn't recognize the Vimy Memorial, erected on French soil to honor fallen WWI Canadians, thought the picture represented New York City's World Trade Center...with naked ladies added.

LEAF NOW

Many Canadians complained when the new $20, $50, and $100 bills displayed not the familiar three-pronged sugar maple leaf, as seen on the national flag, but a five-pronged, highly invasive Norway maple leaf. The Bank of Canada explained that the design was deliberate choice to present a "stylized blend" of sugar and Norway maple leaves to avoid "regional bias."

THAT'S NOT FAIR

The new $100 bill brought on more outrage when Canadians discovered that a picture of a female Asian scientist on back of the new bill had been replaced with a Caucasian woman. In August 2012, the Bank of Canada apologized, saying that it changed the image only because the focus groups said the Asian image stereotyped Asians as "techy" and was insulting because the image had been printed in yellow. The image was not the only source of intrigue for the bill: The Bank of Canada received enough reports that the polymer note smelled like maple syrup that officials publicly denied scenting the bill.

A TUNDRA OF FUN

Enjoy Polar Bear Provincial Park—if you can get there.

DEEP IN THE MIDDLE OF NOWHERE

If you're looking for a relaxing, mellow getaway, the first place you can cross off your list is Polar Bear Provincial Park in northern Ontario. The park, a whopping 23,552 square kilometers (9,093 square miles), is dedicated to the preservation of the area's wildlife habitats—to the point that access is only by air, and all visitors need special permission to enter. In fact, the only remnants of civilization are a few unmanned radar stations left over from the Cold War.

The Canadian government established the park in 1970. Technically part of the Hudson Bay Lowlands, the largest wetland in North America, it occupies the space where James Bay and Hudson Bay meet. Animals of all sorts call the low-lying tundra ecosystem home, from geese and ducks to moose, beaver, and the occasional beluga whale—as well as the eponymous polar bear.

BEAR WITH US

Just getting to the park is itself an expedition. Potential visitors—of which there are no more than 300 per year—must fly a circuitous route to the tiny village of Peawanuck, on the southern shore of the Hudson Bay. Besides Fort Severn, it is the only community to be found within hundreds of miles of the park. Those visitors who have the wherewithal to clear the necessary hurdles for entrance are strongly advised to bring at least a week's worth of extra supplies—not only to survive within the park, but in the event their departure gets delayed due to sudden inclement weather.

Even if you are willing to brave the potential polar bear attacks and frigid temperatures, those residual radar stations may be one dangerous item too many. There are seven stations in the park, each a hazardous site. The Canadian government has made some weak commitments to cleaning up the sites, but seem intent on burying most of the waste to save on cost. Despite these dissuasions, those who tough it out report some of the best trout fishing in the world as well as some stellar views of the Northern Lights. However, you may have to be willing to sleep in a teepee encircled by an electrified fence—one tour guide's preferred way of warding off polar bears.

Shortest-serving prime minister: Sir Charles Tupper (68 days in 1896).

SUPERSTITIONS

These practices will keep safe...unless you're just unlucky.

• In Alberta, picking blackberries after October 11 is bad luck because by that date the devil has already laid claim to those berries.

• In the Canadian prairie, it is custom that if a neighbor brings you a plate of food, you should return the plate dirty. Washing the plate will bring bad luck.

• Some First Nations tribes bless a new home by taking smoldering sage from room to room while saying prayers in order to banish evil spirits and ill feelings.

• A Manitoba urban legend says that if you run around a church called St. Andrews-on-the-Red near Lockport three times at midnight, you'll disappear.

• If you hear frogs croaking in the middle of the day, it's about to rain.

• In Saskatchewan, a red sky on a springtime night portends a windy day to follow.

• Among woodsmen, if a friend gives you a knife, you should give him a coin in return.

• Never place a pair of shoes on a bed; it means someone will die in your family.

• A wild bird flying into a house is a sign of death.

• Do not give cologne or perfume to a partner as a gift, as it will attract someone to break up the relationship. Giving shoes as a gift encourages your partner to break up with you; giving bags encourages him or her to pack up and leave the relationship.

• If your right hand itches, you will soon meet someone new. If your left hand itches, you will come into money.

• Never run out of salt. If you do, you run out of luck.

• Spilling a saltcellar when passing it to a friend indicates the end of the friendship is close at hand.

• After leaving the house for the day, turning back for a forgotten object forebodes disappointment later.

• February 29 is the only day of the year when it is permissible for a woman to propose marriage to a man. It is bad luck for the man to reject the proposal.

Winnipegger Aaron Caissie can balance 17 spoons on his face—more than anyone else on the planet.

HAIR-DRESSING DOWN

Salon professionals face regulations more binding than a hairnet.

CUTS NOT FARE

In Outaouais, Quebec, there are rules on the books that govern nearly all facets of hairdressing, from when hairdressers and barbers can work to the amount of money they can charge. The Joint Committee of Outaouais Hairdressers upholds these regulations, which date back to the 1930s. Hairdressers are forbidden to work on Sundays, close by five on Saturdays, and shut down during evening hours on Mondays, Tuesdays, and Wednesdays. They must also submit their monthly financial records, including business expenditures and wages paid.

If a hairdresser is found working on a holiday or any of the other banned days, he or she can face a fine of $1,000, plus $500 for every employee on the clock. With these limited hours, many Outaouais residents find it difficult to find time to schedule a trim or a shave. Many are forced to cross the Ottawa River and head into Ontario to find open salons or barbershops.

RAZORING PRICES

Hairdressers often have to go "underground," working out of their homes after hours to avoid governmental detection. Strangely, other beauticians (such as manicurists and masseuses) are allowed to work more regular hours. This leads to complications at spas, where beauticians and hairdressers often work together to create "package" deals for clients.

The Joint Committee recently raised the minimum price of an Outaouais haircut at $17, up from the $15 that had been in place for several years. There is a great deal of opposition to the Joint Committee, both inside and outside of the hairdressing community. One hairdresser took the Committee to court—and won—when she refused to turn over her personal information.

Many residents see the overregulation as clear evidence of an out-of-touch government. They say the rules end up promoting illegal activity such as payoffs and graft. Others say the rules are simply outdated, a holdover from a bygone era, and prevent small business owners from expanding. The Committee's defense, that they are ensuring a better standard of living for Outaouais workers, is now met with more skepticism than appreciation.

Don't trip! Sarwan Singh of Surrey has a 2.3 m (7' 9") beard—longer than any other.

A HIT OUT OF NOWHERE

This is the story of Canada's most unlikely hit record.

GIVE THE PEOPLE WHAT THEY WANT

In 1974, former rock musician Hans Fenger was hired to work at a school in Langley, British Columbia. Fenger had never taught music before, but he and his students didn't let their inexperience stop them from making music. Instead of teaching the children traditional choir songs, the iconoclastic Fenger taught them songs by David Bowie, Klaatu, The Beach Boys, and Paul McCartney. Fenger created new arrangements for the songs, and, using an experimental technique popularized by Brian Wilson and Carl Orff, the students accompanied themselves using Indonesian gamelan chimes and percussion instruments. Fenger later said, "I knew nothing of what children's music was supposed to be. But the kids had a grasp of what they liked: emotion, drama, and making music as a group. Whether the results were good, bad, in tune or out, it was no big deal."

FROM BARGAIN BIN TO BESTSELLER

Fenger eventually recorded his charges, some 60 at a time, on a 2-track tape deck during sessions in school gyms in Langley and Metro Vancouver. The recordings were made into 12" LPs and were intended for the students, parents, and teachers. The records might have faded into obscurity, but in 2000, record collector Brian Linds stumbled on them in a thrift store. Enraptured by what he heard, he sent the music to "outsider music" specialist Irvin Chusid. Chusid created an agreement with the Langley School administration and, with the support of Hans Fenger and several former students, marketed them. Ten record labels rejected the recordings until Bar/None Records released them in 2001 as a single CD titled *Innocence and Despair*. The CD met critical acclaim and was hailed as a work of genius. Fred Schneider of the B-52s remarked, " the Langley Project blew me away—a haunting, evocative wall-of-sound experience that is affecting in an incredibly visceral way." David Bowie called the Langley students' rendition of his song "Space Oddity," "a piece of art that I couldn't have conceived of, even with half of Colombia's finest export products in me." The album not only inspired some of the students to continue with careers in music, but also American filmmaker Richard Linklater's 2003 hit *School of Rock*.

CLUB CANADA

Some Canadians go to university to learn skills and enrich their minds and boring stuff like that. Others...join clubs. Weird clubs.

Law Show Club (University of Alberta). Are you a law student—who likes musicals? So much that you've dreamed of making a musical—based on law? Then this club's for you! Every year since 1995 Law Show club members produce one show. Example: "Law Show 2012" featured *Wizard of Laws*, "where we will follow our heroine as she travels through the Land of Laws and make some friends (and enemies) along the way. Will she be able to return home or will she be stuck in the Land of Laws forever?!?" (The show is accompanied by a silent auction, with all proceeds going to local charity.)

Rubik's Cube Club (University of Guelph). This club is for students (university students, we may need to remind you) who love Rubik's Cubes so much they need to get together with other (university) students to talk about, play with, and organize competitions—all based around the Rubik's Cube.

Right-Handed Vehicles Club (University of Manitoba). Membership open only to students who have right-handed vehicles—vehicles produced in or for countries where you drive on the left-hand side of the road—so they can get together to celebrate "the uniqueness of the vehicles we own."

Campus Crusade for Cheese (University of Waterloo). "Do you love cheese? Do you like cheese? Would you be able to work something out with cheese? Say, if the cheese gave you a back rub and set out some nice scented candles first ...?" That's what this club is all about, according to their website's description, but we imagine it also involves eating a lot of cheese.

Kevin Fast of Cobourg, Ontario, pulled a CC-177 Globemaster III airliner 8.8 meters (28' 10")...

POWERLIFTING FOR GOD

The strongest man in the world is a pastor for God.

SUPERNATURAL STRENGTH

Imagine throwing a 25-kg (56-lb) weight straight up in the air and clearing a bar twice as high as you are tall. Now imagine strapping yourself into a harness and pulling a fire truck 33m.

Kevin Fast of Cobourg, Ontario, is recognized as one of the strongest men in the world. Given a set of dumbbells when he was a teenager, Fast, born in April 1963, became a dedicated body builder. While in his thirties Fast learned about Scottish Games, a traditional Celtic athletic competition featuring feats of strength such as the Caber Toss and the Hammer Throw. Although he has no Scottish heritage, Fast joined in and eventually competed at the professional level. In 1997 he heard of people setting world records through feats of strength, such as towing busses through brute force, and decided he could do that too. He has set several Guinness world records. In 2008 he towed a 57,243 kg (126,200 lb) fire truck 100 feet using only the strength in his legs. The next year he set the record for heaviest aircraft ever towed: a 188.83 ton (416,299 lb) CC-177 Globemaster III cargo plane 8.8m (about 28' 10-3/4"). In 2010 he pulled a house that weighted 35.9 tons (79.145 lb) 11.95m (39' 2-1/2"). In 2011 he set two world records: most people ever lifted at one time (22) and heaviest vehicles to be towed 100 feet by two people, with his son Jacob. They lashed together to pull two giant fire engines.

BIG-HEARTED BRAWN

Fast is also a pastor at St. Paul's Lutheran Church in Cobourg. Known as "The Powerlifting Pastor," Dr. Fast uses his feats of strength as part of his ministry. Towing airplanes and fire trucks has got him in the newspapers and on television, including a broadcast of his fire truck pull on the USA's *Live with Regis and Kelley*. He sells sponsorships for his feats to raise money for charity. With the people lift and truck pull records, the modern day Samson raised $60,000 for Habitat for Humanity.

...The airliner weighs 188.83 tons (416,299 pounds).

LITERAL FRENCH CANADA

What does it mean to be French? Being owned by France is a good start.

WANTED: OWNER

In the North Atlantic, just 20 kilometers (15 miles) south of Newfoundland—but 3,800 kilometers west of mainland France—are the Islands of Saint-Pierre and Miquelon. The inhabitants are French citizens and vote in French elections, French is the official language, the currency is the euro, the educational system is French (as in European French), and even TV transmission uses French standards. These two rocky, windswept islands are the only remaining part of France's once-vast colonial empire, which once encompassed much of eastern Canada.

Dominion of the islands passed several times between the British and the French, until after the Napoleonic Wars, when a distracted Britain looked away as France established permanent possession. By that point, it was mainly about the bragging rights. With their cold, wet climate and infertile land, the islands were not considered prime real estate.

WANTED: EXECUTIONER

Saint-Pierre is home to one of the strangest and saddest stories in Canadian maritime history. In 1888, a fisherman, Joseph Néel was convicted of killing a Mr. Coupard and sentenced to death by guillotine. However, no guillotine existed on St. Pierre, and one had to be shipped from Martinique. After it arrived, more problems came up: it wouldn't work without repair, and no one was willing to be Néel's executioner. Finally, a recent emigrant to the island was coerced into doing the deed. Néel's execution was the only time the guillotine was used in North America. (In 2000, the incident was made into a film, *The Widow of Saint-Pierre (La veuve de Saint-Pierre)*, which won the Audience Award at the Toronto Film Festival.)

Since little grows there, the inhabitants of Saint-Pierre and Miquelon have always been fishermen. However, with the collapse of fishing stocks on the Grand Banks and widespread unemployment, the economy has been on the decline for some years. Many young people leave the islands for better prospects elsewhere.

When Canada switched to the metric system in 1970...

THE POPEMOBILE

Think Batman *meets* Superfly*...and you got yourself...a kickin' ride for the pontiff.*

SAFETY FIRST

When Pope John Paul II visited Canada in 1984, he didn't want to wave to his flock from behind tinted limousine windows—he wanted to see and be seen. So Canadians designed a vehicle. Prior to 1984, the Pope would drive through the crowds standing in a convertible or in the back of a truck. Sometimes, he would pop up through a sun roof and wave his blessings at the faithful. After an attempted assassination on Pope John Paul II in 1981 in St. Peter's Square in Vatican City, the papacy wanted more protection. The Thibault Fire Engines Company in Pierreville, Quebec, modified a GMC Sierra pickup truck, so it would be "impervious" but "plush."

TRICKED OUT

While being very "discreet, noble" and luxurious, the 21-foot long limousine was also constructed to withstand an attack. Encased in a two-inch armor plating, the white body of the vehicle displayed the papal crest on both sides and the Vatican flag on the hoods. The pope would sit in a "cockpit" surrounded by bulletproof glass. The gas tanks were lined with a special material designed to withstand an explosion. Thibault made two of the tricked out trucks at $130,000 each. The Popemobile has couch seating for 10, red velour carpeting, a red velvet interior from Italy, dual air conditioners, a state-of-the-art security communications system, and a swivel chair. Thibault, which builds 60 percent of the world's fire trucks, put 200 of its people on the job so the vehicle could be ready in a month's time. While many were not accustomed to seeing the Pope encased in glass, followers could still see him and take his photo through the glass. The Pope was so impressed with his new vehicle that he took one home to the Vatican with him. The car was dubbed the Popemobile (or Papamobile in Italian) and most still call it that, although the Pope in 2002 asked the media refrain from the arguably undignified term. The most current Pope, Francis, has been opting out of the bubble-topped, armor-plated popemobile. In his summer 2013 to Brazil, he chose an open white jeep—along with around 22,000 security staff.

...a group of angry Parliament members opened an illegal gas station selling gas by the gallon.

HAPPY CENTENNIAL!

In 1967, Canada turned 100 years old and the yearlong Canadian Centennial was the biggest celebration ever to hit the nation. Here are some of the quirkier parts of the party.

• Winchester issued a special Centennial version of its famous .30-30 rifle.

• The commission sponsored a 3,200 mile canoe regatta from the Rocky Mountains to Montreal.

• The Centennial flame was lit on Parliament Hill.

• The Cartier Font was commissioned as a distinctly Canadian typeface.

• New works of art were commissioned, including "Canadian Railroad Trilogy" by Gordon Lightfoot and the *Challenge for Change* film series.

• Trumpeter Bobby Gimby and songwriter Ben McPeek wrote "The Centennial Song," also known as "Ca-Na-Da," because of the distinct way the lyrics were delivered by a choir of children. (Two choirs actually; an English speaking group of Young Canada singers sang one version, and a French group sang the French version, "Une Chanson du Centenaire"). The 45 became the most successful single in Canadian history at the time, selling 270,000 copies.

• Ookpik, the Happy Little Arctic Owl, was a popular stuffed toy made of seal skin.

• In 1967, Canadian Prime Minister Lester B. Pearson introduced a unique Canadian toast as part of the Canadian centennial. The toasting word was chimo, which in Inuit means "I'm friendly." Saying "chimo!" was fashionable for about three months and then disappeared into the dustbin of Canadian trivia.

Canada is a world leader in marijuana use, according a U.N. report in 2007.

VIKINGS IN CANADA

The first-ever European settlers in North America came to Canada first.

TRUE DISCOVERY AMID TALL TALES

In 982, Erik the Red reached Greenland, and in about the year 1000, Erik's son Leif Erikson, following up on reports of a land farther west, landed in what is now Newfoundland and established a colony. Some 75 years later, the chronicler Adam of Bremen created the first surviving account of this colony, with additional details later written down in the Norse sagas—thrilling adventure stories that medieval Scandinavians wrote about their Viking ancestors. Of course, the sagas also say that one Viking was killed by an arrow shot by a hopping creature with only one leg, so people were inclined to take the idea of Norse settlement of the New World with a large grain of salt.

JONSSON'S GAMBIT

The first scholar to argue that the Vikings had discovered America was the 16th-century Icelander Arngrim Jonsson. The idea that Vikings had discovered America became a point of pride with Scandinavians. In the 19th century, the works of the Danish historian Carl Rafn began a veritable craze for "Viking runestones" in the States, perhaps the best known of which is the Kensington Runestone, "discovered" by a farmer of Swedish decent in 1898 in Kensington, Minnesota. All of these were demonstrably fake.

The Viking colonization of the New World was nothing more than a legend until, in 1960, the Norwegian explorer Helge Ingstad simply asked the fishermen of L'Anse aux Meadows, Newfoundland, if there were any ruins about. They pointed him the first incontrovertible proof of Norse settlement on the American mainland. Today, L'Anse aux Meadows is a Viking archaeological site, with well-preserved artifacts of what life was like 1,000 years ago.

So, why did the Vikings leave? Why don't Canadians speak Norwegian today? In the later Middle Ages, the climate changed and the sea routes closed off. It was no longer possible for Greenland to be used as a staging base for the Americas. It took another century for the New World to be "rediscovered"—not by Columbus, but by Basques from northern Spain fishing for cod off the Grand Banks.

Canadian Arctic Archipelago consists of 36,563 islands.

CELINE'S SELECTIVES

Celine Dion seems like she might be a very serious person. As it turns out, she's as kooky–and even as bathroom obsessed–as Uncle John (but she has a much better voice).

"My child was not only carried by me, but by the universe."

"Fruits are snacks which are rich in vitamins and can be eaten the whole day."

"I've seen diapers. And believe me, my mother is right. What's in the pooh-pooh is like the Bible. The truth is in there."

"There's something of everything in my bathroom."

"What I am eating I keep in me."

"Everything that I decide to do means something, otherwise I don't do them."

"For me, singing was real life, not two plus two equals four."

"When he's 20 years old what's going to happen to me? I'm gonna marry him." (on her son)

"I've never been cool. And I don't care."

"I smell his feet. They have a scent that's a bit like vinegar." (on her son)

"People used to laugh and call me vampire because I had these big teeth like fangs."

"I often buy myself presents. Sometimes I will spend $100,000 in one day in a posh boutique."

"I wish we were all naked all the time. I have always believed it's what's underneath that counts. If we were all forced to be naked, perhaps we would start to see it a little bit more."

"I am the youngest of 14 children, so I rarely got a chance to speak. If I have an opportunity for talking, I talk."

"Since I was a little child—my nose, I think it is too big."

"I'm not thinking with my head, I'm talking with my heart."

Some Canadians call slushy or broken ice floating in the sea "slob ice."

AM I IN CANADA? ARE YOU SURE?

A look at some weird border and territorial anomalies.

• American president Franklin Roosevelt's family had a retreat on Campobello Island, part of New Brunswick. That makes sense, as you can get there directly from the United States, via a border bridge with Maine. To get there from anywhere else in Canada? You have to take a ferry.

• The town of Hyder, Alaska, is incredibly remote...to the rest of the United States. There are no roads going from anywhere in Alaska (or from anywhere else in the U.S. for that matter) to Hyder. There is, however, a route from Stewart, British Columbia. In other words, to get there, Americans have to go first into Canada, and then back into the U.S.

• Point Roberts, Washington, is accessible by traveling through other parts of Washington State...after crossing two Canadian border stations. The town is bordered by the province of British Columbia, the Straight of Georgia (Canadian waters), and Boundary Bay (which separates Washington state from British Columbia).

• The 600-odd residents of Estcourt Station, Maine, have to undertake international travel to buy a cup of coffee. The residents there have no road access to Maine. To get anywhere, they have to go to Rue Frontiere, which is a road operated by the town of Pohenegamook, in Quebec, on the other side of the border.

• In 1970, three small rural municipalities on the outskirts of Saskatoon merged to form a new district called Corman Park. The vast (1,978 square kilometers), sparsely populated (8,350) area now completely surrounds Saskatoon, the 17th most populated city in Canada.

For the Innu people, Matshishkapeu is the "Fart Man"—the most powerful of all spirits.

BRYAN'S SONGS

Everything Bryan Adams does, he does it for you…even the goofy stuff.

One of the first songs Adams wrote with longtime songwriter partner Jim Vallance was a pop song in 1978 called "Let Me Take You Dancing." It flopped, so Adams's record company had the song remixed into a disco song. While a hit, Adams has never allowed it to be released ever again—because the remix sped up his voice, and he feels he sounds silly, or even feminine.

• In 1981, he wanted to call his second album *Bryan Adams Hasn't Heard of You Either*. A&M Records talked him out of it, and he went with *You Want It, You Got It*.

• Despite being one of the world's biggest Canada-born pop stars, the government did not consider songs from Adams' 1991 album *Waking Up the Neighbors* to fall under "Canadian content" airplay regulations. It was produced by Mutt Lange, who's Australian.

• His biggest ever hit: the 1991 single "Everything I Do (I Do It For You)." That year, former Ku Klux Klan leader David Duke was using it as a theme song for his campaign as Louisiana governor. Adams personally called radio stations in New Orleans and asked them not to play the song anymore. (Duke lost.)

• In 1976, the Vancouver glam rock band Sweeney Todd hit #1 with the song "Roxy Roller." Lead singer Nick Gilder left the band to go solo—and he had another #1 hit with "Hot Child in the City." His eventual replacement in Sweeny Todd—Bryan Adams. He recorded one album with the group, *If Wishes Were Horses*.

• In 2004, Blender placed an Adams song on its "50 Worst Songs Of All Time" list. The song: his 1996 hit "The Only Thing That Looks Good On Me Is You." (The magazine said it just barely edged out Adams' "(I Wanna Be) Your Underwear."

• In 1984, he released as a B-side "Diana," a song he wrote about a little crush on Princess Diana. The British press tried to make a scandal out of it, claiming that Adams had insulted Prince Charles in song. (It eventually died down.)

Canadians purchase 1.7 million boxes of Kraft Dinner each week...

DON'T FENCE ME IN

Canadian women lead the world in hockey, curling, and now, fencing.

WHAT A SCHALM!
Sherraine Schalm is considered one of the best female épéeists in the world. Fencing is an umbrella term for three sword sports: In two of them, foil and sabre, elaborate rules control how you can score points. Épée, however, is pure combat—trying to land a thrust against your opponent with a long, straight sword before he or she does the same.

EN GARDE!
Canada has never won a medal in fencing in the Olympics. However, the thing about the Olympics is that they aren't considered that important in the fencing world—the World Cup is. In 2005, Schalm became the first Canadian to medal in the International Fencing Federation's World Championship, and, in 2006, the first to win the World Cup of fencing. She was a member of the 2004 womens' Olympic épée team, which took fourth—the best Canadian Olympic showing in fencing after another fourth-place finish by the 1984 men's épée team. Early eliminations in subsequent Olympics did little to tarnish her stature in the fencing world.

GETTING AROUND
Born in Brooks, Alberta, and now living in Toronto, Schalm got into the sport because of a junior high school teacher in Edmonton. She lived six years in Budapest to train and has competed across the globe. There were bumps in the road: She once forgot her passport just before leaving a tournament in Cuba (having "safely" stowed it under her mattress), only to have her coach reveal he had recovered it just before she thought she would be unable to board a flight home.

Schalm is married with a young daughter and considering becoming one of the few female coaches in the sport. An active writer with a second book in the works, she related in her memoir, *Running with Swords*, that she was born in fencing stance—with a clubfoot and hip dysplasia.

OOPS, MINISTER!

Proof that even Canadian politicians do stupid things sometimes.

LET THE RIVER RUN. During the 2000 federal elections, Canadian Alliance Party leader and prime minister hopeful Stockwell Day was giving a campaign speech at Niagara Falls, when he promised to put a stop to Canadian jobs going to the U.S. Those jobs, he said, were flowing "from north to south," just like the Niagara River. Political pundits and comedians across the country had a field day over the remark for the next several days, as the Niagara River—which was literally just feet away from Day as he said the words—actually flows straight north. (When later informed of the gaffe by reporters, Day promised to "check the record.")

CONSIDER THE SOURCE. Conservative Ontario minister Bob Dechert was the subject of a scandal in 2011, when it was discovered that the official had sent flirtatious emails to Shi Rong, a Chinese news reporter stationed in Toronto. The emails had been given to reporters by Rong's husband, who had found them in his wife's phone. Dechert, who was also married, defended the messages as innocent flirtations between friends, but apologized for the matter nonetheless. Newspapers called it a very Canadian scandal, due to the mild nature of Dechert's emails to Rong. One of the racier examples: "You are so beautiful. I really like the picture of you by the water with your cheeks puffed. That look is so cute."

FACEBOOKED. In April 2011, Alan Saldanha was running as the Green Party candidate for a seat in British Columbia, when a Vancouver newspaper reported on a quote found on Saldanha's Facebook page: "If rape is inevitable, lie back and enjoy it!" The outcry from women's groups, not to mention other members of the Green Party, was so swift and loud that Saldanha had resigned his candidacy within an hour of the report. Bonus: It was too late for the Green Party to field another candidate, so, even though he was no longer running, Saldanha's name remained on the ballot. (He lost.) Bonus II: Saldanha later said that he thought the quote came from Chinese philosopher Confucius.

Between 1984 and 2008, it was illegal to sell soda in cans on Prince Edward Island...

KNIGHTS OF THE NORTH

Weird as it may seem, Toronto, a modern city of glass and steel, is also a city of shining plate armor and flashing swords.

BY THE BOOK

Everyone's familiar with martial arts like karate, tae kwon do, and kung fu. However, most people don't realize that medieval Europe had a tradition of martial arts, too. Knights had to learn to wield sword, lance, and axe with the same skill as Japanese samurai. Of course, unlike in Japan, there is no living tradition of how to do this. This is where the discipline of Historical European Martial Arts comes in: Using detailed manuals left to us by fencing masters of the past, HEMA practitioners aim to reconstruct how knights actually fought. Toronto's Academy of European Medieval Martial Arts (AEMMA), founded in 1998, is one of the oldest HEMA clubs in North America. Using the manuscripts of Fiore dei Liberi, a medieval Italian fencing master, AEMMA members lovingly re-create and research the fighting skill of the medieval warrior—and then apply them.

In other words, grown men in downtown Toronto dress up in medieval armor and beat the crap out of each other with steel weapons.

BIRDS OF A FEATHER

"When people think of this, they think of some crackpot in his backyard or basement with a sword. But with the Internet, you can find other crackpots in their basements and build a community," joked Brian McIlmoyle, AEMMA's lead instructor.

AEMMA members are more than just "crackpots," though: There's a lot of skill involved. "A lot of people think medieval warfare is all about brutality—smashing and crashing and whoever was strongest won," says Kel Rekuta, a senior AEMMA member. "The reality is, like any other martial art or professional sport, you have to train for it."

AEMMA's brand of medieval mayhem has also won them kudos from academic circles. Students and professors at the University of Toronto have become interested in Fiore dei Liberi, and the group has joined forces with the Royal Ontario Museum to present an annual tournament in the armor gallery.

GENERATION DOUG

Douglas Coupland's first novel Generation X *(1991) named a generation. He never stopped being quotable.*

"If cats were double the size they are now, they'd probably be illegal."

"I don't want any vegetables, thank you. I paid for the cow to eat them for me."

"Christmas makes everything twice as sad."

"Forget about being world famous, it's hard enough just getting the automatic doors at the supermarket to acknowledge our existence."

"If human beings had genuine courage, they'd wear their costumes every day of the year, not just on Halloween."

"Lottery tickets are a surtax on desperation."

"Salad bars are like a restaurant's lungs. They soak up the impurities and bacteria in the environment, leaving you with much cleaner air to enjoy."

"We're rapidly approaching a world comprised entirely of jail and shopping."

"Handmade presents are scary because they reveal that you have too much free time."

"Fondue sets, martini shakers, and juicing machines: three things the world could live completely without."

"The only activities that humans do that have no animal equivalent are smoking, body-building and writing."

"In the future, torture will once again become the recreational sport of the rich."

"Your brain forms roughly 10,000 new cells every day, but unless they hook up to preexisting cells with strong memories, they die. Serves them right."

"Forget sex or politics of religion. Loneliness is the subject that clears out a room."

"Canadians can easily 'pass for American' as long as we don't accidentally use metric measurements or apologize when hit by a car."

The IMAX film system was invented by Canadian Ivan Grame Ferguson to premiere at Expo 67.

OFF THE ICE

So Tim Horton founded Canada's most successful franchise. Big deal–did he ever record a disco album?

WAYNE GRETZKY. In 1991, NBC TV briefly aired *ProStars,* a Saturday morning cartoon starring three big sports stars of the era: Michael Jordan, Bo Jackson, and Gretzky. The cartoon versions of the sports stars had superpowers and a distinct personality, and in every episode the trio would defeat a supervillain, mad scientist, or as they did in one case, recover the stolen Stanley Cup. Gretzky, for some reason, was the jokester of the group and was obsessed with eating. The real Gretzky appeared in live-action bumpers at the beginning and end of the show–voice actor Townsend Coleman performed Gretzky's voice in the animated sequences.

GUY LAFLEUER. At the height of Lafleuer's career and popularity in 1979–he'd just won four straight Stanley Cups with the Montreal Canadiens–Lafleuer recorded an album called *Lafleuer*. It's where Lafleuer's strengths and the trappings of the era collide. It's an album of hockey-themed songs by anonymous studio musicians, as well as monologues of hockey instructional tips from LaFleuer...set to a thumping disco beat. Side one contains six songs: "Skating," "Checking," "Power Play," an extended dance version of "Power Play," "Shooting," and "Scoring. Side two: all of the same songs, but in French.

KEN DRYDEN. For Hall of Fame goalie Ken Dryden, a storied hockey career seems to have been a secondary pursuit. Drafted in 1964, he didn't go pro until 1970 so he could earn a history degree at Cornell University. Three years into his NHL career in 1973, he took a year off to earn a law degree (and intern for a Montreal law firm at the same time). Upon retiring in 1979, he wrote–he's published books about hockey, Canadian history, and the Canadian educational system. And after successful turns in business, law, and serving as the president of the Toronto Maple Leafs, Dryden ran for Parliament in 2004. He represented York Centre until 2011, even making a bid at the Liberal Party's leadership in 2006.

REG HARTT'S MOVIES

Watching a movie with Toronto fixture Reg Hartt isn't just staring at a screen—it's a surreal and singular experience.

THE WAY TO THE CINEFORUM

Strolling along a certain block on one of Toronto's primary thoroughfares, Bathurst Street, you're likely as not to encounter a small sign in a row-house window that reads "Cineforum." Actually, you're just as likely to come across the owner of that row house, and that Cineforum, hanging out on his front stoop, ready to talk about anything from Bunuel to Bugs Bunny, from sci-fi monsters to psychotropic drugs, with anyone who passes by.

Reg Hartt is a film archivist, lecturer and iconoclast-about-town whose Cineforum is actually his front parlor, where he hosts (and annotates, often at length) screenings of old movies ranging from naughty, pre-Hays Code Hollywood arcana to Leni Riefenstahl's Nazi-propaganda classic *Triumph of the Will.* His festivals of "anarchist surrealist hallucinatory films" by Man Ray, Salvador Dali, Luis Bunuel, approach legendary status, as are his occasional spoken-word evenings running the thematic gamut from the life of Christ to "What I Learned From LSD."

MAN ABOUT TOWN

Other Cineforum favorites include Hartt's "sex and violence cartoon fests," featuring the "Censored Eleven" Looney Tunes cartoons that featured blackface characters and other racist depictions, and his transformations of silent films using musical accompaniment he has chosen himself (F.W. Murnau's vampire classic *Nosferatu* set to songs from Radiohead's *Kid A*, for example).

Hartt occasionally takes his show on the road, to Montreal, Ottawa, and elsewhere. But the road trips on which he's most frequently encountered are his bicycle jaunts around Toronto, carrying in his front basket the handmade publicity posters—combining typewritten text with film stills—that have become a hallmark of the city's lampposts and shop windows.

Halifax, Nova Scotia, has more bars per capita than anywhere else in the world.

TORONTO'S FIRST (BOTCHED) HANGING

A city isn't a city until it executes its first prisoner...or comes close.

IN OLD YORK

In 1798, Canada's largest modern-day city was just a five-years-old hamlet, and wasn't yet called Toronto—it was still York. But the city was growing, and so was its crime rate.

In October 1798, an unthinkable, heinous crime took place. An illiterate tailor named John Sullivan and his friend, Michael Flannery, got rip-roaring drunk in one of the town's first taverns. Flannery was so well-versed in Latin proverbs that folks called him "Latin Mike"; Sullivan's skills apparently lay more in the field of artful tracery. Out of cash with their thirst somehow not yet slaked, the two men conspired to fake a banknote for three shillings, which they used to buy more whisky.

HANGING AROUND

The crime was quickly discovered. Latin Mike managed to escape town and across the U.S. border to freedom. Sullivan, however, was caught and jailed in Toronto's brand-new slammer. In short order, Sullivan was tried, convicted, and sentenced by the unforgiving judge to pay for his crime with his life.

Trouble was, the city did not yet have a hangman (and it wouldn't, for another century. Nobody in town was eager to step up and hang a man either. Fortunately, a fellow inmate known only as "McKnight" offered to permanently end Sullivan's reign of terror—for a price. He wanted $100 (about $1,400 in today's money) as well as a pardon. The judge accepted the offer.

Unfortunately, McKnight had no idea what he was doing, and two attempts to tighten the noose and hang Sullivan failed to achieve the desired result. The story goes that Sullivan's last words were something like, "McKnight, I hope to goodness you've got the rope all right this time." The third time was, in fact, a charm.

Women wishing to enter Canada to work as strippers must provide naked photos to get a visa.

FAULKNER'S FLY-BY

William Faulkner wrote fiction, of course, and did it quite well. But examples of the novelist embellishing his life story are legion. Like this one.

THE SOUND...

By 1918, the United States had finally entered World War I, and lots of young men rushed to join the war effort. One of them was Mississippi-born 21-year-old Billy Falkner. But he was only 5'5" tall, and deemed too small to join the U.S. Army. So he hatched a plan to weasel his way into Great Britain's Royal Flying Corps, via its Canadian contingent.

Falkner first learned to change his Mississippi drawl into a phony British accent, changed the spelling of his name from Falkner to "Faulkner" in order to sound more Anglo-Saxon, and he headed to Toronto for pilot training. And if Falkner, er, Faulkner's accounts are to be believed, the RFC accepted him into their ranks in fall 1918 and started training him for combat duty.

...AND THE FURY

Alas, Faulkner never saw the inside of a plane...at least as far as combat was concerned. According to Faulkner, "the war quit on us before we could do anything about it." Armistice was declared on November 11, 1918, and Toronto celebrated. So did Faulkner—he commandeered a biplane, packed the cockpit with bottles of bourbon, and took off over the city.

He attempted a series of trick maneuvers, culminating in a sweeping upside-down loop that was executed perfectly...until he crashed through the ceiling of an airplane hangar and came to rest in the rafters. He emerged with a limp that would plague him for years.

One problem with Faulkner's account: It may not have ever happened. Historians are pretty certain that Faulkner was never in the RFC, never got near a military biplane, and probably faked that lifelong limp. Faulkner biographer Jay Parini dismissed Faulkner's account as an improbable, "testosterone-drenched tale." Still, as Faulkner once wrote, "Most men are a little better than their circumstances give them a chance to be."

KISSING A COD IN NEWFOUNDLAND

When in Rome, do as the Romans do, and pucker up!

BIG JIBS

Newcomers can be forgiven for feeling a bit intimidated when setting foot in Newfoundland for the first time. For starters, the regional dialect may be recognizable as English, but it can be all but indecipherable to a first-time "Come-From-Away," especially when the more mischievous locals (whom you should never, ever call "Newfies") crank up their quirkiness just for sport.

If you really want to ingratiate yourself with the locals, you're likely to find yourself face-to-face with a fish. "Kissing the Cod" is part of an elaborate welcoming ceremony called the "screech-in," which usually takes place in a pub like the ones that line George Street in the provincial capital, St. John's.

The ritual begins with a friendly bartender presenting newcomers with a shot of Screech, a locally produced Jamaican-style rum, and asking, "Are ye a screecher?" The correct response is, "Deed I is, me ol' cock! And long may yer big jib draw!"

This translates as, "Yes I am, my old friend, and may your sails always catch wind."

SEEMS FISHY

After downing the Screech—and taking a moment to recover from the strong, well-named hooch—it's time for the newbies to pucker up. Newfoundlanders aren't oblivious to the hygienic iffiness of planting one on even the freshest of fish, so visitors may be presented with a frozen fish or (particularly since the 1992 moratorium on cod fishing) a replica made from wood or plastic.

Once the shot and the lip-lock are completed, the newcomers are pronounced Honorary Newfoundlanders and presented with a certificate from the Royal Order of Newfoundland Screechers.

IT'S A CONSPIRACY!

All about the bookstore "they" don't want you to know about.

READ ALL ABOUT IT

They can be seen on any given Tuesday afternoon in Toronto's Parkdale district: men skulking along Queen Street with an uncertain gait, then surreptitiously checking every direction—for a zoom lens? for a boom mic? for assassins?—before ducking into a store that treats their paranoid nightmares with the respect they deserve.

Since 2006 the Conspiracy Culture bookstore has established itself as a one-stop shop for those convinced that "the truth is out there." It carries thousands of books, magazines, and DVDs that mainstream booksellers won't, on topics ranging from UFOs to the Illuminati to the Kennedy assassination, as well as T-shirts that read "One Nation Under Surveillance" and "Sodium Fluoride: Poisoning Our Water Since 1945." It also hosts lectures like "The CIA and Military Mind Control," and "The New World Order: A Second Look at the United Nations."

SOMEBODY'S WATCHING

Conspiracy Culture is the brainchild of Patrick Whyte and Kadina Yu, who were stirred by the 9/11 attacks to move beyond their childhood fascinations with Bigfoot and the Bermuda Triangle and consider the vast sea of "alternative narratives" that defy conventional wisdom. Whyte, a former disc jockey, and Yu, a high-school math teacher, decided to open a space where they could sell the publications they were discovering, and offer fellow "free thinkers" a place to share their concerns.

Despite what they call frequent snooping into their affairs by both the Canadian and U.S. governments—including, they claim, routine examinations of imported books by customs officials—they have remained vigilant about providing access to unusual perspectives on the events of the day. "There's the official story, and there's the unofficial story," Whyte told the *Toronto Standard* in 2012. "Once you step into that rabbit hole, watch out, because it just goes and goes and goes."

The actor who played "Scotty" on *Star Trek*, James Doohan, was shot six times on D-Day.

MABEL THE WONDER MONKEY

Why you should "always mount a scratch monkey."

MONKEYING AROUND

Whenever you ask the company's veteran computer guy about reconfiguring or rebooting or another barely comprehensible task related to overhauling your computer, they'll probably first tell you to "always mount a scratch monkey." A "scratch monkey" is, to put things simply, a backup drive—an insurance policy against losing precious or irreplaceable data in case your tinkering goes awry.

The phrase has its origins in the tragic tale of Mabel, a miracle monkey on the campus of the University of Toronto who lost her life because a routine computer fix went wrong.

GOING APE

Mabel was a chimpanzee who became a local celebrity during the late 1970s when researchers at the University of Toronto taught her to swim underwater using a SCUBA-like system controlled by a cutting-edge (at the time) DEC VAX-11/780 computer. While she paddled around a tank, her human trainers pumped various gases through her breathing tube to determine their effects. One day the room-sized computer developed a malfunction, so a technician arrived while Mabel was in the pool. You can guess the rest: The technician fouled up the system regulating Mabel's breathing, there was no backup system, and soon enough the "Swimming Wonder Monkey" had drowned.

Another, slightly more pedestrian (if no less tragic) version of the story concerns a UT experiment that had nothing to do with swimming, but concerned the same computer monitoring the brain waves of five monkeys in a lab. A repair screwup led to the computer emitting electrical signals, rather than receiving them, and two monkeys died.

OCCUPY ICELAND!

Iceland: the turning point of World War II? Sure, why not.

REYKJAVIK OR BUST

The Royal Regiment of Canada got its shiny new name after World War II broke out, but the Toronto-based company had established itself as an elite force as far back as the 1860s, fending off an invasion by Irish-Catholic militants. As the British Empire geared for battle in late 1939, Canadians were eager to join the cause—and soon enough they would be called. The Royal Regiment set sail from Halifax on the *Empress of Australia* the following June, and after a journey across the North Atlantic they saw their first "action"... about 1,000 miles north of mainland Europe.

Of all the things that concerned Winston Churchill in 1940, you'd think Iceland wouldn't have made the list—a peaceful, neutral nation of 120,000, with no standing army. Yet Churchill feared that if Iceland fell to the Nazis, it could lead to them ruling the Atlantic Ocean, so he hatched an invasion plan. And once the British navy had done the dirty work of...well, landing on the island, and mollifying the outraged (if unarmed) locals, Churchill assigned Canadians to maintain the occupation.

TOPS IN SCHNAPPS

And so it was that a few hundred of Toronto's finest—many of whom had never left the city before the war—found themselves hunkered down in drafty huts around places like Reykjavik, Hvalfjörður, and Sandskeið. Eventually joined by soldiers from Ottawa and Montreal—about 2,500 in all—the Royal Regiment spent its first year of duty building airfields and encampments, and keeping warm with shots of a Scandinavian, caraway-flavored schnapps called Brennivin, otherwise known as the "Black Death." Cold and isolated as they were, the Canadians had no idea how good they had it.

They would learn, sadly, when their adventure in Iceland was over—the same regiment suffered brutal casualties during an assault on the French port of Dieppe in 1942.

Dr. Cluny Macpherson, from St. John's, NF, invented the gas mask in WWI.

BED PUSHING

College campuses in the late 1950s and early 1960s were hotbeds of weird fads...like this one.

BAD FADS

In the 1950s, a fad that began in Durban, South Africa, spread to the U.K., Canada, and the U.S.: phone booth stuffing. It literally consisted entirely of seeing how many people could fit into a telephone booth. But fads come and go, and by 1959, phone booth stuffing was passé. Another fad came along to replace it in the U.S.: hunkerin', which involved groups of men squatting on their haunches. What replaced phone booth stuffing in Canada? Bed-pushing.

GO TO BED

Bed pushing was a winter sport, in which a team of students attempted to push a hospital bed, outdoors, the farthest. A team may have been made up by as many as 30 to 40 students. A group of six to eight would take a turn pushing the bed while the rest of the group followed in cars or even in a chartered bus, ready to relieve the pushers when needed. The distances could be vast; a group in Halifax in 1961 pushed a bed 350 miles. Rules could vary. In some, the goal might be to race, with scores being assigned to teams based on distance and time. Other events might involve a boys vs. girls team, "rollers" vs. "pushers," or an objective, such as from one campus to another.

The first instance was traced to the University of British Columbia. The students claimed that they had established a world record in bed-pushing, and since no one had done it before, they were able to hold their title for awhile. But soon, students on college campuses across the country began shattering the UBC record, or setting records of their own. A team from Waterloo Lutheran College got their bed up to 8.4 miles per hour.

But by 1962, bed pushing was dead. A new fad had emerged: Ice cube tossing. Students compete to see how many times they could toss ice cubes back and forth before they melted.

George Ensor and Albert Ganong of New Brunswick invented the chocolate bar.

LEGAL IN CANADA

Liberty reigns in Canada...as long as we're talking chocolate and hormones.

FREEDOM!

While some Americans would have you believe that the liberties of American life are simply unparalleled compared with the restrictive society found in Canada, there are actually quite a few things that are totally legal in Canada that have been outlawed in the U.S.

KINDER SURPRISE EGGS

These chocolate eggs which originated in Italy contain tiny toys inside. Which is exactly why they have never been allowed in the U.S.–the small toys are considered choking hazards for children younger than three. Canadians, on the other hand, don't think they're really for kids younger than three, in part because the packaging would be hard for a toddler to open. As a result, the Kinder Eggs have been available in Canada since the 1970s, and remain a popular holiday treat.

HUMAN GROWTH HORMONE

In Canada, doctors are free to prescribe HGH or various uses, including to help athletic performance or for anti-aging purposes. And off-label prescriptions are widely used, legally in the U.S. For instance, a blood-pressure medication may be prescribed for headaches. But importing HGH into the U.S. is illegal, as is prescribing the drug for off-label uses.

THINGS MADE IN CUBA

Dating back to a trade embargo imposed on Cuba around the time of Cuban Missile Crisis in 1962, tobacco products, including cigars, cannot legally be imported into the U.S.. Americans who buy, sell, or trade Cuban cigars face fines of up to $55,000, as well as prison time. But if you're so inclined, smoke up, Canada: the country never nearly went to war with the tiny Communist nation, so it's perfectly legal to import Cuban cigars.

Canada's top current baby names: Emma and Liam.

ILLEGAL IN CANADA

If you're guilty of anything on this page, get yourself to prison!

TAKING YOUR SPOUSE'S LAST NAME. In most Western countries it's fairly easy for a person to change her (or his) last name upon marriage. The gender equality movement meant that it wasn't automatic, and women were able to keep their last name after marriage. But in Quebec, a law passed in 1981 makes it nearly impossible to do so. The procedures for name change in Quebec leave the decision up to the director of civil status, who needs a serious reason, and the way the law is written, getting married is not a good enough reason.

BABY WALKERS. You know those little wheeled soft seats with their attached disc-like table contraptions your parents put you in when you weren't-quite-walking-yet that allowed you to bump around the house and feel like you were walking? Well, apparently they were pretty much terrible for you. They may delay motor development, and can lead to injury. Canada banned them in 2004. Walkers are illegal to buy and sell, and possession can earn a fine of up to $100,000 and a six-month prison term.

SECOND-HAND MATTRESSES. Canada got serious about bedbugs and has outlawed the import of used mattresses. Anyone moving to Canada is prohibited by the Canada Border Services Agency from bringing their used mattress into the country, unless they can verify that the mattress has been cleaned and fumigated.

PAYING WITH PENNIES. The Canadian Currency Act defines legal tender when it comes to coins. Specifically, a one-cent coin is only legal tender up to 25 cents. So if you buy a cup of coffee and only have pennies to pay with, you could, technically, be in trouble. Nobody's going to arrest you, but the cashier does have the right to reject all-pennies. Likewise, if you only have five cent coins, your money's only good up to $5; it's good for $10 if you have coins that are worth anywhere from 10 cents to less than $1; you can pay for as much as $25 in $1-coins; and as much as $40 "if the denomination is $2 or greater but does not exceed $10." Whew, got all that?

There haven't been mail deliveries on Saturday in Canada since 1969.

HONEST ED'S

At this Toronto landmark, shopping is an adventure.

WHIRLING MIRVISH

In a world dominated by blandly efficient corporate chain stores, Honest Ed's is one of a kind—an old-fashioned emporium, a one-stop shop where filling your cart is an adventure. The retail space, 160,000 square feet spread over two buildings, takes up an entire Toronto city block. The enormous red-and-gold sign outside, modeled after a theater marquee, lights up with 23,000 electric bulbs after dark.

Inside is a mind-boggling array of merchandise—toothbrushes, toaster ovens, cereal bowls, parkas, alarm clocks, Vienna sausages, you name it—all of it marked with hand-painted signage; Ed's employs two full-time sign painters, who at one point could each turn out between 70 and 80 placards a day.

Honest Ed's reflects the larger-than-life personality of its namesake. Ed Mirvish, born in 1914, founded his store in 1948, cashing in his wife's $214 insurance policy to raise money for the stake. Honest Ed's began as a bargain basement, trafficking in factory seconds and fire-sale items. It was a no-frills establishment—merchandise was displayed on orange crates—but it proved immensely profitable.

ED HEADS

Mirvish had a great passion for theatre. He used his fortune to purchase and refurbish playhouses in Toronto and in the U.K.—he was knighted for his work saving London's Old Vic. His sense of the theatrical carried over into the operations of Honest Ed's. Before his death in 2007, Mirvish concocted many publicity stunts, some of which have become community events. On the first Sunday in December, the store gives away 10,000 pounds worth of free Christmas turkeys and fruitcake. And every July, Honest Ed's throws a street party, in honor of Ed Mirvish's birthday.

The store has struggled since Mirvish's death. In fact, the building was put up for sale in July 2013—the store's future is uncertain.

Evansburg, AB, elects a town grouch, licensed to pester and harass.

STREET LEGAL

Two odd, made-in-Canada lawsuits.

PIZZA PIZZA VS. "PIZZA PIZZA"

The Etobicoke, Ontario-based restaurant franchise Pizza Pizza, founded in 1967, has been an innovator in many aspects of its operations. By the company's own account, they were the first chain to use insulated delivery bags to keep their pies warm, the first to advertise with sticky notes on the front page of the Sunday newspaper, and the first to use pineapple as a pizza topping. But its name certainly doesn't break any new ground—it's simple, descriptive, and leaves no doubt as to the nature of the business.

Enter Little Caesars, a massive international chain based in Detroit, Michigan, and its mascot, a cartoon toga-clad Roman who, in the U.S., has spouted the catchphrase "Pizza! Pizza!" since the introduction of Little Caesars' two-for-one special in 1979. The two companies are completely unrelated, and as long as they were not in competition for markets, all was well. But when Little Caesars expanded into Canada, Pizza Pizza took legal action to defend its trademark. As a result, Little Caesars cannot legally use "Pizza! Pizza!" in Canada. Instead, the little Roman uses variants such as "Quality! Quality!" and "Two Pizzas!"

TONY TWIST VS. TONY TWIST

Calgary-born cartoonist Todd McFarlane found fame and fortune in the 1990s with his massively successful horror-tinged comic book *Spawn*, which begat an animated TV show, a movie, and a line of action figures. McFarlane, a huge hockey fan, created a minor character in Spawn with the likeness of NHL player Tony Twist, a tough enforcer for the Quebec Nordiques and the St. Louis Blues. McFarlane even named the character, a mobster, "Antonio Twistelli"—except he preferred the nickname "Tony Twist." The real Tony Twist was not flattered by McFarlane's "tribute." He sued for damages, alleging that McFarlane had profited by unauthorized use of his name and likeness. McFarlane argued that his use of Twist's name and likeness constituted fair use, protected under the US right to free speech, but judges disagreed. After several appeals, Twist received $5 million in damages.

Exeter, Ontario, has a White Squirrel Festival—with real white squirrels—each September.

LET'S GO TO THE MALL!

The West Edmonton Mall is the largest indoor shopping mall in North America. That's not weird, but plenty of odd stuff has gone on there.

• The Mall's amusement park, Galaxyland, was originally called Fantasyland. It was changed after a lawsuit from Disney.

• Among the mall's other attractions: an indoor shooting range, an aquarium, a water park, an interfaith chapel, and a boating lake centered around a large-scale replica of Christopher Columbus' *Santa Maria*.

• Specimens of an invasive cockroach species, native to Asia and not found anywhere else in Edmonton, have been spotted in the water park. The creatures most likely arrived via the park's imported plants.

• The Mall's 18-hole miniature golf course is a scale replica of the famous links at Pebble Beach in California.

• Big retailers can leave big vacancies. When the Mall's IKEA store closed in the mid-1990s, the location stood empty for years, until a recreation complex took over the space in 2002.

• Urban legend: a subway station, ready-built and waiting, sits beneath the Mall in case the city of Edmonton ever expands its light rail system.

• Tragedy struck the Mall in 1986, when several cars from the Mindbender—the 14-story, triple-loop roller coaster—derailed, killing three passengers.

• In 2010, a toddler climbed on a bench on the mall's second story and went toppling over a railing. He miraculously survived when he landed in an ornamental fountain below.

• The Mall houses a 13-screen cinema...complete with an animatronic, fire-breathing dragon in the lobby.

• The Gehrmezian family, who developed the Mall, had *mezuzahs* installed at every entrance. These small cases, containing rolled-up scrolls bearing verses from Deuteronomy, are commonly found on the doorways of Orthodox Jewish homes.

Some of the oldest rocks on Earth make up the Canadian Shield, which covers most of Quebec.

ONLY CANADIAN TO ...

Singular achievements by remarkable Canucks.

...win medals in both the Summer and Winter Olympics: Clara Hughes, who won two bronzes for cycling (1996) and a gold, a silver, and two bronzes in speed skating across three Games (2002, 2006, 2010).

...be named to the *Forbes* 100 Most Powerful Women list: Sue Gardner, executive director of Wikimedia and former director of the CBC's website.

...to make the *Forbes* 2013 billionaires list: David Thomson, whose family controls Thomson Reuters Inc. and *The Globe and Mail*—he's worth an estimated at $20.3 billion).

... win a Grammy in 2013: Drake, who won Best Rap Album for *Take Care*

...win a Latin Grammy: Nelly Furtado.

... command a theatre of operations during WWII: Leonard W. Murray, who was Commander-in-Chief of the Canadian Northwest Atlantic.

... sweep the sprint events at a single Olympics: Percy Williams, who won gold in all of the sprint events in 1928.

... win the Nobel Peace Prize: Lester Pearson, prime minister from 1963 to 1968.

...win the Indianapolis 500: Jacques Villeneuve, in 1995.

...complete a half-marathon in an hour: track and field athlete Jeff Schiebler, who competed in the Olympics twice.

... be awarded the medal of honor in the Vietnam War: Peter Lemon, who while Canadian born, was a U.S. citizen.

...win all three of the top science fiction literary awards: Robert J. Sawyer, who has been awarded the Hugo, the Nebula, and the John W. Campbell Award.

... lose all four limbs in World War I and survive: Ethelbert "Curley" Christian. He not only survived, but was instrumental in establishing Canada's Attendance Allowance program for veterans.

You will not find any snakes, skunks, or poison ivy on the island of Newfoundland.

INCUBUS

Sci-fi-icon. Recording artist. Man's man. William Shatner is all of these. But before his defining role as Captain Kirk, Shatner made one of the strangest movies ever made.

CAPTAIN, MY CAPTAIN

Born in Montreal, Shatner trained for the stage and performed Shakespearean roles at the famous Stratford Festival in Ontario. His first starring role—sporting a bright-blond bleach job—was as the title character in a 1955 CBC production of *Billy Budd*, and soon became the epitome of the jobbing actor, taking whatever role presented itself; he amassed a checkered resume in film, with prestige productions like 1958's *The Brothers Karamazov* alongside the Roger Corman B-movie *The Intruder*, and in TV shows such as *The Twilight Zone* and *The Outer Limits*.

In 1966, shortly before he was cast as Captain Kirk, he was cast in the bizarre supernatural thriller *Incubus*. Directed by *Outer Limits* creator Leslie Stevens, *Incubus* was a weird cross between a Gothic melodrama and an art film. Shatner plays a wounded soldier, passing through a village renowned for its healing waters, who runs afoul of a seductive evil spirit.

ESPERANT-NO

That's a weird enough plot, but the strangest thing about *Incubus* is that it was performed entirely in Esperanto—a constructed language devised in 1887. Esperanto was created by the Polish linguist Ludwig Zamenhof, who hoped that a new common tongue, native to none but understandable by all, would heal divisions between peoples and foster world peace. Stevens had no such agenda; he thought Esperanto would give the film an eerie atmosphere.

In any case, Shatner and the rest of the cast were unfamiliar with the language before shooting began, and learned their lines phonetically. (Esperanto speakers at the time were reportedly dismayed at the improper pronunciation.) Though *Incubus* had some success at film festivals, it was released theatrically only in France. For many years, all prints were believed lost, but the film was rediscovered, restored, and released on DVD in 2001.

The largest lobster ever caught weighed 9.3 kg (20. 5 lbs) and was captured in Nova Scotia in 1977.

MEET THE VILETONES

The story of one of Canada's first—and most controversial—punk rock bands.

THEM. HERE.
Canadian punk in the late '70s tended to be strictly a local affair, with no nationwide touring circuit to speak of. The sheer size of the country, and the prohibitive distance between population centers, made impossible the sort of cheap, speedy touring that allowed punk to propagate in the U.K., and along the U.S. East Coast.

The Viletones were better-travelled than most first-wave Canadian punk bands, even scoring several showcase gigs in New York City; but for the most part, remained Toronto's problem. New musical movements will always face resistance from the established order, but in Toronto of the 1970s, the very idea of punk rock engendered such moral panic that the Viletones' very first gig was greeted with a screaming newspaper headline: "NOT THEM! NOT HERE!"

BAD DOGGIE

To be fair, the Viletones courted controversy. Frontman Steve Leckie performed under the purposely combative stagename "Nazi Dog." Crafting a stage presence that combined the brutal physicality of Iggy Pop with the poetic pretension of Patti Smith, Leckie fostered rumors that he planned to end the Viletones' short career by killing himself on stage. If nothing else, the rumors made the Viletones a can't-miss ticket, since every show might literally be their last. (They still managed to record two albums, in 1977 and 1978.)

These days, the heyday of the Viletones is remembered fondly. They were even the model for the fictional band Screaming Fist in William Gibson's seminal science-fiction novel *Neuromancer*. Steve Leckie took a long hiatus from the music in 1983 and now runs an art gallery. Since 1998, he has occasionally released new music and performed under the Viletones moniker. But in a way, the rumors came true—because when Steve Leckie performs now, he's billed under his real name. "Nazi Dog," he says, is dead.

An *inuksuk* is a human figure made of stone and it is displayed on the Nunavut provincial flag.

POTHEAD PREMIER?

Rules for meeting the Queen: bow or curtsy, and leave the drugs at home.

HATFIELDS OF GREEN

Richard B. Hatfield had served as the premier of New Brunswick since 1970. His primary accomplishments involved economic development in his province, as well as leading the way to help make New Brunswick the first officially bilingual province.

Queen Elizabeth II visited Canada in 1984, as she has many times before and since, and Hatfield was selected to meet and escort her majesty for a spell, along with several other Canadian officials. During a routine inspection before Hatfield, the Queen, and the others were to board a plane, authorities found something in Hatfield's suitcase: 35 grams of marijuana, sitting in an outside pocket.

CHARGING AHEAD

In the weeks following the discovery—and Hatfield's arrest—the 53-year-old conservative premier said of the marijuana, "Obviously I do not know how it got there." He had good reason to deny. Hatfield faced a fine of $750, or up to six months in prison, as 35 grams is a *lot* of marijuana—that amount is generally enough to charge a suspect for "intent to distribute."

Hatfield was found not guilty on all charges. The judge in the case believed the premier's "I don't know how it got there" story, mentioning in his ruling that the marijuana discovery was leaked to the press, saying that a possible motive for planting could have been "the juiciest story ever to crack the media."

But the drug charges weren't the end of Hatfield's troubles. In February 1985, two young men appeared on television and claimed that Hatfield had given them marijuana and cocaine at a 1981 party, and that they witnessed Hatfield smoking pot.

While there were of course calls for Hatfield's resignation, he refused. Hatfield resigned in 1987, when his party lost power in parliamentary elections.

Watertown, Ontario, is home to the world's longest gum wrapper chain: 13,514 m (44,377').

"WILDFLOWER"

Remember the '70s soft rock ballad "Wildflower" by Skylak? It was a Top 10 hit. How? The government.

CANCON DO!

"Canadian Content" rules, introduced in 1971, are now accepted as a way to support homegrown talent and limit American pop culture. At the time, programmers hated being told what to do, and tried to fulfill the requirement to play songs by Canadian acts as quickly or as lazily as possible.

Take the case of "Wildflower." This 1972 soft soul ballad, by Vancouver band Skylark, originally made it to the airwaves only out of spite. The high-powered Ontario AM station, CKLW, had a massive stateside audience for its R&B/soul format; a huge proportion of its advertising sales came from Detroit businesses. Faced with a dearth of Canadian-made soul music, the program director put "Wildflower"—which had not even been issued as a single yet—into heavy rotation for three solid months, solely to satisfy CanCon rules. (The requirement was pretty loose—the law didn't say that the content had to be "*varied* Canadian content," only "Canadian content."

FLOWERS ON THE WALL

At the time, CKLW was the only radio station in North America playing the song. But regional demand in lower Canada and the upper American Midwest for "Wildflower" grew so great that Skylark's record company issued a single, which eventually became a Top 10 hit in both the U.S. and Canada. It also launched the career of keyboardist, songwriter, and producer David Foster (Chicago, Peter Cetera, Celine Dion).

Small consolation to CKLW. Without enough Canadian acts to fulfill the CanCon requirements, the station eventually abandoned the R&B format—and with it most of its Detroit-area African-American listeners. CKLW cycled through several format changes more conducive to CanCon requirements, but could not reverse its ratings slide. Now a news-talk station, CKLW enjoys good local ratings, but has lost virtually its entire stateside audience.

Leamington, Ontario, is the tomato capital of Canada.

MANCE'S TOWN

In 2011, 400 years after the fact, Montreal's city government recognized French nurse Jeanne Mance as one of the city's official "founders."

NUN THE WISER

The roles of women among explorers and settlers frequently are lost to history. But perhaps the most intriguing aspects of Jeanne Mance's new stature are the multifaceted circumstances of her participation in the struggle to establish Montreal, and ensure its early survival.

Having discovered her calling as a Catholic missionary in her mid-30s, Mance eagerly signed on to the fundraising organization that modern-day locals recall as La Société de Notre-Dame de Montréal. (It's often ignored that the full name of that organization was La Société de Notre-Dame de Montréal Pour la Conversion des Sauvages de la Nouvelle-France. That last bit translates rather directly.)

After helping establish the city of Quebec, Mance arrived with Montreal's first French settlers in 1642 as a nurse and bursar, treating the sick and distributing everyday goods such as food... and gunpowder.

NURSE, INFUSION, PLEASE

Mance oversaw the construction and operation of a hospital that treated both the settlers and "savages"...but those local Iroquois proved much more interested in causing injuries than healing them, and Mance was forced to abandon the hospital and retreat into the fort.

She traveled to Paris in 1650 and raised 22,000 livres for the hospital fund from that city's noblewomen—but when she returned to Montreal and saw all the violence around her, she turned over those funds to the military, which used them to acquire more manpower and munitions—a cash infusion credited with saving the city. It took nearly a decade, but eventually Mance was able to return to the hospital and complete her life's work in a fashion more in line with her original ambitions.

WHO YOU GONNA CALL?

The Vancouver Paranormal Society ain't afraid of no ghost.

ZOINKS!

They enter a house armed not with Proton Packs and traps, but with digital cameras and night-vision video equipment. Their aim is not to "catch" or remove a ghost from the premises, and certainly not to summon spirits through séances, but to collect evidence of apparitions' presence and, if possible, make contact with them.

The Vancouver Paranormal Society are "not thrill-seeking ghosthunters looking for notoriety or profits," their website insists; they are serious, amateur investigators fulfilling what they believe is a legitimate need for supernatural research in the modern world.

Founded in 1993, VPS is a team of five human scientists and a dog (just like on *Scooby-Doo!*) that never charges clients for its services. An investigation usually begins with a phone call describing a series of occurrences in a domicile or old building. The investigators descend upon the haunted dwelling, usually at night (because that's when most hauntings are noticed), interviewing the occupants about their experiences and gaining a general history of the building and its previous inhabitants.

SPOOKY STUFF

Then they go to work with their cameras, darkening the house and taking multiple flash photographs, and checking the images for abnormalities—a random shadow here, an unexplainable splotch there. They may attempt to pick up sounds inaudible to the human ear, using an "electronic voice phenomenon recorder"; they may even call out to the spirits, hoping for a response.

The group does not publicize the results of its investigations, but its founder told the *Vancouver Courier*, "We've had members poked, prodded and goosed, and [one was] pushed along a hallway almost like she was possessed." Whether or not a ghost is found in a particular house, she added, "Sometimes people just feel better because we've been there. And that's as far as it needs to go for them."

The world's largest totem pole is a towering 54.94 meters tall and stands in Victoria, B.C.

WE'RE # 1!

Hooray for Canada!

Reputation: In 2013 the Reputation Institute's "Country RepTrak" named Canada the most reputable country on earth— for the third year in a row.

Academic salaries: Average monthly salary of a full-time Canadian professor: $7,196.

Educated adults: 40% of the workforce has a post-secondary college degree, and Canadian students are also the most likely to read for pleasure.

Translators: One in twenty of the world's accredited translators are Canadian.

Coastline: Canada's 151,600 miles of coastline would stretch around the equator six times.

Lakes: Minnesota is the "Land of 10,000 Lakes," but Canada has more than two million.

Space robots: The Canadarm helped shuttle astronauts grab onto orbiting satellites, and Dextre, on the ISS, proved that an orbiting robot could refuel a satellite.

Social media astronauts: Shuttle Commander Chris Hadfield has over a million Twitter followers. (American Buzz Aldrin, the second man to walk on the moon, has 800,000.)

American "brain-drain": When science and engineering Ph.D. recipients from the U.S. choose to work abroad, the majority choose Canada.

Natural capital: In 2012 natural commodities like lumber, rivers, and minerals amounted to CAD $89,000 per capita.

Polar bears: Four out of five of the world's polar bears are Canadian. (Russia and Alaska are home to the rest.)

Hemp food: In 2011 Manitoba's Hemp Oil Canada, Inc. received the world's first safety accreditation for hemp-based food.

Online census: Canada was the first country to have an "online option" for census responses. 54.4% of the 2011 census were completed online.

WE'RE # 1!

Canada is first in the world in bad things, too.

Garbage: In 2009 each Canadian created 777 kilograms of trash—about the same as a large bull moose.

Wasting freshwater: When you have more freshwater than anyone else, you can waste it. In 2006 Canadians used an average of 327 litres of freshwater per day.

Government-approved narwhal killing: In 2008 Ottawa decided to let Inuit hunters kill 500 stranded (and endangered) narwhals rather than use ice-breakers to free them from Pond Inlet. Why? Because the noise from the ice-breakers might be too stressful for the animals.

Low spending on childhood education: In 2007 Canada spent less money on early childhood education than any of the 25 most developed countries.

Freedom from information: Of the world's five Parliamentary democracies, Canada's information laws are the most restrictive.

Time spent online: Canadians averaged 45.3 hours per month online in 2012. What were they doing...

Online video viewing: The average Canadian adult watches 304 videos per month. (The U.S. is second at 286.)

Smoking marijuana: About a third of Canadian teenagers have tried marijuana, the most of any country.

Deaths from fire: 85% of Canadian fire deaths happen in the home. 25% of fatalities are children. Spruce Grove, Alberta, Fire Chief Tim Vandenbrink points the finger at a lack of interest in formulating fire-safety plans.

Opioids usage: Canadians use more prescription opioids (e.g., OxyContin) than anyone else. Ontarians use more than twice as much as the rest of the country.

Unattractive people: According to the French fashion magazine *Maquillage et Motocyclette*. It cited Canadian's tendency to "over-wear warm clothes like sweatpants."

You may not establish a pigsty within 50 feet of a public place in Halifax County, Nova Scotia.

A MYSTERY IS A-FOOT

Sometimes, reality out-creeps even the most macabre fictions.

PLAYING FOOTSIE

On the shores of the Salish Sea around Vancouver, more than a dozen human feet—inside shoes, but otherwise unattached—have washed up since 2007. The series of gruesome discoveries, the most recent of which occurred in a Vancouver dog park in January 2012, has inspired amateur sleuthing and conspiracy theorizing, at least a couple of hoaxes, a Norwegian novel, and an episode of the U.S. television series *Bones*.

The first discovery occurred in August 2007 on the relatively remote Jedediah Island; particularly perplexing was the fact that the shoe, made by Adidas, was sold mostly in India. (Was the owner a victim of the 2004 tsunami?) Six more feet washed up over the next 15 months, including two matching pairs. (Were they bridge-jumping suicides? Victims of grisly murders?) As more feet came ashore, investigators struggled for explanations even as they identified some of the remains, including a local fisherman missing since 1987.

Their efforts weren't aided by the inevitable hoaxes through the years: shoes that were planted on the shoreline with animal feet or raw meat inside.

JUST DO IT

That uncertainty has fed a rumor mill that became more active through the years, with more occasional discoveries—14 in all, as of mid-2013.

• Did the feet detach from the bodies because of the natural impact of water flows?

• Because sea creatures weren't hungry for Nikes?

• Because the shoes' buoyancy (most of them have been sneakers) kept the feet afloat as the bodies sank?

• Or was something more nefarious afoot (sorry)?

No single explanation, for either the deaths or the detachments, has yet proved definitive... so it's likely we'll more headlines like this one from 2008: "Fourth Foot Fuels Flotsam Frenzy."

Garfish, common in the Eastern Atlantic, have green bones.

THE FILIBUSTER

The weirdest day in parlimentary history.

OUT OF ORDER!

Late 19th century prime minister Alexander Mackenzie was known for his brutally honest demeanor, rarely using diplomatic niceties to achieve whatever he wanted. When parliamentary opponents challenged him on rules of order, he would often refuse their requests outright. On the last day of the spring session, a group of French members of the House wanted to continue speaking after a particularly long and drawn-out debate. Opponents clamored to prevent this from happening, appealing to Mackenzie to adjourn the session. When the prime minister blithely denied their request, they came up with an outrageous strategy to tire out the French speakers and hopefully end the session.

The French opposition waited until points of order were introduced to the floor, at which time they began all manner of disruptive activities: making sounds with tin trumpets, banging on their desks, imitating barnyard animals, releasing rubber balloons, throwing their stationery supplies around the room with reckless abandon, and even tossing books of bills and laws onto the floor. The mayhem drowned out the sound of the Speaker of the House as well as the French speakers.

To add further distraction, the opposition began belting out songs ("Marseillaise," "A la Claire Fontaine," and "The Raftsman's Chorus"), which, surprisingly, the songs struck a common chord among members of the House, and soon the entire assembly was singing along. The camaraderie was not to last, though, as when the French speakers resumed control of the floor, the opposition immediately launched into its chaotic assault. The speakers responded with a filibuster of their own, lengthening their speeches with extracts from whatever books and periodicals were at hand.

The madcap exchange, which went on to include a paper-airplane war between the two camps, went on throughout the night. The next day, the sleep-deprived group joined together in an impromptu rendition of "God Save the Queen," thus concluding the bizarre event with an appropriate dash of patriotic spirit.

You aren't allowed to keep a cow in your house in St. John's, Newfoundland.

"THE GREAT WHITE NORTH"

Bob and Doug McKenzie are Canadian icons. It makes sense that they came into existence due to a government demand for Canadian content.

TWO MINUTE WARNING

After two years as a production of the small, regional Global Television Network, the sketch comedy show *SCTV* shifted production to the CBC in 1980. One stipulation: SCTV had to add two minutes to its run time, and, per the requirements of the network and the government's "Canadian Content" regulations, that two minutes had to be distinctly Canadian.

Producers sent the missive down to the creative staff, which included future comedy superstars Dave Thomas and Rick Moranis, who were both cast members and writers. "We thought it was ridiculous," Moranis later told the Chicago Tribute. "We do the show in Canada, we write it here, we're Canadians. How can they ask us to be more Canadian?" So, Thomas and Moranis came up with something that sort of celebrated Canada, but mostly made fun of it, creating two characters to embody every Canadian stereotype they could think of—two slow-talking, beer-swilling, plaid-and-toque-clad, back-bacon-eating goofballs who said "eh" almost constantly. They even gave them Canadian-sounding names: Bob and Doug McKenzie. (Thomas called the McKeznies "a satiric statement on what happens when you try to make entertainment a nationalistic issue.")

THEY TOOK OFF

The McKenzies, portrayed by Moranis and Thomas, made their debut in a sketch on the September 19, 1980 episode of *SCTV*, as hosts of a talk show called *The Great White North*. They immediately (and ironically) became the most popular characters on the show—if not in Canadian TV history. Moranis and Thomas also recorded a #1 album as the McKenzies (with the single "Take Off," featuring Geddy Lee of Rush), not to mention a hit movie (1983's *Strange Brew*), and even an animated series.

Pet tarantulas are forbidden in Toronto.

WORLD'S SMALLEST LIBRARY

If we did our math correctly, this book is bigger than that library.

LIGHT READING

It's always nice to find out that you've set a record of some sort, but in most people's eyes, a record only counts when it's been recognized by the folks at Guinness.

Unfortunately for the folks who run the library in Cardigan, a fishing community on Canada's Prince Edward Island—Guinness doesn't actually have a category in their *Book of World Records* for Smallest Library, but the lesser-known, Guinness rival World Record Academy has decided to go ahead and give them the title anyway.

Operated by John A. MacDonald, the Cardigan library is located in a 3.5 x 3.5 metre building, holds 1,800 books (give or take), operates on an honor system, and only charges $5 for a lifetime membership. The library proudly trumpets its miniscule size with a sign on the side of building, although the words "world's smallest library" feature "smallest" in quotation marks, possibly as a nod to the lack of Guinness approval.

Nonetheless, the books regularly fly in and out of the facility, using only an honor system to ensure that titles are returned in a timely fashion.

OLD MACDONALD HAD SOME BOOKS

In a July 2013 CBC story, MacDonald's daughter, Alexandrea, who assists her father in his literary endeavor, discussed her rationale behind advertising the littleness of the library, explaining, "I think that when they see that, when they're driving by, they're thinking, oh, maybe they're just heading on the way to Montague Library, but then they think, 'Oh, Canada's Smallest Library. That's pretty cool. I'm going to go check that out.'"

You could go to jail for up to 30 days in Nova Scotia if you color a chick.

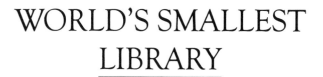

POLI-TALKS

Actual quotes from actual Canadian politicians

"Canada is the greatest nation in this country."

—former Toronto mayor Allan Lamport

"If this thing starts to snowball, it will catch fire right across the country."

—former Alberta MP Robert Thompson

"My conduct had nothing to do with me."

—Ontario MP Al McLean (defending himself against a sexual harassmentcharge)

"What the hell do I want to go to a place like Mombasa? I just see myself in a pot of boiling water with all these natives dancing around me."

—former Toronto mayor Mel Lastman (before departing on an official visit to Kenya)

"Your Majesty, I thank you from the bottom of my heart, and Madame Houde thanks you from her bottom too."

—Montreal mayor Camillien Houde in to King George VI (1936)

"I am not denying anything I didn't say."

—Prime Minister Brian Mulroney

"If I tell a lie, it's because I think I'm telling the truth."

—British Columbia legislator Phil Gaglardi

"My strategy has always been to stay on course unless a change, of course, is announced. And if it is, of course, we will announce it."

—Prime Minister John Turner

"Are you some kind of right-wing commie bastard? Do you want your little wife to go over to Iran and get raped and shot?"

—Toronto mayor Rob Ford (after being asked to be quiet at a hockey game; he was drunk)

"I'm not a genius, obviously, but he makes me look like one."

—former Toronto mayor Mel Lastman, on current Toronto mayor Rob Ford

The world's largest Ceilidh fiddle resides on the waterfront of Sydney, Nova Scotia.

CANUCK PUNK

Without access to traditional outlets for distribution and performance, Canadian punk rock bands were forced to find creative solutions to common challenges.

PRETTY PAPER. Late '70s Newfoundland punk band Da Slyme had done a number of recording sessions for local radio, but had never put out a record. In 1980, the band scraped together enough cash to press a small run of vinyl LPs collecting their radio sessions. When the records arrived, though, they realized to their horror that no record sleeves were included. Lacking the funds to have their own printed, the members of Da Slyme rounded up piles of thrift-store LPs, discarded the records, and repurposed the cardboard sleeves, spray-painting their own logo over the original artwork. These one-of-a-kind jackets are now high-priced collectibles.

BREAKING IMMIGRATION LAW IS PUNK! A ferocious touring band from Ottawa, the Action had been booked for a string of dates opening for the Ramones, with the first gig in Detroit. The band was turned away from border crossings in both Sarnia and Windsor, due to incomplete paperwork. Undeterred, the band made their way to the riverfront and found a pilot who agreed to smuggle them across the border in his boat.

MOB RULE. As a young anglophone band coming up in largely French-speaking Montreal, the 222s were excited to be approached by a manager who promised that he and his organization could get his on the radio. Before long, the 222s realized that they had inadvertently signed up with an organized crime syndicate. The "manager" encouraged the band to embrace a more profitable, pop sound and image. The 222s were forced to record their first single in a basement (with a gun reportedly sitting on the kitchen table upstairs), which was, despite their silent objections, a French pop song chosen for them. The gangsters made good on their end—the 222s' version of "La Poupée qui fait Non" was a hit across Quebec—but the band had broken up before the record even came out.

The Telephone Historical Centre in Edmonton is dedicate to preserving the history of the telephone.

FILLES DU ROI

How your great-great-great-great-great-great-great-great-grandparents met and fell in love.

MEETING MR. RIGHT

Meeting that special someone can be a real challenge. Back when Canada was New France, it was even harder. Few women wanted to pay the cost of an arduous passage and then try to eke out a living out of an unsettled frontier. Therefore, most of the early settlers in New France were men. The gender imbalance worried officials, who saw that the English colonists were rapidly outnumbering the French. Furthermore, many of the voyageurs and *couriers du bois* married Native American women, which gave them an advantage in trading but made French officials worry about settlers going native.

Their proposed solution? Recruit French women to come to the New World. Between 1663 and 1673, around 800 young women took up the challenge. They were known as the "Filles du Roi," (women of the King) because King Louis XIV's government sponsored their passage.

DOWN ON THE FARM

The women, most between 12 and 25, were chosen for their health and good character. Most were lower class, though there were a few impoverished nobility to pair off with officers and gentlemen. Most were also from the cities, which meant that they had to get used to backbreaking agricultural work.

Surprisingly, despite the odds, most of the stories of the Filles du Roi had happy endings. The majority found husbands; the gender imbalance in the colony also meant that those who weren't happy with the men they became engaged to could break up with him and find another.

Thousands of present-day Canadians are descended from the Filles du Roi. And so are luminaries such as Angelina Jolie, Hillary Clinton, and Hockey Hall of Famer Bernie "Boom Boom" Geoffrion.

YOU SAY TOMAHTO, I SAY EH?

We all know Canadians speak English (and quite a bit of French), but there are certain turns of phrase that are uniquely their own.

Arseuver and Headuver. Newfoundland slang for sitting in the back (arseuver) or the front (headuver), especially of a boat.

Ballicatter. In Newfoundland, this is ice that forms along a shore from waves and spray.

Bluenoser. A nickname for a resident of Newfoundland, originally used to describe sailors who were out in the cold until their noses turned blue.

Boonie-bouncing. Going through the woods or logging roads for fun on sport bikes, motorbikes, ATVs, or trucks.

Booter. When you step in a puddle deep enough to soak your foot.

Bunnyhug. A hooded sweatshirt, Saskatchewan.

Coastie. A person from Vancouver with an urban attitude and style of dress—not usually used as a compliment.

Cod choker (or cod chucker). A resident of New Brunswick, based on the area's fishing heritage.

Far as ever a puffin flew. Newfoundland and Labrador contains 95 per cent of the Atlantic Puffins in North America. If a Newfoundlander says that a friend has gone far as ever a puffin flew, well, then they are long gone from those parts.

Hoser. The term comes from hockey. *Hosers* are players that had to hose down the ice after their team was defeated. This clearly comes from the pre-Zamboni days. Calling someone a hoser is the same as calling them a loser, or worse.

Kastaveup. An accident. The term is used in southwestern Nova Scotia.

Lewer day. A day of bad weather when the fishermen stay in, peculiar to southwestern Nova Scotia. What do they do? Work on their lures.

Survey says: 1 in 10 Canadians have had sex in a canoe.

Long may your big jib draw. An old Newfoundlander expression that means, “May the wind always be in your forward sails.” It’s often used as a toast. There’s a longer version that goes: “Deed I is me ol’ cock, and long may your big jib draw.” The first part of the phrase means, “Yes, I am an old friend.”

Making puppies/screwing the pooch. Someone is sitting around doing nothing, or they are slacking off at work. There is a less...dignified expression that is also used, but these two are the printable ones. While originally a military expression, it is quite popular in many Canadian regions and in both French and English.

May 2-4. Of course there is also Victory Day—Queen Victoria’s Birthday holiday—also known as May 2-4. Apparently the 2-4 refers more to the 2-4 packs of beer consumed over the holiday weekend than Victoria’s date of birth.

Muskoka chair. Large, usually wooden deckchair. The equivalent of an Adirondack chair in the United States. It was named after the town of Muskoka, Ontario.

Sook or sookie. A Newfoundlander term for a weak, self-pitying person; a person who won’t go along, especially out of spite; or a crybaby or sore loser. It can also be a term of endearment for pets or children who are extremely affectionate.

Snye. A side-water channel that rejoins a larger river, creating an island.

Tumbler turkeys. Ravens (or crows) found in or around Tumbler Ridge, British Columbia.

Tunk. Knock. Used in southwestern Nova Scotia.

Whadda’yat?. Newfoundlander term meaning, “What are you doing?”

THAT’S NOT VERY NICE

“The beaver, which has come to represent Canada as the eagle does the United States and the lion Britain, is a flat-tailed, slow-witted, toothy rodent known to bite off its own testicles or to stand under its own falling trees.”

—June Callwood

TOE-TALLY GRUESOME

This little piggy became part of Canada's grossest cocktail tradition.

THREE FINGERS . . . AND A TOE

Looking for a test of bravery with your beverage? Then head to the rugged Yukon in the extreme northwest—legendary land of trappers and gold miners. In Dawson City, the Sourdough Lounge in the Downtown Hotel serves the infamous Sourtoe Cocktail. The drink itself is nothing special—often just a shot of whisky. Actually, it can be any drink you like—champagne, scotch, beer, or even a Coke. What makes this cocktail a Sourtoe is not the drink but the garnish. Instead of an olive, onion, or lemon peel, it comes with an actual human toe bobbing in it. The toes come from anonymous donations from sympathetic amputees. The blackened toes have been dehydrated and preserved—packed in a Mason jar full of salt.

The history of the drink goes back to the 1920s during prohibition. As the story goes, the Mounties were hot on the trail of brothers Otto and Louie Liken. They had been hauling illegal rum from Dawson into Alaska. After Otto got his foot wet, his toe went dead from frostbite. The brothers knew gangrene would spread into the foot if they did not take drastic action. In the middle of nowhere and without access to doctors, Louie offered to be the surgeon. Otto uncorked a bottle of his favorite booze and anaesthetized himself. Then Louie performed the delicate operation, blasting his brother's toe off with a shotgun.

AN UNUSUAL MEMEN-TOE

The brothers kept the toe as a souvenir in a jar of alcohol. Flash forward to 1973. When riverboat Captain Dick Stevenson found the preserved digit, he realized he may have a tourist attraction on his hands. He brought the toe to the bar in the Eldorado Hotel, and he challenged all takers to have a drink with the pickled toe floating in it. If they could do it, they'd be a real Yukoner and receive a certificate saying they were officially in the Sourtoe Club. The only rule: Your lips have to touch the toe.

Soused vacationers and locals were captivated by the challenge. For seven years, the standard Sourtoe Cocktail was champagne in a beer glass, topped with Otto's nasty digit.

Taxonomically speaking: Ogopogo is in the genus Zeuglodon of primitive, serpentine whales.

In July 1980, after hundreds of Sourtoes had been downed, tragedy struck. While downing his thirteenth drink of the night, a local miner fell over backwards and accidentally swallowed the toe.

When Captain Dick put out the call for new toes, he received a donation from a woman who had hers lopped off because of a corn. (That must have been one bad corn.) A local trapper also gave his frostbit toe for the cause.

A REAL NAIL BITER

In 1993, Captain Dick handed over his one remaining pickled toe to a friend. That toe found its way to the Downtown Hotel, which has built a thriving line of business surrounding the somewhat macabre tradition. The hotel has given out more than 35,000 certificates to people who have conquered the cocktail. Hotel owners say that every now and then a customer will still swallow a toe. On one festive evening, a firefighter from Ontario chewed a toe up until it was almost unrecognizable and then handed it back.

A Sourtoe Cocktail is now a $5 pour of any drink of your choice with the toe plopped in it. And there is one rule to get a certificate and become a Sourtoer: "You can drink it fast, or drink it slow, but the lips have gotta touch the toe."

* * *

NO GHOSTS FOUND, BUT NEW ONES CREATED

"Emergency crews attend to a woman who fell three storeys at a University of Toronto building. Police arrived at around 2 a.m. in response to reports of a man and woman trying to jump from one level of the building to another. The man was able to make the jump, but the structure the woman was standing on gave way, police said. She fell into a courtyard in the centre of the building. The woman was rushed to St. Michael's Hospital, where she was pronounced dead. The two were hunting for ghosts in the 134-year-old building, which they believed was haunted, according to police."

—CBC News

WEIRD CANADA

Crystal lakes, snow-capped mountains, hockey, Mounties, bilingual traffic signs...and some really, really weird news stories.

NEWS JUNKIE

In 2007 the *Edmonton Sun* interviewed a 70-year-old woman identified only as "Maggie" who claimed she devoured the *Edmonton Sun* every day—literally. For the previous seven years, she'd cut the newspaper into strips and eaten it because, she said, it "tastes good." The woman decided to come forward after doctors removed a massive ball of paper that was lodged in her esophagus.

THESE BANK FEES ARE CRIMINAL

In 2007 Christopher Emmorey tried to rob a bank in Peterborough, Ontario. Instead of asking a teller for all the money, for some reason Emmorey demanded just $5,000. The teller replied that she had only $200 on hand, adding that because he wasn't a customer of that bank, he'd have to pay a $5 withdrawal fee. Emmorey waited while the clerk did the paperwork—which he signed—and gave him $195. He was arrested an hour later.

ICE DANCING WINS

In 2002 a group of softball players met in a Calgary park for a late-night game. At the next field over, a group of croquet players were also playing a late-night game. A few hours later, six players from both groups were in the hospital (two were seriously injured)—the result of a brawl over which sport was the "manliest."

WHO MOVED THE CHEESE?

La Fromagerie Boivin, one of Quebec's largest cheese manufacturers, dropped about a ton of cheese into the Saguenay River in 2004. They thought that aging the cheese underwater for twelve months would give it extra moisture and improve its taste and texture. Did it work? We may never know. In October 2005, the cheesemaker announced that despite the use of thousands of dollars in high-tech locating equipment, divers were unable to find the 2,000 pounds of lost cheese.

...If 14 hippos could get up to the Observation Deck, the glass floor could withstand their weight.

TATTOO YOU

Lane Jensen, an Alberta tattoo artist, has a tattoo of a large-breasted cowgirl on his left leg. In 2007 he decided his cowgirl didn't look buxom enough. So his tattoo got "breast" implants—dime-sized bags of silicone inserted into his leg under the tattoo. Two weeks later, Jensen lost a liter of lymphatic fluid from his leg—his body had rejected the implants. "I guess my girl wasn't meant to have 3-D breasts," he said.

WHAT GOES AROUND...

In 2007 a 15-year-old in Hamilton, Ontario, was sledding one night and decided he wanted to tag a local bridge with some graffiti. He left his gloves and cell phone in the sled and rappelled down the side of the bridge. Suddenly the rope shifted and the boy panicked. He tried to scurry back up but somehow ended up hanging by his feet, upside down. As he tried to wiggle free, his shirt came off. And it was February. And it was –5°F. He was there for two hours before someone finally heard his screams for help and saved him.

THE SMOKING GUN

Keep It Simple, a bar in Edmonton, was in danger of being closed in 2003 when officials found out it was not abiding by the citywide smoking ban. The only place smoking is legal is in liquor licensed bars. But Keep It Simple is a bar for recovering alcoholics—it doesn't serve alcohol. It does allow smoking, which helps many alcoholics not to drink. But because it didn't have a liquor license, it was illegal for people to smoke there. So in order to let its nondrinking customers smoke, Keep It Simple applied for and received a liquor license, which it doesn't use, because it doesn't sell liquor.

HOME COOKING

Health inspectors in Granby, Quebec, shut down the Comme Chez Soi restaurant in 2000 when the owners were caught re-serving foods such as tartar sauce, coleslaw, bread, and fondue that had been discarded from previous customers' plates. They'd even used bread slices with bites out of them to make bread crumbs. They were also caught reusing discarded food from rooms in a motel they owned. (Comme chez soi means "just like home.")

A tagged Monarch butterfly was released near Ontario and recovered four months later in Mexico.

WEST JEST

WestJet is a low-cost, no-frills Canadian airline. They're also known for pilots and flight attendants that are free to be as funny as they want. Here are some real quips made by West Jet employees.

"People, people we're not picking out furniture here, find a seat and get in it!"

"To operate your seat belt, insert the metal tab into the buckle, and pull tight. It works just like every other seat belt; and, if you don't know how to operate one, you probably shouldn't be out in public unsupervised."

"Please take care when opening the overhead compartments because, after a landing like that, sure as hell everything has shifted."

"Ladies and gentlemen, we've reached cruising altitude and will be turning down the cabin lights. This is for your comfort and to enhance the appearance of your flight attendants."

"Please be sure to take all of your belongings. If you're going to leave anything, please make sure it's something we'd like to have."

"There may be 50 ways to leave your lover, but there are only four ways out of this airplane."

"Thank you for flying West Jet Express. We hope you enjoyed giving us the business as much as we enjoyed taking you for a ride."

"Whoa, big fella. WHOA!"
—a pilot, upon descent

"In the event of a sudden loss of cabin pressure, masks will descend from the ceiling, stop screaming, grab the mask, and pull it over your face. If you have a small child traveling with you, secure your mask before assisting with theirs. If you are traveling with more than one small child, pick your favorite."

"Ladies and Gentlemen, welcome to Regina. Please remain in your seats with your seat belts fastened while the Captain taxis what's left of our airplane to the gate!"

Canadians consume 23.4 pounds of cheese per person per year.

"Weather at our destination is 50 degrees with some broken clouds, but we'll try to have them fixed before we arrive."

"Your seat cushions can be used for flotation; and in the event of an emergency water landing, please paddle to shore and take them with our compliments."

"We love you, you love us, we're much faster than the bus."

"Ladies and gentlemen, one of our passengers is flying to Calgary to meet her boyfriend. Thats right, her boyfriend from the internet whom she's had for a year and has never met! Let's congratulate her on a job well done, and wish her the best on her 'layover' in Calgary!"

"We are pleased to announce that we have some of the best flight attendants in the industry. Unfortunately, none of them are on this flight."

"We'd like to thank you folks for flying with us today. And, the next time you get the insane urge to go blasting through the skies in a pressurized metal tube, we hope you'll think of us."

"If you wish to smoke, the smoking section on this airplane is on the wing. If you can light 'em, you can smoke 'em."

MORE SKYWARD SILLINESS:

• The company also likes to make big, public April Fool's Day pranks each year. In 2012, company vice president Richard Bartrem appeared in a phony advertisement announcing that WestJet was introducing child-free flights—as its new KargoKids program would just place all of the kids in the plane's cargo hold with the luggage.

• In April 2013, WestJet announced that it was "easting restrictions on pets in the cabin." In other words, "Furry Family" would allow passengers to take any kind of pet with them on board—they released a video featured travelers bringing along their ducks, lizards, raccoons, fish, and bears.

• The joke in 2008—WestJet's new "sleeper cabins." A press photo showed a flight attendant happily lounging in a plane's overhead storage bin.

OGOPOGO MONSTER

A prehistoric lake monster is slithering through the depths of Okanagan Lake in British Columbia—or so the legend goes.

FLIPPED-OUT FISH

The First Nations tribe calls him Naitaka (N'ha-a-itk) or Lake Demon. Like Nessie in Scotland, Ogopogo is a lake monster who has been (supposedly) swimming through these waters for hundreds of years. He has been "seen" by thousands—yet he remains elusive. Like Sasquatch, Ogopogo is called a *cryptid*—a creature who has been seen and rumored to exist, yet there is no conclusive proof that he is real. Some believe Ogopogo is a surviving plesiosaur from the age of the dinosaurs. Other experts peg Ogopogo as a form of primitive whale—*basilosaurus cetoide*.

Based on various sightings over the decades, the monster appears to be black or tan and stretches to about 50 feet long. He is three feet wide . . . with humps.

ROUGH PUNISHMENT

Some local legends say that Ogopogo was a demon-possessed man who had murdered another local resident. The murdered man went by the name of "Old Kan-He-Kan," and that's how Okanagan got its name. To pay for his heinous crime, the gods condemned the murderer to live forever as a lake serpent, tortured by an eternity of remorse.

Sightings of the beast by the "white man" go back to the 1860s. One day back then, trapper John McDougall was towing a team of his horses across the lake, pulling them along as he rowed his canoe. He had made similar trips, and he would often bring a small animal—a chicken or tiny pig—which he would drop in the middle of the lake as a sacrifice for the creature. Once, he forgot his peace offering. Halfway across, the horses began to sink and McDougall suspected an angry Ogopogo may be dragging them to their deaths. His horses were pulled to the bottom of the lake, and he would have been as well if he hadn't quickly cut the tow rope with his knife and paddled ashore.

The Canadian maple leaf flag was not adopted until 1965.

UNSEEMLY SIGHTINGS

Over the decades, mysterious drownings have been attributed to the beast.

In the 1930s, two boys boating on the lake say they saw the monster quickly rise from the lake, snatch a seagull from the air in its maw, and within seconds, plunge back into the deep.

• *In 2000*, a swimmer taking a dip in the lake claims to have seen two of the critters swimming by.
• *On April 18*, 2002, a fourteen-member crew spotted Ogopogo while filming a documentary. A crew member said, "We saw two humps undulating in and out of the water. It was huge, black, and shiny." Some thought its head was spewing out water.
• *In 2004*, a mother was watching the lake with her three children. She heard a fast, repeated "thump thump thump thump" that made the water spray up. She said it was much louder than a beaver slap. Then she spotted three smooth, shiny humps gliding across the surface of the water.

There are scores of stories like these, and if you go on the Web you can see photos of things that may or may not be the lake monster. Skeptics say that the creature is just a long log. Tens of thousands of logs have been cut down by the timber trade, and they often float barely beneath the lake's surface.

*   *   *

MY FUNNY SERPENTINE

A long-necked, horse-headed creature known as Cadborosaurus (named for Cadboro Bay, near Victoria, British Columbia) is a legendary sea creature that swims the BC waters. Nicknamed Caddy, the sea serpent has been spotted by folks in the area for centuries. In 1937 at the Naden Harbour whaling station in the Queen Charlotte Islands, some flensers (workers who strip whales of their blubber) thought they had real proof of the monster. They found a bizarre animal in the stomach of a harvested whale. It was unlike any creature these fishermen had ever seen—a camel-like head, long serpentine body, and a distinctive tail and flippers. Tissue samples were taken and sent off to be identified, but they vanished. Photos of the creature exist, and they persist in stumping scientists. Sightings continue to this day.

Four hummingbird species nest only in Canada...

THE MILKSHAKE MURDER

Her milkshake brought all the boys to the...graveyard.

KILLER DRINK!

White Spot is a popular family dining chain with more than 60 locations across western Canada. For more than 80 years, the chain has served up signature burgers (with secret "Triple-O Sauce" of mayonnaise and hamburger relish), hand-cut fries, and triple-thick shakes. Many love the creamy shakes, and they were a favorite of Esther Castellani, the wife of Rene Castellani, a radio promotional manager in Vancouver.

In the early 1960s, Rene was working for CKNW. He was known for his outrageous publicity stunts. To help the BowMac car dealership sell more automobiles, Rene stayed perched on top of the 10-story BowMac sign for eight days. He vowed not to leave the top of the sign until every car was sold. (The sign, which is still standing on West Broadway, is a Vancouver landmark.) Rene also started a rumor that a maharaja wanted to buy British Columbia. He also once posed as an Indian prince and drove around town in a limousine with bodyguards and dancing girls.

APPEARANCES ARE DECEIVING

Between pulling crazy stunts, he made time to be a devoted husband. He brought his wife of 19 years a daily treat of a vanilla White Spot milkshake. Esther Castellani, who was busy as a saleswoman at a clothing store, appreciated the thoughtful treats from her husband.

Oddly enough, in 1965 Esther's health began to fail with each shake that she drank. She started to get stomach and lower back pain that kept her out of work. Around this time, she found a love letter in Rene's pocket and confronted him about it. But Esther's health was the bigger concern. She began to have bouts of nausea, diarrhea, and intense vomiting. Her fingers and toes went numb. She couldn't walk or use her hands.

For two months, Esther was hospitalized as doctors puzzled over her condition. Some suspected gall bladder issues or poor diet (such as milkshakes) as the culprit. But they couldn't find the answer or cure. In August of 1965 Esther died at age 40, leaving behind her husband and their 12-year-old daughter.

...the Ruby-Throated, Black-Chinned and two types of Rufous.

KILL HER WITH KINDNESS

It turns out that the love letter Esther found was a sign of Rene's infidelity. He was carrying on an affair with a strawberry-blonde receptionist at the radio station. He intended to marry her. But to do so, he needed Esther out of the way. Instead of asking for a divorce, Rene opted for murder. And he might have gotten away with it, too, if it weren't for an intern at the medical examiner's office who suggested an autopsy be performed.

The autopsy revealed that Esther had 1,500 times the normal level of arsenic in her body. The medical examiners determined that she was ingesting it for more than six months—including while she was in the hospital. Where was she getting it? Those daily milkshake deliveries from her husband.

A HAIRY SITUATION

Police made a search of the Castellani home and found Triox weed killer beneath the kitchen sink. It was missing the exact amount of poison that was estimated to have been in Esther's body. Esther's hair held more evidence. Strands had arsenic in them and were used to provide a timeline of when she was being poisoned. Scientists could chart the amount of arsenic Esther consumed each day from a strand of her long black hair. Curiously, the hair revealed that during the eight days that Rene was on top of the BowMac sign—when the milkshake deliveries were interrupted—there was no sign of poison in her system.

About three months after the murder, Rene applied for a license to marry the receptionist. Two days later, the police arrested him. He was convicted of murder and sentenced to life in prison. However, he was released after 12 years, and both Rene and his mistress wound up marrying other people.

*　　*　　*

YOUR AD HERE

To raise money for her son's education, Karolyne Smith, a Utah woman, decided to sell advertising on her body. Whoever bid the highest could have a permanent tattoo on her forehead. Smith held an eBay auction that attracted more than 27,000 hits and 1,000 watchers. Bidding reached $999.99 before one company clicked "buy now" and met Smith's $10,000 asking price. Goldenpalace.com, an Internet gambling company centered in the Mohawk Territory of Kahnawake, Canada, had the winning bid and asked Smith to tattoo its URL on her forehead.

Pabulum, the baby food, originated in Toronto's Hospital for Sick Children.

THE FLAMING SHIP

Don't worry–that ship in the Northumberland Strait isn't really on fire. It's just a ghost! (Gulp!)

DESPERATION IN SIGHT OF SHORE

The Maritimes are an unforgiving place to eke out a living on the seas. Managing the "living" part can be hard enough on its own.

> Late one evening, approaching dusk, a ship [was] sighted in the harbor which appeared to be in peril. Some distance out in the channel was what appeared to be a huge three-masted sailing vessel ablaze from bow to stern. A group of men boarded a small boat and rowed toward the flaming ship, in hopes of rescuing as many of her crew as was possible. While they still were some distance from the craft, it disappeared into the mist and appeared to vanish completely.
>
> –*Folklore: Prince Edward Island by* Sterling Ramsay

Since the 1700s, numerous residents on the coast of Eastern Canada have reported spotting a huge ship that appears to be ablaze sailing through the Northumberland Strait, which separates Prince Edward Island from Nova Scotia and New Brunswick. The three-masted square schooner appears to be swallowed by flames, and those on board are frantically running on deck to put out the fire or jumping overboard. The ship, which usually sails at a very high speed moving eastward, is often spotted just before rough weather comes in–typically around October. Several times, rescue parties have frantically gone after the ship to save those trapped on the vessel. But as they near the ship, it disappears.

EYEWITNESS ACCOUNT

A witness describes seeing the ship during the 1960s:

> "At the time I first saw the Phantom Ship it was early evening in the fall of the year, November 26, 1965, just turning dark. I was busy with my housework, having no thought of such a thing as a Phantom Ship. I was standing near my kitchen window, and when I looked up, I was so startled that I could hardly believe my eyes. There was this ship, on fire and sailing down the Strait. The telephone was right beside me on the wall, so as I watched the ship, I called some of my neighbors up the road that keeps close to the shore. Those others looked and saw what I was seeing, and the word spread up the Cape [this sighting

Don Cherry got the nickname "Hot Lips" when he kissed NHLer Doug Gilmour.

> is from Cape John]. Many, as they told me afterwards, stood at their back doors and saw for the first time in their lives the Phantom Ship of which they had heard. As we watched, the ship just seemed to disappear. There was no mistaking it for a real ship.
>
> "But that wasn't the end of it. Two nights later, almost under the same circumstances, I saw the Phantom Ship for the second time. Again I phoned others to make sure I wasn't seeing things. They, too, as before, saw that same ship. Word was flashed to River John, some six miles away, and soon our Cape road was crowded with cars, loaded with people eager to catch their first sight of the ghost ship. And they weren't disappointed. That time the Phantom was visible to hundreds of people for a half hour, and then, like the other time, it just seemed to fade away, and where the bright light had been, there was only the blackness of the water."

Some scientists have explained that the "ship" may be actually be a bank of fog reflecting the moonlight. In 1905, Willima Ganong attributed the vision to underwater coal beds that release methane gas, which rises to the surface playing Jack O'Lantern tricks on unwary humans. That would be a good explanation, but there is no evidence that "underwater coal beds" are located there.

* * *

VISIT HUDSON BAY: YOU'LL FEEL LIGHTER

Trying to lose weight? Want to get lighter instantly? Visit the Hudson Bay area. Just being there decreases your weight (compared to what it is in other parts of the world). In the 1960s, scientists began charting the Earth's gravitational fields, and they found that gravity actually has a greater pull in some areas than others. Large parts of the Hudson Bay area are said to be "missing gravity."

There are two theories as to why this happens. One is that convection pulls the Earth's plates downward in that area, which decreases the mass and gravity. The other theory states that the Laurentide Ice Sheet is the cause. The Ice Sheet melted 10,000 years ago and left a huge indent in the Earth, which may have altered the gravity. So, how much gravity is missing? Scientists say that the gravitational force in Hudson Bay is about 1/25,000 of a percent less than normal. For those wanting to lose weight instantly, you should head to the Hudson Bay area to drop 4/1000ths of a percent of your body weight.

WINDIGO-A-GO-GO

When this man said, "We're having the family for dinner," he wasn't kidding.

STRIKING APPEARANCE

The Windigo is a mythological creature that is legend among people of the First Nations from the Rockies to Quebec. The beast also goes by Wihtikow, Witigo, Witiko, Windigo, Weendigo, Windago, Windiga, and Wee-Tee-Go. It supposedly feasts on human flesh, and the more it eats, the hungrier it gets.

Ethnohistorian Nathan Carlson in Edmonton has described the creature as "an owl-eyed monster with large claws, matted hair, a naked emaciated body and a heart made of solid ice." Other stories paint Windigo as a lanky, 15-foot tall phantasm, complete with glowing eyes, long, yellowed canine teeth, and a hyper-extended tongue. Some say the monster is hairless, covered with jaundiced skin, and has stag-like horns. The creature often looks starved or has the rotting-corpse look that comes from losing parts of the skin to frostbite. Despite the rotting, a Windigo is very fast and strong with very large feet.

To make the horror of the Windigo even worse, the creature was thought to have been a human who transformed into the beast. The spirit of the Windigo could supposedly possess people and make them into wide-eyed, violent flesh eaters.

POSSESSED BY THE WINDIGO

Swift Runner, a Cree trapper in Alaska, wandered into the mission in St. Albert in the spring of 1879, claiming that he was the only one of his family to survive the harsh winter. However, the priests grew suspicious of him, as he looked well nourished and weighed over 200 pounds. At night, he screamed in his sleep. They reported him to the police, who escorted Swift Runner back to his family campground in Edmonton only to make the horrific discovery.

He murdered and ate eight members of his family. He was sentenced to death, but even up to the moment he was hanged Swift Runner insisted that he was possessed by an evil spirit that made him butcher and eat his family.

TOUGH LOVE

Other cases of Windigo possession in Canada have involved the person begging to be killed so they would do no harm to their families. Eyewitness reports describe the possessed as having swollen bodies and enlarged lips and mouths. The mental condition gained the named of "Windigo psychosis."

The Edmonton Sun published a story about an incident in 1887 where Marie Courtereille, 40, died from ax blows from her husband and son. Testimony at the trial said that Courtereille had begged her family to kill her because she thought she was possessed by a Windigo and would eat her family. She roared like an animal and attacked her husband. The woman was tied down and watched around the clock until her husband and son decided to kill her. The community supported the family's decision.

Jack Fiddler may be the most famous Windigo hunter. Fiddler, a Cree Indian, and his brother killed 14 people, all of which he claimed were Windigos. In 1907, he was arrested for killing his brother Joseph's daughter-in-law.

CHENOOS

The Wabanaki tribe of the Maritimes and Quebec believed in evil, man-eating ice giants called Chenoos. A Chenoo was similar to a Windigo. It was once a human being who either became possessed by an evil spirit or committed a terrible crime (especially cannibalism or withholding food from a starving person). This turned the person's heart to ice. In a few legends, a human who has become a Chenoo has been successfully rescued. Usually, however, once transformed into a Chenoo, the person can escape only through death.

PRACTICAL ADVICE

Windigos are notoriously hard to kill. By one account, Windigos have few weaknesses, and only a weapon of iron, steel or silver can kill one. One method involves shattering the creature's ice heart with a silver stake and then dismembering the body with a silver axe.

If you find yourself alone and very hungry in Canada, get something to eat fast and resist any forces that might be changing you into a Windigo.

Car license plates in Ontario were made of leather in 1903.

CANADA THE BIG

Canada is a big country and has an abundance of incredibly huge–and strange–things.

Object: A Prominent Pierogi

Place: Glendon, Alberta

Story: In 1990, Mayor Johnny Demienko wanted to put Glendon on the map. One night, when eating his favorite meal of pierogis (also spelled perogies and pyrogys), he had a flash of inspiration. The town should erect the world's largest monument to his beloved Eastern European dumpling (Glendon has a long Ukrainian and Polish heritage). The first version of the giant pierogi was designed without a fork. But Demienko said that many people didn't know what it was supposed to be; some thought it was a giant cow pie. The fork made it clear. If you drive down Pyrogy Drive and head to Pyrogy Park, you will see the 8-meter (27-foot) high, 2,700-kilogram (6,000-pound), fiberglass and steel pierogi (on a fork). Glendon, which has dubbed itself the Pyrogy Capital, also has the Pyrogy Park Café and the Pyrogy Motel and Restaurant. The town is now a popular tourist attraction where you can count on getting authentic pierogis in local restaurants. There is an annual pierogi festival and souvenirs—T-shirts, hats, glasses, and more. Glendon even has an official song "Volaré," rewritten with "pierogi" replacing the title word.

Object: An Enormous Easter Egg

Place: Vegreville, Alberta

Story: Vegreville, Alberta, is the largest Ukrainian settlement in Canada, and its majority hails from a region where the "pysanka"-style Easter egg is popular. Coming from the Ukrainian word *pysaty* or "to write," pysankas are colorful and intricately decorated. To attract tourists to its town, Vegreville built the world's largest pysanka in 1975. Utah computer scientist Ronald Resch created the mathematically designed pattern. Made of aluminum, the 8-meter- (26-foot-) tall egg rotates in the wind like a weathervane. Every July, the town celebrates with its annual Pysanka Festival where the townspeople dance, drink, and eat, Ukrainian-style. Visitors to the celebrations can even learn how to make their own pysankas.

"It's hard to make predictions—especially those about the future." —Toronto mayor Allan Lamport

Object: Super Sausage

Place: Mundare, Alberta

Story: Canadian Ukrainians seem to like to do things big. The proud citizens of Mundare have honored their Ukrainian roots with a giant sausage. Mundare is home to Stawnichy's Meat Processing, which is famous for its kielbasa. The Stawnichy family began a meat-smoking business there back in 1959. Stretching toward the sky at almost 13 meters (42 feet) high and weighing over 5,400 kilograms (12,000 pounds), the brown fiberglass sausage is often called "the giant turd" by locals. And an expensive turd it is, costing an estimated $120,000 to build.

OTHER MINOR GIANTS

- In Kimberly, B.C., "Happy Hans" emerges from the world's largest standing cuckoo clock and yodels.

- The largest curling rock is in Arborg, Manitoba, where it serves as a marker for the local curling rink.

- A 5.8-meter- (19-foot-) pipe weighing about a ton and a half in St. Claude, Manitoba, pays tribute to the town's namesake in France, where the main industry was pipe manufacturing.

- The world's largest lobster presides over the "Lobster Capital of the World," Shediac, New Brunswick. A life-size fisherman stands between the mighty pincers of this 10.7-meter- (35-foot-) long crustacean.

- Do not activate the 6.4-meter- (21-foot-) tall transformer robot in Port Hope, Ontario. Made of old truck, scooter, and lawnmower parts, the statue promotes Primitive Designs, a store that sells smaller robots.

- Bring your entire extended family to take a load off in Meaford, Ontario, on the record-setting 11-meter- (36-foot-) porch swing.

- A 7,000-kilogram (eight ton) tomahawk extending 16.5 meters (54 feet) in length and jutting through the top of a large concrete teepee brings the wow factor to Cut Knife, Saskatchewan. Built in 1971 in Tomahawk Park, the sculpture commemorates the signing of treaties with local Indians from a hundred years earlier.

THE MAN WITH A WINDOW IN HIS STOMACH

Before there was informed consent...there were fur trappers.

BEGIN WITH ONE HOLE...

When the Canadian fur trapper Alexis St. Martin was accidentally shot at close range by a musket, he could have easily died. The musket fired on June 6, 1822, on Mackinac Island in Lake Huron blasted through his ribs and stomach and exposed his internal organs. He lost muscle tissue, rib bones were broken, and a hole was torn in his stomach. Many expected the 20-year-old to die.

Dr. William Beaumont, a U.S. Army surgeon from nearby Fort Mackinac attended to St. Martin's wounds. For 17 days, St. Martin could not digest food. Everything he ate came out of an opening in his side. He had to receive nutrition through enemas to stay alive. Gradually, he healed and his eating returned to normal. But the hole that had torn through his abdomen, and his stomach never fully closed. In fact, he healed in a very peculiar way. The edge of the hole in his stomach fused to the edge of the hole in his skin creating a "window" into St. Martin's digestive tract.

...ADD A LITTLE KNOWLEDGE...FOR A PRICE

Scientists at the time knew very little about how the digestive system worked. Seeing the unique way that St. Martin was healing, Beaumont saw an opportunity. In an arrangement that would be seen as entirely unethical today, the doctor convinced St. Martin to work as his servant. He would be paid to chop wood and fetch bundles. The young man also allowed Dr. Beaumont to experiment on him.

Dr. Beaumont tied quarter-ounce bits of food to string and dangled them into the hole in St. Martin's side. The food items were "high seasoned alamode beef," raw salted lean beef, raw salted fat pork, raw lean fresh beef, boiled corned beef, stale bread, and raw cabbage. After inserting the food, the doctors would send St. Martin back to work. After different time intervals–one, two, and three hours–he'd pull the food out and note how the food had been digested. The doctor used not only his fingers and instruments to examine St. Martin but also his tongue. Dr. Beaumont thought he could obtain a measure of alkalinity by "tasting" the wound for sourness. Dr. Beaumont also removed gastric juices from St. Martin and observed how they reacted with a piece of corned beef in a "test tube–style" environment.

The young man suffered through much probing and physical distress. Beaumont remarked that "the boy complained of some pain and uneasiness at the breast." After two months of prodding and experiments, St. Martin returned to Quebec, where he married and had children.

STIR AS NEEDED

Over the next eight years, St. Martin returned to visit with the doctor and conduct further experiments. In June of 1829, St. Martin brought his wife and family. Among other things, Dr. Beaumont learned that gastric juice needed heat to digest and that vegetables took longer to digest than other foods. Because St. Martin became understandably irritable during some tests, the doctor was able to determine that anger hindered digestion. The doctor was living in Wisconsin at this time, and when the round of experiments was completed, St. Martin and his family actually traveled by canoe and portage back to their home in Montreal.

In 1832, the two met one last time. The doctor observed the effects of sausage, mutton, and "boiled salted fat pork" being placed in St. Martin. One time, he put 12 raw oysters directly into his stomach. He found that exercise helped the production and release of gastric juice. Along the way, the doctor also made the groundbreaking discovery that digestion was mainly a chemical (as opposed to mechanical) process.

FOLLOW WITH JUST DESSERTS

After Beaumont's experiments came to an end, he took his copious notes and wrote a book titled *Experiments and Observations of the Gastric Juice and the Physiology of Digestion*. The book became an important guide for scientists and others who wanted to understand more about human digestion.

St. Martin, who was expected to die as a young man, lived until the ripe old age of 78. The doctor died at age 68 from a slip on some icy stairs.

EDIFICES EXTRAORDINAIRE

It's not just the nature in Canada that's so amazing it doesn't seem possible. The buildings boggle the mind, too.

HAVE A BALL

Free Spirit Spheres on Vancouver Island are unique, circular treehouses that give visitors a chance to sleep suspended in the forest canopy as if in a nest. Rented by the night, these globular units look like giant nuts or seeds hanging from the trees. Inside, they feature two porthole windows to give a bird's eye view of Mother Nature. With inside diameters of about 3.2 meters (around 10 feet), each orb squeezes in fold-out tables and mirrors, curved loft beds and benches, and tiny appliances.

To enter a sphere at the "treesort" in Qualicum Beach, you climb up a spiral staircase that wraps around the trunk and then cross a short suspension bridge to get in the front door. Made from light, bendy woods like Sitka Spruce and Yellow Cedar, they weigh about 500 kilograms (1,102 pounds). The builders borrowed heavily from techniques used for sailboat construction. The spheres are tethered to three separate trees in a manner mimicking a spider web, so the affect of the wind's movement is minimized. They sway gently in the breeze but move much more abruptly when someone inside changes position.

Tom Chudleigh, the inventor and manufacturer of these tree-mounted spheres, says that being in the sphere is "like being in a nut shell that's decorated like a palace. It feels like you are floating in the canopy among the sleeping birds. When it's stormy it can be tense, but nothing like a storm at sea." The spheres are for sale as well—a wood unit (wired, insulated, heated, and plumbed) goes for about $150,000, and a fiberglass unit (insulated and wired) for about $45,000.

LIVING INSIDE MARILYN MONROE?

Southwest of Toronto, in Mississauga, Ontario, a condominium complex is breaking out of the cereal-box mold of skyscrapers. The residential Absolute Tower 1 has been dubbed "Marilyn Monroe" by the locals because the building is extra curvy. The voluptuous skyscraper rises up 56 stories, and it has a shorter, less buxom twin that is 50 stories tall. Ma Yansong, who designed the building when he was just 30, said he was trying to "express nature in the big cities." The floors of the Absolute Tower are increasingly oval, which maintains the curved and twisted outline. One continuous spiraling balcony adds to the condo's curviness. A three-story recreation and exercise facility, which is both indoor and outdoor, features areas for basketball, baseball, and volleyball. Residents enjoy a heated outdoor pool complete with patio and fireplace. In 2012, when these modern towers were completed, the Council on Tall Buildings and Urban Habitat awarded the towers the prize of Best Tall Buildings in the Americas.

PYRAMID-POWERED WINE

In Kelowna, British Columbia, a great pyramid of wine rises. Overlooking Kelowna's Okanagan Lake, the Summerhill Winery has a very unique feature—a huge four-story pyramid where wines are aged. When Stephen Cipes first visited the Okanagan in 1986, the New Yorker thought that area would be ideal for producing intensely flavored small grapes. In 1991, he established his 45-acre, all-organic winery, using no pesticides or herbicides. Wines are aged for 30 to 90 days in the concrete replica of the Pyramid of Cheops. Cipes believes that the sacred geometry of the pyramid clarifies and enhances liquids. The winery, which is the most visited in Canada, produces Riesling, Chardonnay, Pinot Noir, Gewurztraminer, Ehrenfelser, and Pinot Meunier. In addition to the pyramid, the winery uses some other very unique techniques to create its award-winning organic vino. The vineyard takes rainwater mixed with the manure from a lactating cow to produce a biologically-active fertilizer which is then sprayed on the vines. The mixture is supposed to suppress fungus and mildew.

WHY DOES THIS PLACE MAKE ME THIRSTY?

Edouard Arsenault, the lighthouse keeper at Cap-Egmont in Prince Edward Island, sure liked bottles. He accumulated a massive collection, and at age 66 he decided it was time to start building houses out of them. Between 1980 and 1984, he cemented together 25,000 bottles to build three fantasy houses. The structures include a six-gabled house and a chapel. In the 1990s, the buildings were deteriorating and had to be rebuilt using more stable foundations.

Vancouver visitor to child: "Does it ever stop raining here?" Child: "How should I know? I'm only six."

GREAT LAKES

In Canada, even the lakes have personality.

THE DISAPPEARING LAKE

It's not unusual for a lake to fill in the summer from melting snows or glacier waters and then get lower in the fall and winter as less water flows in, as most lakes are fed and drained by rivers and streams. What makes Medicine Lake in Jasper National Park different is that there appears to be no outlet for draining. Water pours in from the Maligne River, but there is no river leading out. How does the water leave the Medicine Lake? Through the bottom, just like a tub. The water escapes through a cave system of soluble limestone rock and surfaces about 16 kilometers (10 miles) away in Maligne Canyon. This is one of the largest known "sinking rivers" in the Western Hemisphere, and the caves may be the largest inaccessible caverns in the world. Every year as the melting glacier water comes in, the lake fills faster than the sink holes can drain it, and then by winter, the lake disappears, turning into mudflats.

WHOLE GREATER THAN ITS POOLS

The Spotted Lake (Kliluk) is really 365 separate pools of highly concentrated minerals. The First Nations consider this lake near Osoyoos between the Okanagan and Similkameen Valleys in British Columbia to be a sacred medicine spot. Pools rich in magnesium sulfate, calcium and sodium sulfates, and 12 other minerals including traces of silver and titanium are clustered close together to make up this "lake." Although the waters supposedly have healing powers, a fence surrounding it prevents public access. Visitors can only see it from about 700 meters (about half a mile) away.

SCUBA DIVING IN THE MOUNTAINS

When you take the gondola ride to the summit of Banff's Sulphur Mountain in Alberta, you might want to pack your scuba gear. At Lake Minnewanka, a summer resort village was established in 1888 with streets, avenues, hotels, restaurants, and cruise boats. In 1941, a dam was built that raised the water level 30 meters (98 feet), submerging the village, which had been there over 50 years. Now scuba divers visit this glacier lake to explore the site of the submerged town,

Elvis Presley's favorite female singer was Anne Murray.

Minnewanka Landing. Lake Minnewanka means "Water of the Spirits" in Nakoda, and divers have reported seeing spirits in the underwater town. Because the lake is high in the Rockies, this is cold water diving—so don't jump in with just your swim trunks.

YOU CANNOT SINK IN LITTLE MANITOU LAKE

Located in central Saskatchewan, just north of Watrous, this lake gets its name from the Algonquian word meaning "mysterious being." And indeed, this body of water is mysterious—it's unusually buoyant due to its dense concentration of salt, magnesium, and potassium. The mineral density is greater than that of the Dead Sea. Some say you can lie on your back in these waters and read a newspaper without getting it wet. However, the water is saltier than the ocean, so keeping it out of your eyes is essential; otherwise, stinging and tearing begin. Those who don't shower after a dip get an extra-white back from a coating of minerals.

Since the early 19th century, visitors have come to the lake for its curative powers. Local legend has it that medicine men would take their sick to the beach to be cured. The area has been called the Carlsbad spa of Canada, and in the 1920s and 30s, Little Manitou Lake—which covers 13.3 square kilometers (five square miles), with an average depth of 3.8 meters (12 feet), became a very hot attraction for folks living in the prairies. People flocked to the resort town for mineral swimming pools, massage rooms, medical clinics, dance halls, brothels, and bootleg whisky. Tourism declined during the Depression.

During the 1980s, a new spa was built, and the old 1928 Danceland building was restored, making the area a destination for vacations and conventions. As far as any local can tell, no one has ever drowned in the lake.

* * *

TRUE OR FALSE: Most beer produced in Canada is stronger than American beer.

FALSE. Despite the rumors that Canadians make a more potent brew than their neighbors in the States, most Canadian beers have an alcohol content of 4% to 6%, just like American beers. A regular Molson has 5.1% alcohol, and a Budweiser has 5.0% alcohol.

Vancouver bartender Robyn Gray makes a drink with meat-infused cognac and a foie gras-stuffed cherry.

BUCKLEY'S MIXTURE

A witch's brew of foul ingredients provides cold relief to generations.

A HISTORY OF BAD TASTE

William Knapp Buckley made his fortune by leaving a bad taste in the mouths of millions. He created a cough and cold remedy that is a household name in Canada because it is undeniably horrible tasting. After graduating from Ontario College of Pharmacy in 1915, the native of Wallace, Nova Scotia, moved to Toronto in 1914. Here, he became owner of a drug store in 1919 and began experimenting with different natural ingredients that could relieve coughs and colds.

MOTHER NATURE'S NASTY, NASTY CABINET

He came up with a formula combining Canada balsam (some would call this a fancy name for turpentine), pine needle oil, ammonium carbonate (used in smelling salts to jolt a person awake), potassium bicarbonate, camphor (from the camphor tree), menthol, a tincture of capsicum (hot pepper), extract of Irish moss, and dextromethorphan (a known cough suppressant). The result was truly awful tasting and nasty smelling, as Buckley would tell you. But it relieved cold symptoms and suppressed coughs. Buckley decided that there was no need to hide the horrible flavor of his medicine. Instead, he used it as a selling point. After all, strong medicine should have a strong taste to at least seem effective.

STIR IT UP

He mixed up his early batches in a butter churn and sold the elixir for 75 cents a bottle. Despite the shudders and winces of his pharmacy customers, they gave the product positive reviews. He sold 2,000 bottles in the first year. Buckley formed the company W.K. Buckley Limited in 1920 and began marketing his product. That year, Buckley's rang up sales of $40,000. By 1935, Buckley sold his drug store to focus all his energies on the production and sales of Buckley's Mixture.

Buckley was a born salesman and marketing pioneer. He concentrated his sales efforts in print and radio advertising during the rapid growth of broadcasting. His son Frank has said that his father was ahead of the curve in recognizing how effective radio advertising could be, and his use of broadcasting was instrumental in making Buckley's a hit in Canada.

Some of the memorable ad lines were:

"It tastes awful. And it works."

"We're #1, but we taste like #2."

"Not New. Not Improved."

"People Swear By Us and At Us."

In January 1978, W. K. Buckley died, but his son kept up with the clever slogans, including "I came by my bad taste honestly; I inherited it from my father," and "I wake up with nightmares that someone gives me a taste of my own medicine."

SOURPUSSES SELL

Some say that people bought Buckley's for others to take just so they could watch their grimaces as they tasted the product. One TV campaign showed the many facial contortion of customers swallowing the syrup. In the runup to the federal election in 2006, the TV comedy show *This Hour Has 22 Minutes* spoofed the ad with a skit showing a number of people making the same screwed-up faces as in the Buckley's ads. The skit revealed that they were making their faces after putting an "X" by Stephen Harper's name as they voted.

EXPANDING THE FRANCHISE

Along the way in the company's history, Buckley's introduced White Rub and Jack and Jill's children's cough syrup. In time, the firm expanded its sales to the United States, the Caribbean, New Zealand, Australia, and Holland. After all, why should only Canadian get to enjoy the horrible taste of Buckley's.

Because he also had a passion for thoroughbred racehorses, W.K. Buckley also created a treatment for respiratory ailments in horses called Buckley's Zev.

In 2002, drug company Novartis bought the Buckley's brand and formulas—and stuck with promoting its foul flavor. The company recently had a "Buckley's Bad Taste Tour," where it passed out spoonfuls of the mixture to random people, recording video of their reactions and for its website.

THESE BOOTS WERE MADE FOR EATING

And that's just what they did.

THE PUNISHING YUKON

"I'll eat my boots" may seem like hyperbole, but at one time stranded adventurers really did resort to it. Sir John Franklin's men, starving as they mapped the northern coast of Canada in 1820 ate their boots. The famed "Lost Patrol" of Canadian Mounties, led by Francis Fitzgerald into the Yukon's heavy snow and −62°C weather, ate their dogs and tried eating their boots before they perished in 1911 near Fort McPherson. But the most successful Canadian boot-eater was Yukon missionary and bishop, Isaac Stringer.

It was September, 1909; Bishop Stringer had just finished substituting for another bishop in the Northwest Territories' Mackenzie River area. With missionary worker Charles Johnson as companion, Bishop Stringer set off on an 800 kilometer (500 mile) hike across the vast Yukon to return to his diocese and visit his parishioners.

But like other adventurers beaten by weather, the two men were soon lost in an early storm, their compass thrown off by the magnetic north pole. They had little food and only two blankets. After struggling onward, surviving into October on berries and small game, the men were getting desperate. They could no longer find birds or squirrels to hunt, and the weather was getting worse. All they had left to eat was their boots.

RECIPE FOR BOOT STEW

Today's shoes and boots contain all kinds of chemicals; which make the leather impervious to insects, mold, and weather. It also makes the leather impervious (and likely poisonous) to humans. Boots, after all, are not really intended to be eaten. Stringer and Johnson's boots, however, came from a more "natural" era. The soles were made of walrus skin, the uppers were made of sealskin, and the skins were not tanned.

They cut their boots one piece at a time and boiled each piece for hours, trying to rehydrate the skin into something edible and meaty. After boiling, they roasted each piece over the fire to a "palatable" consistency, Stringer wrote in his journal. Evidently the walrus was superior to the seal. On October 20, they ate "breakfast from the top of boots. Not so good as sole."

RESCUE

On the day they finished eating their boots, Stringer and Johnson discovered sled tracks and freshly-cut trees. As they staggered on to the native campsite, emaciated and weather-beaten, they were quickly recognized; reports of their disappearance had been spread far and wide. Stringer and Johnson had been lost for over a month and had shed 50 pounds, surviving those final few days on only their boots. A local man, Andrew Cloh, took the two men to his home where he gave them their first real meal in weeks: fish and rabbit.

* * *

BOSSY SIMS

While human daredevils have walked across the Niagara River on a tightrope, only one cow has made the trip. Her owner, George Sims, farmed and operated Prospect Point Incline Railway, which carried travelers to the top of the gorge near the Falls. At the time, cows were not fenced in to keep them on a certain property, so Bossy felt inclined to travel the countryside at will, including wandering into the river, which often took her to within 10 meters of the American side of the Falls, or a location that became known as the "Brink of Doom." Although no one knows for sure what caused Bossy's frequent dips into the Niagara River, taking her almost to the point of no return, a few theories exist. One theory is that she simply enjoyed the succulent grasses near the river's edge—and without looking just sauntered into the river, wading and grazing until she reached the edge.

But there's another theory that may actually be more likely. In a 2004 column in the *Niagara Falls Reporter*, Bob Kostoff included a letter he'd received in reaction to his previously printed column that detailed Bossy's amazing walks in the river. The letter was from Anne Brophy, a descendant of George Sims. According to Ms. Brophy, the story in the family was that tourists would try to pet Bossy, and they annoyed her. In true diva fashion, she simply took to the river to get away from them. Some stories say she even reached Goat Island on one of her ramblings.

Bandleader Guy Lomabardo was also a speedboat-racing champion.

THE TIDE IS HIGH

When the tides come in at the Bay of Fundy in Nova Scotia, ...run.

MAY THE FORCE BE WITH YOU!

Stretching about 274 kilometers (170 miles) long and 15 meters (50 feet) wide, the Bay of Fundy has tides that can rise above 15 meters (50 feet) in height. At Minas Basin, the ocean reaches 16 meters (53 feet) high, and the tides increase by about 20 percent during a full moon. Compare that to the average tide of one meter (3 feet). Scientists say that the bay's natural funnel shape contributes to the extreme tides. Because it becomes narrower and shallower at the end, water is forced higher up onto the shore.

Like all tides, these waters spectacularly climb and drop twice a day. To get the full sense of how high the tides can be, visitors often come for a low and high tide. On average, there's about six hours and 13 minutes between high and low tides, so visitors can expect to see at least one high and one low tide during daylight hours. The dramatic tides have created a unique shoreline with cliffs and sea stacks. You can safely walk out more than three-quarters of a kilometer (half a mile) in some places.

UNUSUAL INHABITANTS

The ocean has worn away red sandstone and volcanic rock to reveal fossils from over 300 million years ago. Millions of organisms live half the day underwater and the other half revealed. Walking along at low tide, you can find sea glass, shells, starfish, and assorted flotsam. At low tide, fishing boats that were bobbing in the water dockside are sitting on the ground against the wharf. Sometimes, unusually warm temperatures in the water bring exotic, normally tropical fish to the area, such as the mola mola, or ocean sunfish.

The unique tides also cause some other water anomalies, such as tidal bores. These are fronts of water that "bore" their way up a river against the normal river flow. The tides can also create whirlpools. In the Western Passage of the Passamaquoddy Bay toward the mouth of the Bay of Fundy, "Old Sow" spins. It's the largest whirlpool in the Western Hemisphere and the second largest in the world—second only to the Maelstrom Whirlpool of Norway. It got its name from the distinct sounds that come out of these churning waters.

A favorite Inuit snack is *muktuk*, a combo of whale skin and blubber.

A POWERFUL CURRENT

While the folklore of the Mi'kmaq First Nation tribe attributed the extreme tides to a giant whale splashing in the ocean, the gravitational pull of the moon and the sun really moves about 100 billion tons of seawater in and out of the bay. Because of this massive source of power, one of the three tidal power plants in the world and the only one in North America is located here. The Annapolis Tidal at the mouth of the Bay of Fundy went online in 1984. By harnessing the energy of the tides and converting it into electricity, the plant generates roughly 80 to 100 megawatt hours of electricity, depending on the tides. That's enough energy to produce more than 30 million kilowatt hours per year and power about 4,500 homes. The energy is fed directly into the Nova Scotia Power Corporation's utility system.

Capturing this power, however, has been challenging. Nova Scotia Power, which had a turbine test spot on the Bay of Fundy, abandoned further research into tidal energy after powerful currents destroyed a $10 million turbine less than a month after it was set up in November 2009. Other companies are still pursuing the possibility. Tidal energy is part of Nova Scotia's plan to generate 40 percent of its electricity from renewable resources by 2020.

* * *

DEFYING GRAVITY

There are a few places on Earth that seem to defy gravity, and Magnetic Hill, New Brunswick, is one of them. For years, travelers have been driving their cars to the bottom of the hill, putting them in neutral, and then watching them roll backward back up the hill. The locals have been puzzling over the phenomenon since the 1800s. Farmers with horse-drawn carts would notice how their horses struggled down the hill and how their wagons would almost crash into their horses' feet as they went up the hill. In reality, there is no supernatural phenomenon at work here—the hill is an optical illusion. The landscape creates a unique perspective where downhill appears to be uphill and vice versa.

Facial creams using snail slime are banned in Canada.

BORDERING ON THE STRANGE

Canadian and U.S. citizens share a rich history...of weird and failed smugglings.

TALES FROM THE BORDER CROSSINGS

Canadians and Americans share a large border, and they generally traverse it with élan. But the Web is filled with funny stories of folks being questioned at the Canada-U.S. border with suitcases full of toilet paper, Cuban cigars, and more. Some of the rules controlling what you can bring into America from Canada are downright wacky.

RUN FOR THE BORDER

People on the north side of Canusa Avenue are Canadian and live in Stanstead, Quebec. People across the street on the southern side are American and live in Derby Line, Vermont. This is the only part of the Canada–United States border that runs directly down a street, appropriately named Canusa for Canada and USA. Whenever residents on the American side pull out of their driveways, they are officially in Canada, and they must report to border post, conveniently located on the corner. There are security cameras on light poles to help patrol the area. Citizens on both sides of the street once passed more freely into each other's country, but after 9-11, security tightened in the area.

FOR WHEN YOU JUST CAN'T DECIDE

In addition to Canusa Avenue being a security concern, the Royal Canadian Mounted Police and the United States Border Patrol keep a watchful eye on the nearby Haskell Free Library and Opera House. The building is located on Church Street in Rock Island, Quebec, and on Derby Line in Rock Island, Vermont. Straddling the border between the two countries, the building has black tape running across the reading room and beneath the opera house seats, marking Canada from the States. Visitors like jumping back and forth between the two countries or having one foot in Canada and the

Bill and Hillary Clinton named their daughter after Joni Mitchell's "Chelsea Morning."

other in the United States—all inside a library. The parking lot is in Canada, but the main entrance is in the States. If you walk to the checkout desk to take out a book, you'll be back in Canada. You can sit on the U.S. side of the audience and watch the performers on stage in Canada.

The building was constructed by American sawmill owner Carlos Haskell and his Canadian wife Martha Stewart Haskell. They wanted Canadians and Americans to have equal access to the library and opera house ...so they built it on both borders.

MOON THE BALLOON

In Sarnia in Ontario, an estimated 200 people took a stand in favor of personal privacy and against public surveillance with a mass dropping of their drawers. In the summer of 2009, the U.S. Department of Homeland Security, carrying a $1 million surveillance camera on the border, tested a spy balloon outside of Sarnia, Ontario. The camera was sensitive enough to read the name of a ship from about 14 kilometers (almost 9 miles) away. The 15-meter-long (about 49 feet) Aerostat balloon and camera were being tested on Sarnia's waterfront, where it would scan many homes and private businesses. Sarnia Mayor Mike Bradley and many citizens called the balloon an invasion of Canadian privacy. In protest, 200 people gathered in Centennial Park on August 15 on the St. Clair River. At about 5 p.m., protestors lined up, and upon the announcer's count of three, they all mooned the balloon. Unfortunately, the balloon wasn't in the sky that day, much to the dismay of the cheeky protestors. Protestors still hoped their message came across.

Martin said he wanted to make it clear to the United States that Sarnia residents do not like being watched.

SHELL-SHOCKED

In Halifax Harbour, antiterror officials installed a 1.6-kilometer (1-mile) orange security fence to protect Navy ships against terrorist attacks. The military poured about $3.5 million into the superstructure, which was designed to thwart small boats loaded with explosives from making any sort of strategic attack on the Royal Navy. The floating barrier was thought to be almost impenetrable. Unfortunately, military commanders didn't count on a hidden menace. Mussels and kelp weighed down the structure, rendering it useless. The fence was dismantled.

Baffin Island is more than twice the size Great Britain.

WEIRD CANADA

Crystal lakes, snow-capped mountains, hockey, Mounties, bilingual traffic signs...and some really, really weird news stories.

DON'T EAT THE YELLOW SNOW

In 1991 British artist Helen Chadwick came to Canada to create a series of 12 artworks: bronzed "urine flowers." She formed round piles of densely packed, fresh snow, and peed on them (to turn them yellow). Then she had a male friend "draw" (pee) a circular pattern on it. The combined result looked something like a daisy. Then, before it could melt, Chadwick made a bronze casting of the snow, to create a lasting, one-of-a-kind sculpture. (She sold all 12 for $2,000 each.)

DIRT DU JOUR

Canadian research scientists have developed a program called Instrumental Neutron Activation Analysis, used to determine the nutritional value of rural Ontario dirt. Their finding: the average scoop of soil contains many essential vitamins and minerals needed for a healthy body, including iron, calcium, magnesium, and potassium. But if the thought of eating dirt makes you sick, don't worry—it also contains the mineral kaolinite, which can soothe an upset stomach.

GOAL!

Corey Hirsch, goalie for the 1994 Canadian Olympic hockey team, threatened to sue the Swedish government in 1995. Sweden planned to issue a postage stamp commemorating the Swedish hockey team's come-from-behind defeat of Canada to win the gold medal at the 1994 Winter Olympics. Hirsch's objection: The stamp would depict Peter Forsberg scoring the game-winning goal—against Hirsch. That, said Hirsch, is "not the way I want to be remembered." (Sweden issued the stamp anyway.)

EAT MY SHORTS

Alberta police stopped David Zurfluh for driving erratically, suspicious that the teenager was drunk. But before he could be given a breath analysis, Zurfluh, who was sitting in the back of the squad car,

The chance that a public road is unpaved in the U.S. is 1%; in Canada it's 75%.

ate his own underwear. Questioned in court, Zurfluh later admitted that his intention was to eat enough cotton so that it would absorb the alcohol in his system. Amazingly, it may have worked: the breath test showed his blood alcohol level to be at the legal limit. Zurfluh was acquitted of all charges.

DRILLED TO MEET YOU

Donald Wright was installing a sliding glass door in his Toronto apartment building when he fell off a stepladder and knocked himself unconscious. When he woke up, he discovered that he'd fallen head first onto a power drill, which had bored three inches into his right temple. He tried to pull the drill out, but it wouldn't budge, so he set it on reverse, turned it on...and removed it from his head. (Doctors later removed bone fragments from Wright's brain.)

WHO WOULD HAVE SUSPECTED?

In April 2001, police in Vancouver, British Columbia, ended a three-year crime spree when they arrested 64-year-old Eugene Mah and his 32-year-old son, Avery. The Mahs had been stealing assorted lawn and garden items from homes in their neighborhood, including garbage cans, lawn decorations, recycling boxes, and realty signs. They even reportedly stole a neighbor's doormat...and each of the 14 other doormats the neighbor bought as replacements. Why did they steal them? Nobody knows. Eugene Mah is a real estate tycoon worth a reported $13 million.

DEATH MERCHANT

Roman Panchyshyn, a 47-year-old Winnipeg retailer, upset some of his fellow residents when he started selling $65 sweatshirts that read "Winnipeg, Murder Capital of Canada—Escape The Fear" in his store. The shirts showed the city skyline dripping in blood. "We spend hundreds of thousands of dollars yearly to promote Winnipeg to the world," complained City Councillor Harry Lazarenko, "and I don't want this to give us a black eye." So he contacted the premier to see if Panchyshyn could be stopped. He couldn't—the shirts are accurate. Winnipeg has the highest murder rate in Canada. Said the unapologetic Panchyshyn, "The truth hurts."

The Pocket Desert in Osoyoos, B.C., is the only "true" desert in Canada.

MOTHERLAND OF INVENTION

Whatever is in the air and water of Canada has sparked some innovative thinking.

ABDOMENIZER

Canadian chiropractor Dennis Colonello's product may not have been revolutionary, but his way of selling it was. When Colonello invented the abdomenizer, it was one of the first fitness products sold an entirely new way: the infomercial—now the most popular and successful way to sell fitness and weight loss products.

The abdomenizer was basically a piece of plastic with handles. It included a hollow space to protect the lower back. It was a way for people to do sit-ups without injuring their lower back—something Dr. Colonello was familiar with. Users could sit on it, grab the handles, and "rock, rock, rock their way to a firmer stomach."

Dr. Colonello invented this exercise tool in 1984 and it was manufactured and distributed by a company called Fitness Quest, based in Canton, Ohio. He said the reason it worked is that the hollow for the lower back caused the user's pelvis to tilt, isolating the abdominal muscles and making sit-ups safer.

The one-minute infomercial, which can still be found on YouTube, opened with a sloppily dressed woman doing sit-ups and acting like they were causing her pain. Cut to the svelte, shapely blond woman on the abdomenizer, doing sit-ups with ease and without pain. Shoppers could buy this amazing product for the low price of $19.95. And they could buy a second abdomenizer for just $9.95 more.

The infomercial was a huge success, perhaps because of its timing. In North America, people were beginning to take exercising much more seriously, creating an "exercise craze." By 1992, 1.5 million had been sold directly to consumers through infomercials and another 2 million were sold through stores. Sales continued until the early 2000s when the distributor, Fitness Quest, stopped offering the product so it could offer a different product with a higher profit margin.

After his success with the abdomenizer, Colonello decided to capitalize on it and invent a few more products. His amazing abdomenizer was followed by the Back Therapy System, Nordic Rower,

In parts of Canada, McDonald's serves a McLobster sandwich.

Nordic Power, and Nordic Ab Works. He also served as the treating doctor for various members of the National Hockey League teams, the Los Angeles Lakers, Oakland Raiders, Dallas Mavericks, Miami Heat, and the Canadian Olympic women's basketball and wrestling teams. Eventually, he moved to Beverly Hills and became a chiropractor to celebrities such as Gavin MacLeod (of Love Boat) and Dick Van Patten (*Eight is Enough*).

And creative Canadians and other North American users of the abdomenizer discovered that even if it didn't flatten their stomachs, it made a great sled. After a few people got hurt using it that way, Fitness Quest included a warning on the box that said, "This is not a sled!"

DID THE INUIT INVENT SUNGLASSES?

You might think of sunglasses as a fairly modern invention, but the Inuit of the Arctic might deserve some credit. A pair made from walrus ivory was found in northern Baffin, Quebec, dating from between 1200 and 1600 AD. Sometimes the Inuit cut the sunglasses from caribou antlers. The Inuit made them to protect their eyes from snow blindness. They're basically strips with little slits to see out of. The slits cut back the bright light but still give a large field of view. The glasses are now in the collection at the Canadian Museum of Civilization, located in Gatineau, Quebec.

WOODEN UNDERWEAR

When you see acres of majestic white pines, you might not think underwear—but that's what popped into one young French designer's mind. Sophie Young takes harvested fibers from white pines of Canada to create Lenpur, fabric used to produce wooden underwear. The company says the fabric offers the comfort of silk, the feel of cashmere, and the coolness of linen.

The resulting pieces have surprising thermal-regulating and antistress properties. Young swears they will not give you a splinter. Her company—called g=9.8, which physicists will recognize from $g = 9.81$ meters/second^2, the equation for gravitational acceleration—touts the eco benefits of these ethical undies. The fabric is biodegradable, and because it's made from wood scraps, no extra water is required to produce the product. The makers claim that the underwear is more hygienic than conventional private attire because it has more microscopic holes.

Zero Energy Experimental Pile (ZEEP) in Ontario was Canada's first nuclear reactor.

URBAN LEGENDS

Hey, did you hear about the Mountie who chased down hockey-playing moose on foot? We heard it from our neighbor's friend's dog's cousin's aunt-in-law...and she swears it's true!

LEGEND: An American tourist was visiting Canada when he suffered cardiac arrest. After he was rushed to a hospital, doctors found traces of nicotine in his blood, which he is severely allergic to. "I don't even smoke!" insisted the patient. He told doctors he hadn't had anything different to eat or drink since he got to Canada ... except for a coffee at Tim Hortons. Subsequent lab tests of the restaurant chain's coffee showed trace levels of nicotine. The highly addictive chemical was also found in their baked goods ... which explains the long lines at Tim Hortons.

HOW IT SPREAD: Another scary email forward, going back at least as far as 2002.

THE TRUTH: If you don't believe Tim Hortons' insistence that their food has no nicotine, MSG, or any other rumored substances, the CFIA (Canadian Food Inspection Agency) backs them up. Tim Hortons are so good simply because of good ol' caffeine, sugar, and fat.

LEGEND: A hundred years ago, a little girl from Niagara Falls escaped from a farmhouse fire. Screaming, and with her clothes burning, she ran down a hill and into a tunnel...where she succumbed to the flames. Today, if you go into the center of the 16-foot-high, 125-foot-long "Screaming Tunnel" and light a match, you'll hear the doomed girl's screams...and then the match will go out.

HOW IT SPREAD: Around campfires, at slumber parties, and other places where ghost stories are told. This legend is particularly popular due to its close proximity to one of Canada's most visited tourist spots. The details of the legend vary—one version says the girl was burned by her abusive stepfather; in another, a local butcher, obsessed with the girl, burned down the farmhouse to flush her out. But the story always ends with her screams.

THE TRUTH: Paranormal investigators and adventure seekers have entered the tunnel to light matches and listen for screams for decades. Indeed, the matches usually go out, but that's because of the strong

Ottawa-born impressionist Rick Little once hosted *The Tonight Show* in Johnny Carson's voice.

winds present in the tunnel. The creepy location no doubt adds to the allure of this legend. But there's no evidence that a little girl ever died here. One theory as to the source of the legend: There once was a farmhouse in the woods above the tunnel. A mentally unstable woman was reported to have lived there. To relieve stress, she would hide in the center of the tunnel and scream at the top of her lungs. Over time, as the stories got passed down, the troubled woman became a ghost girl.

LEGEND: This is the "actual transcript" of a radio conversation that took place between a U.S. Navy carrier captain and Canadian authorities off the coast of Newfoundland in October 1995.

> **American:** Please divert your course 15 degrees to the north to avoid a collision.
>
> **Canadian:** Recommend you divert YOUR course 15 degrees to the south to avoid a collision.
>
> **American:** This is the Captain of a U.S. Navy ship. I say again, divert YOUR course.
>
> **Canadian:** No. I say again, you divert YOUR course.
>
> **American:** This is the aircraft carrier *USS Lincoln*, the second largest ship in the United States' Atlantic fleet! We are accompanied by three destroyers, three cruisers, and numerous support vessels. I demand that YOU change your course 15 degrees north, or countermeasures will be undertaken to ensure the safety of this ship.
>
> **Canadian:** This is a lighthouse. Your call.

HOW IT SPREAD: Most recently, via the Internet. But variations of this story go back to the years following World War II.

TRUTH: This exchange never took place, but that doesn't stop motivational speakers from using it as a "real" example of what happens when you let your bullheadedness get in the way of the facts. When asked by the *Virginia Pilot* if this scenario is even possible, a U.S. Navy spokesman said it's "completely bogus." Even in heavy fog (which doesn't even appear in most versions of this legend), a state-of-the-art military ship would not mistake a lighthouse for a vessel. But if you don't believe the U.S. Navy, a lighthouse keeper from British Columbia named Jim Abram told the business magazine *Fast Company*, "I've been lighthouse keeping for 21 years, and no one's ever thought that I was in anything but a lighthouse."

Patrick Burns, a meat packer from Oshawa, started his successful biz with the name "Burns Meats."

UNCANNY CANADIAN CREATURES

The fabulous fauna of Canada attest to the nation's vastness and diversity.

HOW CAN THAT BE A PET?

Jim and Linda Sautner of Spruce Grove, Alberta, love their pet bison and do all they can to show him a good time. They take him to a local bar, where he enjoys a bottle of beer or root beer. He likes to lounge in front of the TV and be read to. And like most great pets, he's housebroken. But people take notice when they see the 700-kilogram (1,600-pound) Bailey Jr. being driven around town in a modified red Pontiac convertible. Apparently, Jim has a real affinity for buffalo. His wife calls him the bison whisperer.

Jim had befriended and tamed another bison before this one—that's Bailey Sr.—who died at age 8 when he got his leg caught in some agricultural equipment on the Sautner farm. Jim was broken-hearted, until he got a call from a friend about an orphaned buffalo.

The Sautners took the new calf into their home, bottle-fed him, and named him Bailey Jr. When he was "little," Bailey Jr. would jump into bed with the Sautners. But Jim said he took up too many blankets, so they moved him outside. Besides going to the local bar, the Sautners have taken him to a china shop—where he didn't break a thing—and to a local bank. Jim said Bailey made a deposit there, but it came out the wrong end.

FROGSICLE

Common to the Maritimes and southern British Columbia, the wood frog has a rare trait that helps it survive through brutal winters. When the temperature drops to between –6 and –1 degrees Celsius (21 and 30 degrees Fahrenheit), these amphibians basically become frog ice cubes. The frogs hibernate underground; as the soil freezes, so do the frogs. Two-thirds or more of their body is water. The eyeballs and brain freeze. The heart and breathing stops. The wood frogs can't stand temperatures much colder though. If the mercury drops below –7 degrees Celsius (19 degrees Fahrenheit), they can die. But snow and soil often act as natural insulators. Once the thawing process is completed over the course of a few hours, come spring the hearts restart and off the

The highest recorded temp in Canada was 45 °C/113 °F in Midale, Saskatchewan, in 1937

frogs hop. Because these frogs go through complete cardiac arrest and their hearts start up again without harm, scientists are studying the creatures to see if the freezing and thawing process may help humans.

MOOSE MANIA

Just like the beaver, these antlered quadrupeds are definitively Canadian. These largest members of the deer family are vegetarians. In fact, the word *moose* comes from *mooswa*, which is Algonquin for "twig-eater". Moose have a flap of skin that hangs beneath their throat called a bell. It's uncertain if the bell has a purpose, but investigators have postulated that a moose gets urine-soaked mud on its bell to attract a mate. The nostrils have a unique ability for directional smelling—they can point toward a smell to better identify it.

THERE'S BLOOD IN YOUR EYE

Horned lizards, sometimes wrongly called "horny toads" and common to southwestern Canada, have a strange protection mechanism. When attacked, they squirt blood from their eyes. If a fox or coyote picks one up in its mouth, the lizard squirts the blood; apparently the taste is so foul that it will drop the lizard.

SLITHERING LUNGLESS WONDERS

Fundy National Park is one of the world's great havens for salamanders. Seven species reside there, including the yellow-spotted, red-backed, and two-lined. The red-backed, two-lined, dusky, and four-toed are all considered "lungless." These amphibians undergo a process called cutaneous respiration. They take oxygen in through their skin, which acts like gills; their skin then releases carbon dioxide.

* * *

WAR PLAN BED

"All my sisters would fight over who got to sleep with me. I was always thinking up all the games, telling all the stories, and had the best clothes. I was the entertainment. We didn't have television and we didn't have movies, and I was always the boss. Once, I had this idea that we'd put all the beds on top of one another so there would be only one bed, but it would be a really big, tall bed. Then we'd take turns sleeping on that bed while everybody else slept on the floor. Like, for a month. Everyone thought that was a great idea. I don't know why. I guess because we grew up way, way out in the country and we never had any neighbors."

—Jennifer Tilly

Before Canada was named some choices were New Britannia, Laurentia, Ursalia, and Vesporia...

COINS OF THE REALM

All about Canadian coins and bills.

• In 2011, the Mint rolled out two 25-cent pieces in honor of cryptids. One depicts Memphré, a serpent-like creature with a dragon-like head peering from the waves as its snaky body propels it through the waters of Lake Memphremagog. The other coin shows Mishepishu, which means great lynx, with its wildcat shape. This is a mysterious beast from Ojibwe legend that lurks in the depths of Lake Superior. Myth has it that Mishepishu swims the waters of the Great Lakes and protects the precious copper found in the stones there.

• In 2004, Canada made history when it introduced the world's first colored coin. The Canadian quarter proudly displayed a bright red poppy that year. The poppy is Canada's flower of remembrance, paying homage to the nearly 117,000 Canadians who have died in war since the birth of the country. The coin triggered a bizarre reaction among U.S. Army contractors traveling in Canada, who had never seen anything like it. They erroneously thought that there was nanotechnology built into the coin and that Canada might somehow be using the coins as devices of espionage. The U.S. Department of Defense issued a warning about these supposed spy coins, suggesting that transmitters in the coins might secretly track people. The Department of National Defence soon realized its error and retracted all warnings.

• In 2007, the Mint created what was then the largest coin in the world. The Canadian coin had a face value of $1 million. Made of pure gold, the coin weighs in at 100 kilograms (220 pounds) and features Queen Elizabeth II on the face and Canada's national symbol—the maple leaf—on the back. The coin measures 50 centimeters (about 20 inches) in diameter and 3 centimeters (just over an inch) thick. The mint took about six weeks to produce the coin. In 2010, the coin was auctioned to Spain's Oro Direct, a precious metal company, for just over $4 million. (It lost the largest-coin title in 2011, when Australia issued a coin that was 10 times heavier.)

• The Royal Canadian Mint killed the penny in 2012. Pennies are no longer being produced, and as they return to financial institutions, they are being melted down. Why eliminate the penny? The government says it costs about $11 million a year to supply pennies. With other coins, the government says it "earns more from the sale of coins at face value than it pays to the mint for their production."

• Canada introduced a new $20 bill in 2013, and it is almost indestructible. The bills, which are made out of polymer rather than cotton fiber, are impervious to boiling water, unaffected when set on a hot plate with a temperature of 85° Celsius (185° Fahrenheit), and unharmed when put in a deep freeze of −45 degrees Celsius (−49 degrees Fahrenheit). The bill is also designed to thwart counterfeiters with a hologram of the Queen and a metallic Peace Tower that shines and subtly changes colors when tilted. The new material means that the bills will be in circulation longer. The government is expected to save $200 million over the next eight years from not having to print as many new bills.

• The design of the new bill has caused concern among some Canadians because it features an image of the Vimy Memorial in northern France, the largest monument overseas for Canadian soldiers lost in the First World War. The memorial has naked figures representing Justice, Peace, and Hope. Some were offended to see three nude women on their currency.

* * *

MYSTERY EARTHQUAKES SWARM NEW BRUNSWICK

McAdam, a tiny, quiet town in southwestern New Brunswick, is all shook up. At least, that's how the townspeople felt in the spring of 2012 when a series of 35 minor tremors struck the town in a five-week stretch. The shocks were generally under 3 in magnitude—not enough to do much damage but enough to rattle windows, get floors creaking, and jolt pictures off the walls.

Some locals describe hearing a loud bang or boom along with the movement of the earth. One local said it was like a thud you hear when someone falls out of bed, and another said it was similar to a dynamite blast. Scientists call the phenomenon an "earthquake swarm," but they're not sure why McAdam was feeling the bad vibrations. They are exceedingly rare, though, and that it could be a sign that a big earthquake could be coming in the future. Since the swarm, there haven't been any reports of earthquakes but some residents are waiting for the next, bigger shoe to drop.

The highest recorded temp in Canada was 45 °C/113 °F in Midale, Saskatchewan, in 1937

THE LANGUAGE POLICE

You say frittata, I say melee....

WATCH YOUR MOUTH

If you're a business owner in Quebec, you have to be careful about how you use language or you could be fined. While Canada is officially bilingual, in 1977, the Charter of the French Language defined French as the language of the majority of the population, and thus the official language of the civil service and of business in private workplaces in Quebec with over 50 employees, and it banned the use of languages other than French from commercial signs.

In time, all of the bilingual traffic signs became exclusively French; STOP/ARRÊT signs were replaced by the unilingual ARRÊT. Critics of this change have said that *arrêt* isn't even proper French. *Arrêt* would be more appropriate for a bus stop, and in French the word used to describe coming to a halt at an intersection is *stop* or *stoppez*. As such, in France, stop signs read STOP. Some have said that misunderstandings over the meanings of the signs have led to accidents.

Nevertheless, in upholding the French identity of the province, Office Quebecois de la Langue Francaise (fondly called "the language police") "safeguards" the language, which is spoken by about 94 percent of residents there. (Outside of Quebec, only 4 percent of Canadians percent speak fluent French.) The work has not been without its *contretemps*.

FINICKY FRENCH

In 2013, a language inspector told the owner of an Italian restaurant in Montreal that words such as *botiglia*, *pasta*, and *antipasto* should have a French translation written next to them on the menu. Prompted by public outcry, the head of Quebec's Office of French Language, Louise Marchand, resigned. The office eased off the pasta edict, but the establishment was still not permitted to use the word *ristorante* outside. Here are some other language police orders.

- A British-themed restaurant had to change *fish and chips* on its menu to *poisson frit et frites*.

• A restaurant was forced to mask out the word *redial* on its phones.

• Another eatery was told to remove *WC* (short for water closet) from its toilets.

• A pet shop owner was threatened because it had a parrot named Peekaboo that only squawked out phrases in English.

• A high-end restaurant was commanded to remove the word *steak* from a blackboard in the kitchen that the chef used as a shopping list. They told him to change it to *bifteck*. The same restaurant owner was asked to cover up the words *on/off* on a hot water switch.

• The tiny apostrophe has often been a target of the language police. The French use an apostrophe but not for the possessive. That's why Tim Horton's became Tim Hortons. Somehow, McDonald's has been allowed to keep its apostrophe.

• In Quebec, Kentucky Fried Chicken is known as PFK, or Poulet Frit Kentucky.

* * *

AIMEZ-VOUS FRANCAIS?

The strict attitude toward language has a long history in Quebec. In the 1630s, Quebec's founder, Samuel de Champlain, would not tolerate blasphemy and issued an order prohibiting it. If you were caught, the punishment was having your tongue cut out.

More recently, in an effort to sustain the purity of the French language, France recently banished the word hashtag and introduced mot-dièse, which means "sharp word." In related news, a Federal Court judge in 2011 awarded an Ottawa couple $12,000 for Air Canada's failure to serve them in French. Bilingual computer technician Michel Thibodeau ordered a Sprite in French and received a 7 Up.

THE GREAT MAPLE SYRUP HEIST

Some crooks don't know the first rule of crime: don't stick around.

STICKY-FINGERED THIEVES

Over the years, there have been many stories of robberies that captured the imagination of the public, from the Great Train Robbery, to the stories of thefts completed by Butch Cassidy and the Sundance Kid and Bonnie and Clyde. People have long heard about the heists of such valuable items as cash, gold, diamonds, and even oil. In 2012, another very unexpected robbery was added to that list: The theft of maple syrup from the Global Strategic Syrup Reserve (GSSR) in Quebec.

Located about two hours northeast of Montreal in Saint-Louis-de-Blandford, the GSSR truly lives up to its name. According to a December 19, 2012 *New York Times* report, the province can produce as much as 75 percent of the world's supply of maple syrup. The GSSR is the brainchild of the Federation of Quebec Maple Syrup Producers, an organization given the authority by the Canadian government to set supply quotas for producers as well as local prices. Since some seasons (which are only about 24 days long) produce more syrup than others, the Federation thought it would be a good idea to have a reserve of syrup on hand for those leaner years; hence the GSSR. The Federation compares the GSSR with the United States' strategic oil reserves. Except believe it or not, barrels of maple syrup are more valuable than their "slick" counterparts: grade A syrup sells for about $32 per gallon, or $1,800 per barrel. The New York Times estimated syrup to be three times more valuable than crude oil.

GETTING TO THE BOTTOM OF THE BARREL

The GSSR had stored about 20.9 million kilograms (46 million pounds) of this expensive stuff in part of a rented brick warehouse while building the facility that would be the GSSR's permanent home. The Federation had hired an accountant, Michel Gauvreau, to audit the inventory at the warehouse. During his audit, he discovered that some barrels were empty and some contained water. After about two months of going through the inventory, Gauvreau and inspectors discovered that 6 million pounds of syrup, or about $18 million worth, had been stolen from the facility. A *BusinessWeek* report calculated that it would take more than 100 tractor trailers to transport that much syrup.

AN INTERNATIONAL CRIME TEAM CRACKS MYSTERY

The Canadian government took the theft of its precious maple syrup quite seriously. The Royal Canadian Mounted Police and the U.S. Immigration and Customs Enforcement investigated the crime, issuing 40 search warrants and questioning about 300 people. Police arrested Richard Vallières as the ringleader, and a total of 23 people were charged. Canada's *National Post* called the group the Maple Syrup Mafia (which is better than the Maple Syrup Gang, which would sound too much like a Walt Disney movie). It turns out the thieves were pretty blatant about the whole thing. They rented space in the same warehouse and simply moved the syrup from one section of the warehouse to another and then out onto a loading dock. From there, they presented themselves as legitimate producers to buyers in the neighboring province of New Brunswick, and eventually the illicitly gotten syrup ended up in the United States, where the trail turned cold. Since there's no bar code on containers, and you can't stamp serial numbers on syrup, people in the United States are probably unwitting possessors of stolen property, and eating it on their pancakes.

*　　*　　*

A MAPLE A DAY KEEPS THE DOCTOR AWAY

When most people think maple, they also think syrup and pancakes—not health food. But Quebec maple producers want people to start thinking differently. In spring 2013, maple water was launched as an "ideal thirst-quencher in the summer or for rehydrating after physical exercise." The Federation of Maple Syrup Producers is touting the beverage as a historic tonic that First Nations people and fur traders originally drank for energy and hydration. A spokeswoman for the product compared it to drinking "fresh maple water directly from the tree." And for those worried about packing on the pounds from drinking the maple beverage, Maple water has 25 calories in a 250-millileter (8.5-ounce) serving.

WEIRD CANADA

Crystal lakes, snow-capped mountains, hockey, Mounties, bilingual traffic signs...and some really, really weird news stories.

HOT CHEESE

Brick cheese, which is commonly used on pizzas, sells for one-third of the price in the States as it does in Canada. In the fall of 2012, three men from Fort Erie, Ontario, were arrested for running an illegal cross-border cheese operation. The idea behind their scheme was simple. They bought brick cheese cheaply in America, snuck it across the border, and sold it in Canada. The smugglers packed cases with brick cheese and drove it across the border without paying duties on it. Authorities say the trio purchased more than $200,000 worth of food and sold it at a profit of more than $165,000.

NO HARD FEELINGS

Dany Lariviere, mayor of the small town of St-Theodore-d'Acton in Montreal delivered a 20-ton boulder topped with a pink ribbon to his ex-wife in the summer of 2011. The enormous stone was spray painted with the message "Happy birthday, Isa." Lariviere jokingly compared his "gift" to a giant diamond ring, saying he gave Isa 18 to 24 carat-tons. Because he owns an excavation company, Lariviere transported the rock through the town in the wee hours one Saturday using one of his front loaders. Needless to say, the split between the two has been contentious.

WHO WANTS SOME STANBITS?

In the 1992 movie *Wayne's World*, Wayne and Garth hang out at a Chicago doughnut shop called Stan Mikita's. It's a subtle Tim Hortons joke likely lost on the film's largely American audience. Co-writer and star Mike Myers is Canadian, and a huge hockey fan—and so very familiar with Tim Horton, both as a hockey player and doughnut seller. *Wayne's World* takes place in Chicago, so the characters congregate at Stan Mikita's—Mikita being a legendary player for the Chicago Blackhawks in the '60s and '70s. A replica of the movie Stan Mikita's was built in 1994 for the Kings Dominion amusement park in Virginia. Sadly, it was eventually turned into a *Happy Days*-themed restaurant.

A TRULY ENTRANCING ACT

To entertain its students at the end of the school year, Collège du Sacré-Coeur in Sherbrooke, Quebec, hired a young hypnotist. Maxime

Norma Macmillan, born in Vancouver, was the voice of Casper the Ghost and Gumby.

Nadeau performed his act for a small group of 12- and 13-year-old girls in June 2012. His act was going well until the end. When he told the girls that the act was over, several of them remained mesmerized and couldn't snap out of it, no matter what Nadeau did.

Nadeau remained calm and called his mentor, Richard Whitbread, who made the hour-long trip from his home in the town of Danville to the school. Whitbread discovered that several of the girls were still under the effects of a mass hypnosis. Whitbread described the girls as "eyes wide open but nobody home." To break them out of the spell, the master hypnotist made the girls think they were being rehypnotized and then brought them out using a stern voice. One described it as an out-of-body experience. Others who were hypnotized described feeling like their limbs were heavy. Many felt spaced out. One question arises: are spaced-out students different from the norm?

* * *

T.O.'S VERY OWN BIRD MAN

In 2010, a group of scientists from the University of Toronto invented an aircraft powered by human flapping. Called the Snowbird Human-Powered Ornithopter, the invention is the first man-powered aircraft that requires the pilot to continuously flap wings to soar in the air. The team was inspired by da Vinci and set out to create a device similar to his ornithopter (an aircraft that is powered by flapping its wings). To take to the skies, a car pulls the aircraft to launch it as a pilot pumps a set of pedals that are attached to pulleys that cause the wings to flap. The Snowbird is actually a bit of a baby chick that's just learning to fly.

Weighing a light 94 pounds (43 kilograms), the invention has maintained altitude for just 19.3 seconds so far. It's traveled 145 meters (476 feet) at a speed of 26 kilometers (16 miles) per hour. Todd Reichert, an engineering student who piloted e Snowbird, said, "Throughout history, countless men and women have dreamt of flying like a bird under their own power, and hundreds, if not thousands, have attempted to achieve it. This represents one of the last aviation firsts." Obviously, kinks need to be ironed out before all of us are flapping through the sky like pigeons. Plus, Reichert admits that he had to lose 8 kilograms (a little over 17 pounds) to get the machine in the air. Many may choose to remain earthbound if they have to lose that much weight to fly.

Saskatoon comes from the Cree "Mis-Sask-quah-toomia" meaning "fruit of the much wood."

SENSATIONAL PREMIER STIRS UP A RUCKUS

Personality overcame mistakes for this political icon.

A VERY HUMAN HERO

Rarely have politicians survived, much less continue to be honored, when they make personal mistakes. Whether it's having an affair or abusing drugs or alcohol, when the situation is revealed, it's the end of that politician's political career. That is not the case with John A. Macdonald, Canada's first prime minister. This very human man made mistake after mistake, yet he is still considered a great man and the Father of the Confederation.

When looking at his achievements, it isn't hard to be impressed: He's credited with the construction of the Canadian Pacific Railway, the transcontinental railway; building the Canadian confederation with the addition of Prince Edward Island, the Northwest Territories, Manitoba, and British Columbia; and he created the Northwest Mounted Police. He served as prime minister twice, once in July 1, 1867 to November 5, 1873, and his second term from October 17, 1878, to June 6, 1891. His personal magnetism and drive were two characteristics that made him stand out and succeed, despite some very serious personal and political disasters.

SCADS OF SCANDALS

Macdonald's public career and success were also fraught with equally public scandals. His binge drinking, which began in 1856, was never a secret. From being so inebriated he could barely make decisions while being in charge of the militia during a rebellion to public intoxication during a political debate, he made no efforts to hide his drinking. Yet despite this, he continued to win elections and serve in positions of great responsibility—even the highest responsibility in the confederation.

But this wasn't Macdonald's only scandal. He also had financial problems, at one point amassing debt of $1 million by today's value. The negotiations for the construction of the Canadian Pacific Railway just happened to occur during his 1872 election campaign. He and

Early Canadian explorers suffered from mal de *raquette*—snowshoe sickness.

his colleagues received very large campaign contributions from Sir Hugh Allan, who was designated to lead the syndicate of railroad construction companies. Macdonald claimed that since he had not profited personally, he was innocent of wrongdoing. But this became a big enough scandal after the elections that Macdonald was defeated when he ran again in 1874.

OUT OF THE ASHES

But the weird thing is, despite the drinking and the scandals, he won the election of 1878, just four years later, and became prime minister, again. Perhaps it is just because Canadians are a forgiving lot. Or maybe it's because Macdonald's personal tragedies were also well known. He had witnessed the murder of his brother when he was five years old, his first wife and their first son had died, and his daughter was born with hydrocephalus. But what may have also contributed to his successful election and made him a real hero is the fact that he had overcome his binge drinking problem by 1876.

*   *   *

CANADIAN WHISKY FACTS

• It can be made from any mixture of cereal grains, such as corn, wheat, barley, or rye, and has to be aged for a minimum of three years...entirely in Canada.

• Most Canadian whiskys are blends of other, made-in-Canada, single-malt whiskys.

• It's called whisky, not whiskey to uphold the Scottish tradition.

• Canadian whisky nickname: "brown vodka."

• Distiller Glen Breton makes a whisky that has been aged for 10 years in barrels normally used to make ice wine.

TRADE YA?

Here's how to turn a red paper clip into a house in Saskatchewan.

START SMALL

In 2005, 25-year-old Kyle MacDonald and his girlfriend, were living in Montreal in a small, $600-a-month apartment. MacDonald had dabbled in travel writing and worked occasionally for his father, but he needed better employment. As he thought about ways to advance his life, he looked down at his résumé, held together by a red paper clip. As a teenager, he had heard of a game called Bigger and Better, which was a type of scavenger hunt. The idea was that you would go door to door with a small item and ask for something bigger. He'd heard about one fellow who had started with an old shoe and ended the night with a car.

In a moment of inspiration, MacDonald decided that he would trade the red paper clip and try to end up with a house. On July 12, he placed a photo of his red paper clip on Craigslist with a notice that he was looking to trade up for something bigger.

...THERE'S A WAY

In his first trade, he got a wooden fish pen. He bartered that for a knob made by a potter in Seattle. The knob was swapped for a Coleman grill in Massachusetts, which was promptly exchanged for a generator in California. A man from Queens offered a vintage Budweiser sign, and MacDonald drove to make the exchange. As he reported his progress on his blog, he gained some attention. A Montreal radio host heard of his quest and offered his snowmobile. The media was now paying more attention to MacDonald. On a news program, he joked that he would trade the snowmobile for anything but a trip to Yahk, British Columbia. The next day he was offered a trip to Yahk.

His mission was picking up momentum. At a quick pace, he traded for a van, then a recording contract, and then a year of rent. Through his blog he was gaining fans who were rooting him on with each trade forward. Then, at one point he traded a day with Alice Cooper for a KISS snow globe. Many in his growing base of fans were outraged. How could he have made such a stupid trade! He received hate mail. People began calling his quest a sham—where was the quest for the house?

The most common crime in Canada is "theft under $5,000".

JACK OF ALL TRADES

But about a week later, MacDonald had parlayed the snow globe into a speaking role in a Hollywood film with Corbin Bernsen. About one year and 14 exchanges later, MacDonald traded the movie role for a house in the town of Kipling, Saskatchewan, population 1,140.

On July 12, 2006, he accepted the keys to the house in a ceremony that included many of the people he had made trades with along the way. At the event, he asked Corinna Haight, who now had the famous red paper clip, if he could borrow it. He twisted the clip into a ring and asked his girlfriend to marry him. She accepted and wore the ring for that day, then returning it to the owner.

*　　*　　*

EATON TRIFLES

Irish-Canadian immigrant Timothy Eaton founded T. Eaton Co. Limited in the 1860s, which grew from a dry goods business into Canada's largest retail chain by the mid-20th century. Notably, it was the first Canadian store to utilize mail-order catalogs.

• The oddest item ever offered through the Eaton catalog: a house. The Neils Hogenson House (eventually named after its owner) was mail-ordered in 1917. Everything from the largest doors and windows to the individual bolts and screws were packaged in Winnipeg, put on a train, and shipped to Stirling, Alberta, where it was paid for at the station. The total cost: a whopping $1,577, which, thankfully, included assembly instructions. The house remains in Stirling, in its original state.

• A Saskatchewan town was named Eaton, after the stores, in 1919. Two years later, it was changed to Eatonia to avoid confusion with the nearby Eston.

• When Timothy Eaton died in 1907, his son and heir, John, spent some of his newfound inheritance on a private rail car. It was extremely opulent, featuring three bedrooms, a living room, dining room, and a steward's quarters. Since 1972, it's been on display in Heritage Park Historical Village, a living-history museum in Calgary.

100 Mile House is a town in B.C. named because of its distance from Lillooet.

HARVESTING THE FROZEN GOLIATHS

In Newfoundland and Labrador, icebergs are a big deal for both tourists and corporations.

THE COLD, HARD FACTS

Every spring and summer (mostly between April and June) off the coast of Newfoundland and Labrador, a new crop of icebergs floats by off shore. Broken away from glaciers over 10,000 years old (usually from western Greenland), the icebergs drift into the area from the Arctic. Annually, about 40,000 medium- to large-sized icebergs break off, or calve, from Greenland glaciers. Only about 400 to 800 make it as far south as St. John's, Newfoundland, although climate change may be to blame for their more sporadic appearance in recent years.

Twillingate, a small island in the North Atlantic, is located on the edge of what's known as "Iceberg Alley." The townspeople call it the Iceberg Capital of the World. Locals say that tourism accounts for about half of the income generated in the town, with several businesses running iceberg-watching boat tours. Visitors come to admire the floating ice piles with their shades of aquamarine and white. Illuminated by reflections from the sea, the icebergs have been called "cathedrals of ice." If you're there at the right moment, you may see and hear one break apart, causing a great wheezing sounding that climaxes with a huge bang.

ICEBERGS ARE (VERY) BIG BUSINESS

Fishermen in this area have also found another source of income in harvesting water from icebergs. Once they capture chunks of the ice, they melt their "prey" and sell the water to vodka, beer, wine, and bottled water companies that are creating products using iceberg water as a hook. The Canadian Iceberg Vodka Corporation produces high-quality vodka from iceberg water, which it claims is the cleanest water on Earth. The company says that sales have been strong. Quidi Vidi Brewing sometimes has trouble keeping up with demand for its Iceberg Beer. Auk Island Winery makes several wines with berg water.

"In Canada, there are 9 months of winter and 3 months of road repair." —Peter Hansen

A skin-care line now features environmentally friendly products made from iceberg water (along with seaweed, caviar, and berry extracts). Ossentra Wondrous Earth says the pH, or acidity, level of the iceberg water is 5.0, almost the same as the pH of skin.

BREAKING THE ICE

Scouting for the bergs takes patience and diligence. When an iceberg hunter spots a candidate drifting along, he has to calculate the trajectory and plan how to best approach it. Those scouting bergs often go to icebergfinder.com, which provides charts showing the last known location of icebergs in Iceberg Alley. The icebergs are tracked through visual sightings from on-the-ground ambassadors and satellite detection from Canadian Space Agency technology.

FINDING THE TIP OF THE ICEBERG

Getting a chip off the old block isn't such an easy process. Iceberg hunters, all with permits from the provincial government to capture pieces of the giants, will sometime go at the ice with chainsaws and hatchets. Some icebergers shoot the ice with a rifle; the sonic waves will cleave off a chunk. Another method is to use a massive hydraulic claw to rip off chunks. These ice harvesters have to be very careful because icebergs are often very unstable. Varying degrees of melting and breakup can cause them to tip or roll suddenly. They can roll completely over in seconds without any apparent reason. Iceberg hunters often haul their harvest to bigger ships in massive nets dragged along by motorboats. Huge hydraulics lift the piece from the sea and onto the deck of a vessel. Workers use high-pressure steam or potable water to rinse the ice. Then they cut it into pieces and store them in barrels. Some is melted and pumped into holding containers. The hard work, potential hazards, and patience of iceberging is worth it for many of the harvesters because there's money in the big ice cubes. During a good season, an ice man can bring in a haul worth several hundred thousand dollars.

* * *

MORBID JOB MARKET

Something in the water? Between 1996 and 2006, the number of female funeral directors in Canada doubled, from 720 to nearly 1,400.

HAUNTED HAUNTS

Ghost stories abound in the Canada, and they often have tragic tales behind them. Here are some of our favorite spooooky places.

GHOSTLY GOALS

Hockey fans are accustomed to hearing the sound of crying when their team misses a shot, but those who visit the Hockey Hall of Fame may hear the eerie crying of a ghost named Dorothy, who is said to haunt the halls. The building that houses the Hall of Fame had been a Bank of Montreal for 100 years before it was converted into a hockey shrine in the early 1990s. Lights have mysteriously flickered on and off, windows and doors have opened and closed without anyone near them, and screams and cries have been heard echoing throughout the building. In 1995, a boy touring the Hall started screaming, "Don't you see her? Don't you see her?" The boy claimed to have witnessed a woman with long black hair going in and out of the walls. Legend has it that Dorothy was a teller who killed herself in the bank over a romantic affair with a bank manager gone wrong. No one knew the story of who Dorothy really was until the Toronto newspaper *The Star* did a little digging in 2009 and discovered that the spirit may be that of Dorothea Mae Elliott. She shot herself early in the morning on Wednesday, March 11, 1953, with the bank's revolver, a .38 caliber, in a women's washroom on the second floor of the bank. She died 22 hours later at St. Michael's Hospital.

PASTA FA-GHOUL

The Old Spaghetti Factory, in Vancouver, British Columbia has a famous spirit is connected to Trolley Number 53, which sits in the middle of the restaurant. The train car was once a part of the British Columbia Electric Railway Company's fleet of electric trams for public transport. It was built in 1904 and decommissioned in 1957. After closing, staff have spotted a uniformed conductor sitting on the trolley, always at the same table. Witnesses have seen table settings move and felt unexplained cold spots aboard old Number 53. The conductor reportedly died in an underground collision below where the restaurant now stands. Others say the ghost came with the car. While the conductor may be the most famous spirit at the Old Spaghetti

Singer Tom Cochrane of Ontario sold a toy train set at age 11 to raise money for his first guitar.

Factory, the hauntings don't end with him. Some female diners claim that a pint-sized, red-haired, ruddy-faced ghost has spooked them in the ladies' room. A ghost boy named Edward has been spotted hiding under tables, and a little girl spirit holding a balloon has been seen at a table in the front window.

GOING OFF THE RAILS ON THE CRAZY GHOST TRAIN

Late at night, visitors to a stretch of abandoned railway track on a dirt road in St. Louis, Saskatchewan, swear they see ghostly lights coming along where the rails were once located and then disappearing into the mist. The story goes that an engineer for the Canadian National Railway was examining the tracks in St. Louis one night in 1929 and didn't notice a train barreling straight at him. The speeding train struck the poor fellow, and he died in its oncoming lights. For more than 80 years, various people have spied the lights and some video footage has even been captured. Witnesses think the engineer is driving a phantom train along that stretch. Others say the lights are from a conductor who was decapitated in the area and keeps coming back with a light, searching until he finds his missing head.

IN THIS THEATER, THE ACTORS MAY BOO YOU

In the early 1900s, Laurence Irving and Mabel Hackney were popular stage actors in England. In early 1914, the couple performed in four plays in Winnipeg, including *The Importance of Being Earnest* by Oscar Wilde. When the final curtain went down on May 23, Irving and Hackney jumped a train to Quebec City so they could catch their boat, *The Empress of Ireland*, which was departing on May 28 to Europe. In the St. Lawrence River, their boat collided with another ship, the coal freighter SS *Storstad*, and the couple drowned on May 29, along with more than a thousand other passengers. Since the drowning, visitors and staff at the Walker Theater have heard singing, shouting, applauding from unoccupied seats, and stage performances—all when no actors were around. A steel door has closed on its own. Recordings have captured the eerie sounds that have all been attributed to the doomed duo. On one recording made when the theater was dark, you can supposedly hear a voice whispering, "Please."

In Chinook, "high muckamuck" means feast.

YOU CALL THAT ART?

Artists are known for their "unique" way of viewing the world. Here's a collection of Canadian creations that stand out for being particularly unusual.

THIS DRESS IS A CUT ABOVE

Twenty years before Lady Gaga shocked the audience of the 2010 MTV Video Music Awards by wearing a dress made of raw beef, Montreal artist Jana Sterbak constructed an outfit hand-stitched from 23 kilograms (50 pounds) of raw, unrefrigerated, salted flank steak. *Vanitas: Flesh Dress for an Albino Anorexic* was displayed in the National Gallery of Canada in Ottawa, which purchased the distinctive dress. In the weeks following the installation, 200 people mailed food scraps to the gallery to protest the work, which Sterbak explained as dealing with issues of vanity and bodily decay. It was also meant to communicate that no matter how we drape ourselves, we are still just meat on bones. When the dress decomposed, which took about six weeks, it was replaced with another $300 worth of raw meat; the gallery staff was trained to piece it together.

LEAVING ITS MARK

Maskull Lasserre wants to put city dwellers a little on edge. Using urethane rubber, the native of Alberta has cast the footprints of various predatory creatures and then attached them to the bottoms of shoes. When people put on his shoes and then walk through the snowy city streets, they leave behind the tracks of cougars, bears, deer, and the occasional Big Foot. He said that the human footprints he always saw in the snow looked a little lonely, so he created these animal prints as companions. You may spy his handiwork—or fancy footwork—near his studios in Montreal and Ottawa.

A PEDAL TO THE MEDAL

Michael de Broin of Montreal (and Berlin) is a true conceptual artist. He suspended the largest mirror ball (constructed of 1,000 mirrors) ever made from a construction crane 50 meters (164 feet) above the ground in the Jardin du Luxembourg during the Nuit Blanche event, an annual all-night arts festival. He created a star in New Orleans

In 1999, Aashrita Furman pogo-sticked up the 1,899 steps of the CN Tower.

from lampposts that were torn down by Hurricane Katrina. In 2005, De Broin stripped the inside of an '86 Buick Regal of its engine, suspension, transmission, and electrical system, reducing its weight considerably. He equipped the vehicle with four separate pedal and gear mechanisms so that passengers could power the vehicle via pedaling. With four pedalers aboard, the *Shared Propulsion Car* could reach top speeds of 15 kilometers (9 miles) per hour. When the artist took the car for a spin in Montreal, with tea lights sitting in place of light bulbs at the front, police pulled over De Broin and issued him a ticket for driving an unsafe vehicle. The artist argued his case in court, where Justice of the Peace Patrick Marum didn't see De Broin as much of a danger. He threw the case out.

A DANGEROUS YARN

Howie Woo has a soft spot for thrilling things. The 35-year-old artist from British Columbia grew up wanting to play with various weapons but never had the chance to. After taking lessons in Amigurumi, the Japanese art of crocheting or knitting stuffed characters, Woo decided to crochet versions of dangerous items that he always wanted to play with as a young lad. He poses in photos featuring himself in action using his crocheted grenades, sticks of dynamite, UFOs, and ray guns, all hand-made from harmless wool.

HOW MUCH IS THAT BANANA IN THE WINDOW?

Artist Michael Fernandes caused a stir in 2008 when he placed a banana in the window of Gallery Page and Strange in Halifax with a price tag of $2,500. Anyone who bought the banana would not just be buying a piece of fruit; it was a concept. Fernandes changed the banana every day to a progressively greener one, and he would eat the old banana. He was making a comment about the transitory nature of things. "We (humans) are also temporal, but we live as if we are not," he wrote. Despite the exorbitant price tag, two collectors placed holds on the piece, which was titled *Banana*. The gallery's co-owner, Victoria Page, wanted prospective buyers to absolutely understand what they were getting for their money. "Collectors are contacting us; they've seen the picture on our website, and they're asking us what medium he's using," she said. She made sure to tell collectors: "It's a banana; you understand that it's a banana?"

Des Sawa Jr. of Tobermory made the largest golf tee in the world—over 2.1 m (7') feet tall.

CANADIAN CYBORG

Some people really get close with their gear.

LIFE ON TWO WHEELS

French artist and copy editor Guillaume Blanchet loves his bicycle. In fact, he spent 382 days on it—*never* leaving. He cooked, he ate, he slept, he flirted, and he washed his clothes on a bicycle for all of 2011 and more. And he made sure to film a lot of his experience. Blanchet did everything on the go, constantly pedaling. While remaining on his bicycle seat, he handled frying pans, shaving kits, laptops, telephones, Rubik's cubes, and musical instruments. He kept a roll of toilet paper on the handle bar, which does raise the question of how he did some things while remaining on his bike.

PART MANN, PART MACHINE

For more than 20 years, University of Toronto engineering professor Steve Mann has lived his life as a cyborg. He wears a web of wires, computers, and sensors. His devices are designed to enhance his vision, boost his memory, and track his vital signs. A small camera/computer called the EyeTap connects into his skull. He carries documents from his doctor explaining that the EyeTap is physically attached to his head and cannot be removed without special tools. Because of his unusual appearance, Dr. Mann has been accosted. In 2002, security personnel at St. John's International Airport in Newfoundland strip-searched him and destroyed $56,800 worth of his equipment, including the eyeglasses that serve as his display screen.

THE REAL STEPFORD WIFE

Those looking for the perfect woman might want to contact inventor Le Trung. The science genius has built his own ideal female robotic companion. The native of Brampton, Ontario, named her Aiko, which is Japanese for love child. Aiko plays multiplayer Xbox games, helps to clean the house, and can fix drinks. When they go on romantic country drives, Aiko gives perfect directions. She recognizes faces and says hello to those she has met. The 37-year-old whiz is so in love with his perfect woman that he has brought her home

Canadian Jack MacKenzie is the oldest person to ski to the North Pole, at age 77.

to spend Christmas with his parents. Aiko opened her presents and joined in the family tradition of playing quiz and board games. She's programmed to speak 13,000 sentences. The fembot does not like it if you get fresh with her, though.

If you grab or squeeze her too hard, she will slap you. The silicon beauty with the hourglass figure even has sensors in her private parts, but Trung emphasizes that he has not slept with her. Trung originally started building Aiko as a robot that would help take care of the elderly, but he evidently strayed from his original plan.

He has spent at least $23,000 so far creating his dreambot. Trung has said, "Aiko doesn't need food or rest and will work almost 24 hours a day." For the right person, she is the ideal companion.

* * *

SKYROCKETS IN FLIGHT

British Columbia boffin Ken Schellenberg is a rocket enthusiast. The chief scientist and CEO at Antigravity Research Corporation—a company in Chilliwack devoted to state-of-the-science professional pop-bottle water rocketry—has already broken the world record for shooting a water rocket to the highest altitude ever. His small carbon fiber–reinforced pop-bottle rocket, fueled by compressed nitrogen and foamed water, hit an altitude of 378.5 meters (1,242 feet).

Schellenberg's next goal is to launch a 2-liter (half a gallon) pop bottle into outer space. His company sells products that allow rocket enthusiasts to build their own high-flying bottles. They're made by attaching plastic or cardboard fins to an empty bottle, punching a hole in the bottle top to act as a nozzle, and pressurizing the bottle with air from a bicycle pump. Water and dish soaps often propel the rockets to higher heights. His project to get a bottle rocket in space is still in the works, but he has developed plans for a two-stage reinforced vessel with ultra-strong carbon fiber fueled by liquid CO_2. He also wants to do everything legally and without interfering with other technology that is in orbit, so he intends on launching his creation from a military facility such as the one in Cold Lake, Alberta.

The longest marriage in the world is 80 years, between Joseph and Annie Jarvis of Yukon Territory.

BATHROOM NEWS

Uncle John lifts the lid on these toilet tales.

THE $2 MILLION OUTHOUSE

Alberta's Banff National Park has more than just acres of unspoiled wilderness. As of September 2008, the park is home to what may be the world's most expensive outhouse. Called the super-biffy (slang in scouting terms for outhouse) by the locals, the bathroom at Lake Minnewanka generates its own power, heat and hot water through solar power collected in panels on the roof. The solar panels also generate electricity that provide light for all those seeking relief, and a battery pack stores electricity on days when there is no sun. You wouldn't know for the looks of it that it is a deluxe privy. It looks more like a large new barn. Though the building is environmentally progressive, many critics were outraged by the amount spend on a toilet. According to the *Calgary Herald* it will take 576 years to pay itself off. Visitors have remarked that the stalls are very small, as are the sinks, which are made of plastic. The *Calgary Herald* and other publications have strongly criticized the outhouse, wondering how it could cost so much for a few urinals, a few washbasins, and a few stalls. Since publicly funded Parks Canada owns the land, the cost especially seems outrageous.

DON'T FLUSH THAT SQUIRREL

In June 2013, a Winnipeg woman was awoken by her dogs barking extra early. She wasn't sure what was disturbing them at first until she heard a splashing coming from underneath the lid of her toilet. Although she was nervous about looking inside, she flipped the lid and discovered a soaked squirrel clinging for dear life. Angela Campbell had no idea how the furry creature got in there, but she knew she had to react fast to save the critter's life. She ran to the kitchen and grabbed a pair of barbecue tongs. Then, she snagged the water-logged rodent and plopped him in her bathtub. The animal was filthy and smelled horrible, so she gently rinsed the dazed tree-dweller. After the little beast was cleaned up, she grabbed him again with tongs and placed him on her patio, where he scampered back into the wild.

Gopher comes from the French for the rodents' tunnels: "gaufre gris," literally "gray waffle."

AWARD WINNING POTTY PALACES

Cintas, a Canadian company that provides work uniforms and restroom supplies, holds a Canada's Best Restroom Contest every year to honor the spiffiest biffy. Some of the "Hall of Fame" crappers:

• **The Langely Street Loo, Victoria, British Columbia.** This public potty is open to the public and wins high praise for its graffiti-proof coating and "a lit sign that makes it easy to find at night." We have a nightlight in our bathroom that makes it easy to find, but so far we have not won a toilet Oscar.

• **e11even, Toronto, Ontario.** This upscale restaurant took the grand prize for a washroom that provides "luxury and an intimate ambience" where guest can "relax and indulge in a private space." Sounds like a place you may never want to leave.

• **The Cactus Club Café, Vancouver, British Columbia**. Padded furniture, televisions, glass floor-to-ceiling stall doors, and hardwood walls make this restroom a sexy superstar.

*   *   *

HEALING HEN

In Newfoundland, historical records recall the tale of a boy whose hand became wounded and infected from a fishing hook. His hand swelled, and a dark color spread up his arm. Although there was no doctor in the area, an old Eskimo woman lived nearby and was known for her healing powers.

When the boy was brought to the old woman, she saw his injury and acted decisively. She cut open his wound where it had healed. She then cut open a live chicken at the beak and inserted the boy's hand into the chicken. Reports say the dark color drained from his arm. When it completely disappeared the hen died. The boy was made well, and the old woman had the chicken buried so the dogs wouldn't eat it and swallow the poison that had drained into the chicken.

CIRQUE DU SOLEIL

Everything you ever wanted to know about Canada's preeminent whimsical French circus.

SOMETIMES CLOWNING AROUND PAYS OFF

Guy Laliberte, the founder of Cirque du Soleil, is the first billionaire clown in outer space. The Montreal-based circus company has been a phenomenal success, developing many touring shows. Having started the wildly popular Canadian circus, Laliberte owns 95 percent of the shares in the company and has an estimated worth of more than $2.5 billion. In 2009, Laliberte plunked down $35 million to ride aboard the Soyuz TMA-16 spacecraft to the International Space Station. He was accompanied by U.S. astronaut Jeffrey Williams and Russian cosmonaut Maxim Surayev.

To send off Laliberte, his girlfriend, Claudia Barilla, a former model, donned a yellow clown nose and joined friends in a rousing rendition of Elton John's "Rocket Man."

WHERE NO CLOWN HAS GONE BEFORE

The clown tycoon used his trip to increase awareness about the shortage of clean water here on planet Earth on behalf of his charity organization called One Drop. An unexpected outcome of his space travels was the series of beautiful photos he took of Earth. The snapshots are abstract images of our world taken from a great distance.

Laliberte has certainly come a long way from his humble beginning as a fire-breathing street performer and poker shark. He founded the Montreal-based circus with a gang of street performers in 1984 using some funding from the Canadian government. Over a period of almost 30 years, the operation has grown into an entertainment empire, although the business has suffered in recent years because of poor tickets sales for some shows, including the Las Vegas production of *Viva Elvis*. One of the biggest moneymakers for the company is a spectacle called *Michael Jackson: The Immortal*. In 2008, Laliberte sold 20 percent of his holdings to two firms in Dubai for $600 million. So the former street clown has some extra cash to take a trip into outer space every now and then:

• To get attention from the Quebec government to help fund the formation of an early circus troupe, Gilles Ste-Croix, a partner of Laliberte's, walked 56 miles (90 km) from Baie-Saint-Paul to Quebec in 1979. This first circus troupe was led to Cirque du Soleil. The stunt worked. The government gave Laliberte, Ste-Croix and their third partner, Daniel Gauthier funding to launch the circus.

• Cirque du Soleil was not an overnight success. The troupe experienced a roller coaster of successes and failures for about a decade before the circus became truly popular. In Toronto in 1986, their show was playing to houses that were just one-quarter full. Ste-Croix, always game for a publicity stunt, walked through downtown Toronto dressed as a monkey. The circus had written hundreds of thousands of dollars in bad checks. In many ways, it didn't look like it would survive. But financiers came through with backing to keep the show going.

• Cirque du Soleil's hugely popular tribute to Michael Jackson is a strange as the pop star himself. The show features a human-sized dancing white glove. Some critics have compared it to a glamorous version of the Hamburger Helper mascot. An actor dressed as Jackson's beloved chimp Bubbles ascends on a platform. Dancers leap from a giant pair of Michael Jackson's shoes.

• Some shows feature an obese adult baby who goes up to audience members calling them "papa," squirting water on them, dumping popcorn over their heads, and making them wear a diaper on stage. Several audience members have complained that having a fat adult baby harass them wasn't very fun or funny.

* * *

WANT TO GET HIGH?

Guinness World Records has acknowledged the CN Tower in Toronto for having the highest external walk. Those who do not have a fear of heights can try walking hands-free along a 1.5-meter- (about 5-foot-) wide ledge that circles the top of the tower's main pod at 356 meters (about 1,168 feet) off the ground. Guests are securely tethered to a rail in a harness and can lean back over the edge. The EdgeWalk attraction opened on August 1, 2011, and is closed during the winter, electrical storms, and high winds.

The world's largest Scottish country dance saw 512 kicking up their heels in Toronto in 1991.

HAIRY TERROR

Call the big guy what you will, just don't call him late for dinner.

READY FOR YETI

The Squatch is a gigantic, ape-like creature that seems to be part human. The mythic creature stands 1.8 to 2.7 meters (7 to 9 feet) tall and weighs between 270 and 400 kilograms (600 and 900 pounds). A Sasquatch has never been caught but there have been hundreds and hundreds of sightings. And there seems to be a similar creature stalking the mountains of the Himalayas of Asia—the famous Abominable Snowman or Yeti. Legends of the Sasquatch in Canada goes back centuries. First Nation tribes have stories of the beast and his name is Salish for "hairy giant."

KEEPING UP APPEARANCES

While Sasquatch has been spotted in the northwestern U.S., Canada may have the first recorded "evidence." David Thompson was working in 1811 as a trader in Jasper, Alberta, when he found huge footprints in the snow. They were 36 centimeters (14 inches) long and 20 centimeters (eight inches wide). Plus, the beast that left the prints only had four toes. The *Daily Colonist*, a newspaper in Victoria, British Columbia, published a story in 1884 about the capture of a Sasquatch, although it was smaller than in later descriptions. The paper wrote the following account:

> Jack, as his captors have called the creature is something of a gorilla type, standing about four feet seven inches in height and weighing 127 pounds. He has long black hair and resembles a human being with one exception, his entire body, excepting his hands or paws and feet are covered in glossy hair about one inch long. His forearm is much longer than man's forearm and he possesses extraordinary strength, as he will take hold of a stick and break it by wrenching it or twisting it, which no living man could break in the same way.

About a week later, though, another newspaper in the province claimed the report was a hoax.

LOSING YOUR HEAD

In 1924, Albert Ostman was a lumberjack who claimed that a Big Foot picked him up in his sleeping bag and brought him back to his Sasquatch family. Ostman said the family—a mother and father Sasquatch and their children—kept him captive but did not harm him. He remarked that the beasts were vegetarian, eating roots, grass, and spruce tips.

PAYING THE FERRYMAN

As recent as 2005, video was taken of a massive, hairy figure walking along the shore of the Nelson River, about 500 kilometers (311 miles) north of Winnipeg. It was about 6:30 a.m. on a Saturday morning when Bobby Clarke, a ferry operator, was working to transport vehicles across the Nelson River. Clarke looked about 250 meters (820 feet) across the river and spied a huge, hairy creature, walking upright through the bulrushes at the water's edge, and he grabbed his camera. Many skeptics who have seen the video say that it has made them believers.

* * *

THE TWISTED TREES OF ALTICANE

Normal quaking aspens stand tall and straight, majestically reaching heights of 20 to 25 meters (66 to 82 feet). They are also called trembling aspens or quaking poplars, and so named for the way their leaves flutter in the breeze. But in a grove in Alticane, Saskatchewan, grow peculiar poplars like none other in the world. These twisted and gnarled trees are a genuinely eerie sight.

But what is at the root of these deformed versions of the graceful aspen with its dancing leaves? Locals attribute the contorted trunks to aliens or ghosts. A farmer claims to have spied aliens urinating in the area before the trees began growing in the 1940s—Alticane is located in an area well known for UFO sightings. Visitors to the area report a strange energy in the grove, getting dizzy as they stroll along the wooden walkway. Even cattle avoid the patch of trees.

While there is no definitive explanation for the unusual occurrence, some believe the gnarled trees are genetic mutations caused by contaminated soil—possibly from meteorites that crashed to Earth in that area ages ago. Rick Sawatzky from the University of Saskatchewan has taken cuttings from the trees... which, even away from the forest, again grew in the same twisted formation.

A karate team demolished a 10-room house with their bare hands in Saskatchewan in 1996.

COW CRAZINESS

Canadian cows udderly fascinate their human keepers.

BUILDING A BETTER COW

Carbon emissions may be contributing to global warming, but the world's 1.5 billion cows emit dozens of polluting gases, including lots of methane—two-thirds of all ammonia comes from cows. University of Alberta scientists are looking into ways to breed cows that will not unleash as many methane-rich "emissions." While researchers have already found ways to change the cow diet to lower their methane output by up to 25 percent, they are now trying to develop a genetic means of producing a gas-free bovine. Many farmers in Alberta now feed their livestock a diet rich in edible oils, which ferment less than grass and low-quality feed, leading to fewer waste gasses. Some farms are even producing energy from the methane gas trapped in manure. In a typical system, the cow waste is pumped into a huge sealed concrete tank known as a digester, where it is kept at a temperature of 38 degrees Celsius (101 degrees Fahrenheit). Anaerobic bacteria break down the organic matter, which produces a mix of methane and other gases, known as biogas. The gas is then burned in an engine that runs an electric generator.

YOU WIN?

Gambling and cow patties make a winning combination at fairs and charity events in Canada. The game is cow-patty bingo, and it's proven to be a popular fund-raising event. Here's how it works: 150 squares are drawn on a street or field. Each square has a number in it. Players buy a numbered ticket for $10 each. Then the cows are let loose. If an animal plops a flop on a square, the ticket holder with the matching number wins a prize. Unlike regular bingo, it would be almost impossible for cows to happen to poop in five squares in a row. The fundraisers have refined cow-patty bingo over the years. In the past, the squares were painted bright pink, which apparently scared the animals and often prevented pooping.

A SPICE-Y STORY

The University of Saskatchewan has a cow named Spice with a hole in its side that leads directly into one of its four stomachs. Students

She's part material Canuck: Madonna's mother is of French Canadian descent.

can put their (gloved) hands directly inside the cow. Making this type of *fistula*, or abnormal passageway, in a cow is done on occasion at veterinary schools. After surgically creating the opening, doctors fitted Spice's hole with a sealing cover called a cannula. As a result, investigators can observe how Spice is digesting her food.

BED OF GRASS

It makes sense that well-rested cows are more productive. That's why a company in called CowMatsCanada.com makes mattresses for cattle that are the ultimate in comfort—for cattle. A big selling feature is the slightly raised center that allows fluids to drain off—something we all might desire in a mattress.

A MOO-VING MEMORIAL

People for the Ethical Treatment of Animals (PETA) in Winnipeg has been fighting for a roadside memorial for cows who have died in highway crashes in Manitoba. The group wants to set up a sign along the road where 71 cows died after a semi collided with a train on January 31, 2012.

*　　　*　　　*

BIRD BRAIN

A racing pigeon from Japan took off with 8,000 of his fellow racing pigeons on May 10, 2013, from Sapporo, Japan. It was due to fly 600 miles but it took a wrong turn somewhere and wound up 4,000 miles away on Vancouver Island at the end of June. Pigeon professionals believe the feathered adventurer had to hitch a ride on a ship to make it so far. Rescuers found the bird starving and exhausted, but they were able to trace the bird back to its owner in Japan. Hiroyasu Takasu was grateful to hear his bird was still alive and coming back to health. Although he missed his bird, Takasu asked that the pigeon not be returned because the trip would endanger its health. The Mid-Island Racing Club in Nanaimo on Vancouver Island has adopted the long-distance flier. Trainers want to pair it with a suitable female to breed champion racers.

THE TROUBLE WITH TRACY

Viewers remember great television. Uncle John helps you keep in mind the not-so-great.

THE WORST TV SHOW EVER?

Canadians have very few television shows that are known outside of Canada. *Second City Television* (SCTV) is famous for all the comedians that got their start there—John Candy, Martin Short, Eugene Levy, and Rick Moranis, to name a few. *The Kids in the Hall* is well-known for its innovative, absurd comedy, and the teen drama *Degrassi Jr. High* became a huge franchise. Still, there aren't too many shows that have become famous outside the country, but one more is known by many television buffs—mostly because it has been called one of the worst television shows ever made. *The Trouble with Tracy* was a sitcom from the early 1970s made by CTV to meet requirements of a law mandating that it air at least 60 percent Canadian-made content. CTV had very little money to spend, so it decided to use old scripts from a dated 1940s radio comedy called *Easy Aces*.

HOW TO MAKE A FLOP

The sitcom was filmed on a single set in Toronto with one camera. The actors had been criticized for lacking any sense of comedic timing, and the production value often seems worse than cable public access. The laughtrack couldn't save the show, either, and in fact, probably made the program a whole lot worse by forcing laughs where none were to be found. Flubbed lines and bloopers often made it into the program because CTV could not afford to reshoot any scenes.

The Trouble was about a young advertising executive and his wife trying to make it in New York City. In fact, the young couple were actually *named* the Youngs. The ditzy and naïve Tracy Young usually wears a miniskirt, and her ever-loving husband, Doug, rolls his eyes and puts up with her antics while never losing his temper. In a typical episode, Doug doesn't want to watch Tracy's favorite TV show because he thinks the cheesy mystery is beneath his intelligence. However, many of the events in the TV show start playing out in real life, starting with a neighbor who needed help carrying a truck to his car. Many eerie coincidences unfold, leading to comedic misunderstandings. The show was not only bad, there was so much

Jerry Seinfeld got his start opening for Anne Murray.

of it. CTV filmed and aired 130 episodes of the stinker in just two years (1970 and 1971). The 60-percent Canadian content meant that CTV couldn't simply cancel the show. It needed the programming by law.

NOT EXACTLY AN ENCORE

The actors survived the show, but they didn't exactly rise to stardom. Steve Weston (Doug) appeared on *The Hart and Lorne Terrific Hour*, starring Lorne Michaels. Diane Nyland (Tracy) returned to TV only once more in 1992 to act in *Street Legal*, a hit drama. Franz Russell, who plays Doug's weirdo brother-in-law Paul, became a well-known voice actor and lent his voice talents to advertisements for AT&T, Budweiser, Chevron, Duracell, Juicy Juice, PBS and Shake & Bake.

In March 2003, The Comedy Network in Canada announced that it was reviving the show, sending a shudder through TV viewers everywhere. Nyland even appeared at the press conference. Fortunately, they made the announcement on April 1 and it turned out to be a practical joke.

* * *

UNEXPECTED CANADIAN EXPORTS

Hot dog mustard. Saskatchewan is the largest producer of mustard in the world with 300,000 to 400,000 acres dedicated to growing the plant. In 2005 speech, Saskatchewan's Premier Lorne Calvert said, "Every drop of mustard on a Yankee Stadium hotdog now comes from Saskatchewan." He isn't wrong. Canada is also the world's largest exporter of the mustard seed.

Uranium. In 2008, the Saskatchewan uranium mines accounted for more than 20 percent of the world's total uranium production.

Potash. Potash is a potassium compound or salt used in fertilizers. It gets its name from the Dutch word *potaschen* or pot ashes. The potash substance can be obtained by leaching wood ashes—the white residue left behind is "pot ash." Most of the world's reserve of potassium started as sea water deposits that evaporated. The potassium salts crystallized into beds of potash.

John Lennon's favorite cover of "You Won't See Me" was by Anne Murray.

URBAN LEGENDS

Did you hear about the Mountie who chased down a speeding drunk driver on foot? We heard it from our neighbor's friend's dog's cousin's aunt-in-law...and she swears it's true!

LEGEND: In 1985, while filming the gritty CBS police drama Night Heat in Toronto, the crew dressed the clean street with trash to make it look more like an American city. When the crew went to lunch, a Toronto sanitation crew swooped in and swept up all the trash. The director was miffed when he returned.

HOW IT SPREAD: A 1987 *Chicago Tribune* article about *Night Heat* seems to be the source of this urban legend: "Toronto's sanitation department has been known to 'accidentally' clean it up while the cast was on its lunch break." From there, the story grew: Some versions say it's a movie crew; and some say that the crew was only on a five-minute coffee break when the cleaning took place.

THE TRUTH: It's very unlikely that an outdoor filming location in the middle of a city would be left unattended while the entire cast and crew went to lunch. That's why production companies hire security. Most likely, this legend began as a bit of "artistic license" by the *Chicago Tribune* playing into Canadian stereotypes.

LEGEND: Canola oil is poisonous! It's made from the rapeseed plant! Rapeseed is the chief ingredient in mustard gas! Canola oil causes blindness, emphysema, respiratory distress, anemia, constipation, Mad Cow Disease, and irritability! Don't eat it!

HOW IT SPREAD: This fear-mongering chain-email started circulating in 2000, compiled by a woman named "Darleen Bradley" (about whom we couldn't find any info). "Here are just a few facts everyone should know before buying anything containing canola," began her tirade. "Canola is not the name of a natural plant but a made-up word." And then she goes on to basically say that it will harm anyone who touches it. According to the Department of Nutrition of the University of Manitoba, most of the email's "facts" came from a 1996 article by John Thomas in the Canadian health magazine *Perception*, and has since been reprinted in other holistic health magazines.

Fancy a trip to Hell? An area of turbulent water on the Fraser River is called Hell's Gate.

THE TRUTH: Canola oil is safe. This urban legend falls under the "don't trust Big Agriculture" category. The email is true in that Canola is a made-up word, and that it does come from the rapeseed plant, which in its pure form contains a dangerous chemical called erucic acid. However, in the 1970s, Canadian farmers used cross-breeding, not "genetic engineering" as the legend charges, to grow rapeseed plants with the much safer oleic acid. In fact, *Canola* is short for "Canadian oil, low acid."

LEGEND: A Cadillac with Michigan plates was driving through Saskatchewan when an RCMP officer pulled it over for a minor infraction. As the Mountie approached, four men (all wearing expensive suits) got out and automatically assumed the "spread eagle" position up against the car. The bemused Mountie told them that that won't be necessary. One of the men responded that, where they're from, it is.

HOW IT SPREAD: By word-of-mouth in the 1980s. Some stories say the men are from Detroit; some say they're from New York.

THE TRUTH: This is yet another urban legend that reinforces stereotypes—all Americans are criminals, all Canucks are polite—but there's no evidence that it ever happened.

LEGEND: The Fox News Channel is banned in Canada because the CRTC (Canadian Radio-Television and Telecommunications Commission) enforced new rules to prevent news networks from deliberately distorting the truth and misleading viewers.

HOW IT SPREAD: In February 2011, Toronto's *Globe and Mail* reported that Conservative P.M. Stephen Harper's campaign to launch a Fox-style propaganda news channel was rejected by the CRTC. The urban legend grew out of this news story.

THE TRUTH: By the time the CRTC ruling was made in 2011, Fox News had already been available on Canadian cable-TV carriers for eight years. The new rules only apply to Canadian-run news outlets, which dashed Harper's hopes. But in today's highly polarized political climate, an inflammatory headline such as "Fox News Banned In Canada" spread like wildfire, even though it wasn't true.

Laura Secord walked 20 miles to warn Brits of an impending attack in the War of 1812.

THE WONDERBRA

An uplifting story about one of Canada's most important inventions

FIRST IMPRESSIONS

The first bra is thought to have been created in 1914 by a New York debutante who was preparing for a dance. With the help of a maid, she strung two handkerchiefs together with pink ribbon and fitted herself with the first bra. The world hasn't been the same since, and designers—mostly men—have been tinkering with new bra looks for decades.

In the 1940s and 50s (and maybe ever since), full-breasted women like Marilyn Monroe, Jayne Mansfield, and Jane Russell were considered the sexual ideal. Many women began stuffing their bras to achieve that fully endowed look. When brassiere companies realized that women were trying to look bustier, they took decisive action—creating padded bras so women wouldn't have to stuff. In 1948, Frederick Mellinger, who started Frederick's of Hollywood, introduced the first push-up bra, the Rising Star. A type of uplifting bra called the Torpedo was popular around this time, too; it made each breast look like a projectile about to be launched. Maidenform sold one called the Bullet Bra.

The push-up bra was well appreciated and inspired other bra designers to create bras that made women seem fuller and rounder and enhanced their cleavage. In 1964, Canadian Louise Poirier created the Wonderbra for Canadelle, a Canadian lingerie company. The bra is actually an intricate piece of precision engineering with 54 design elements coming together to lift and support without compressing the breasts or using much padding.

PHENOMENAL SALES CURVE

The bra was popular but not an instant smash. After its invention, the Wonderbra was produced in Europe and had steady but unspectacular sales—mostly in Europe. In the 1990s, sales really began to take off. An estimated 11 million Wonderbras had been sold as of 1991. In 1992, sales were climbing at a rate of 22,000 per week and the manufacturer had difficulty keeping up with demand.

Biggar, Saskatchewan's slogan is "New York is Big...but this is Biggar."

At this time in the 1990s, a company called Gossard owned the license for the Wonderbra. But its license to produce the product would expire on January 1, 1994. Sara Lee Corporation, which is perhaps best known for its baked goods, had acquired Canadelle in 1991. The company owned the rights to the Wonderbra. Seeing sales climb steadily, Sara Lee intended to take over production of the Wonderbra and reintroduce it to the world with a major marketing campaign. Gossard, not wanting to lose business, decided to create its own version of the Wonderbra called the Ultrabra. Equipped with multimillion-dollar marketing budgets, both companies began a bra war, blanketing the world with titillating ads to gain control of the market for cleavage-enhancing bras.

PUMPING PROFITS

In May 1994, the Canadian-born Wonderbra, which was 30 years old, was re-introduced to America. With a suggested retail price of $26, the bra flew off the racks. They were selling at a rate of one every 15 seconds. First-year sales hit $120 million, making it one of Sara Lee's top 30 selling products. Women lined up outside stores to try to buy the coveted bra. By the end of 1994, the Wonderbra was a fashion phenomenon. Ethel Klein, president of EDK Associates, a New York–based marketing firm specializing in women's fashion, said, "Wonderbra has become sort of like Kleenex, in that it's the product name that defines the category. It's the brand name associated with the product."

A Canadian had created one of the most popular, industry-changing bras of all time.

In 2001, Wonderbra introduced the Air Wonder model for "high-altitude cleavage." With this futuristic model, a woman can pump up her bra cups to the size she chooses. A mini pump is included in each package. The brand continues to generate huge sales across the globe.

* * *

THE TRUTH IS OUT THERE ...OVER THERE

The X-Files was filmed mostly in Canada, and for fans of the show, a pilgrimage to the corner of Mulder Avenue and Scully Way in Ottawa may be necessary. The similarity between the names of these streets and those of the show's main characters is said to be a coincidence, however.

PROSEBUSTERS!

Who are you going to call when you need government or corporate documents translated from gobbledygook into plain English? Prosebusters! This Ottawa-based company edits hard-to-comprehend documents to help their clients find "the shortest distance between a concept and its readers." Here are a few before-and-after examples taken from real documents that they've edited.

Original: "To make these determinations requires a flow of information that allows appropriate and timely action to be taken in relation to activities that are consummated within a very short time span."
Prosebusted: "Good judgements require a steady stream of accurate information even when events happen quickly."

Original: "In the context of a climate of serious financial restraint within the federal government, there are now strong imperatives to manage resources with improved efficiency thereby reducing the longer term costs to the government's administration."
Prosebusted: "The federal government, facing severe financial restraint, must cut costs and manage more efficiently."

Original: "The most critical area of exposure to athletes is without a doubt the immediate playing environment. It is important that a visual inspection of the facility occur, and deficiencies be rectified, prior to the competition."
Prosebusted: "For athletes' safety, look over the playing field and fix any problems before competition begins."

Original: "Active involvement had taken place concerning the departmental restructuring of the exercise through the formation of a branch committee to deal with and advise on all human resource aspects of the exercise."
Prosebusted: "We have started a committee to help employees affected by transfers and layoffs."

July 14, 1968: In five minutes, 17.8 mm (.7") of rain fell on the city of Winnipeg.

Original: "Since the plan reflects the department's developing vision of the future, it will be amended annually to incorporate those changes in the vision which occur as it matures."

Prosebusted: "The plan will be reviewed every year and changed as needed."

Original: "Some combination of these meetings should be attended on an ongoing basis."

Prosebusted: "Go to these meetings occasionally."

Original: "We have agreed to concur on the recommendations for the two staffing processes."

Prosebusted: "We accept the recommended candidates."

Original: "This document is the overarching and enabling pivot that plows the field and accelerates the implementation of all major activities in an attempt to realize the Office's Vision."

Prosebusted: "Meaningless tripe."

* * *

FACEBOOK FOR NARCISSISTS

If you like yourself—if you really, really like yourself—Adam and Kirk Johnson have the social network for you. The duo from Petersborough, Ontario, have created the Web service ilooklikeyou.com so people can find others who look just like they do and perhaps strike up an online relationship. Users of the free social network upload a front-facing photo of themselves, and then that photo can be matched with members from the network's global community. Users choose which other members they think most resemble them and then display their lookalikes on their profile page for others to see.

The founders say that the site can help reunite identical twins who were separated at birth. And it may also be able to help find missing persons; if someone recognizes a posted face and can post a match, there's a chance that the missing person can be located.

Born in London, Ontario, actor Hume Cronyn was once an Olympic-level boxer.

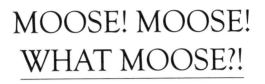

MOOSE! MOOSE! WHAT MOOSE?!

Interesting interactions between humans and moose don't happen only in Canada, of course. They just happen there a lot more often than in other places. Here are a few examples.

MOOSE! An RCMP officer was driving down a rural road in northern British Columbia at around 1 a.m. one night in October 2012, when two moose—a bull and a cow—appeared out of the woods and began to cross the road. There was a car coming the other way, so the Mountie, trying to ensure that the driver of the other car saw the gigantic, car-destroying creatures in the road, drove up close to the animals so his headlights would reveal them. That, apparently, annoyed the bull moose. It charged the Mountie's car and jumped on its hood, kicking off the bumper and smashing the grill in doing so. Then it jumped on the car's roof, breaking the windshield on the way. Atop the car now, and still kicking furiously, it then somehow smashed out the car's driver side window, and managed to kick the mountie in the shoulder. The moose then jumped off the back of the car, and, according to an RCMP statement, "Both the culprit and accomplice departed the area on hoof." They were not seen again. The Mountie was okay. "Although they are likely more scared of people than we are of them," the RCMP statement concluded, "we believe our officer would disagree."

MOOSE! In July 2013, Chris Nicholas of St. John's, Newfoundland, posted a video to YouTube showing his front yard, and the street in front of his house at night. In the silent, black-and-white video, lights can be seen coming from the right of the screen. Then a moose appears. It nonchalantly runs down the middle of the road, and past the house. A few seconds later, a police car appears, all its lights blazing. Driving very slowly, it follows after the moose, and disappears to the left of the screen. Some seconds later, more lights are seen coming from the right of the screen. A second moose appears. It nonchalantly runs by the house. A few seconds later a second police car appears, all its lights flashing, slowly following after the second moose. Nicholas wrote a note to accompany the video: "Police chasing two moose up my street. Pretty standard Newfoundland sight I suppose." Police later told reporters that the Royal Newfoundland Constabulary officers engaged in the "slow-speed pursuit" of the moose through the streets of St. John's for several hours, until wildlife officials were finally able to shoot the moose with tranquilizers, after which they were released back into the wild.

WHAT MOOSE?! On the evening of May 7, 2012, Michelle Higgins of Norris Arm, Newfoundland, was driving down the TransCanada Highway, on her way to her night shift job in Gander. When she arrived at work about a half an hour later, her co-workers immediately rushed outside. They asked her if she was okay, she asked why, and they replied, "You're bleeding—and look at your car! The hood had several dents in it, the entire windshield was completely caved in, and the roof was torn back to the back seat. "The roof was like a sardine can!" Higgins said. "I thought, 'this is impossible!'"—because she had no memory of being in an accident. Her co-workers got her to a hospital, where she was diagnosed with two fractured vertebrae in her neck, along with what became extensive bruising of her face.

Meanwhile, police found a massive, and unfortunately dead, moose along the side of the highway. Higgins had hit the animal, taking the full impact of the huge beast in her windshield ... and had simply continued driving ... for 25 miles. That included driving through one small town, going through traffic lights, and making three turns. And she arrived at work on time. And she still remembers absolutely nothing about it. Higgins made an appeal to the public, asking if anyone saw someone driving a completely smashed-up car that evening. "I'd like to know," she explained to reporters, "if I was driving safely."

* * *

PORKY'S 2

In related animal poop news, scientists at the University of Guelph have genetically engineered a less-polluting pig that they have dubbed *enviropig*. The genetically modified swine can digest more of the phosphorous in its food, thereby reducing the amount of harmful phosphorous in its manure.

July 28, 1981: A severe hailstorm in Calgary caused $150 million of property damage.

SEND IN THE CLOWNS

Those rowdy, fireman-bashing clowns.

A GRAND NIGHT OUT

In July 1855, Toronto was a fast-growing city of 40,000 with new immigrants arriving at a steady clip. S.B. Howes' Star Troupe Menagerie & Circus knew they'd find a good crowd in the budding metropolis, so they came that summer with their big cats, elephants, acrobats, trick horse riders, and clowns.

After a sold-out show one night, the clowns decided that they needed a little entertainment themselves. So they wiped off their pancake makeup and packed away their squirting flowers and headed to the local brothel.

PSYCHO CIRCUS

As is turns out, the brothel at the corner of King and Jarvis was also a hangout for many of the local firemen of the Hook & Ladder Fire-fighting Company. A little backstory: The H&LFCC had a reputation for stirring things up. Since there wasn't a centrally run fire department at this time, independent fire brigades raced to the scene of a fire to be the first to claim the job. A few weeks before the clowns arrived, the firemen of Hook & Ladder arrived at a blaze on Church Street at the same time as another fire company. Each brigade insisted that the fire was theirs to extinguish. But instead of fighting the flames, the firemen fought and rioted in the streets. As the building turned to smoke and ash, the police arrived and were drawn into the brawl. The firemen were charged with assault.

So when the clowns came barging into this house of ill repute, it may have come as no surprise that another fight erupted. No one is sure what triggered the brawl. Some say a loudmouthed bozo lit the fuse of a short-tempered fireman. Or that the circus performers cut in line or that one knocked off the hat of a fellow. One thing is certain: The clowns flattened the firefighters—two were seriously hurt and the others hightailed it into the night.

DON'T CRY OUT LOUD

The clowns returned to the brothel to make whoopee, but that wasn't the end of the trouble. The firemen were members of a Protestant

Coffins rose to the surface in spring thaw in Herschel Island, Yukon Territory, in 2001.

political group called the Orange Order. All the important jobs in Toronto belonged to the Orangemen, including police positions. So, the day after the brothel incident, an angry Orange crowd gathered round the circus and the tension mounted. In a short time, a devastating riot erupted. Stones were thrown, carts overturned, fires set, and tents were pulled to the ground.

Wielding axes and pikes, firemen were set on revenge and destruction. Their numbers were now no match for the clowns, who were beaten silly. Fast as possible, the circus packed their gear and left town. The police arrived, but as they were Orangemen, they did little to stop the clown melee. (They did, however, stop one rioter from torching the animal cages.) In time, the Orange stranglehold in Toronto was broken and the entire police force was thrown out and replaced. But that night in Toronto history will always be remembered as the Circus Riot of 1855.

* * *

IT TAKES TRUE GRIT

Calgary is called "Cow Town" because of its long cowboy heritage, and every year during the early part of July the city celebrates with the Calgary Stampede. As part of the festivities, Buzzard's Cowboy Cuisine holds the Testicle Festival, during which it serves a variety of dishes featuring prairie oysters, or bull testicles.

Traditionally, ranchers would send their cattle off to graze in the spring. Before they did so, they would brand them so they could identify them when the fall roundup came. While they had the males on the ground for branding, they would often castrate them to maintain genetic integrity in the herd.

The cooks would take the balls and prepare them for meals. The balls look a bit like oysters, so that's how they got their nickname.

Depending on the menu for the year at the Testicle Festival, you might enjoy a plate of crunchy testicles coated in panko crumbs or biscuits, balls, and gravy. It might help that the restaurant, with its rustic cowboy décor, has 140 beers on tap to help wash them down.

Chute Montmorency is a French-Canadian term for waterfall.

HAIL THE NEW KING OF ROCK 'N' ROLL

The king will never be dead.

TREAT ME LIKE A FOOL

Collingwood, Ontario, a small town on the Georgian Bay, has a special claim to fame: every year it hosts the annual "Elvis Festival," a four-day extravaganza celebrating the life and music of Elvis Presley. Tens of thousands of visitors descend upon the town to participate in events such as a karaoke pub crawl, a vintage-car cruise (featuring several Cadillacs, the King's favorite ride), round-table discussions with former friends and associates of Elvis, and, of course, plenty of live music provided by Elvis impersonators from all over the world. Special VIP guests (including past members of Elvis's bands) are on hand to perform as well.

The festival began in 1995 as a loose gathering of 35 Elvis impersonators looking to pay homage to their hero. In 1996 they aligned with Elvis Presley Enterprises to license the event, and the following year it was formally rechristened the Collingwood Elvis Festival. In 2003 the town of Collingwood took charge of the festival, turning it into the area's main summer tourist attraction. Today it boasts over 130 Elvis Tribute Artists (known as ETAs) providing entertainment with such shows as "Spend an Evening with Elvis," "Elvis Under the Stars," and "Colonel Tom's Tiki Lounge."

DOUBLE TROUBLE

Now recognized as the largest Elvis festival on the planet, the event has featured such exploits as 94 ETAs singing "All Shook Up" simultaneously (officially counted by the mayor of Collingwood, who claimed it was her strangest duty as an elected official thus far). For the duration of the weekend, Elvises are seen everywhere—some in full Las Vegas–era regalia, others in "cone-head" Elvis wigs and gold-rimmed sunglasses—trading favorite songs, stories, legends, and sartorial tips. Whole families attend in costume, perusing the wares of street merchants selling Elvis-based gifts.

Rush recorded a rendition of "O Canada" for the soundtrack of the South Park movie.

Each year the festival has a specific theme. These have included "Elvis's Canadian Appearances" and "Welcome Home, Elvis," a look at Elvis's time in the U.S. Armed Forces. The highlight of the weekend, however, is the Tribute Artist competition on Sunday evening. Impersonators compete in either the "Early Years" or "Concert Years" category, singing their hearts out for a chance to be crowned "the King" and represent Collingwood in the "Ultimate Elvis Tribute Artist Contest" in Memphis, Tennessee. Collingwood is one of two original qualifying locations for the Memphis contest. Up-and-coming ETAs can compete in a youth division, honing their chops for future festivals.

HARUM SCARUM

If all this wasn't enough, Collingwood has even bigger plans for the annual gathering. The town would like to increase youth participation and add an "arts education" component, showcasing the importance of music in childhood development. Organizers hope to make the event more environmentally friendly. And, of course, they are always on the lookout for more ETAs to break the record for most Elvis impersonators gathered in one place—currently a whopping 814, assembled in the Welsh town of Porthcawl in 2012. The song they chose to sing together to commemorate the event? The King's 1956 smash hit, "Hound Dog."

* * *

@BORING

In 2010 Tamara Small, a professor at Mount Allison University in Sackville, New Brunswick, conducted a study of Canadian political Twitter conversations. While Small concluded that the media and political junkies were using Twitter effectively to further political discourse and reporting, she found that the least interesting political tweets, scientifically speaking, were from Canadian politicians. The professor explained that Canadian politicians spent too much time writing about themselves—where they were traveling and what they are doing—and not enough about actual politics. "It isn't a very interesting study because politicians aren't doing anything interesting with Twitter," said Small.

"Bungee" is a dialect of English that was first spoken north of Winnipeg.

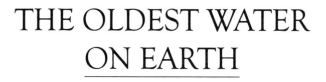

THE OLDEST WATER ON EARTH

Primeval water reveals Earth's history.

PRISTINE DATA

When multicellular life began on planet Earth, it needed water. The water that helped this life begin has been found in a pocket in a copper and zinc mine in Timmins, Ontario. Dating back 1.5 billion to 2.64 billion years, the oldest flowing water known to man has been uncovered by miners drilling deep underground in northern Ontario, according to a paper published in the journal *Nature* in May 2013. The H^2O is flowing out of fractures and bore holes drilled by the miners 2.4 kilometers (about one and a half miles) from the Earth's surface. Barbara Sherwood Lollar, a geologist from the University of Toronto, who is co-leading a research team on this project, has said that ancient isolated water may be found in several regions of Earth in geological formations below the surface. Mining projects have helped unearth these sources of water as they dig deeper than ever to uncover copper, zinc, and gold, which has shot up in price. Scientists collected samples from one fracture that was pouring out at a rate of two liters (a little over half a gallon) per minute.

EVIAN IT AIN'T

The water is rich in hydrogen and methane, which could support life, so scientists are testing the water to see if such life is there. Microbes that have been isolated for tens of millions of years have already been found in other underground water sources. This water is salty and filled with bubbles containing ancient gasses. Scientists already know that hydrogen-rich water from hydrothermal vents deep in the ocean can sustain microbial life, and that 2.7 billion years ago there was a huge hydrothermal vent system on an ancient seafloor beneath the Earth's crust. Professor Sherwood Lollar says that life on the plant very well could have started far below the surface protected from the ultraviolet radiation and meteorites that were showering the earth at that time, and she speculates that we might find similar energy rich water beneath the surface of Mars.

Minnedosa, Manitoba, gets its name from the Sioux phrase *minne duza* which means "fast water."

NO SELL-BY DATE

When you find something that's been in your freezer for six months or a year, you might chuck it out because it's just not good any more. That's why scientists from the University of Alberta were surprised to find that plants they found frozen in glaciers for 400 years could be brought back to life. In Ellesmere Island in the Canadian Arctic, researchers discovered moss in a glacier that showed signs of being dormant rather than being dead. A large ice mass at Ellesmere had been melting and shrinking at a rate of about three or four meters (about 10 to 13 feet) a year since 2004. While it's unfortunate that the glacier is disappearing, the melting had revealed large areas of plant life for scientists to analyze. The researchers are focusing on bryophytes, which are super-simple plants like moss. The moss was well preserved despite being buried in centuries of ice, amazing scientists. Much of the moss was still green and after the moss was exposed, the scientist observed bright green stems emerging from the vegetation. However, thawing out and reanimating plants is far different than bringing a living creature, such as a wooly mammoth or caveman, back to life should one be discovered. Because the bryophytes are so hardy, investigators have a notion that they possibly could survive beyond this planet. With increasing interest in sending people to Mars and possibly colonizing the Red Planet one day, scientists wonder if a plant like a bryophyte might hold a key for sustaining life on the fourth rock from the sun.

* * *

AND PINGOS WERE THEIR NAME-O

Pingos are unique, earth-covered ice mounds, and Tuktoyaktuk in the Northwest Territories is loaded with them. In fact, this area has the highest concentration of these hills anywhere in the world. About one-quarter of the world's pingos—1,350—dot the Tuktoyaktuk Peninsula in the western Arctic region. Basically, these landforms are made from ground ice that develops when the temperatures plunge in the winter months. They're slow growing, expanding only a few centimeters each year. At their peak, they reach up to 70 meters (230 feet) in height and up to 600 meters (2,000 feet) in diameter. In time, pingos break down and collapse, but they generally last about 1,000 years. Because the pingos are made of ice, some native Inuit hunters reportedly hollowed some out and used them as freezers to store their meat.

Hockey star Hector "Toe" Blake got his name from a younger sister who said his name "hec-toe."

SNAKES ON A PLAIN

Narcisse, Manitoba, is no place for ophidiophobes.

NAR-HISSSSSS

The greatest concentration of red-sided garter snakes in the world lives 90 minutes north of Winnipeg. The combination of limestone dens and marshes makes it an ideal environment for snakes. Just after the snow melts in late April and early May, tens of thousands of red-sided garter snakes congregate at the surface, rising from their winter homes at the Narcisse Snake Dens. It is said that you can see more snakes at a glance here than anywhere else in the world.

The serpents slither out of their subterranean limestone caverns and begin their frenzied mating ritual. The cavorting reptiles writhe in the warm weather in great tangled heaps. It's not unusual for 10, 20, or even 50 male snakes to pounce on an adult female snake, which can be three times the size of a male. Forming a mating ball, the excited snakes make a unique rustling sound and give off a musky odor. After successfully mating, the female emits a hormone that warns other snakes to stay away. When the males are done mating they want to eat; a favorite meal is frog.

BRUMATION STATION

Despite the feverish activity of the mating ritual, the reproductive cycle for garter snakes is surprisingly slow. Snakes do not breed for at least three years, and only once every other year after that. A female's first brood is usually no more than five young, of which approximately 80 percent do not survive their first winter. Fifty percent of snakes born in a given year die before the next mating season. As female snakes age, they get more productive: an adult female (classified as anything over 80 cm) can give birth to up to 40 snakes every other year.

After the mating season, the snakes disperse from the area above the dens to their summer feeding habitats. The females give birth to live young in wetland areas up to 20 kilometers away. Prime summer habitats are moist areas with expansive ground cover and plenty of invertebrates and amphibians to feast on. Unfortunately, in recent

The rock group 54°40, based in Tsawwassen got its name from a U.S.–Canada border dispute.

years drought and excessive land development have led to a decrease in available feeding habitats.

In late August and early September the snakes return to their winter dens. When the weather turns colder, they make their way deep underground and pass their winters in a state known as brumation, where their body temperature cools to around 4 degrees Celsius, the temperature of the surrounding air.

THE LONG AND WINDING ROAD

Every year, about 45,000 visitors come to wend their way through the snakes' pits on viewing platforms. Visitors are even allowed to handle the snakes, and while the serpents might bite, their undersized teeth don't usually break the skin. The larger danger of snake wrangling is getting pooped on. Garters generally poop when they are scared, and a pungent and unpleasant smell from their output can hang around for quite some time. So while visitors have little to fear except stinking, the garters themselves must watch out for crows and other birds looking for a tasty meal. Seems these flying predators think nothing of ripping the liver from the snakes' bellies, leaving the lifeless garter remains splayed out for visitors to see.

In 1995, to promote tourism in the area, the tiny town of Inwood, located near the main garter dens, constructed an impressive garter statue. Designed by Marlene Hourd and built by volunteers, the base stands 4.6 meters high and consists of granite and limestone rocks. On top of the rocks are two slithering garters affectionately known as "S-s-sam" and "S-s-sara." These snake statues are around 8 meters long and are made from re-bar, polyurethane foam and fiberglass.

In 1999, a bout of harsh weather killed tens of thousands of Narcissa's snakes before they could return to their winter dens. This prompted concern about the snakes' migratory patterns, particularly their crossing the heavily trafficked Highway 17. A combination of fences that force the snakes into underground tunnels beneath the roadway as well as increased signage to warn drivers have greatly reduced unnecessary snake deaths.

A six-pack of beer was called a "poverty pack" during the Great Depression.

CANADIAN SUPERHEROES

Not all superheroes fight for the "American Way." Here are some of Canada's greatest men and women in tights.

CAPTAIN CANUCK. Over the years, Captain Canuck has been the secret identity of three different Canadian secret agents: Tom Evans, Darren Oak, and David Semple. He wears a red-and-white costume based on the Canadian Flag, with a red Maple leaf on his forehead.

WOLVERINE. Wolverine was born in Alberta in the 1880s to the wife of a wealthy farmer and a groundskeeper named Logan, with whom she had an affair. Wolverine is a mutant who has retractable claws and regenerative powers that keep him from aging. In the late-20th century, Wolverine was a part of Canada's Weapon X program, where his memories were wiped out and he had adamantine fused onto his bones, making him even stronger. A member of Marvel's X-Men, Wolverine is regularly voted one of the most popular superheroes in the world.

DEADPOOL. Wade Winston Wilson is the secret identity of the villain-turned-antihero Deadpool. Like Wolverine, Deadpool is a product of the Weapon X program, a super-secret attempt to breed ultimate soldiers conducted by the Canadian government.

CENTRIX. DC's tree-hugging, new age, crystal-loving Centrix is the Canadian member of the Global Guardians, an international team of super heroes originally backed by the U.N. Centrix can shoot energy beams at his enemies and quote Carlos Castaneda to them.

ALPHA FLIGHT. All of the members of Alpha Flight—a superhero team based on The Avengers—are Canadian, many from the First Nations. They include Guardian, Box, Sasquatch, Diamond Lil, Yukon Jack, and Northstar, who was the first openly gay Marvel superhero.

NORTHGUARD. Northguard is a "realistic" superhero. He does not live in a fantasy universe where superpowers are real. He lives in the "real world" of Montreal. With no superpowers, Northguard simply

An "Alberta Clipper" is a high plains wind with speeds of 60 km/hr and gusts close to 100 km/hr.

dons a costume because he thinks it will be easier to battle evil if he has a secret identity.

FLEUR DE LYS. Northguard's Quebecois partner, she also has no actual superpowers. Her name is taken from the stylized lily that is the symbol of both France and Quebec.

NELVANA OF THE NORTHERN LIGHTS. As World War II was under way and U.S. entry seemed likely, the value of the Canadian Dollar began to plummet in exchange with greenbacks. In December 1940, Canada passed the War Exchange Conservation Act, which, among other things, banned the import of U.S. comic books. Canadian publishers stepped up to fill the void, creating the first Canadian patriotic superheroes. One of these was Nelvana of the Northern lights, one of the first female superheroes (she predates Wonder Woman by four months). Nelvana was inspired by a hideous witch from Inuit mythology. She was immortal, could fly faster than the speed of light, turn invisible, and communicate telepathically.

JOHNNY CANUCK. The original Johnny Canuck appeared in newspaper editorial cartoons in the 1880s. A working-class, tall-tale hero in the mold of Paul Bunyan, he sometimes appeared as a lumberjack, at other times as a farmer or a rancher. In 1942, in answer to the war and to the comics ban, the character received a reboot and was resurrected as a Nazi-fighting aviator and secret agent by 16-year-old Leo Bulche, who got the job after a chance encounter with the owner of Dime Comics. Later still, the lumberjack version of Johnny Canuck was adopted as the logo for the Vancouver Canucks, and he occasionally makes appearances on their uniforms on "retro nights."

CANADA JACK. Montreal Educational Products published a comic called *Canadian Heroes*, which profiled real-life Canadians. However, with the need for fictional heroes brought on by the comics ban, they also created a fictional superhero, Canada Jack. Canada Jack had no superpowers. He was just a great athlete and acrobat who turned to fighting Nazis on the home front. He battled saboteurs and black marketeers in a tank top with a red leaf on his chest.

For a few months in 2011, Canada banned the Dire Straits song "Money for Nothing."

CAMPY COUNCILLORS

An iconic national leader had mysterious ways.

HEADY TIMES

William Lyon Mackenzie King served longer than any other prime minister. During his 22 years in office, King guided Canada through World War II, working as a key partner with Winston Churchill and Franklin Roosevelt. He set up the British Commonwealth Air Traning Program, which trained more than 130,000 air crewmen in Canada for the Allied war effort. He introduced Canada's system for old age pensions, and established unemployment insurance and welfare programs. After he died in 1950, the public learned of some of his unusual policy-making methods. His papers and diary revealed that he was a spiritualist.

MAKING THE MAN

A devout Christian, King suffered great personal losses in a short period—his sister Bella died in 1915, followed by his father in 1916, his mother in 1917 and his brother Max, in 1922. After visiting his brother on his deathbed, King wrote in his diary: "I spoke of love being stronger than all else and of my belief in immortal life." His brother told him that the two of them would be together always. In a 1925 consultation with a medium King saw the spirits of his mother and his brother. He also learned that he would win a hard-fought election campaign.

In the 1930s, King attended a few séances and was thrilled to "communicate" with mother, father, grandfather, brother, and sister. He wrote in his diary, "There can be no doubt whatsoever that the persons I have been talking with were the loved ones and others I have known and who have passed away. It was the spirits of the departed." And they were good for tips. He journaled on his grandfather's birthday, "My actions today and utterances have been in large part the result of our talk together last night."

In 1945 he was unsure how to proceed with a Russian espionage case, so he asked his long-dead brother, as well as the recently deceased Franklin Roosevelt. As his interest in communicating with spirits grew, he sought advice from Leonardo da Vinci, President Theodore Roosevelt, and former Canadian Prime Minister Wilfred Laurier.

"Brin bag" is a Newfoundland term for a burlap sack.

MULTIPLE SOURCES

Not entirely surprisingly, King was superstitious. He believed numbers 7 and 17 were lucky He also habitually talked with his dogs—shooting the breeze with his Irish terrier, Pat, and tapping him for political advice as well.

King found significance in formations in his shaving cream; he would read the shapes like tea leaves, which—go figure—he also consulted.

*   *   *

DREAM WEAVERS

Jayne Gackenbach at Grant MacEwan University in Edmonton has a dream job—literally. She explores dreams and their relationships to modern media use, including video games and social media. Gackenbach describes dreams as the "gold standard" for presence or the sense of "being there" in video games. According to Gackenbach's research, most video gamers report the same level of this feeling of being there while playing video games as they do while dreaming.

Gackenbach's theory, which has been proven to be true in more than one study, is that video gamers do not experience nightmares as often as others, which Gackenbach theorizes could be for several reasons. First, playing video games is considered a kind of therapeutic experience in which gamers can act out their defense against an attacker. Gackenbach has also discovered that frequent gamers cite the ability to control their dreams, much like they control their avatars in games. Gamers also frequently call their nightmares "exciting" rather than "scary." And her research found that gamers tend to have better spatial skills and are less likely to get motion sickness. All of this is evidence that playing video games does have a few advantages.

Some rural Ontario couples have a combined stag party called "a buck and doe."

QUIRKY CANADIAN TV

Is TV full of garbage...or just misunderstood?

SHOW: *Yvon of the Yukon*

YEAR: 1999

DETAILS: The premise of this animated series: a French sea captain and explorer named Yvon Ducharme set out from France sometime in the past, and not knowing how to read a map, became lost. He ended up in Arctic waters north of Canada, was knocked off his ship—and became frozen in a black of ice. He remained frozen in that block of ice...for three hundred years...then he was freed. How? A dog from a passing dogsled peed on the ice block, causing it to thaw. Yvon then goes on to try to conquer the fictional Inuit town of Upyer Mukluk, Yukon, in the name of France's "King Louie." Amazingly, the show lasted three seasons.

SHOW: *The Starlost*

YEAR: 1973

DETAILS: This CTV series was created by acclaimed American science-fiction author Harlan Ellison. Premise: Earth is going to be destroyed, so humans build a gargantuan space craft—200 miles long and 50 miles wide—to escape. The ship has several seperate and huge biospheres where people of different cultures live. Something goes wrong, the crew is killed, and the biospheres are locked down. Centuries later, the people in the biospheres don't even known they're on a spaceship—but a young man discovers the truth—and is branded a heretic. It sounds promising, but the budget didn't match the ambition. The special effects camera created for the show didn't work, and the sets looked like something from a high school play. Ellison quit the project before the first episode aired, and demanded that his name be taken off the credits. In the end just sixteen episodes were made.

SHOW: *Party Game*

YEAR: Produced locally at a small TV station in Hamilton, *Party Game* was a game show broadcast nationally from 1970 to 1981.

DETAILS: And how did the contestants compete to win fabulous cash

"The Butterfly" is a goaltending move where the player drops to the ice, splaying his legs like a butterfly.

and prizes? Charades—they played the tedious party game of Charades. One team, the "Challengers," consisted of a contestant and two minor celebrity guest stars, played the "Home Team," with series regulars/ B-list celebrities Jack Duffy, Billy Van, and Dinah Christie. Bonus: If viewers sent in a Charades suggestion used on the air, *Party Game* sent them a small cash prize. (And although it was made by a Hamilton station, it was taped, on the cheap, in a room at a Toronto hotel.)

SHOW: *Kevin Spencer*

YEAR: 1999–2005

DETAILS: The cartoon revolves around the Spencer family, mostly around troubled 14-year-old Kevin. The show's theme song says it all, really: "Kevin Spencer/you better not cross his path/Kevin Spencer/ he's a chain-smoking alcoholic sociopath." That's not all—Kevin is also addicted to cough syrup (as are his equally alcoholic and chain-smoking parents). Kevin has anger issues, commits violence, gets into trouble, and isn't very smart. His only friend is Allen the Magic Goose, who is imaginary, and who talks Kevin into doing bad things. Needless to say, *Kevin Spencer* was very controversial; the first season episode "The New Mr. Franklin," was aired once—then banned from Canadian TV forever, because, among other reasons, "excessively graphic scenes such as those involving the theft and use, as a plaything, a severed human head from an accident site."

* * *

D'OH! A DEER! A FEMALE DEER

In July 2013, Alexandra Beraru was driving down a highway north of Calgary when she struck a large female mule deer. She immediately pulled over, and she and her passenger found a tiny fawn, no bigger than a small dog, standing in the road. They initially thought it must have been with the doe they'd hit, and they had simply not seen it, but then they noticed something: "We were like, 'why is it still slimy?'" Beraru told reporters later. They then noticed the deer they had struck: it was dead in the ditch, and its stomach had been ripped open. That's when they realized that the deer had given birth to the fawn, as it were, upon being hit by the car. The fawn was taken to a wildlife center, where it was given to a new mother to be raised

A "Calgary Redeye" is a combination of beer and tomato juice.

THE MYSTERIOUS DEATH OF TOM THOMSON

He captured the fascination of his countrymen in life...and in death.

THE YOUNG PRODIGAL

Thomas Tom Thomson was an Ontario native who went on to become one of the most famous Canadian artists of the twentieth century. Born near Claremont, Ontario, in 1877, his family moved to Leith, close to Owen Sound, Ontario, on Georgian Bay. With his many siblings (the family would grow to ten children in all), he enjoyed a rusticated boyhood. Here his love for the natural world was born as he wandered through the surrounding woods, fished, and hunted. Here too his love for the arts blossomed: young Tom began to sketch and paint very early in his life, pastimes enhanced by his fondness for music (he played the mandolin and sang in a church choir) and poetry.

Thomson took an apprenticeship at a machine shop in 1899. This did not last long—a mere eight months—before he attempted to enlist to fight in the Second Boer War. Rejected on account of his flat feet, he found a job as a fire ranger in Algonquin Park in central Ontario before heading off to business school in the town of Chatham in 1901. Restless as ever, he dropped out less than a year later to follow his brother to Seattle. Here he worked at a photo-engraving firm and began to pursue painting with greater vigor. Three years later, he returned to Ontario.

WOODSMAN AND ARTIST

Thomson continued to support himself by working at several different photo-engraving companies, culminating in a position at Grip Limited in Toronto. At Grip, a prestigious design firm, he met a diverse group of up-and-coming artists. Many of these artists would come to be known as the "Group of Seven" (also known as the Algonquin School). After work hours they would meet at the Arts and Letters Club of Toronto for lengthy discussions about the nature of art, and on the weekends they would often decamp for the countryside around Toronto to paint in *plein air*.

After a brief stint at another design firm, Thomson had an artistic breakthrough with the painting *A Northern Lake*. The canvas won a prize of $250 at the 1913 Ontario Society of Artists exhibition. With his newfound success, Thomson was able to leave the commercial world and focus exclusively on his own work.

In 1914 the National Gallery of Canada acquired one of Thomson's paintings. The three years that followed were his most prolific, when he generated such signature canvases as *The Jack Pine*, *The West Wind*, and *The Northern River*. Committed to showing the Canadian landscape in all its rugged beauty, Thomson's art touched deep nationalistic sentiments and incorporated the "handmade" qualities of the Arts and Crafts movement.

James MacCullum, a well-known Toronto ophthalmologist, became Thomson's patron during this time. MacCullum helped many developing artists by constructing the Studio Building in the Rosedale neighborhood in Toronto. He quickly secured a studio for Thomson. It became the artist's custom to divide his time in the city with prolonged stays in his beloved north country, often to Algonquin Park. Here he honed his skills as a woodsman as well as an artist.

AN ENDURING INFLUENCE

On July 8, 1917, Thomson went out for a routine canoe trip on Canoe Lake in Algonquin Park. The canoe was seen floating upside down later that day; just over a week later, on July 16, his body was discovered. The cause of death was initially listed as "accidental drowning," though several of his friends wondered how such an experienced outdoorsman exploring one of his most routine routes could have made such a tragic mistake. He was buried near Canoe Lake but reinterred in Leith at his brother's request. In September 1917 Thomson's friends, funded by MacCullum, erected a memorial cairn at Hayhurst Point on the lake, still standing today.

The mystery surrounding Thomson's final hours has led to much speculation over the years. While most theories are simply conjecture, historians at the Great Unsolved Mysteries in Canadian History project have put forth some very plausible ideas: Was Thomson murdered by poachers, worried that a witness would report their illegal activity? Was he the victim of a freak logging accident, a rapidly expanding industry at the time that threatened to undo the very ideal of untamed wilderness he helped propagate? We may never know the truth, but one thing remains certain: Tom Thomson is still revered today as an almost mythic cultural figure in Canada, an artist who helped shape an entire nation's self-perception.

A "Caribou" is a potent Quebec drink of one part red wine and six parts grain alcohol.

ODDBALL FESTIVALS

Some weird gatherings from around Canada

Festival: The Yukon Sourdough Rendezvous Festival

Location: Whitehorse, Yukon

Details: The Yukon Sourdough Rendezvous Festival is not only the coldest festival in Canada, but one of the oddest. It's been held every February since 1962, though it began in 1945 as Yukon Carnival Week. The following year saw merchants encouraged to decorate their establishments in the style of 1898—old-timey décor being one hallmark of the Festival—while things began to get weird in 1947 with the beard-growing contest (which was, in fact, mandatory for all male residents). Today, the Beard Growing Contest still continues, complemented by the Moustache Growing Contest and the Hairy Leg Contest for women, as well as weird dancing and athletic contests.

Festival: World Championship Bathtub Race

Location: Nanaimo, B.C.

Details: The 36-mile World Championship Bathtub Race has been held by the Loyal Nanaimo Bathtub Society in the last weekend of July every year since 1967, and is part of Nanaimo, BC's Marine Festival. A competitive bathtub must be built around a facsimile of an old-fashioned roll-top bathtub, and is limited to an 8-horsepower engine and a minimum weight of 350 pounds.

Festival: Windsor Pumpkin Regatta

Location: Windsor, Nova Scotia

Details: Another weird water race, the Great Pumpkin Race sees competitors growing their own boats. As the self-proclaimed "pumpkin capital of the world," Windsor commemorates every October with a pumpkin race on Lake Pesaquid. About 50 or 60 boats compete in three classes: motor, experimental, and paddling. The boats can be made of nothing but pumpkin. Some start out with 450-kilogram (1,000-pound) specimens from the gourd family. Once hollowed out, the half-ton orange behemoths float—as long as you sit in the right place. The race was founded in 1999 by Danny Dill, son of Howard Dill, the breeder who developed the Atlantic Giant Pumpkin.

In Newfoundland, they pour coady (a sauce of molasses and butter) over their boiled pudding.

In the 1970s, Howard Dill put Windsor on the map when he engineered mammoth pumpkins and created the seed for Dill's Atlantic Giant. Dill was recognized four times by Guinness World Records for growing big pumpkins. The town wanted to find a way to capitalize on its history as the birthplace of giant pumpkin growing. Howard's son Danny suggested that they hold the giant pumpkin races—with people actually inside the pumpkins.

Despite skepticism from some townspeople, the Great Pumpkin Regatta was launched in 1999. Five people entered and about 2,000 watched the event that first year. But nowadays more than 10,000 people flock to the town and entries range between 50 and 60. Contestants go to great lengths to hollow out and decorate their pumpkin ships. Before the race, paddlers march in a parade with their PVCs (personal vegetable crafts). While Windsor was first to hold a pumpkin race, other towns, including Cooperstown, New York, and Elk Grove, California, also hold races. Windsor also has another claim to fame in the world of sports: It is the birthplace of hockey.

Festival: Islendingadagurinn

Location: Gimli, Manitoba

Details: Dating back to 1890, the Icelandic Festival is the second oldest continually-held ethnic festival in North America (after an Irish festival in Montreal). Participants dress in both historically accurate and fanciful Norse dress and play games such as Islendingadunk, where contestants try to knock each other off a soapy pole suspended over the harbor. Other events include demonstrations of Viking life, Viking warfare and tactics, and Viking beach volleyball.

Festival: Poutine Festival

Location: Drummondville, Quebec

Details: If deep-fried peanut butter and banana sandwiches aren't to your taste, how about the Quebecois delicacy of French fries, gravy, and cheese curds? The Poutine Festival in Drummondville features all the poutine you can eat, plus bands so you can dance off the calories.

Digby chicken is no bird—it's smoked and salted herring in Nova Scotia.

THE MYSTERIOUS FATE OF HENRY HUDSON

A search for an explorer's final resting place.

TRUE NORTH

Henry Hudson was one of the most steadfast, determined, and resolute of all the early explorers, singularly obsessed with finding the Northwest Passage. The thinking of the day was that, because the sun shines for three months out of the year, there might be an ice-free route north of Canada from the Atlantic to the Pacific oceans, allowing Europeans easier access to the fantastic wealth of Asia. Alas, this was not so, and Hudson and his crew aboard the *Discovery* spent the winter of 1610–11 iced into the bay that now bears his name.

After a harsh winter, Hudson's crew wanted to return home. He, however, wanted to press on westwards. They mutinied and put Hudson, his son John, and seven crewmen who were either loyal to him or ill aboard a small open boat. Hudson and his men tried to row after the *Discovery*, but soon fell behind and were never heard from again, lost to history.

NO BONES ABOUT IT

What happened to Henry Hudson and his men? Their fate is one of the unanswered questions of Canadian exploration. They had been set adrift in June, so there would have been plenty of time for them to build shelters and lay in provisions for the winter. They might have also traded with Native Americans for food and were perhaps taken in by a local tribe. However, the fact that Hudson had previously attacked and robbed the peoples he had found makes it unlikely.

A stronger possibility was that their interactions with natives was less friendly. In 1959, a stone with the words "HH captive 1612" was found along the banks of the Ottawa River near the town of Chalk River. Had Hudson and his men been taken prisoner and perhaps enslaved by Native Americans? Or was the stone a forgery? Adding to the difficulty was the fact that the stone was smashed by vandals in 2005. There are other tantalizing hints as to Hudsons' ultimate fate.

Canadian referee Ron Foxcroft invented the Fox 40 whistle used at sporting events.

For instance, the Cree also have a legend that a white man had lived amongst them for a time.

Though the search for Henry Hudson's final resting place will never have a satisfactory ending, the search for the Northwest Passage concluded with an interesting twist. The explorers of the seventeenth century couldn't find an all-water route to Asia because none existed at the time. Sea ice made the journey impossible. The first to travel it entirely by sea was the Norwegian Roald Amundsen, and it took him from 1903 to 1906. However, that all changed in the twenty-first century. By 2007, thanks to global warming, the sea ice had retreated to allow routine commercial shipping to sail from the Atlantic to the Pacific.

* * *

TURN DOWN THOSE FALLS

Is the roar of Niagara Falls a little too loud for you? You could ask them to turn it down a bit. Power-generating plants in Canada and the United States really do control the flow at Niagara with hydro gates that are set up before the falls. When they reduce the flow going over the falls, they are able to force more water into the hydro generation plants to create additional power. But June to August is peak tourist time, and the power authorities want to keep the tourist business booming, so they let the water flow at 28,317,000 liters (7,480,500 gallons) per second during the day. That amount of water would fill up 50 Olympic-size swimming pools in one minute. In the evening and the off season (November to April) though, they cut back the amount of water flowing over the falls by half. Those who have been there during the day and then at night will tell you that the volume difference is clearly noticeable. They say it almost seems quiet.

GO FOG DEVILS!

Canadian hockey stretches far behind the seven native NHL teams and into hundreds of minor and junior league teams in almost every town in the country. Unfortunately, all the best names have already been taken.

Team: Saint-Georges Cool FM 103.5

Story: Many teams around the world have been named after the corporations which founded them, such as the NFL's Green Bay Packers (named for original sponsor the Indian Packing Company) and major league soccer's New York Red Bulls (named for an energy drink). But since 2010, Saint-Georges' team in Quebec's semipro Ligue Nord-Américaine de Hockey has been the first—and only—hockey team in the world named after the local soft rock radio station. Bonus: For five years before that they were known as the Saint-Georges CRS Express, after the trucking company whose owner also owned the team.

Team: St. John's Fog Devils

Story: Located along the North Atlantic Ocean on the eastern tip of Newfoundland and Labrador, St. John's is one of the foggiest cities in Canada. So when the Quebec Major Junior Hockey League put a team there in 2005, it was only natural that they name the team after the climate, adding the word "Devils" to make them sound tougher. However, the team didn't last, presumably because nobody could find their arena through all the fog. In 2008, they moved, and are currently known as the Blainville-Boisbriand Armada.

Team: Penticton Vees

Story: Since forming in 1961, Penticton's entry in the British Columbia Hockey League has, on three occasions, been called the "Vees," but not after the 22nd letter of the alphabet or in reference to British Columbia's nearby major cities of Vancouver or Victoria. No, the Vees are named for the three varieties of peaches—veteran, valiant, and vedette—that are indigenous to the area.

Nova Scotia leads the world in exporting lobster, wild blueberries, and Christmas trees.

Team: Fort McMurray Oil Barons

Story: The proximity to the Athabasca Oil Sands has caused this rural northeast Alberta town to grow, and in 1981, it was awarded a team in the Alberta Junior Hockey League. The Oil Barons have won their league championship three times, which must have been difficult considering the risk of playing hockey while wearing a monocle and twirling a handlebar moustache (just kidding).

Team: Asbestos Aztèques

Story: In 1997, the Ligue Nord-Américaine de Hockey gave a team to the town of Asbestos, Quebec, so named because of the town's Jeffrey Mine, the world's largest natural source of asbestos, a carcinogenic mineral and former building material. For their nickname, they looked to the indigenous Mexican people who were conquered by the Spanish in 1521 (and who never set foot anywhere remotely near Quebec). As befitted their nickname, they did not last very long, folding after the 2002–03 season.

Team: Regina Pats

Story: Founded in 1917, this Saskatchewan-based team in the Western Hockey League is the oldest continuously operating junior hockey team in the world. Also, they've got to be the only junior hockey team in the world technically name after a princess. First known as the Regina Patricias (and shortened to the Pats), the team was named after Princess Patricia, the granddaughter of Queen Victoria and daughter of Prince Arthur, the tenth Governor General of Canada.

Team: Calgary Hitmen

Story: "Hitmen" is certainly a very intimidating name for a hockey team, but it wasn't chosen for solely that reason. One of the Hitmens' first investors and owners when it joined the WHL in 1994 was Calgary-born wrestler Bret "The Hitman" Hart.

A 2,377-foot chicken dog was made in 1985 by Maple Lodge Farms in Norval, Canada.

THE NEWFIE PALATE

The people of Newfoundland have their own very unique tastes.

SEAL AS A MEAL

At one gourmet restaurant in Montreal, customers pack in to try a seared dark red loin. Diners describe the flavor as similar to beef but a bit gamier. The meat is not beef, but seal.

While there are no seal burger chains open in Canada, seal has experienced a small resurgence in popularity. Top chefs are preparing seal steaks with caramelized onions and cranberry sauces. Some make a seal sausage that resembles pepperoni and can be used as a pizza topping. Cooks in Montreal are making seal mousse, seal tartare, and smoked seal, which some compare to brisket.

Seal hunting is controversial but still legal in Canada. Every year, the Canadian government allows more than a quarter of a million seals to be killed. There's a small seal hunt by the Inuits in the Arctic, but the big hunt takes place on ice floes in the Gulf of St. Lawrence in March and April. The government wants to thin the herd, which is often estimated at about five and a half million.

Seals are either shot or hit over the head with a spiked club called a hakapik, which animal rights activists say is cruel. The European Union has declared sealing inhumane and has banned imports of seal products. All of Canada's major political parties have said they are in favor of the hunt, and parliamentarians have staged events where they've eaten dishes such as double-smoked, bacon-wrapped seal loin in a port reduction to show how delicious seal can be.

THEIR LIPS ARE SEALED

Newfies have long been known for their seal cuisine. Many Sunday dinners in Newfoundland have featured roast seal—often with flippers still attached. The seal dish most well known in the province is a delicacy called seal flipper pie. Independent sealers still sail into St. John's Harbor every spring and sell young harp seal flippers off the wharf. In April, community clubs all over the city hold flipper pie dinners. There has been debate in some religious circles about whether seal is meat or fish because devout Catholics may abstain from eating meat on Good Friday. The flippers are tender and delicious, but it's said that few mainlanders acquire a taste for them.

The biggest ice cream sundae weighed 55,000 pounds and was created in Alberta in 1988.

Recipes call for dipping seal flippers in flour and pan-frying them in pork fat. Then you pour a gravy of Worcestershire sauce and flour over the flippers, cover with pastry dough, and bake.

MORE NEWFIE FOODS COMESTIBLES

Try these other odd eats for a good munch in the Maritimes.

Scrunchions: Small pieces of pork rind or pork fatback fried until rendered and crispy. They're usually an essential ingredient in fish and brewis, a dish common in Newfoundland.

Bang Belly: A round, pungent molasses-and-salt pork cake that is often served on Christmas Eve. You can bake, fry, or boil it in a stew like dumplings.

Cod Tongues: The gelatinous piece of flesh from the cod's throat is a local delicacy . . . and an acquired taste. The tongue used to be a part of the fish that most people discarded with the fish head. Poorer folks would gather the heads to feed their families. During the Depression, kids would head to the docks to sift through piles of discarded fish heads and cut out cod tongues. Back in the day, they were sold for 15 cents a dozen; now the local grocery sells them for $8.50 a pound. Upscale local restaurants serve them—sometimes lightly battered, fried, and topped with scrunchions. A common way to prepare them is to soak them in milk, dip in seasoned flour, then sauté in hot oil until nicely browned on both sides. Boiled cod cheek meat is also a big hit in Newfoundland.

Jiggs Dinner: This traditional meal is commonly prepared and eaten on Sundays in many regions around the province of Newfoundland and Labrador. It consists of a roasted turkey or chicken stuffed with dressing and served with a combination of side dishes that would all traditionally be cooked in a single pot.

Figgy Duff: Often served as part of a Jiggs Dinner, this popular bag pudding is not so figgy any more. It's commonly made today with raisins in place of figs. Typical ingredients are breadcrumbs, raisins, brown sugar, molasses, butter, flour, and spices. Ingredients are mixed and put in a pudding bag, wrapped in cheesecloth, or stuffed into an empty can and then boiled, usually along with vegetables.

Fish and Brewis: This stoical standard meal includes salted codfish and hard bread or hardtack (a cracker-like, dried biscuit). Brewis or brewes was the name for oat cakes.

Jack Graney of St. Thomas, Ontario, was the first person to pitch to Babe Ruth in the Major Leagues.

WEIRD CANADA

Crystal lakes, snow-capped mountains, hockey, Mounties, bilingual traffic signs...and some really, really weird news stories.

STEP RIGHT UP

In 2005 the Canadian postal service notified Christine Charbonneau of Orleans, Ontario, that they would no longer be delivering mail to her door. Reason: her front steps were 30 cm (12 inches) high, and regulations say that mail carriers are not required to climb steps higher than 20 cm (8 inches). Charbonneau said that the mail had been delivered to her door for the last 17 years and added that her 77-year-old mother-in-law—who is on oxygen— uses the stairs regularly.

BEAUZEAU LE CLOWN

In 2001 Quebec Premier Bernard Landry proposed the province spend $11 million to increase the number of clowns and other performers graduating from Quebec's National Circus School. The school was only graduating ten students a year, and when it comes to clown training, said Landry, Quebec must "maintain and enhance its leadership position."

UH, DOCTOR?

Rebecca Chinalquay of Saskatoon, Saskatchewan, sued the Meadow Lake Hospital after she was left alone in the delivery room while in labor. She called for help, but no one came, and she ended up having the baby by herself. The hospital's excuse: Chinalquay was being uncooperative and wouldn't allow nurses to monitor her condition, preventing them from knowing that the baby was coming.

SHOW ME THE MONEY

The Toronto-Dominion Bank loaned businessman Edward Del Grande $3.5 million in 1990. In 1995, when he didn't pay them back, they sued him. Del Grande countersued...for $30 million. His charge: the bank ruined him by loaning him too much money. Case dismissed.

More Canadians live in Los Angeles than in Ottawa.

LOTT O' LUCK

A man from Sherbrooke, Quebec, sued the provincial lottery, Loto-Quebec, for fooling him into believing he could actually win. He said that they sold only losing tickets, something he could prove by showing the $840 worth of losing tickets he'd bought in the month of March alone. The man, who is on welfare, sued the lottery for $879.58. The case was settled out of court.

SNOW DAY

In January 2002, a 30-year-old Ontario man named Nona Thusky was charged with public drunkenness and violation of probation. He was kept in custody awaiting sentencing on a previous conviction for assaulting a police officer when, two weeks later, he was suddenly released. Why? Because it snowed. Mr. Thusky is a member of the Algonquin tribe from the Barriere Lake reservation, and he's the only community member who knows how to operate the snowplow. After a severe February snowstorm, judge Jean-Francois Gosselin decreed that "community service"—for instance, clearing snow from the streets—made more sense than jail time.

BEYOND THE CALL OF DOOTY

In 1943, 17-year-old Hugh Trainor enlisted in the army and passed a preliminary test in his hometown on Prince Edward Island. He then traveled by ferry to an army barracks in Halifax, Nova Scotia. Once there, he failed his medical test and never officially became a member of the armed forces. But Trainor claimed that his time on the ferry—about a 10-mile ride—qualified as "war service," because German submarines had previously attacked ships in Canadian waters. In 2002 the Federal Court of Canada ruled that 75-year-old Trainor was entitled to veteran's benefits for his service and awarded him $1,000 a month for the rest of his life.

NIZE GUYZ FINISH LAZT

By adding another "z" to his last name, Zeke Zzzyzus (formerly Zzyzus) regained his status as the last name in the Montreal phone book. His competition for the honor: "Pol Zzyzzo" and "Zzzap Distribution."

GOING WITH THE FLOW

North America's most famous falls are best appreciated from a distance.

OVER THE FALLS IN A BARREL

Some people come to the biggest falls in North America to marvel at their beauty and enormity. Other people come and think, "I should go over those falls in a barrel." In 1901, Annie Taylor was the first to experience the falls via barrel. She was able to create pressure in her airtight barrel by having air pumped in with a bicycle pump. After going down the falls, Annie emerged bruised and battered but alive. In 1911, Bobby Leach plummeted over the falls inside of a steel barrel. He broke both kneecaps and his jaw. (Years later he died from gangrene, which he got after slipping on a banana peel.) In 1920, Charles Stephens tied himself to an anvil, climbed into his barrel, and headed over the falls. Afterward, the only thing found in the barrel was his left arm. In 1930, a Greek waiter named George L. Statakis suffocated to death after his barrel became trapped behind the falls for more than 14 hours.

TAKING THE PLUNGE

A Canadian mechanic nicknamed "Super Dave" Munday plunged over the falls in a barrel in 1985. He loved it so much he repeated it in 1993. In 1995, Robert Overcracker drove his jet ski directly over the falls in a campaign to promote homelessness awareness. He planned to open a parachute as he went over the falls, but the shoot did not open. His body was never found. Kirk Jones of Canton, Michigan, holds the distinction of having gone over the falls in nothing but the clothes on his back. On October 22, 2003, he crossed into Canada, swam out into the current, and dropped 53.3 meters (175 feet). He passed the Maid of the Mist tour boat as he swam to shore. He had a friend videotape the whole thing, but his friend wasn't working the camera correctly and nothing was recorded. The authorities picked him up and fined him $2,300. He was banned from entering Canada for the rest of his life.

AN AMAZING TALE OF SURVIVAL

Niagara Falls is actually a collection of falls that includes Canada's Horseshoe Falls. On June 9, 1960, Jim Honeycutt took family friends Deanna and Roger Woodward on a small boat past the hydro dam.

Roger was just seven years old, and his sister Deanna was 17. The dam was considered the point of no return for all small boats, and Honeycutt and his passengers swiftly realized they were in trouble. They tried to drive the boat to Goat Island, a small island in the Niagara River. Unfortunately, the boat overturned. Deanna, who had on a life jacket, was able to swim close enough to shore for two tourists to pull her out about 20 feet before the drop, but Roger and James went over the falls. Roger, who was also wearing a life jacket, miraculously survived the drop to the bottom. Jim Honeycutt, who was not wearing a life jacket, died. His body was found four days later downriver. Roger Woodward literally went down in history as the first person to survive a trip over Niagara Falls wearing only a life jacket. He was rescued by the crew aboard the *Maid of the Mist* tour boat. Moments after being rescued he asked about his sister. Relieved to hear of her rescue, he then asked for a glass of water. "I had probably drank half the Niagara River, but I was pretty thirsty," Roger said.

*   *   *

THESE CHANGING TIMES

Sandford Fleming did a lot of things. In 1851, at age 24, he designed Canada's first postage stamp (it had a beaver on it), and he invented the world's first pair of inline skates. But his "day job" was as a surveyor for railroads, and later as an engineer. Perhaps Fleming's most lasting contribution, however, is that of the 24-hour international clock. On a visit to Ireland, Fleming missed a train because the schedule mixed up the AM and PM sections. Frustrated, but seeing an opportunity for a more logical, systematic approach to timekeeping, he came up with the idea of a worldwide clock, divided into time zones based on Greenwich as the median. He introduced his idea at the International Prime Meridian Conference in Washington, D.C., in 1884—a gathering he also helped spearhead. The idea was adopted, though left up to individual countries to implement. By 1929 most all the world was on board.

Humorist Thomas Chandler Haliburton popularized the phrase "raining cats and dogs"...

ONLY IN CANADA...

Let your freak flag fly.

...can non-natives hunt polar bears.

...are guide dogs trained specifically for blind teenagers.

...can the killing of seals be filmed.

...are classical-style apprenticeships still offered to oil drillers.

...is ice wine production consistent and stable.

...can you find a narwhal—the unicorn of the sea!

...are the facilities regularly called "the washroom."

...are foods "glycemic index" ratings displayed on the package.

...is fishing the endangered porbeagle shark allowed.

...are legal rights constitutionally guaranteed to people with a mental illness.

...has trade with Cuba never been interrupted or stopped.

...is parents spanking children explicitly legal.

...are helicopter pilots trained to land on water.

...can you be officially certified as an "asthma educator."

...is there no federal department of education (among first-world nations).

...Is Coca-Cola not labeled "Coca-Cola Classic"—just Coca-Cola.

STEPHEN LEACOCK

Every country has its signature humorist. The U.S. has Mark Twain. Ireland has Oscar Wilde. Canada has Stephen Leacock (1869-1944).

"The Lord said, 'let there be wheat' and Saskatchewan was born."

"Men are able to trust one another, knowing the exact degree of dishonesty they are entitled to expect."

"It takes a good deal of physical courage to ride a horse. This, however, I have. I get it at about 40 cents a flask, and take it as required."

"I detest life insurance agents. They always argue that I shall some day die, which is not so."

"Advertising is the science of arresting the human intelligence long enough to get money from it."

"Writing is no trouble. You just jot down ideas as they occur to you. The jotting is simplicity itself—it is the occurring which is difficult."

"A sportsman is a man who every now and then simply has to get out and kill something."

"Many a man in love with a dimple makes the mistake of marrying the whole girl."

"Astronomy teaches the correct use of the sun and the planets."

"I am a great believer in luck, and I find the harder I work, the more I have of it."

"Electricity is of two kinds: positive and negative. The difference is, I presume, that one comes a little more expensive, but is more durable; the other is a cheaper thing, but the moths get into it."

"In ancient times they had no statistics, so they had to fall back on lies."

"Newspapermen learn to call a murderer 'an alleged murderer' and the king of England 'the alleged king of England' to avoid libel suits."

"There are two things in ordinary conversation which ordinary people dislike: information and wit."

THE GREAT FARINI

Some people life live on the edge.

BORN TO BE WILD

William Hunt was born in New York in June 1838, but his family soon moved to Port Hope, Ontario. His upbringing was strict, with Hunt's parents trying and failing to reign in their wild and impulsive son. For example, he loved swimming, but his parents thought he did it too much. So, his mother sewed up the collars and sleeves of his clothes so he could not shed them and go swimming. But that didn't stop Hunt. He would either dive in fully clothed and then run around until dry, or he would rip off his clothes, swim, and have older girls sew up the clothes again.

At a young age, Hunt snuck into a traveling circus and he was mesmerized, bitten by the show biz bug. When his parents were not around, Hunt secretly developed his muscles and his ability to do acrobatics. Even though he was just a boy, he put together a small show of music and various circus-like entertainments. Kids came and enjoyed themselves, but parents hated the idea and complained to his parents. Enraged by his son's frivolous pursuit, his father beat him. But Hunt continued to practice his acrobatics and tightrope walking.

THE WIRE

In 1859, at age 21, Hunt said goodbye to his old self and changed his name to something more fitting of a showman: Signor Guillermo Antonio Farini, or "The Great Farini." His first public stunt: he strung a rope between two buildings—80 feet in the air, and above the roaring Ganaraska River—and then he walked across. His first stunt sparked such interest that by the time he crossed his second river, 8,000 spectators attended, more than double the population of Port Hope. The major highlight of that walk: When he arrived at the midway point, the Great Farini stopped and stood on his head.

Less than a year later he was upping the ante:

- In 1860, he challenged the legendary French stuntman, Blondin, to walk across the Niagara Gorge near Niagara Falls.
- During a walk across the Falls, Farini reached midpoint and then attached a rope to the tightrope. He proceeded to lower himself

onto the deck of the *Maid of the Mist* 200 feet below. After enjoying a glass of wine and speaking with the passengers, he ascended back up the rope and continued his performance.

- On another walk, he carried a man on his back across the rope.
- One time he wore a sack covering his entire body.
- He learned to perform high-wire somersaults.
- He once hung from the high wire by his feet.
- On September 5, 1860, Farini attached an "Empire Washing Machine" to his body and walked out on his rope, over the Niagara Gorge. He lowered a bucket to the river beneath him and let it fill with water. He then proceeded to fill the machine and wash a dozen handkerchiefs, all given to him by female admirers.

He performed throughout the United States, and in 1866, he made it to Europe where he was a sensation. But in 1869, the Great Farini bid farewell to the tightrope because at age 31, he felt he might injure himself.

THE SHOW MUST GO ON

Still, the Great Farini would not give up show business, training and managing other acrobats. Eventually, he became an impresario, exhibiting pygmies and "Dwarf Earthmen." In 1885, he partnered with P.T. Barnum for an exploratory trip to Africa. With his adopted son and onetime aerial partner Lulu, Farini traveled through the Kalahari Desert in 1885 and found a colossal lost city there. An exhibit on "The Lost City of Kalahari" was mounted in London. Farini published a book on his explorations titled *Through the Kalahari Desert*, under his real name.

Farini ultimately learned seven languages, and during World War I, he and his wife, Anna, translated and transcribed daily war events from the German newspapers. Somehow, Farini found the time to invent folding theater seats, a modern-day parachute, and an apparatus that could fire a human like a cannonball. He devised improvements from steam engines and can-packing machines. He even served as vice president of the Rossland Gold Mining Development and Investment Company.

Truly, the Great Farinia lived a full life, and there never was a dull moment. He died at the age of 91 of influenza in 1929.

The Thousand Island Railway in Ontario was North America 's shortest railway at 5.43 km

SPACE FOOD

Canadians are in outer space. And they brought snacks!

LOOKING FOR MR. GOODBAR?

Canada has a great history of explorers, and it sure has a lot of space, but what about Canadians exploring space? Believe it or not, Canadians also excel at space exploration. No less than eight Canadians have traveled aboard shuttle missions and the International Space Station: Dr. Marc Garneau, Dr. Roberta L. Bondar, Dr. Steven G. MacLean, LtCol. Chris A. Hadfield, Dr. Robert (Bob) Thirsk, Bjarni V. Tryggvason, Dr. Dafydd (Dave) Williams, and Capt. Julie Payette. But how to take a bit of home with you into the wild black yonder?

Food is one of the top ways astronauts keep their morale up 70 kilometers above the earth. However, not just any munchies will make the grade. Food for space needs to be selected on several criteria.

The first is shelf life: There's no refrigeration on the International Space Station, and it won't do any good to have food rotting in space. The second is ease of eating in microgravity. Puddings and stews stick to a spoon long enough to eat, while salad can be a bit more challenging. This also means that nothing crumbly is allowed, since in microgravity, crumbs can litter the inside of the space station and become an inhalation hazard. For instance, tortillas are sent up instead of bread. Poutine, obviously, is right out. Finally there's the ability to prepare in the ISS's galley, which only has a convection oven and water for rehydrating food.

AND THE WINNERS ARE...

After an exhausting search, thirty-five great Canadian food products were chosen. The winners? For starters, candies and snacks like Whistler Pocket Chocolate and HapiFoods' Holy Crap Cereal make good space food, since they're packaged in discreet bundles. There was also a lot of preserved fish—SeaChange salmon and Brunswick sardines and herring were all deemed space-worthy. For drinks, Four O'Clock maple herbal tea and Tim Hortons coffee all made the cut—meaning that Tim Hortons is now literally "the most Canadian place in the universe."

Here is the full list, as published by the Canadian Space Agency:

(*items selected through the Snacks for Space contest):

- Les Canardises Duck Rillettes
- Trails End Buffalo Stix Cranberry Craze*
- SeaChange Candied Wild Smoked Salmon*
- SeaChange Smoked Salmon Pate*
- SeaChange Smoked Sockeye Salmon
- West Coast Select Salmon Jerky Original
- Brunswick Seafood Snacks Herring in lemon and cracked pepper
- Brunswick Sardines in mustard sauce
- Brunswick Sardines with hot peppers
- SoSoya+ Crunchers unsalted (soy nuts)
- HapiFoods Group Holy Crap Cereal*
- Profitapom CroustiPom (dried apple chunks)*
- Taste of Nature Nova Scotia Blueberry Fields Snack Bars
- Honey Bar Trail Mix Bar
- Sun-Rype FruitSource Blueberry Pomegranate Fruit Bar*
- Sun-Rype FruitSource Strawberry Fruit Bar*
- Sun-Rype Fruit-to-go Wildberry Fruit Snack
- Sun-Rype Fruit-to-go Raspberry Fruit Snack
- Dole Squish'ems! Apple Strawberry Squeezable Snack
- Fruit d'Or Dried Cranberries Original
- Leclerc Praeventia - Orange zest with green tea extract cookies*
- L.B. Maple Treat Maple Syrup Cream Cookies*
- Turkey Hill Sugarbush Maple Syrup*
- Citadelle Maple Hard Candies
- Four O'clock Maple Herbal Tea
- Tim Hortons English Toffee Cappuccino
- Tim Hortons French Vanilla Cappuccino
- Brookside Dark Chocolate Covered Cranberries
- Whistler Pocket Chocolate – Milk*
- Reese Bites (Reese Bouchées)*
- Mars Candy Bar*
- Smarties*
- Honibe Honeydrop*
- Rogers Chocolates – Maple Chocolate, Dark Chocolate, Milk Chocolate Bars
- Rocky Mountain Chocolate Factory – Milk, Dark and White Chocolate Maple Leafs

Canadian Troy Hurtubise invented a $150,000 Mark VI robo-bear suit for bear encounters.

POUTINE SUPREME

Fries, cheese curds, and gravy—poutine is a food so Canadian that it's a Canadian cliché (as well as "the National Dish of Canada"). But it doesn't have to be so...ordinary.

On a 2010 episode of *Iron Chef*, in which the secret key ingredient was Candian lobser, Quebec chef Chuck Hughes beat celebrity chef Bobby Flay. Maybe it wasn't a fair fight with that particular ingredient, but Hughes sealed the victory with a traditional poutine topped with lobster.

• Au Pied de Cochon, a restaurant in Montreal serves two nontraditional poutines. One is prepared with fois gras—the rich, buttery liver of a fattened goose. The other is a poutine temaki—a bite-sized appetizer in which the ingreidents are rolled up in seaweed like a piece of sushi.

• Soleil Westwood, is a Los Angeles-based French restaurant. Poutine is the signature dish there, or rather dishes—they serve more than 10 different varieties. All are made with the standard fries and cheese curds, plus unique ingredients such as Bolognese sauce (Poutine Celine), cognac-pepper sauce (Poutine Christine), sausage and peppers (Poutine Simon Chen), peas and chicken (Poutine Sheridan), and filet mignon and mushrooms (Poutine Marat).

• Bouchard's in Toronto dresses poutine like the cheeseburger that comes with plain old fries—it's fries topped with melted American cheese slices, ketchup, and pickle slices.

• The Jan Jette is an offering at the hot dog chain Tubby Dog. It's a poutine hot dog—a 1/3 lb. frankfurter covered with mustard, ketchup, fries, cheese curds, gravy, and the house sauce.

• The Big Cheese Poutinery in Calgary didn't think that poutine had nearly enough (or any) meat on it. So it took a poutine and slathered it in pulled pork, smoked bacon, and Italian sausage.

A "Yukon Gold" is a drink combining Yukon Jack and Goldschlager.

• Even Burger King Canada added poutine to the menu in 2011. It came in two varieties: Angry Poutine (the usual poutine ingredients, plus jalapenos, spicy fried onions, and a spicy sauce) and Poutine With Bacon (the usual poutine ingredients...with bacon).

• Sweet poutine! The Epic Meal Time podcast made a dessert poutine—deep-fried Kit Kat bar pieces (the "fries"), marshmallows (the "cheese curds"), and caramel sauce (the "gravy").

• Sweeter poutine! Try the Iced Poutine at Koko Ma Boule in Montreal. Instead of fries there are chocolate wafer cookies, instead of cheese curds there are marshmallows and caramel popcorn, and instead of gravy it's caramel syrup. And it's all placed on top of a huge bowl of vanilla ice cream.

• Liquid poutine! Jones Soda makes a variety of artisanal sodas in traditional soda flavors, but has one they sell only in Canada: poutine. You can really taste the gravy, the potatoes, and "fatty, cheesy notes."

* * *

THE HILLS ARE ALIVE

The sandbanks near Belleville, Ontario, make up the largest freshwater sandbar and dune in the world. In the mid-19th century, farmers removed most of the trees around to graze cows on the dune grass. The soil eroded, and sand dune grew phenomenally—the sandbanks devoured the town! In 1921, the Ontario government finally got the soil erosion problem under control, and in the early 1960s Sandbanks Provincial Park opened to the public.

Another kooky thing about this place: During low tide, freshwater flows down the park's Grepesy Brook to the ocean and at high tide, salt water flows up the brook to Heron Pond. This means that the animals and plants that make this waterway their home have to tolerate both salt and fresh water conditions. Not too many ponds contain salt-tolerant plants and waterfowl.

Whiskey-jack is not a drink. It's another name for the Canada jay bird.

LIFE, DEATH, AND PEMMICAN

The jerky precursor was so important that a battle was fought over it—a battle that decided the fate of the Canadian frontier.

WOOL FOR SKINS

You may know the Hudson's Bay Company as a chain of retail stores, but the company began as fur traders, trading European goods, especially "point" blankets, to Native Americans for beaver pelts. Point blankets were made of wool, and were named for the fact that each was worth a certain number of points. A one-point blanket was about 1 × 2.5 m (32" × 8") and was worth one prepared beaver skin. The Hudson's Bay Company became so powerful that much of western Canada was under its direct control.

Against the British-controlled Hudson's Bay Company was the North West Company, aided by the old kings of the frontier—the Métis, that is, people of mixed European and First Nations ancestry. It was very common for French voyageurs to marry First Nations women. This was necessary as much for survival as companionship: First Nations women could speak the local languages, knew what foods were safe, and could act as go-betweens between natives and Europeans. The Métis formed a distinct and wholly Canadian ethnic group, and were vital to the frontier economy. Groups would go down to the American plains, hunt buffalo, convert the meat to pemmican by slicing it into strips, mixing with fat, and pounding and drying it—and bring it back to Canada for fur traders to use on their long voyages.

WHERE'S THE BEEF?

In 1814, Miles MacDonell, the governor of the Red River Colony around what is now Winnipeg forbade the export of pemmican from the colony. The intent was to ensure supplies for the Hudson's Bay Company at the expense of the North West Company, but this antagonized the local Métis population. Led by Cuthbert Grant, they seized a supply of pemmican that had been stolen from them, intending to sell it to the North West Company. Robert Semple, an American

The whiskey-jack bird gets its name from a mispronunciation of the Cree *weskuchanis*.

businessman who had replaced MacDonell following the latter's nervous breakdown, went out to stop them, and a battle, known as the Battle of the Seven Oaks, ensued. Semple and 20 of his men were killed, against only one of the Métis. The Métis were cleared of any charges.

The battle went a long way towards easing the Hudson's Bay Company's stranglehold over the Red River Colony and ensuring the Métis' rights and survival as a people. The conflict only really ended, though, when the North West Company and Hudson's Bay Company finally merged in 1821—making the Canadian frontier a whole lot less wild.

*   *   *

FAILED DIPLOMA-CY

In the French language, verbs must agree with their either masculine or feminine subjects. This simple grammatical principle—one learned by Canadian students everywhere—was the cause of an embarrassing error in Montreal, where the Ministry of Education gave out 130,000 poorly worded diplomas at high school graduations in 2013.

The diplomas contain the phrase "We, the undersigned, attest..."; since the signatories of the diplomas were Quebec Education Minister Marie Malavoy and Deputy Minister Bernard Matte, the form of the verb "undersigned" should have been in the masculine (soussignés). However, as previous deputy minister was a female, the feminine version (soussignées) remained on the diplomas. On *all* of the diplomas.

Two students first brought the error to the ministry's attention. After some cost evaluation, it was determined the botched diplomas would cost $225,000 to fix. Officials decided against this, but gave students the option of requesting a new, grammatically correct diploma if they so desired. The story soon took on political dimensions. The Parti Québécois, a provincial political party that fights for the cause of Quebec independence, had just come into power at the beginning of the 2012–2013 academic year. As the party is fiercely devoted to the preservation of the French language, many in the Canadian press thought it ironic that its education ministry couldn't nail basic grammar.

In 2004, Canada banned importing, selling, or advertising baby walkers.

EVERY CITY IN THE WORLD

Hundreds of movies and TV shows have been shot in Toronto... even if you can't recognize it.

Hollywood producers have frequently chosen Toronto as a filming location over the last 40 years. Some say it's because location costs are so much less, while others say it's because the city is a perfect stand-in for just about any major metropolitan area.

Here's a list of just a few of the films that have been shot there... and where they were "supposed" to take place.

- ***Hollywoodland*** **(2006):** Hollywood
- ***The Adventures of Pluto Nash*** **(2002):** The moon
- ***The Gospel of John*** **(2007):** The Holy Land
- ***Ararat*** **(2002):** Armenia
- ***Where the Truth Lies*** **(2005):** New Jersey
- ***Vendetta*** **(1999):** New Orleans
- ***Chicago*** **(2002):** Chicago
- ***Three Men and a Baby*** **(1987):** New York
- ***RED*** **(2010):** Cleveland
- ***Detroit Rock City*** **(1999):** Detroit
- ***Land of the Dead*** **(2005):** Pittsburgh
- ***Hairspray*** **(2007):** Baltimore
- ***Fools Rush In*** **(1997):** Las Vegas
- ***Fever Pitch*** **(2005):** Boston
- ***The Virgin Suicides*** **(1999):** Grosse Pointe, Michigan
- ***Thomas and the Magic Railroad*** **(2000):** British Isles
- ***Rumor Has It*** **(2005):** Pasadena
- ***Good Will Hunting*** **(1997):** Cambridge, Massachusetts
- ***The Prince and Me*** **(2004):** Madison, Wisconsin
- ***Pacific Rim*** **(2013):** San Francisco
- ***The Ref*** **(1994):** Connecticut
- ***Dawn of the Dead*** **(2004):** Milwaukee
- ***Wrong Turn*** **(2003):** West Virginia

- *Twister* (1996): Oklahoma
- *Brokeback Mountain* (2005): Wyoming
- *Tommy Boy* (1995): Ohio
- *A Cool, Dry Place* (1999): Kansas
- *A History of Violence* (2005): Millbrook, Indiana
- *The Adventures of Bob & Doug McKenzie: Strange Brew* (1983): Toronto
- *Murder at 1600* (1997): Washington, D.C.
- *Dracula 2000* (2000): London

* * *

THREE GOOFY GAME SHOWS

***The Lawbreaker* (1970)** Contestants watched short silent films of a character named "The Lawbreaker" who was shown breaking obscure Canadian laws. Competitors had to guess what law was being broken. (The Lawbreaker was played by Paul Soles, who was voice of Hermey the Elf in Rudolph the Red-Nosed Reindeer.) Because the films were silent, you never heard Soles's distinctive voice.

***Strategy* (1969)** This was one of the first game shows ever hosted by Alex Trebek. In Strategy, teams of couples could move forward along a huge board, space by space, if they answered questions correctly. Their goal was to make it to the center of a huge maze. Players could block their opponent, and occasionally they would land on spaces that were booby-trapped.

***Just Like Mom* (1980)** Mothers and their sons or daughters spun a wheel and answered questions. For the middle round, they competed in a bake-off. The kids made the food, and the mothers had to eat it.

THE KINKY KILLER COLONEL

A family man and military man transforms into an underwear fetishist and horrific murderer. Did jogging and photography lead to his descent?

REVEALING REVEILLE

In 2007, at age 44, Colonel David Russell Williams was a respected member of the Canadian Armed Forces. He was a decorated pilot who had served 20 years in the Canadian military. By 2009, he would be the commander of Canada's largest air base, in Trenton, Ontario. He and his wife had been married for 16 years, and owned a home in a suburb of Ottawa and a cottage in Tweed. Williams helped out at charity events and posed at press events.

STRANGE HOBBY

Williams's interests in golf, fishing, jogging, and photography, however, seemed to help feed a deeply hidden perversion. During runs near his home, Williams began scoping out the neighbors—and specifically the female residents. He closely observed when the houses with young women were empty, and one day, he picked up his camera and started a new hobby: breaking into the neighbors' homes and photographing himself wearing girls' underwear.

He would then leave with several pairs of underwear, which he neatly stored in his own home. He reportedly broke into at least 48 homes along the way, including one house on nine separate occasions. Williams gradually built a large collection of women's underwear, as well as a library of thousands of photos of himself wearing the underwear.

REVEALING ENCOUNTER

His perverse behavior gradually escalated. On one occasion, he hid in a woman's backyard to observe her getting into the shower. He then took off all his clothes, left them outside, and broke into the woman's home completely naked. In September 2009, his behavior became more violent. He broke into a woman's home near his cottage in Tweed. He knocked her out with a flashlight. He sexually assaulted her and took photos of her and of himself with her underwear draped over his face.

Just hours after the violent assault, Williams went to a professional conference, accepted a donation for a wounded veterans' group, and dropped the puck for the season opener of a junior hockey team.

KILLER OBSESSION

Two weeks later, he committed a similar horrible attack. But by November 2009 his violent behavior became more extreme. He broke into the house of a female corporal who worked at his base. She found him hiding behind the furnace in the basement. Williams murdered her, and three hours later he drove to a meeting. When the female corporal's body was found, Williams sent a letter of condolence to her father.

Then on January 29, 2010, he struck again. Williams kidnapped a young woman on a highway not far from Tweed and killed her. He dumped her body in the woods, and the next day he piloted a troop flight to California. Because the victim was not found right away, she was treated as a missing person. At the victim's home, an officer had noticed a suspicious SUV parked in a nearby field on the day of her disappearance. The police photographed the tire tracks left behind.

TRACKED DOWN

On February 4, police set up roadblocks in the area, checking cars with the hope of finding a clue to the woman's whereabouts. Officers also had a copy of the tire print left behind near the victim's house. When Russell Williams pulled through a checkpoint in his SUV, one diligent officer noticed that his tires matched the photo of the tire print. On February 7, Ottawa police called Williams in for questioning. Inspector Jim Smyth treated Williams with great respect and slowly revealed the evidence the police had against him. Over the course of 10 hours, Williams confessed. He couldn't explain why he committed the crimes, but it was clear that he wanted to make things as easy as possible for his wife. After he signed a confession, he wrote his wife a note of apology and asked her to take good care of their cat. Williams was given two life sentences for murder, plus 120 years for the other crimes.

SHADES OF GREY OWL

Even in the Great White North, things aren't always what they seem....

CONSERVATIONIST, HERO, FAKE

From 1930 to 1938, a man named Grey Owl was an international superstar—a gripping public speaker, environmentalist, and philosopher. He declaimed powerfully on the need to preserve unspoiled wilderness, and he upheld a strong Native identity for Canada. "I want to arouse in the Canadian people a sense of responsibility they have for the north country and its inhabitants, humans and animal," wrote Grey Owl. His goal was to establish wildlife sanctuaries throughout Canada. He was also interested in restricting commercial traffic in animal skins to protect animal life. Grey Owl wanted to prevent Native culture from becoming commercialized and fueled by European fashion trends. He tried to convince white Canadians to support a conservation plan, arguing that an untamed North within Canada was vital to its national identity. He wrote the best-selling books, *Pilgrims of the Wild* and *The Adventures of Sajo and Her Beaver People*. He made movies and traveled on lecture tours throughout North America and Europe. He presented before the royal family in England, saluting King George VI and speaking a few words in Ojibwe.

ALL THAT GLITTERS

For Victoria Day 1923, Belaney organized a "war party" in Biscotasing, Ontario. Belaney played the role of Indian chief and tied a symbolic white prisoner to a pole. He told the man of the wrongs white men had committed against Native people. The event was a great success, and the local paper published an account of the drama.

In time, Belaney grew to believe trapping was wrong. After adopting a pair of beaver kittens, he recognized that they were affectionate, intelligent creatures, and he could no longer justify killing these animals.

AUTEUR, AUTEUR?

When Belaney died in 1938, details of his background caused some surprise and consternation: His given name was Archie Stansfeld

Belaney, and he was raised by two maiden aunts in Hastings, England. The press had often called the blue-eyed Grey Owl a "full-blooded" Indian, though Belaney had said he was half Apache and half Scottish. Actually, he had zero Native blood.

At age 18, he immigrated to Canada. His desire was to live in the wilderness. He learned trapping from a band of Ojibwe and a woodsman named Jesse Hill. He worked summers as a guide or forest ranger, and in winter he trapped and sold furs.

Belaney wasn't always a saint. Before he became Grey Owl, he was a hard-drinking, womanizing rogue. He abandoned two wives, a girlfriend, and a total of three children. He was a notorious drunkard. He would go on two- to three-week binges—even as Grey Owl—because he feared his identity might be uncovered.

As he grew older, he became so captivated by Indian culture that he wanted to become a native. He dyed his brown hair black and darkened his fair skin with henna.

After the posthumous revelation of his identity, many forgave his transgressions, appreciating the efforts he made for conservationism. You can visit the grave of one of Canada's greatest naturalists and imposters in Prince Albert National Park in Saskatchewan.

* * *

A NEWFOUND WAY TO TELL TIME

There's something more than just the laid-back pace of life on Newfoundland and Labrador that makes time feel like it's moving differently. The province has its very own time zone, Newfoundland Standard Time, which it shares with no other inhabited region.

And while most of the world—including the rest of Canada—calculates its local time in differences of whole hours from Greenwich Mean Time for the sake of convenience, NST doesn't. It's 30 minutes ahead of Atlantic Standard Time, used by the closest parts of the coastal mainland.

The only other place in the world that varies from the rest of its home country by a fraction of an hour is Eucla, an isolated region of West Australia that is perpetually 15 minutes out of synch with its neighbors.

THE GREAT ONE'S GREAT TIPS

In his 1990 autobiography, Gretzky, *Wayne Gretzky took it upon himself to outline a 10-point plan for revamping the NHL. Some of it actually came to fruition.*

1. Expand. Develop teams in new cities to generate wider interest. Outcome: The NHL has added eight teams since 1992, including the San Jose Sharks, the Ottawa Senators, and the Columbus Blue Jackets.

2. Rename the conferences. The "Prince of Wales Conference" and the "Clarence Campbell Conference" had a poetic ring to them, but geographical-based names were easier for fans to understand. Outcome: In 1994 the NHL renamed them the Eastern Conference and Western Conference, respectively.

3. Realign the conferences. Conferences were "stacked" so that certain teams were virtually guaranteed to win, such as the Chicago Blackhawks and the Toronto Maple Leafs. There were also too many repeat matchups, making it hard for fans to get to know new players. Outcome: In 1998 the Western and Eastern Conferences were split from two to three divisions apiece.

4. Bring on free agency. Many remember the league lockout in 1994–1995, which partially stemmed from Gretzky's concern. He felt that it would be better for the league if players were allowed to seek the team that suited them best. Outcome: Since the lockout, the league has allowed for greater leeway for free agency.

5. Institute a week-off plan. Gretzky felt players were overworked with exhibition games and playoffs in addition to the regular season. A rotating rest period for teams would help sustain a long-term, quality level of play. Outcome: This one never caught on.

6. Let the players help make the rules. Perhaps a bit controversial, Gretzky believed that the players' perspective on the game would be

Quest University in Squamish, B.C., is the smallest Canadian university: 220 students.

useful in updating outmoded regulations. Outcome: Again, this was a tough one to implement.

7. Pay the refs more. Underpaid referees with limited benefits were not good for league morale. Raising their salaries and ensuring solid pension plans would ensure their dedication to the sport. Outcome: After striking in 1993, referees and NHL officials reached an agreement that included a salary increase as well as additional retirement benefits.

8. Bring back ESPN: The cable giant had an interrupted history of broadcasting NHL games: first from 1980 to 1982, then 1986 to 1989. At the time of *Gretzky*'s publication in 1990, the station was not broadcasting games, cutting out a wide segment of potential American viewers. Outcome: It resumed again from 1992 to 2004. (Games now air on NBC in the U.S.)

9. Let pros play in the Olympics. Remember the American "Dream Team"? It was a collection of top players from the NBA fielded to play in—and subsequently dominate—the 1992 Olympics in Barcelona. Gretzky had similar visions for the NHL, which did not allow its players to participate in the Games because of conflicts in schedule. Outcome: The NHL finally allowed player participation in the 1998 Winter Olympics.

10. End the fighting. Gretzky wanted to curb the brawling that distracted from the purity of the game. Outcome: Yeah, right.

* * *

A BAD JOKE

- Q: How do you get 26 Canadians out of a swimming pool?
- A: Yell, "Everybody out of the pool!"

GROLAR BEARS

These mysterious bears were once considered a legend. Until one appeared.

WHEN A GRIZZLY LOVES A POLAR

A "grolar" is the offspring of a grizzly bear and a polar bear. The "gr" comes from "grizzly," and the "olar" from polar. (Grolars are also sometimes called "pizzly bears.") Grolars, pizzlies, whatever you want to call them, can also be spawned by two other species of brown bears (meaning no grizzly, but a polar is still needed), although they're rarely bred in captivity. As of 2013, only 17 are held in zoos.

Grolars typically behave more like polar bears but they possess features distinctive of both breeds. For example, their bodies tend to be smaller than those of polar bears but they usually have humped shoulders like grizzlies.

BEARLY REAL

But they're incredibly rare in nature and, until a few years ago, wild grolars were considered a legend since no one had ever managed to track down hard evidence of their existence. You see, brown and polar bears live in ecologically diverse regions which makes the chances of them encountering one another, let alone breeding, all but impossible. (Nor do most humans who value their lives go messing around with wild bears of any kind.)

Brown bears prefer temperate forests whereas polar bears, needless to say, typically live in much chillier climates. Their "bedroom habits" are also different. While their breeding seasons overlap, brown bears prefer to mate on land; polar bears prefer ice flows.

THE GRIZZLY TRUTH

Native American legends surrounding grolars date back to at least the mid-19th century. In 1864, a group of Inuit hunters shot and killed an enormous bear in the wilds of what is now the Northwest Territories. They were mystified by its odd fur and donated the pelt and the skull to a naturalist named Robert MacFarlane. MacFarlane turned over the remains to the Smithsonian Institution. Their researchers

Sandford Fleming of Ontario invented time—he came up with the idea of Standard Time.

weren't convinced they were anything special and placed them in storage.

Years later, in 1918, a zoologist named Clinton Hart Merriam came across "MacFarlane's Bear" in the institute's archives and inspected the remains. He came to the conclusion that they were from a female bear unlike any other that had been identified up until that point. The teeth and skull were different than that of a grizzly and Merriam was baffled by the pelt. He decided that they belonged to a previously undiscovered species and gave MacFarlane's Bear a new scientific title: *Vetularctos inopinatus*.

In the years that followed, other researchers investigated "mystery bears" like this one, but their findings were rarely taken seriously. As for MacFarlane's Bear, some scientists theorized it was a wild "grolar"; others wrote it off as a anomaly.

A LEGEND BECOMES REALITY

Two grolar cubs were born at a zoo in Osnabrück, Germany, in 2004, but it wasn't until two years later that one was finally discovered in the wild. An American big game hunter named Jim Martell teamed up with Roger Kuptana, an Inuit tracker, for an expedition on the NWT's Banks Island in the spring of 2006. Martell shot and killed what he thought was a polar bear. Upon further inspection, he and Kuptana realized what they had on their hands was infinitely more rare.

DNA evidence later confirmed that their bear was, indeed, the first confirmed grolar ever discovered in the wild. Scientists in British Columbia controversially returned the bear to Martell, which he has since dubbed "Polargrizz." As of 2007, he was keeping the stuffed grolar in his trophy room next to a Canadian wolf. It all happened again in April of 2010. A hunter named David Kuptan killed what he thought was a polar bear outside of Ulukhaktok, NWT. It turned out to be another wild grolar.

Scientists still consider the bears to be exceptionally rare in nature, but the likelihood of a population boom could increase as grizzlies are driven further north by civilization and as polar bears are driven further south by global warming.

This may come as no surprise—a Canadian invented the snowblower.

THE RICHARD RIOT

Sometimes the biggest fights in hockey happen off the ice...and by the fans.

THIS IS A STICK-UP!

It was a perfect storm of culture and politics, of burgeoning ethnic pride and social consciousness, and old-fashioned excitable sports fandom. Whatever the root cause, the rioting that followed the suspension of Montreal Canadiens legend Maurice "Rocket" Richard exposed a schism in Canadian society.

On March 13, 1955, during an away game against the Boston Bruins, Richard was high-sticked, and he retaliated. Richard brutally pummeled Bruins defenseman Hal Laycoe repeatedly, eventually breaking his stick across Laycoe's body. When a linesman tried to intervene, Richard also punched him senseless. Richard was tossed out of the came, and after a hearing later that week, NHL president Clarence Campbell suspended Richard...for the rest of the season.

CAMPBELL'S SOUP

Montreal fans were furious—at the suspension of their star player, certianly, but mostly at the high-handed tone of Campbell's ruling. Campbell accused Richard of "temperamental instability" and "willful defiance of authority." Many Quebecers felt that the ruling was part of a longstanding pattern of discrimination against French-Canadian players. Indeed, Richard himself had once written a newspaper column that referred to Campbell as a "dictator" for his hypocrisy in dispensing what he thought were harsher penalties to French-Canadian players than to their Anglo counterparts for similar offenses.

Campbell was unmoved by the protests, and stoked fan resentment with his insistence on attending the next Canadiens home game in person, which was both a public relations move and a sign to the team, and its fans, that he was watching them.

RIOTING NIGHT IN CANADA

It was a misguided effort—the game on March 17, 1955 was a debacle. More than 6,000 demonstrators gathered outside the Montreal

Forum, awaiting the conclusion of the game against the Detroit Red Wings. That couldn't come fast enough for some fans—the opposing team was pelted with garbage for six solid minutes upon their arrival at the arena. Some fands tried to crash the gates, which led to police intervention. Nevertheless, one fan made his way through police, the gates, and security, into the stadium...and punched Clarence Campbell.

After a tear gas bomb was set off inside, the fire brigade evacuated the Forum, and the rioting spilled out onto St. Catherine Street. Windows were smashed, cars overturned, bystanders assaulted, and stores looted within a 15-block radius of the Forum. The damage toll included 37 injuries, as many as 100 arrests, and an estimated $100,000 worth of damages—or about $850,000, in today's dollars.

VIVE LE QUEBEC?

In the aftermath, Richard gave a national TV address in both French and English, appealing for calm. But the riot had roiled the simmering ethnic tensions in Quebec, and is sometimes cited as a harbinger of the "Quiet Revolution" that would transform Quebecois society in the 1960s.

The events of 1955 continue to resonate in pop culture. Singer Jane Siberry immortalized the incident with a line in her 1989 song "Hockey": "They rioted in the streets of Montreal when they benched Rocket Richard." Richard's life story (including the riot) has been adapted for film several times, most recently in *The Rocket* (2006).

* * *

NO TOUCHING!

In April of 2006, commuter trains in the Toronto area flashed a concerning message about the prime minister: "Stephen Harper eats babies." Apparently, the prank was the work of a hacker who tapped into the system and changed the message using a wireless device that cost about $25. Gerry Nicholls, vice president of the National Citizens Coalition, responded to the incident: "I worked with Stephen Harper for five years and never once did he in that time eat a baby."

POLE DANCING FOR ALL!

This is your fault, Canada.

VERTICAL HORIZON

The idea of exercising with the use of a vertical pole goes back nearly 1,000 years to the Indian gymnastic sport called mallakhamb. But turning those gymnastic gyrations into a sexy dance is a more recent phenomenon. Some trace the first combination of vertical poles and stripping to a 1968 at an Oregon bar called Mugwumps. Others claim that topless go-go dancer Carol Doda began pole dancing at the historic Condor Club in San Francisco as early as 1964. Regardless of where it started, pole dancing is now permanently associated with strip clubs.

Sometime in the 1990s, people began to realize that pole dancing could be more strenuous than simply spinning and gyrating around a vertical pole. Some of the more fit erotic dancers integrated acrobatic moves into their pole dances, using core and limb strength to climb, spin, and dance up and down the pole. It wasn't long before the idea of pole dancing for fitness—for non-strippers spread.

BLUE MONDEY

Canadian exotic dancer-turned-body builder Fawnia Mondey is credited with helping to spread the popularity of pole dancing to non-strippers, and she produced the first-ever pole dancing DVD. She also founded a Pole Dancer Instructor Certification program and is on the board of the Pole Fitness Association (yes, it's real).

By 2007, major newspapers and magazines like the *New York Times* were running articles about pole dancing spreading to suburban New York housewife circles, and poles even being found in limos, as part of college fundraisers and even at bar mitzvahs. While pole dancing had a fitness component, it was still laced with a "bad girl" vibe.

JUNIOR DIVISION

But leave it to some enterprising Canadians to turn the trend into child's play. Literally. Tammy Morris, a former exotic dance champion (yes, that's real, too) from Vancouver got international attention for offering pole dancing classes at her studio, Tantra Fitness, to nine-year-olds, with private instruction available for kids as young as five. Morris told Fox news in 2010, "Moms had brought their kids to classes for one reason or another, maybe lack of child care. If that was OK with the parents, that was OK with us."

Morris says there was nothing inherently sexy about the classes, despite class titles such as "Pussycat Dolls," "Promiscuous Girls," "Bellylicious" and "Sexy Flexy."

IF THEY JUMPED OFF A BRIDGE...

Morris thinks that pole dancing is innately about fitness, and anything tawdry is purely secondary or not applicable. "Our classes are very fitness focused," she said. "We're not teaching how to grind or undulate, we're teaching a gymnastics style class on the pole." Besides, Morris points out, mothers can judge for themselves if it's appropriate to bring along their daughters, and that demonstrations of fitness pole dancing have been shown on family-friendly daytime TV shows, like *The Oprah Winfrey Show* and *Ellen.*

"Children have no (erotic) association with the pole whatsoever," she added. "Unless you teach someone how to grind and make reference to taking off your clothing, there's nothing wrong with it."

Morris isn't alone. Kristy Craig of The Twiste Grip Dance and Fitness Studio, in Duncan, B.C., offered a "Little Spinners" pole dancing class to kids—girls and at least one boy—as young as five, saying that, "My existing students were asking about it for their children. They were saying, 'My daughter plays on my pole at home all the time, I'd love her to actually learn how to do things properly and not hurt herself."

* * *

CAPTAIN OF THE UNIVERSE

In 2009, a fan wrote William Shatner a letter, suggesting that he nominated himself to be Canada's governor general. Shatner set his sights higher. "My intention is to become prime minister of Canada, not governor general, which is mainly a ceremonial position," was his official reply.

THEY DID THAT ON TELEVISION

How a low-budget kiddie TV show from Canada gave rise to an entertainment empire.

MADE IN CANADA

The world is getting smaller. It seems that these days, kids everywhere all watch the same TV shows—Japanese cartoons, the Disney Channel, and *iCarly,* for example. But there was a time when children in the U.S. and Canada had more distinct and separate TV cultures. American kids in the '80s watched *Sesame Street*, then *Punky Brewster*, then *Saved By the Bell.* Canadian kids had *Mr. Dressup* and *The Littlest Hobo* and *Degrassi*. But for now grown-up kids of a certain age on both sides of the border, there's a point of convergence: the scrappy CTV sketch comedy *You Can't Do That On Television!*

SKETCHING IT OUT

You Can't Do That on Television! began production in 1979 at Ottawa's CJOH-TV, and quickly became a local sensation with its blend of juvenile *Laugh-In* setups and bargain-basement *Monty Python*-style surrealism, performed by an all-child cast with a single adult foil, veteran comedian Les Lye. But its strange second life began when it was licensed to the fledgling U.S. cable network Nickelodeon in 1981.

In those days, Nick was not the zillion-dollar multi-platform behemoth it is today; indeed, as a start-up channel it was a perpetual money-loser. In its early days, Nickelodeon was only on the air for 12 hours a day, and was perpetually scrambling for inexpensive programming to fill those hours—most of that was an Ohio-based puppet show called *Pinwheel*, as well as children's educational programming imported from the U.K. and Canada.

But *You Can't Do That on Television!* was pretty much the only game in town for kids on weekday afternoons—Saturday morning cartoons and a couple of kids' shows in the mornings on public television was all that was available at the time. *You Can't Do That on Television!* had a captive Stateside audience for its after-school time slot. In short order, the show had become Nick's first hit and most-watched show.

A survey in 1995 reported that 38% of Canadian women preferred chocolate to making love.

I DON'T KNOW

American audiences latched on to host Christine "Moose" McGlade's deadpan comic timing, the comic grotesquerie of Les Lye's adult characters, the broad humor of the sketches, and the kid-friendly one-liners. Some highlights:

• Anytime a cast member said "water," a bucket of water fell on their heads, as if by magic, humiliating them.
• Anytime a cast member said "I don't know," a bucket of bright-green slime fell on their heads, as if by magic, humiliating them.
• "Don't encourage him!" became a popular catchphrase, usually said by one adult to another about a kid acting up.
• Among the most popular recurring sketches was "Barth Burger," the world's most disgusting fast-food restaurant.
• Another recurring–and dark–sketch: a cast member tied up to a post, about to be executed, trying to worm their way out of their inevitable fate. ("Wait a minute, wait a minute! Stop the execution!")
• The kid and teen cast members portrayed "themselves," and were always addressed by each other's first name. Lye, however, portrayed Ross, the permanently exasperated, crafty, and vaguely child-hating stage manager.
• Lifted from *Laugh-In:* a wall of lockers, from which the cast members pop out and sell silly jokes.

SLIME TIME

Production on *You Can't Do That on Television!* ended in 1990, with Nick continuing to air reruns until 1994. Lye passed away in 2009; McGlade is now a communications and media executive. (Some person named "Alanis Morissette" was a cast member for a while, too.) But though the show is long gone, many of the running gags have become an enduring part of Nickelodeon lore. The infamous green slime has become a Nick trademark–literally. A trademark injunction was filed to name the stuff "Nickelodeon Slime"), and a highlight of the annual Nickelodeon Kids' Choice Awards is the sliming of a popular celebrity.

IT'S A TRADITION!

Do hockey players win games because they work hard and try their best? Nah, it's because of all the pre-game rituals and fan traditions.

W**ayne Gretzky** had a very specific intermission beverage routine. Right off the ice, he'd drink a Diet Coke, followed by an ice water, then a Gatorade, and then another Diet Coke. It had to be in that order.

• **Glenn Hall** got nervous before games for almost his entire career. To calm himself down, he'd vomit before the game started.

• **Stephan Lebeau** would chew a massive wad of 25 pieces of gum, just before the game. Once the game clock had been running for two minutes, Lebeau spit out all the gum (not onto the ice).

• **Red Coupille** is a little-known player from the 1930s. During games, he'd keep a bottle of Coca-Cola in his shoes, in the locker room. He claimed the superstition would guarantee he'd score a goal...although he only ever scored 12 times in eight years of play.

• **Stan Mikita** would smoke a cigarette between each period of play. When he was done, he tossed the butt into the trash—always over his left shoulder.

• **Bill Ranford** wouldn't let linesmen take the puck out of his goalie glove. First, he had to toss it in the air and land it on the back of the glove.

• **Stéphane Quintal** refused to talk to anyone after 1:30 p.m. on game days.

• **Joe Nieuwendyk** would eat two pieces of toast—with peanut butter—before every game.

• **Sidney Crosby** won't call his mother on a game day, because on the days of the the three games in which he'd been injured were also days he'd talked to his mother.

• **Ken Dryden** had to end his goalie warm-ups with a save, not a goal. If a teammate practice-scored on him, he had them shoot again so he could make a save.

• **Kyle McLaren** wore a yellow, not clear, visor. It started as a prank—his teammates changed it because McLaren is colorblind, and would have no idea that it had been changed. But McLaren scored that first night, so he kept the visor as a good-luck charm.

• **Ray Bourque** changed his skate laces before every individual period, and never used the same pair twice. He played in 1,826, which amounts to 10,956 pairs of laces.

• **Patrick Roy** had two weird superstitions. When skating to his goaltending position, he'd hop over the blue and red lines—he didn't want to touch them. He'd also talk to his goalposts throughout the game.

• **Jocelyn Thibault** would pour water over his head exactly six-and-a-half minutes before the start of a game.

• **Karl Alzner** would tap his stick to the ice exactly 88 times during the playing of the Canadian National Anthem. As he did so, he'd trace the outline of the maple leaf in time to the music.

• **Bruce Gardiner** played from 1994 to 2005. During that span, before every game, he dunked the blade of his hockey stick into the locker room toilet. (Bruce Gardiner is now Uncle John's all-time favorite hockey player.)

• Here's a nice team-wide superstition. In 1987, the Winnipeg Jets faced the Calgary Flames in the first round of the NHL playoffs. The Flames had a tradition for home game fans to show up wearing the team's red uniform color—it made the stands a sea of intimidating red, known as the "C of Red." In response, the Jets came up with their own tradition based on their own color: home fans showed up in entirely white to create the "Winnipeg White Out." The Jets won the series, and carried on the tradition for home playoff games—even when the team relocated to Phoenix.

Estevan, Saskatchewan is the sunniest place in Canada—2,540 hours of sunshine a year.

PIERRE BERTON VS. THE CUISINART

The real-life Canadian inspiration behind a riotously famous TV gag.

SAVE THE LIVER!

During his stint on *Saturday Night Live*, Ottawa-born Dan Aykroyd famously parodied Julia Child in a 1978 sketch where the TV chef cut the dickens out of her finger and proceeded to bleed all over her kitchen set. Although fellow chef Jacques Pepin has claimed that the sketch was based on a real incident which took place while he and Child were prepping for an appearance on *Tomorrow with Tom Snyder*, a not-entirely-dissimilar situation—this one in front of the camera—unfolded during an episode of CBC-TV's *90 Minutes Live*.

Host Peter Gzowski's guests that evening were comedian David Steinberg and esteemed journalist Pierre Berton, with Berton taking the opportunity to demonstrate the then-new Cuisinart and its remarkable ability to simplify the process of making scalloped potatoes. In the process of slicing spuds, however, Berton accidentally sliced two of his fingers open while trying to stop the device's blade. "Now, you see, that's what you shouldn't do," muttered Berton before quickly asking the age-old question, "Is there a doctor in the house?"

A BLOODY MESS

Attempting to laugh it off, Berton continued onward with his potato preparations, but Gzowski's nervousness about the increasing amount of blood was palpable. Steinberg quipped, "I think I'll pass on eating those potatoes, thanks," but only in an effort to keep things light after having already nervously suggested that Berton slip backstage to have someone look at his wound. Although citing the classic line "the show must go on," Gzowski nonetheless cut to commercial. The following evening, Berton reappeared on the show, his fingers profoundly bandaged, and soldiered on with the demonstration, but the original moment of bloodshed remains a highlight of Canadian TV history.

SKIRTING THE ISSUE

The archetypical Sixties garment turned European heads…in the 1760s.

TO THEIR HEALTH

Did the miniskirt originate among the indigenous cultures of 18th-century Canada? A close reading of the diaries of several European explorers seems to affirm the theory. "The men wore no trousers, the women a short, thin skirt," wrote Swedish-Finnish explorer Peter Kalm when traversing the Iroquois country along the border of New York and Canada in 1750, a description that evokes that piece of provocative contemporary women's wear.

To pull off such a fashion statement, Iroquois women must have been in great shape—and, by all accounts, they were, as were as their male counterparts. Lieutenant James M. Hadden, who served under British General John Burgoyne, described a group of Native Canadians as "tall, active and well made" in his journal of Burgoyne's 1776–1777 military campaign. Diarist William Wood, spoke of "Indians Northward" as being "straight bodied, strongly composed, smooth-skinned, [and] merry countenanced."

TOTALLY ORGANIC

What were the reasons for the natives' healthy and vigorous physical appearance? Well, the abundance of natural foods, for one: bountiful wild game, fruits, and vegetables were nourished organically. More importantly, the natives did everything by hand, from building their lodgings to planting their crops to combing the landscape for firewood. Having to walk everywhere to glean food and other material, as well as transport it over great distances, ensured a peak level of fitness. Add to this the common day-to-day tasks such as washing clothes and dressing game, and one can see how these populations were so robust.

In the end, we may never know the exact origins of the miniskirt. The garment (worn by both men and women) has cropped up throughout history, from ancient Greece to the knights of the Middle Ages (who supposedly wore them under their armor). But accounts like Kalm's make a strong case for the Iroquois as the modern-day pioneers.

The sun is not seen almost nonstop for three months in the northern Yukon.

ODD DEATHS

Everybody's gotta go sometime. (Warning: these are pretty grim.)

OWEN HART

While the world is widely aware that (spoiler alert) professional wrestling is heavily staged, there's still considerable opportunity for its participants to be injured or even killed, but sometimes the damage has nothing to do with what moves take place in the ring. On May 23, 1999, during a pay-per-view event called *Over the Edge*, the Alberta-born Hart was latched into a harness and being lowered by grapple line from the rafters of Kansas City's Kemper Arena into the ring when he accidentally trigged the quick-release mechanism on the harness, falling 78 feet and landing chest-first on the top rope of the ring.

TV viewers were spared the sight of Hart's fall, as a pre-match film was airing at the time, and upon returning to the arena, the camera focused on the audience while Hart received medical attention, but announcer Jim Ross clarified the situation and repeatedly reiterated that the events which were unfolding weren't part of a World Wrestling Federation "storyline."

Although he was quickly moved to Kansas City's Truman Medical Center, Hart died as a result of his injuries. The WWF actually continued airing the rest of the program—Hart's death was announced to viewers but not to those in the arena.

TAYLOR MITCHELL

Although only 19 years old, Halifax-born singer Taylor Mitchell seemed to be well on her way to a successful career, having just earned a Canadian Folk Music Award nomination for Young Performer of the Year. While on an afternoon hike in 2009 on the Skyline Trail in Nova Scotia's Cape Breton Highlands National Park, Mitchell was attacked by a pack of three coyotes. The animals were feeding on her, when additional hikers happened upon the scene and scared the animals away. Although she was transported to a hospital by emergency crews and subsequently airlifted to Queen Elizabeth II Health Sciences Centre in Halifax, she succumbed to her injuries that night.

A Toronto design studio stuck a car in a pothole to promote its exciting pothole app.

In an interview with the CBC, retired Department of Natural Resources biologist Bob Bancroft observed, "In situations like a national park [where] usually there's no hunting and no trapping allowed, [coyotes] can get used to a human presence and not have much fear of any retribution. They may have snuck up on her and knocked her over before she even knew what happened. They may have just capitalized on a situation where a young person was acting vulnerable and very frightened by their presence." Still, such occurrences are so rare that the attack on Mitchell made her the first adult on record to have ever been fatally attacked by coyotes.

GARRY HOY

A co-worker at Garry Hoy's lawfirm described Hoy as "one of the brighter lights at the firm, just a super nice guy, a very generous fellow," he earned instant immortality—albeit in a very unfortunate fashion—due to the very unfortunate way in which he met his death in 1993. In order to demonstrate to the firm's articling students the unbreakable nature of the office windows in the Toronto-Dominion Centre, Hoy decided to hurl himself at the glass. The first time he did it, he bounced off. The second time he did it, he most decidedly did not. When Hoy hit the glass, the window frame gave way, sending him hurtling out of the 24th story window and falling to his death. At the time, a *Toronto Star* article about the incident featured a quote from a Toronto Metro police spokesperson describing Hoy's demise as being treated as a "death by misadventure," with the officer noting that "the frame and blinds are still there."

Regrettably, if not entirely unsurprisingly, Hoy's death made its way into an episode of *Mythbusters*, receiving a shout-out of sorts during a scene in the sitcom *Billable Hours*, and earning the spotlight on Spike TV's *1000 Ways to Die*. None of this pop culture success likely served as consolation to Hoy's firm, Holden Day Wilson, which closed in 1996 in part because it never successfully recovered from the notoriety surrounding Mr. Hoy's death.

* * *

"If you're not annoying somebody, you're not really alive."

—**Margaret Atwood**

WEIRD CANADA

Crystal lakes, snow-capped mountains, hockey, Mounties, bilingual traffic signs...and some really, really weird news stories.

TAKING A BITE OUT OF CRIME

Aaron Helferty, 31, was drinking in an Edmonton bar when a group of men he didn't know began berating him. He ignored it...until one man approached him, silently stared at him, then suddenly lunged forward and started chewing on his nose. Two bar employees broke up the fight and threw out the attacker, who'd managed to bite off (and swallow) part of Helferty's nose. Helferty plans to get reconstructive surgery; police can't find the attacker.

YOU WANT THE TOOTH, OFFICER?

Outside Sarnia, Ontario, in June 2010, a driver flagged down a police officer on Highway 402 to warn him of a semi truck meandering all over the road. The officer caught up to the truck and pulled it over. The driver's explanation for his erratic driving: He was attempting to pull out one of his teeth. No longer able to deal with a toothache, he tied one end of a piece of string to the bad tooth and the other to the roof of his cab. "One good bump" and it would come right out, he told the officer. As it turned out, he was right—the officer could tell by the bloody tooth on a string sitting on the seat.

BEEFY VINO

In Japan, Wagyu cattle are fed beer and massaged with sake each day. The result is the richly flavored and expensive (more than $100 a pound) Kobe beef. Seeking to create his own specialty beef market, Bill Freding of Southern Plus Feedlots in Oliver, B.C., has developed his own booze-based method: wine-fed cows. Like the cattle at other high-volume beef producers, Freding's cattle eat a diet of primarily grain. But they also drink a liter of wine every day for 90 days prior to slaughter. The red wine is from wineries in the Okanagan Valley of British Columbia, and Freding claims the beef tastes "sweeter."

PLEASE KNOCK FIRST

For Valentine's Day 2010, the Toronto restaurant Mildred's Temple Kitchen pulled out all the stops for romantic diners—serving intimate meals for two...and openly encouraging couples to "couple" in the restrooms. A handful of concerned citizens reported the Mildred's promotion to the Toronto Public Health office. The agency investigated and found nothing wrong with the idea, as long as frisky patrons stayed out of food-preparation areas.

DIRTY YOUNG MEN

Professor Simon Louis Lajeunesse of the University of Montreal's social work department began a project in December 2009 investigating how pornography affects the way men view and relate to women. Part of that research required a "control group" for comparison, so Lajeunesse advertised around Montreal to recruit 20 young men who did not view pornography. He received zero responses.

BAN-ADA

In the 1910s, Toronto police had full authority over movies, including the right to ban films they considered offensive. The criteria: Any movie that showed a pro-America attitude, murder, or an extramarital romance could be banned. Any movie. In 1911, an inspector reported, "I witnessed a moving picture show of *Hamlet*, written I think by Shakespeare. That's all very well to say it's a famous drama, but it doesn't keep it from being a spectacle of violence." A few weeks later, the same inspector banned a film version of *Romeo and Juliet.*

YOUR (CANADIAN) TAX DOLLARS AT WORK

In June 2006, the federally funded Council for the Arts gave a $9,000 grant to a performance artist named Jess Dobkin. Her performance: She set up a bar called "Lactation Station" where patrons could sample human breast milk. Dobkin modeled the event after a wine tasting, providing milk from six different women. In similar news, the Ontario provincial government gave $150,000 to researchers at Laurentian University to study the sex drive of squirrels.

SOMEONE TO WATCH OVER ME

In the spring of 2013, Google Earth captured an image of a mountainous region that looks like a gigantic Mayan Chieftain in full headdress. The locals call the figure "The Badlands Guardian," and it can only be seen from high in the sky.

Ponoka, Alberta, once forbade the building of mud huts and houses with straw roofs.

ODD-LYMPICS

Canada goes a little nutty over winter sports.

DANCE, CANADA, DANCE!

The closing ceremonies of the Olympics are more or less a giant party—at least after the flame is passed on to the next city, the torch extinguished and the TV cameras go off. At the end of 2010 Winter Olympics in Vancouver, Neil Young sang "Long May You Run" and the network coverage feed went out. The live audience then got to witness a comedy routine from William Shatner, a bizarre performance from Michael Bublé in disguise, a troupe of dancers in Mountie costumes, a dancer dressed as a hockey puck, a life-size reenactment of a tabletop hockey game, and, finally Nickelback.

IT'S GONNA COST YA

Montreal won the right to host the 1976 Summer Olympics in 1970, promising citiziens that it would cost the Quebec provincial government $310 million, which would be offset by the massive cash windfall once the Games began. Instead, cost overruns and labor strikes pushed the final cost to $2 billion. About $800 million of that went to Olympic Stadium, with its state-of-the-art retractable roof on which construction finished...in 1987. Quebec did finally pay off its billions of debt. It enacted a tobacco tax, which erased the Olympics debt... in 2006.

GO PLANET!

The Montreal Olympics velodrome was supposed to cost $5 million to build. Instead, it came it at $59 million. After the Olympics it was repurposed into a biosphere.

UNCLE JOHN APPROVES

The downhill skiing course in 2010 was named the Dave Murray Course, after the legendary Canadian skiier. That's the most normally named part of the track. Individual sections of the three kilometer course are named "the Loveshack," "the Weasel," "Boyd's Chin," "Fallaway," "Coach's Corner," and, "the Toilet Bowl."

The only walled city north of Mexico is Québec City.

HOCKEY? WHO CARES?

At the 2006 Olympics, which were held in Torino, Italy, more than five million Canadians watched the curling events. That's more Canadian viewers than even men's ice hockey.

HEAVY MEDAL

The Vancouver Games had the "greenest medals" in Olympics history. They were made of recycled materials, from reclaimed electronics garbage. Also, no two medals are the same. In a nod to the Olympics spirit of community, medal designer Corrine Hunt first created a giant "patchwork quilt" of all of the medals put together. Each medal is a piece of that artwork.

NO BEARS ALLOWED

In an Olympics first, bears were a major security threat at the Vancouver games, particularly on the perimeter of the athletes village at the Whistler sports facility. But rather than just have armed guards shoot angry bears, conservation officers were charged with bear patrol duty.

YES TO SITTING, NO TO SMOKING

The 1988 Winter Olympics in Calgary marked the first time that competing athletes were allowed to sit in the stands and watch events (not their own events, obviously). The Calgary games were also the first Olympics where smoking was banned.

STAY SAFE

Olympics world record: in 2010, Vancouver Coastal Health, Canadian Foundation for AIDS Research, and British Columbia Centre for Disease Control passed out 100,000 condoms to people in town for the 17-day Games. It's the most prophylactics ever passed out at an Olympics.

*　　*　　*

Ontario Premier Ernie Eves: "Mr. McGuinty just says whatever pops into his little, sharp, pointy head because he thinks that's what you want to hear."

Ontario Liberal Leader Dalton McGuinty: "What if I spear you with my head?"

SUPER NOVA

Nova Scotia has its share of strange foods, slang, ghost ships, and legends.

THE SHAG HARBOUR UFO CASE

On a beautiful, dark but clear evening at about 11:20 pm on October 4, 1964, dozens of people from Shag Harbour, on the southern tip of Nova Scotia, saw many strange lights in the sky, including a huge orange sphere. Some, including members of the Royal Canadian Mounted Police, saw a series of flashing lights that suddenly crashed into the harbor at a 45° angle. A pale yellow light was seen moving underneath the water, before it disappeared.

Fishermen rushed out in their motorboats to try to save any survivors of what was assumed to be a plane crash, but they only found a patch of yellow foam that smelled of sulphur. Authorities put out a call to see if any aircraft were missing, but there were no reports of missing planes or other aircraft. While something had crashed into the water, no one knew what it was. Teams of military divers were sent to search for wreckage. Townspeople reported that they pulled something from the water and drove away with a package, but they would not tell anyone what they found.

The truth about what actually crashed on that night may never be known, but the incident remains one of the most widely seen sightings of what was, technically, a UFO. Each August, the town usually holds a UFO Festival with a barbecue, parade, and people sharing memories of the event.

BRIGHT BLUE LOBSTER

The odds of finding a vibrant blue lobster are one-in-two-million according to the University of Maine's Lobster Institute. But in June of 2012, Bobby Stoddard, a lobster fisherman from Clarks Harbour, Nova Scotia, found one. He and his father have been fishing the waters around Nova Scotia for decades, and Stoddard says that his father actually caught one about 45 years earlier and hadn't seen one since. Stoddard, who hauls in an average of 3,000 lobsters on a good day, is keeping the bright blue one in a tank in his office for folks to come and see.

The Blackberry smartphone was developed in Waterloo, Ontario.

JEROME THE MYSTERY MAN

On September 8, 1863, an unidentified man missing both of his legs was found at the beach of Sandy Cove on the coast of the Bay of Fundy. While the area's residents took him in and cared for him, the man refused to explain how he got there or even give his name. The Acadians dubbed him "Jerome" based on the sound of his grunts; the man spent the rest of his life in almost total silence.

The mystery man became an attraction, and people came from far away to see him. Rumors spread about his true identity: Some said he was an Italian nobleman who had been mutilated out of revenge, others said he was an Italian naval officer who had been abandoned after losing his legs. Still others thought him to be a lumberjack who had lost his legs in an unfortunate accident and was left to die.

The mystery man Jerome has inspired many Acadians and Nova Scotians who have paid tribute to him in song, film, and paintings—but his true origin remains unknown.

EARLY HOCKEY PUCKS WERE HORSE POOP

The boys at Canada's first college—King's College School, established in 1788—played a field game called hurley. A hurley was a wooden stick used to hit a leather ball. Teams would try to get the ball into their opponent's goal. Some students took the game to the ice and ice hurley was invented. That game evolved into ice hockey, and players used skates to zip along the ice more speedily. Boys often played with wooden pucks, but pucks were also made from whatever material was available—heels from boots, compressed tin cans, lumps of coal, and frozen horse droppings, which they referred to as "horse puckies," or "horse apples."

The rubber puck came into play in the late 1880s. Whole balls were originally used as pucks, but when the sport moved indoors, rink owners found that a slice from the middle section of a lacrosse ball made a more manageable puck.

CHIN UP, SURF'S UP

It's hard enough to balance on a surf board, but Doug McManaman can balance a surf board on his chin. In fact, this sturdy-jawed 68-year-old from Cumberland County, Nova Scotia, holds the record for balancing a surfboard on his chin for the longest amount of time—51.47 seconds.

Jordan Tootoo, Cal Clutterbuck, Zarley Zalapski, and Hakan Loob are all real Canadian hockey players.

McManaman calls himself "The Balance King" and holds more than 340 other records, most of them for balancing things on his head. He once balanced a bowling ball, a golf club, and a hockey puck on his head… at the same time.

A GAELIC OLD TIME

Nova Scotia (which in Latin means New Scotland) is the only region outside Scotland where the Gaelic language and culture remain everyday aspects of community life. Gaelic speakers came from the highlands and islands of Scotland to Canada starting in the 1700s. Late in the 19th century, about 100,000 residents of Cape Breton spoke Gaelic.

Today, between 1,000 and 2,000 speak it in the province. Interest in Gaelic heritage is growing again in the area–you'll see Gaelic words on signs, and the language is even taught in high school in Mabou. The Gaelic College of Celtic Arts and Crafts in St Ann's is dedicated to preserving the language. It hosts more than 1,000 students each summer from around the world, who study the language, piping, fiddling, singing, dance, and other customs. A few Gaelic words that have become part of the local dialect in Nova Scotia are : *boomaler* (an oaf), *sgudal* (garbage), and *skiff* (snow)

YOU CAN GET THERE FROM HERE

In July 2010, Italian couple Valerio Torresi and Serena Tavoloni boarded a plane in Rome that they thought was heading to Sydney, Australia. When they touched down in Halifax, Nova Scotia, they weren't concerned. They thought they were merely changing planes for the final leg of the journey. While they did change planes, their final destination was off by about 16,818 kilometers (10,451 miles). They arrived in Sydney–but Sydney, Nova Scotia.

Their travel agent had goofed and booked them on a flight to the wrong city. The wayward travelers were rewarded for their misadventure.

They enjoyed free accommodation and a lobster dinner, and an Italian-speaking local gave the couple a grand tour of the sites before they were able to get a flight to the slightly more popular Sydney, Australia.

In Nanuvut, the farthest Northern part of Canada, cabbage can cost $28 and chicken $65 a pound.

MORE CANADA THE BIG

More big (and weird) stuff from a big (and weird) country.

Object: A huge hockey stick

Place: Duncan, B.C.

Story: It's only natural that a hockey-loving nation has the world's largest hockey stick and puck. A 62.5-meter- (205-foot-) stick made of Douglas fir and reinforced with steel adorns the community center in Duncan on Vancouver Island. Forty times life-size, the stick weighs in at a whopping 27,700 kilograms (61,000 pounds). The government of Canada commissioned it as part of the Expo '86 World's Fair Exposition in Vancouver. *Guinness World Records* officially recognized Duncan's stick as the world's largest on July 14, 2008, after a 20-year battle. Eveleth, Minnesota, also had "the world's largest hockey stick," but it's a puny 32.6 meters (107 feet).

Object: The big apple

Place: Colborne, Ontario

Story: A nearly 11-meter- (35-foot-) apple—complete with an observation deck and a restaurant inside—shines in Colborne, Ontario. The apple is part of a small enterprise called The Big Apple, which sells pies and sandwiches. The attraction lures in visitors with a rabbit-petting park and miniature golf.

Object: Mucho dinero

Place: Ontario

Story: Sudbury is home to a 9-meter- (30-foot-) tall 1951 Canadian nickel. It is the only item left from what was to be a "numismatic theme park." (Nothing says "action park" like coin collecting!) In Campbellford, Ontario, an 8-meter- (27-foot-) tall two-dollar coin looms over the villagers. Campbellford is the hometown of the artist who drew the polar bear on the "toonie." In 1992, Echo Bay, Ontario, paid a similar honor to local Robert-Ralph Carmichael who designed the loonie. The town erected a big replica of the coin along the highway.

A study in Institute of Physics' journal found that global warming could kill outdoor hockey.

Object: Big bunnocks

Place: Macklin, Saskatchewan

Story: When you think Macklin, think enormous horse anklebone. A nearly 10-meter- (32-foot) fiberglass horse anklebone greets travelers at the town's tourist information center. Bunnock is the name of that bone, and it's also the name of a game played in Macklin. It originated with German and Russian soldiers posted in Siberia in the late 1800s. The "game of bones" was brought to the Macklin area by Russian and German settlers in the early 1900s. The game has been called a cross between bowling and curling—two teams square off on opposite sides and try to knock over their opponent's row of standing bunnocks by throwing bones at the bunnocks. The town still hosts the World Bunnock Championship every year.

Object: A huge, horned human

Place: Gimli, Manitoba

Story: A 4.6-meter- (15-foot-) tall Viking stands watching over the shores of Lake Winnipeg in Gimli, Manitoba. Gimli boasts the largest Icelandic population outside of Iceland. In Norse mythology, Gimli is the home of the Gods. In the 1870s, Icelandic settlers established the Republic of New Iceland in Gimli and surrounding towns. In midsummer, the Icelandic festival known as "Islendingadagurinn" attracts about 30,000 people—many wearing Viking helmets. Costumed re-enactors depict life in Viking times and demonstrate Viking weapons and warfare. Contests include pole vaulting and Islendingadunk, a combination pillow fight and jousting match where opponents sit on poles suspended over water and try to dunk each other.

Gimli is also the setting for the creepy and expressionist Guy Maddin film *Tales from Gimli Hospital*. And Gimli is home to the *Gimli Glider*, an Air Canada jet that, in July of 1983, ran out of fuel at 12,500 meters (41,000 feet). The crew was able to glide it to a safe emergency landing. How can a plane not have enough fuel? The metric system is partially to blame. The accident happened shortly after Canada converted from the imperial system to the metric system, and the fuel tank was filled inadequately due to a misunderstanding of the newly adopted system of measurement.

Actor Leslie Nielsen's brother Erik was the Deputy Prime Minister of Canada.

OTHER MINOR GIANTS

• A 9.8-meter- (32-foot-) tall Tin Soldier stands guard over New Minster, British Columbia.

• A colossal cowboy casts a very long shadow in Airdrie, Alberta. He stands about nine meters (30 feet) tall in a cowboy hat and moustache.

• Visit Medicine Hat to see the "World's Largest Teepee," a metal-pipe construction 68.5 meters (215 feet) tall. (But then where do you go to see the world's largest medicine hat?)

• The world's largest dinosaur (25 meters, 82 feet tall) continuously bares its fiberglass teeth in Drumheller, Alberta.

• For moose fans, the largest of these beasts is Mac in, naturally, Moose Jaw, Saskatchewan. The world's most sizable moose is made of over 9,000 kilograms (10 tons) of concrete and steel.

• The biggest furry tree gnasher resides in Beaverlodge, Alberta. Built in 2004, the 4.5-meter- (15-foot-) tall bucktooth critter perches on a 6-meter- (20-foot-) long log and weighs over 1,300 kilograms (a ton and a half).

• A depiction in flight, the statue of the giant duck in Andrew, Alberta, was erected to spotlight the duck breeding grounds in the local wetlands. With its 7-meter (23-foot) wingspan, the fowl flies above a local playground, and some jokingly warn about the huge droppings that the big quacker might leave behind.

• Montreal, Quebec, has a gargantuan fruit—a three-story plastic orange that's been serving orange juice since 1942.

• The biggest furry tree gnasher resides in Beaverlodge, Alberta. Built in 2004, the 4.5-meter- (15-foot-) tall bucktooth critter perches on a 6-meter- (20-foot-) long log and weighs over 1,300 kilograms (a ton and a half).

• A 3-meter- (10-foot-) tall buffalo reminds travelers to Wainwright, Alberta, that this was the site of Canada's biggest buffalo herd.

• The world's largest tractor weathervane calls attention to the Canadian Tractor Museum in Westlock, Alberta. The museum displays rare and just plain interesting vintage tractors.

Canada won most gold medals ever (14) at a Winter Olympics (2010).

EVEN HOSERS HAVE HOMETOWNS

Many of Canada's cities and provinces have unusual, even downright wacky, nicknames.

TORONTO

• **The Big Smoke:** Home to several mega-story smokestacks.

• **Hogtown:** This is not a derogatory reflection of Toronto citizens, but a reference to the fact that for many years the city was home to several pork processing plants.

• **Muddy York:** In its early days, the city was called York. It earned this nickname because the streets were unpaved and lacked storm drains. Every time it rained, the streets became huge mud pits.

BRITISH COLUMBIA

• **Skookum:** A "big and mighty" province deserves this nickname with the same meaning in Chinook, a language developed with words from French, English, Salish, Nootka and other local languages.

VANCOUVER

• **Lotusland:** Vancouver gained this nickname due to the fact that residents enjoy an apparently more idyllic lifestyle than elsewhere in Canada. Lotusland is a reference to a section of Homer's *Odyssey*. In this part of the classic tale, Odysseus visits a land where the native residents live under the influence of an edible narcotic lotus.

• **North Hollywood:** Vancouver's earned this nickname due to the large number of movies filmed in the city thanks to its ability to look like any large metropolitan area. (See page x.)

• **Gastown:** In its very early days, what is considered the city's core downtown area was first settled. One of the very first settlers in this area was John "Gassy Jack" Deighton, a riverboat pilot who opened a saloon there. The area soon became known as Gastown, after Gassy Jack. Don't worry though, in those days people were called gassy if they talked a lot, not because of . . . well, you know.

VICTORIA

• **Chicktoria:** There are a few theories for this nickname: the women in Victoria are

In spring 2013, waves of ice 9 meters (29'6") destroyed at least six homes in Ochre River, MB.

particularly attractive; there are more women there than men; or the city's colleges attract a large number of female students.

• **The Little Smoke:** As opposed to Toronto, "The Big Smoke."

• **The Island:** What Vancouver residents call Victoria.

CALGARY

• **Cowgary:** Calgary is the ranching capital of Canada and home to the Calgary Stampede, one of the largest rodeos in the world.

EDMONTON

• **The Big Onion:** New York is known as The Big Apple. This nickname was given to Edmonton in an effort to compare it with New York.

• **Deadmonton:** People use this nickname for one of two reasons: the city was often thought of as a boring place to be, and in recent years, it's been home to an increasing murder rate.

• **Redmonton:** It's a more liberal area of the country, electing few Conservative candidates.

HAMILTON

• **Steeltown:** The steel industry has always been central to the economic life of Hamilton.

• **The Hammer:** Another reference to steel manufacturing.

OTTAWA

• **Bytown:** This was the original name of the town, named after Colonel By, a British engineer and one of the city's founders.

WINNIPEG

• **Winterpeg:** Yes, winters are very cold in Winnipeg. The average low temperature in January is about -9 degrees F and the average high is 10 degrees F.

ST. JOHN'S

• **The City of Legends:** St. John's earned this nickname because it is theorized to be the oldest major city in North America, founded before 1620.

• **Sin City:** A mispronunciation of the St. in St. John's led to this nickname.

HALIFAX

• **Dalifax:** Dalhousie University is located in Halifax. Or some people just refer to the city as The Fax.

QUEBEC

• **La Vieille Capitale City:** Literally "the old capital city," which it once was.

MONTREAL

• **The 5-1-4:** Montreal's area code.

• **Real City:** Break apart Montreal and you've got Mont and Real—hence the nickname.

• **La Metropole:** So called because the city was once the economic capital of Quebec and the biggest "metropolitan" area there.

KITCHENER AND WATERLOO

• **K-W:** These two cities share everything, almost as if they're one and the same city.

SASKATOON

• **Toontown:** Catchy nickname taken from the city's actual name.

WINDSOR

• **Motor City C-A:** It's the leading car manufacturer in Canada.

* * *

DEVON ISLAND

Imagine a place so remote, so barren, that it's been used as a doppelganger for the surface of Mars. A place so barren, that almost nothing grows there. This place is Devon Island, the largest uninhabited island on earth.

Known in Inuit as *Tatlurutit*, Devon is located in Baffin Bay, Nunavut. It's a polar desert: Except for the Truelove Lowland, which supports a small population of musk oxen, foxes, and polar bears, the climate is too cold and dry for much plant or animal life to grow. Even during the summer, the temperature seldom gets above 10 degrees Celsius, and in the winter it can get as low as negative 50 degrees.

There were some attempts to settle Devon Island in the 1930s and 40s, but the climate proved too inhospitable. Nothing remains today but some ruins and the graves of some of the settlers. However, though there are no permanent residents, the Mars Society established a simulated base there from 2001–2009. "Astronauts" lived in a simulated Mars base according to the Martian solar cycle, performed simulated "extravehicular activities," and tested equipment that might one day be used to explore the Red Planet. Though all activities outside the station took place in spacesuits, one "out-of-simulation" crew member was required to come along on all trips outside the base. Their job? To watch out for the very non-Martian danger of polar bears.

In Nova Scotia, "some" is used as "very." As in: "It's some hot out."

THE STOPWATCH GANG

They pulled off the biggest gold heist in Canada's history and more than 100 bank robberies–usually in under two minutes.

QUITE THE RÉSUMÉ

Stephen Reid was a born criminal. By the age of 21, in 1972, he had put together a pretty good resume of criminal activity–shoplifting, drug dealing, and robbery. A series of robberies earned him a 10 year sentence in Warkworth Penitentiary in Campbellford, Ontario. A year and a half into his stretch Reid had earned points for good behavior setting up athletics programs for the other inmates. His good deeds earned him a day pass to attend a seminar on prison fitness programs. On the way back he asked the guard to stop for some Chinese food. Food in the prison was pretty bleak after all. During the meal he excused himself to go to the bathroom, slipped out a window, and escaped. It was a bold first step on what proved to be a truly audacious career.

THE GREAT GOLD HEIST

Reid settled in Ottawa and teamed up with Paddy Mitchell and Lionel Wright, two well established criminals. In an Ottawa bar one night the three of them overheard an Air Canada employee describing how gold bars that were being shipped from an Ontario mine to the Royal Canadian Mint were often left unattended overnight at Ottawa International Airport. The three professional robbers hatched a plan. Mitchell knew a petty thief who worked at the airport and could get them inside. Reid led the way, disguised as a baggage handler. The three men waylaid the guard, slipped a hood over his head, and handcuffed him to a pipe, gaining access to the gold room. But they didn't carry anything out of the airport. In yet another audacious move, they simply shipped the gold bars to themselves. They boxed them up, slapped a shipping label on them, and left them in the cargo area. "Air Canada very generously delivered them to us in Windsor the next day," said Mitchell. The six gold bars were worth $700,000–the biggest gold heist in Canadian history.

FAST WORK

The three men went on a crime spree that has become the stuff of legend. They robbed over 100 banks. Their robberies were both spectacular and meticulous. Their tactics were so clever that Hollywood often copied them, notably in *Beverly Hills Cop II* and *Point Break*. Reid came up with the idea of phoning in a bomb threat across town to distract the police. Mitchell came up with the disguises they wore, including, famously, masks of ex Presidents. But their most famous tactic was the stopwatch. Reid would wear a stopwatch around his neck and keep time during a heist. They would be in and out of a bank, usually, in under 90 seconds. Although they used guns, they were extremely polite to the people they robbed. Their motto was "nobody gets hurt," and nobody ever did, earning them the nick name The Gentle Bandits. But it was the name given them by the FBI that eventually stuck. They were called The Stopwatch Gang.

In 1975 Reid and Mitchell were pinched and sent to Millhaven Maximum Security Prison. Three years later, Reid was transferred to a minimum security penitentiary where he was captain of the prison hockey team and studied to be a hair stylist. In 1979, Reid got another day pass and he escaped again in the very same way. He convinced the guard to stop for fish and chips and then slipped out the back of the men's room. He was so cheeky this time that he had arranged to be picked up at a nearby Holliday Inn beforehand.

About two weeks later, Mitchell suffered an apparent heart attack and was rushed to a hospital. Two attendants wheeled him from the ambulance into the emergency room, and then came running out to tell the guards that Mitchell had jumped off the gurney and fled down the hall. The guards gave chase. In a few minutes, the two attendants wheeled someone out of the hospital and into the same ambulance. Then they drove away. The attendants were Reid and Wright, and Mitchell was on the gurney. Once again, the gang's daring had beaten the hapless police.

SOUTH OF THE BORDER

Canada being too hot for the gang now, they headed for the States. They settled in Arizona and began the final leg of their legendary spree. At this time there was a series of bank heists going on up and down the West Coast, and the Stopwatch Gang became the most

File under "Hard to Verify": A dog sled team can kill and devour a man in under 3 minutes.

notorious bank robbers in a crowded field. They were extremely careful and methodical. Mitchell would search death records for people who were about the same ages as them and then order duplicate birth certificates. They would carefully pick a bank and begin to case it. Using their fake IDs, they would open bank accounts, gaining access to the banks methods and systems. Nobody was suspicious of three new customers coming in, chatting with the tellers, and watching the guards. They would figure out the schedule of the armored cars. When they had the routes and timing down, they would strike. They rented cars and then stole license plates to hide the vehicles identities. They entered the bank ahead of time and waited for the armored cars to arrive. They would wait for the first bags, with the coin, to pass and then strike when the bags of cash were brought in. They would pull their guns and make everyone lie down on the floor, grab the bags and the guard's gun, and then split. They were the quickest heists ever. Once they had fled the scene they would strip out of their disguises and drop them into a garbage bag. Lionel Wright would dump it into a dumpster that was about to be picked up while Reid and Mitchell switched the license plates back. Then they would just drive away.

Their run of success was amazing. They lived for years in Arizona under the guise of successful concert promoters, giving them a good reason to travel. Reid even befriended the local sheriff and once, when the Sheriff asked him what he did for a living, Reid replied "I rob banks." The Sheriff thought that was funny.

THE END

In September 1980 the Stopwatch Gang pulled off its biggest bank heist, hitting a Bank of America in San Diego when two armored cars were making a morning delivery. They made away with $283,000, but they were sloppy. Wright dumped the disguises into the wrong dumpster and the police found them before the garbage truck picked it up. They soon found where the cars had been rented. This led to a tip as to the gang's whereabouts. They were busted and sent back to prison yet again.

While locked up this time, Reid wrote a novel titled *Jack Rabbit Parole*. A copy made its way to Canadian poet Susan Musgrove, who was so impressed with the writing that she arranged to meet Reid.

The two fell in love and ultimately got married and had a baby girl. In 1986, Reid busted loose again. He was serving time in an Arizona prison when he escaped through an air conditioning vent, but He was recaptured not long after. In 1987, Reid got parole and reportedly enjoyed his family life for 12 years. By 1999, addicted to heroin and deeply in debt, another bank robbery landed him back in prison. He was paroled in 2008. Mitchell died of lung cancer while in a prison in North Carolina. Lionel Wright's whereabouts are unknown.

* * *

BETTER WEAR NEW SHOES

The emperor may need new clothes, but the Canadian Minister of Finance must have new shoes. In an unusual tradition, the Minister of Finance is supposed to buy and wear new shoes on the day he or she delivers the country's budget. This occurs on a day aptly named Budget Day. The first mention of new shoes appeared on March 31, 1960, when Donald Fleming was finance minister. A newspaper report refers to the new shoes as a budget tradition, but mysteriously there seems to be no other mention of it prior to Fleming.

Finance ministers have since gotten a little creative with the tradition—John Crosbie wore used mukluks to present the budget in 1979. In 2008, Jim Flaherty wore resoled shoes to show he was being financially conservative. The tradition has spread to the provincial finance ministers. In 2005, Colin Hansen in British Columbia sported new running shoes when presenting the budget. In a twist, Stockwell Day, Alberta's treasurer in the late 1990s, showed off inline skating gear and a crash helmet to highlight his budget's new direction. Nunavut finance minister Kelvin Ng donned a new pair of caribou-skin boots when he unveiled his government's first budget in 1999. That same year, British Columbia's Joy MacPhail wore a pair of second-hand shoes to sell a bad-news budget when she was the New Democratic Party's (NDP's) finance minister. Her successor, Paul Ramsey, bought discounted suede loafers to deliver the NDP budget. He thought the economical shoes made a statement about the budget, which would serve the needs of families.

Actor Brendan Fraser's grandfather was a member of Royal Canadian Mounted Police.

THE ROCK 'N' ROLL LIFE OF THE STANLEY CUP

The most famous trophy in sports has probably led a more interesting life than you have.

THE ULTIMATE AWARD

The Cup, which stands almost a meter (about three feet) tall and weighs 15.5 kilograms (34.5 pounds), has traveled from the tops of mountains to strip clubs and churches. It has served as potato chip bowl and used to store horse feed. It has been aboard motorcycles, traveled to a war zone, and held under Niagara Falls. Why has the Cup led such an adventure-filled life? It's because of a unique tradition—every player on every championship team gets at least 24 hours to do virtually whatever he wishes with old Stan. Here are some tales from Stanley's Canadian winners:

• In 1905, one of the very inebriated Ottawa Silver Seven (now the Senators) was dared to drop-kick the Stanley Cup into the city's Rideau Canal. The only problem was the canal was frozen solid. When the kicker and his partying teammates heard the beloved Cup bounce and skid across the ice, they realized their mistake and wisely decided to go home and sober up. The next day they returned to reclaim a battered and newly dented Stanley.

• In 1907, the Montreal Wanderers came together for a photo shoot and left the Cup behind. The photographer's mother used it as a flower pot until someone came to collect it a few months later.

• In 1924, the Montreal Canadiens won the Stanley Cup and threw it in the trunk of a car before heading to a victory party. On the way, the car got a flat tire so the trophy was taken out to get the spare. They quickly fixed the flat and were on their merry way, except for one thing—they had left the trophy in a snow bank at the side of the road.

• In 1927, after the Ottawa Senators won the Cup, King Clancy used it to hold junk mail, pencils, gum, and cigars.

• In 1964, Red Kelly, a Canadian who played on eight Stanley Cup–winning teams, sat his little son in the Cup, and the boy proceeded to urinate. Kelly laughs every time he sees players drinking from it now.

• In 1979, Guy Lafleur of the Montreal Canadiens placed the trophy in his front yard in Thuro, Quebec, so all the neighbors could see and enjoy it.

• At least two players have allowed the family dog to eat from the polished chalice. In 1980, Clark Gillies fed his dog out of Stanley. Then in 2006, Anaheim Ducks' Sean O'Donnell gave his dog Buddy, a black lab who had lost one leg to cancer, the chance to dine from the trophy.

• When the Edmonton Oilers took the championship in 1987, the Cup wound up on the runway with an exotic dancer at the Forum Inn, just across from the Northland Coliseum.

• In 1991, Mario Lemieux of the Pittsburgh Penguins found the Cup at the bottom of his swimming pool. It had served as a giant cham¬pagne flute the night before.

• Martin Brodeur, a goalie with the New Jersey Devils, drove around Montreal with it strapped in the passenger seat so all could see it in 1995. In 2000, he took the Cup to the movies and his kids ate popcorn out of it.

• Sylvain Lefebvre, who played with the Colorado Avalanche, baptized his daughter in the Cup in 1996.

• In 1997, Detroit Red Wing Steve Yzerman could not bear to part with the trophy he had worked for 14 years to win. After the Red Wings crushed the Flyers in four games, a sleepless and very joyful Captain Yzerman took a shower with Stanley.

• In 2001, Rob Blake of the Colorado Avalanche took Stanley back to his family's farm in Simcoe, Ontario. While there, his little brother David hoisted the shiny prize onto the roof of a combine.

• In 2004, when Jay Feaster, general manager of the Tampa Bay Lightning, wanted a tour of the space shuttle *Discovery*, he was told to bring the Stanley Cup along in exchange. Throughout the day a long line of NASA employees—quality assurance specialists, technicians, and inquisitive scientists—all waited to pose for photos with the Cup and celebrate the hometown team's Lightening victory.

Alex Trebek's first hosting job in the U.S. was for a show called *The Wizard of Odds.*

• On its way to a charity event in Vancouver in 2010, the Cup was routed to another Canadian city. It was soon discovered that Stanley's large and unmarked case had not one, but *two* listed destinations—Vancouver and the trophy's hometown of Toronto. It was later recovered by an Air Canada employee. As the CBC reported, "For the record, the Stanley Cup made a subsequent trip to California unscathed."

The Stanley Cup now has a bodyguard and protector who is with it 24 hours a day—except when the winning players have it. The Keeper of the Cup or the Cup Cop keeps a watchful eye on the prize and transports it to various events around the world.

However, there is a caveat: In another odd twist to the Stanley Cup saga is the fact that there is really more than one beloved Cup. So the Cup that the Cup Cop watches over is not, in fact, the original. Until 1970, the winning team was given the original trophy. After that the original Stanley—too brittle to be taken on the road—was put on permanent public retirement in the Hockey Hall of Fame in Toronto. The winning team today takes home what is known as the Presentation Cup. This accounts for the first two versions. The third Cup, known as the Replica Cup, was created to make appearances when the presentation cup is not available.

* * *

CANADIANS LAUGH IT OFF

Canada is known for producing some great comedians—John Candy, Mike Myers, Jim Carrey, The Kids in the Hall, etc. It's no wonder that the first ever laughing competition was held in Montreal in October 2010. Ten of Quebec's jolliest residents brought their best guffaws to the Grand Laughing Championship. Filmmaker Allen Nerenberg created the contest, touting the health benefits of laughter: He says it's good for the heart and the immune system, and relieves stress. Judges at this first laughing event selected Nicole Veillette of Ste-Eustache, Quebec for having the best, most contagious laugh. It is contagious: laughing championships have since been held in the U.S., the UK, France, the Czech Republic, Slovenia, and Japan. Depending on the competition, top laughers might vie for titles such as "Best Maniacal Laugher," "Best Alabama Knee Slapper," and "Most Contagious Belly Laugh."

Winnie the Pooh was inspired by a bear cub from Canada named Winnipeg.

THE SOUTHERN MENACE

Planning for hostilities between Canada and the United States has been very real.

STRANGE BUT TRUE COLORS

It may seem strange in this time of prolonged peace between the United States, Canada, and Great Britain, but in the late 1920s and early 1930s American military personnel drafted a plan to attack Canada in the event of a trade war with England. As it was purely a contingency plan, it was never close to being implemented. However, the American government invested $57 million just to build air bases on the Canadian border—so there was definitely a degree of seriousness involved.

Dubbed "War Plan Red," it was one of several strategies for potential attacks by other world powers. "War Plan Green" focused on Mexico, "Orange" on Japan, "Yellow" on China, and "Black" on Germany. (There was even one plan, "White," drawn up in the event of a domestic uprising!) To add to the strangeness, War Plan Red had several "sub-shades" for other British-related nations: "Crimson" for Canada, "Scarlet" for Australia, and "Garnet" for New Zealand.

CHARGE OF THE LIGHT RIFLES

Anti-British sentiment was at a high during the American Great Depression, as England owed the United States $14 billion incurred during the fighting of World War I. A particularly tense 1927 Geneva Naval Conference didn't help. While military planners knew a war to be unlikely, governmental pressure to keep strategic and tactical skills up-to-date lent extra motivation to War Plan Red.

The thought was that, in the event of an attack, Britain would use Canada as an entry point into the U.S. In defense, War Plan Red called for the capture of the port city of Halifax, preventing the British from resupplying; taking over power plants near Niagara Falls; and having the U.S. Navy block access to Canada's Atlantic and Pacific ports.

Additionally, the plan had American troops invading Canada on three distinct fronts: storming Winnipeg via North Dakota to shut down operations of the major railway center there, marching through Vermont to take over Montreal and Quebec, and capturing valuable

What does Canadian company Stinky Moose sell? Cloth diapers.

nickel mines in Ontario. Additional battalions of "light rifles"—the nickname for soldiers who could both run and fight—would work to control bridgeheads in Buffalo, Detroit, and Sault Ste. Marie.
If all this wasn't enough, the Americans had a plan for a hypothetical British-Canadian victory in which the U.S. would be forced to cede Alaska. The response? To use the build-up of American naval forces to take Bermuda and the UK's other Caribbean territories.

A LEAK IN AMERICA'S ROOF

While most of the planning was theoretical in nature, the Americans did some actual reconnaissance, including sending Charles Lindbergh to Hudson Bay to scout possible areas for land invasion. In December 1930, the U.S. Naval attaché in Ottawa reported to the Joint Board of the Army and Navy that Canada "had no idea of trouble with any other country" and was thus unprepared for war.

In 1934 an amendment approved bombing Halifax, Montreal, and Quebec City if need be, as well as authorized the use of chemical weapons. The following year the plan was updated further to specify which roads were best for an invasion—Route 99 to Vancouver, for instance, easily accessed through Bellingham, Washington. It was also the year the plan to build the aforementioned air bases was leaked by the Government Printing Office in a printing mix-up; the office's published report, "Air Defense Bases: Hearings before the Committee on Military Affairs, House of Representatives, Seventy-Fourth Congress," was picked up by the New York Times and ran on the front page of the May 1, 1935 edition.

A hole in the War Plan Red was America's ill-preparedness for the possibility of Canada declaring its neutrality. One thing was for certain, though: if America staved off British attack, captured land would not be returned: "Blue intentions are to hold in perpetuity all CRIMSON and RED territory gained," an appendix to the plan boldly declared.

TOUR PLAN RED

With America secretly on the offensive, history showed that both the UK and Canada had plans to invade the U.S. going back several years before War Plan Red. "Defence Scheme No. 1" was the Canadian plan, drafted by Lieutenant Colonel James Sutherland "Buster" Brown, a World War I hero and then-Director of Military Operations and Intelligence. Created in 1921, a full nine years before the American plan, Defence Scheme No. 1 called for immediate Canadian takeover of

Seattle, Spokane, and Portland. This would be followed by an invasion of Albany, Minneapolis, and Fargo, as well as a marine attack of Maine. As troops withdrew they would be instructed to demolish bridges and railroads. The ultimate goal of the many-faceted invasion was to buy time while waiting for British backup.

Brown did his own reconnaissance for the plan, taking a cohort of plainclothes lieutenants-colonel into American territory. The reconnaissance mission had an air of tourism about it, as the Canadians snapped photos with their own cameras and picked up free maps at various filling stations.

With a strong streak of isolationism running through Canada at that time, Defence Scheme No. 1 didn't make much of an impact with the top brass. In 1928 Chief of the General Staff Andrew McNaughton withdrew it from discussion and destroyed many related documents. It has never been confirmed whether the Americans and Canadians knew of each other's plans.

BACK ON (THE LAUGH) TRACK

The British, too, had a strategy for war with the U.S. While not as formalized as the plans by the Americans and Canadians, the general consensus among Royal Navy officers was that the U.S. was simply too powerful to invade; they would have to intercept any American fleets coming across the Atlantic from a territory such as Bermuda, and call upon Canada to attack American ports and disrupt trade.

War Plan Red was finally declassified in 1974. While it is now an object of curiosity, the 94-page document is a reminder of how unstable the geopolitical climate was in the years following World War I. U.S. President Franklin Roosevelt assured Canadians he had no plans for war in 1935, and later dismissed any intent to invade the UK as "wholly inapplicable."

* * *

SOLVE THIS PUZZLE

The artist and designer Josh Chalom works in an interesting medium—Rubik's Cubes. In 2013, the Toronto-based Chalom unveiled his mosaic depicting the skyline of Macau, China, made from 85,794 puzzles. Stretching 67 meters (220 feet) long and 4 meters (13 feet) high, the artwork claimed the title of biggest Rubik's Cube mosaic ever. It may come as no surprise: Chalom says that he loves to play with Rubik's Cubes.

A message in a bottle washed up in Croatia 28 years after being thrown into the sea off Nova Scotia.

HAUNTED HAUNTS

Ghost stories abound in the Canada, and they often have tragic tales behind them. Here are some of our favorite spooooky places.

THE KEG MANSION

The Keg Mansion is a Toronto restaurant housed in a gothic manor that has the classic look of a haunted house. (In fact, it was used often for exterior shots on *Alfred Hitchcock Presents.*) The home became part of The Keg Steakhouse franchise in 1976, but prior to that it had been owned by the industrialist Hart Massey, who founded Massey Ferguson, a farm equipment and tractor producer. Massey's daughter, Lillian, died in 1915 at age 61 on the second floor of the mansion. Many said that her health declined after her husband died six years earlier. And that's not the only untimely death in the house. As the story goes, a maid was so distraught over Lillian's death that she hung herself in the vestibule.

The mansion also had a secret underneath it—a tunnel connecting to the original Wellesley Hospital building. Hart Massey used it to quietly bring his son, Frederick, in for tuberculosis treatment. Many who visit the restaurant today say they feel a presence in the women's restroom on the second floor. One woman reported that she hung a bag containing a bottle of wine on the back of the stall door. She heard the bag rustle and then saw it move off the hook. Instead of crashing to the floor, it gently lowered to her feet. Another diner said that the stall door unlocked and was opened by an unseen force. Also spotted: a woman with a noose around her neck, while others have heard children's footsteps coming from the second floor, when no one was up there. A young boy has been spotted running up and down the staircase and is sometimes seen looking down on diners.

BANFF SPRINGS HOTEL

Often shrouded in the mists of the Canadian Rockies, the deluxe, castle-like Banff Springs Hotel can sometimes have an eerie air about it. While the hotel, which dates back to 1888, denies that it is haunted, there are a few legends of guests who checked in and never checked out. One of the hotel's ghostly tales concerns room 873, known as "the missing room." Although there is a room 773 below the eighth floor and a room 973 above, there is no room 873 where you would expect. As you walk

Charles Fenerty, a poet from Halifax, was the first person to use wood fibers to make paper in 1844.

down each hallway, there is a light above each room's door. Where room 873 should be, there is a light above but no door—just a wall. At the baseboard, there is a cut marking where a door should be, and if you knock on the wall, it has a hollow sound.

The story is that at some point many decades ago, a mother, father, and at least one little girl were murdered in room 873. After a police investigation, the room was cleaned up, refurbished, and rented out to tourists again. But some of the new guests heard hollow screams and others saw bloody handprints appearing on the mirrors in the room. As the legend goes, the hotel decided to finally seal off the site of the horrific crime. But some visitors have reported seeing the spirits of the family roaming in this hallway.

Then there is the story of the doomed bride who either tripped on her wedding gown and fell down the stairs to her death or brushed against some candles, lighting her gown on fire and taking a deadly spill down the stairs. Guests swear they have seen the image of a woman with a burning wedding dress abruptly disappear into thin air.

The ghost of Sam McCauley also shows up occasionally, and this is one apparition with a history that is easily traced. Sam worked at the hotel for more than 40 years, and he told everyone that he'd be sure to haunt the hotel after he died. Some guests have spotted a bellhop in full uniform who fits McCauley's description. An older couple who was visiting swore that an older man helped them with their bags, but at the time none of the bellhops were over the age of 30. There have been sightings of a headless bagpiper and a ghostly bartender who warns guests when they've had too much to drink, but some of these visions may have been from just that—too much to drink.

THE GIBRALTAR POINT LIGHTHOUSE

In 1815, J. P. Rademuller—the first lightkeeper on the Toronto islands—met an untimely end. To make some extra money, he smuggled beer from the United States and sold it to the Canadians. Supposedly, some drunken soldiers from Fort York came to get beer from Rademuller one day and he refused to sell them any. Enraged by his refusal, they beat poor Rademuller.

Even after being clobbered, he refused to sell the soldiers beer. They didn't take too kindly to his refusal, so they killed Rademuller by hacking his body apart and buried him around the lighthouse. It's been said that on foggy nights, Rademuller's ghost can be seen lurking about the premises, and his moans can be heard rising from

Buttertubs Drive, Dingle Bingle Hill Terrace, and Jingle Pot Road are streets in Nanaimo, B.C.

beneath the sea-soaked floorboards.

THE WEIRD JOURNEY OF CHARLES FRANCIS COGHLAN

Charles Francis Coghlan was a popular actor in Europe and North America in the late 1800s. While visiting Galveston, Texas, in 1899 at the age of 57, he made his "final exit." He specified in his will that he wished to be buried on Prince Edward Island, where he had bought some property for his retirement. His body was placed in a metal casket until the final arrangements could be determined. Nearly a year after his death his body still had not been moved. When the Galveston Hurricane of 1900 struck, his coffin was swept away. On January 15, 1907, the *New York Times* reported that a hunter had found his casket partially buried in a marsh, 29 kilometers (18 miles) inland from Galveston.

That report was accepted as the final word on Coghlan's ending—until 1929. That year *Ripley's Believe It or Not* reported that Coghlan's casket was found by fishermen off the coast of… Prince Edward Island. His coffin had apparently been caught in the Gulf Stream and had mysteriously made it to its proper resting place. Now that tale is generally accepted as folklore. But one question does remain unanswered: What happened to the body of Charles Francis Coghlan?

* * *

A LIGHT READ

Many of us have to put on reading glasses when we crack open a book. If you want to read *Teeny Ted from Turnip Town*, however, you'll need to have your electron microscope handy. Measuring just 0.07 millimeters by 0.10 millimeters (.003 inches by .004 inches), *Teeny Ted* is the world's smallest book. To get an idea of how small this tome is, the head of a pin is about 2 millimeters (.08 inches). So the book is at least 20 times smaller. Physicists in the nanoimaging lab of Simon Fraser University (SFU) in Burnaby, British Columbia, created the book with 30 microtablets, using a gallium-ion beam and an electron microscope. The SFU team made 20 copies, and the book even has an International Standard Book Number (ISBN-978-1- 894897-17-4). The cost: $20,000. It may be a hefty price for a microscopic read, but you'll always have room for it.

MAD MUSEUMS

Who needs paintings, sculptures, and dinosaur bones when you've got gophers, potatoes, and Star Trek?

Museum: Gopher Hole Museum

Location: Torrington, Alberta

Details: Have you ever dreamed of seeing a gopher dressed as Mountie? Or maybe you've fantasized about gophers working as hairdressers and styling each other's locks. How about a gopher dressed as a preacher or an angel gopher with a halo and harp floating in the air above his head? At the Gopher Hole Museum in Torrington, Alberta (just north of Calgary), these visions are all on display for you to behold and admire. About the size of a garage, the museum displays 44 dioramas with 71 stuffed gophers (really Richardson's ground squirrels, to be accurate) elaborately dressed as townspeople doing a wide range of activities, including bank officer, robber, and firefighter. Don't miss: The gophersmith hammering at his anvil; the clown gopher clutching his balloons; a '50s-style female gopher showing off her poodle skirt while holding hands with a young male gopher in a leather jacket.

Museum: Canadian Potato Museum

Location: O'leary, PEI

Details: Potatoes are an important crop for the residents of Prince Edward Island, so it's no surprise that O'Leary has its own potato museum. The museum is serious for the most part, displaying information about the history of potato farming and the numerous types of potatoes. Visitors can see an expansive collection of farm machinery and implements. Don't miss: Tiny coffins, each holding an infected potato that has gone on to the great spud farm in the sky.

Museum: Bata Shoe Museum

Location: Toronto

Details: From the long, pointed sabatons of medieval times to Nike Air Jordans, you can learn a lot about history from what people wore below the knees at the Bata Shoe Museum. Housed in a unique, modern wedge of a building that resembles a shoe box, this is one of the most extensive collections of footwear in the world with more than 10,000 items spanning a history of 4,500 years.

...the same day 10 of them got laid off.

Intricately crafted beaded moccasins tell a story about trade patterns in Native North America. Dutch wooden clogs were perfect for working the wet bog in the Netherlands. The museum displays every kind of footwear—ancient funerary sandals, Chinese silk shoes, haute couture pumps, chestnut-crushing clogs from France, and sumo wrestling shoes called geta.

This shoe shrine showcases the foot-gear of the famous as well—Marilyn Monroe's red high heels, the blue Adidas running shoes worn Terry Fox, Elvis Presley's blue suede shoes, and Justin Bieber's burgundy, Supra SkyTop II high-tops he delicate paper shoe sculptures of French artist Thierry Agnone.

Museum: Vulcan Tourism and Trek Station

Location: Vulcan, Alberta

Details: If you're a Trekkie, you'll want to put on your pointy ears and boldly go about an hour southeast of Calgary to the tiny town of Vulcan (population 2,000), named not after Spock's home planet but the Roman god of fire. Seeing how the popularity of *Star Trek* swelled in the decades after the television show first aired in 1966, the townspeople of Vulcan said, "*Chaw' maH tlhap vam qep ghoS!*" That's Klingon for "Let's get this party started!" the town started small in 1995 by erecting a replica of the *Enterprise*, starship. In 1998, the Vulcan Tourism Trek Station was opened, which is a visitor center and museum shaped like a spaceship and packed with *Trek*-related items. Visitors are greeted in English, Vulcan, and Klingon. The center is a chance to slip into costumes, sit in Kirk's chair, and have their photos taken as crew members of the *Enterprise*. Don't miss: After the museum closes, visitors can let loose with Klingon Karaoke, Lunar Liquor, or stop by Tribbles Small Dog Grooming. Green women even take the stage at the strip club.

In 2010, Leonard Nimoy, at age 79, made his first visit to the museum and the town, saying, "I've been a Vulcan for 44 years. It's about time I came home." Of course, he couldn't leave without giving his blessing to the locals: "May each and every one of you live long and prosper." They unveiled a bronze bust of Mr. Spock during his visit. Nimoy contributed a handprint, giving the famous Vulcan peace sign. It was cast in bronze and placed below the bust.

Museum: Niagara Apothecary

Location: Niagara-on-the-Lake, Ontario

Details: The museum itself is Canada's oldest apothecary—a pharmacy that operated between 1820 and 1964 and is now restored to its 1869 state. The museum's most famous collection is bottles and jars first imported from Britain in about 1830 used to store medicinal remedies. Visitors often seek out a handsome piece of glazed white china dating back to the 19th century. The 50-centimeter-(20-inch-)tall container features a perforated lid to assure a suitable degree of ventilation for its contents—leeches.

Don't miss: The Victorian-era enema box looks especially uncomfortable. Those who needed to...ahem...loosen up a bit would impale themselves on an ivory projection and then push down on a plunger to send fluid up.

Museum: Sardine Museum and Herring Hall of Fame

Location: Grand Manan Island, New Brunswick

Details: A collection of three historic smoke sheds houses artifacts from the days when smoking herring was a major industry on the island. The museum also displays an extensive collection of sardine tins from around the world. Michael Zimmer, who founded the museum, was known to float around the cove in a boat that resembled an open can of sardines; his boat is on display.

Museum: Corkscrew Inn Wine Museum

Location: Vancouver

Details: Upon first walking into the Corkscrew Inn Wine Museum, the walls may appear to be decorated with implements of torture. But once you start to take a closer look, you realize that you're surrounded by devices to remove cork. Most people don't give a corkscrew a second thought, but the Corkscrew Inn Wine Museum has collected scores, some dating back to the 1700s. Not all were made strictly for wine either; some were made to open medicine, cologne, and shoe polish bottles. Others are specifically designed to open certain beers. A few of the highlights are a ladies' gold and mother of pearl pocket corkscrew made in France in the mid-19th century, corkscrews hidden in figurines of clowns and knights, and elegant Art Deco designs from the Austrian designer Karl Hagenauer (1898–1956). Don't miss: The Corkscrew Inn also has unique stained glass windows with images of corkscrews and a collection of wine-related antiques, including vine-pruning shears, grape-picking knives, wine bottles, and wine glasses.

Yellowknife has a Ragged Ass Road.

Museum: Anne Murray Centre

Location: Springhill, Nova Scotia

Details: For some Canadians, Anne Murray is a superstar on the level of Elvis, and going to the Anne Murray Centre is like going to Graceland. For those who aren't fans of the 70s soft rock icon, this place can seem very strange. The museum displays minute details of the singer's life. There's the first record player she owned, the dress she wore representing Nova Scotia in the 1971 Rose Ball Parade, and the outfit she wore at the Vancouver Olympics. Fans can walk down the rows of gold and platinum albums. Don't miss: Murray's grade school report cards.

Museum: Accordion Museum

Location: Montmagny, Quebec

Details: Everything you ever wanted to know about accordions is waiting for you at the Accordion Museum. The accordion has had an influence on music in the Quebec region, and the museum traces the history of the instrument and displays many different types, including an ancient Chinese version that dates back 4,000 years.

* * *

A GROSS (BUT REAL) CANADIAN CARTOON

The main characters on *The Brothers Grunt* (1994) share their names with famous crooners—Bing, Dean, Frank, Perry, Sammy, and Tony, all voiced by one person (Doug Parker)—but they're actually some of the most grotesque creatures ever to appear on TV. The show followed five of the brothers' adventures after they left their monastery home on a quest to find the sixth, Perry and bring him home to fulfill his destiny as his people's "Chosen One." Less human than some sort of toad-like creatures, the linguistically-challenged Brothers Grunt meandered through 27 episodes, puking, farting, and rarely wearing more than underpants, with their theme song summing up the problematic nature of their brotherly endeavor: "It's hard to find that for which you hunt / When your speech is a bunch of grunts/ And when you have incredible needs / For cold martinis and melted cheese." TV critic Charles Solomon warned viewers, "Parents who dislike *Beavis and Butt-head* won't want their children exposed to gags about used condoms, urinals, police beatings, and nipples."

Lameque, NB, has a peat moss festival and the locals decorate their homes and offices with bales of peat.

THE GENTLE GIANT OF WILLOW BUNCH

While he was tall in measure, Edoard Beaupré had a short life spent mostly as a circus attraction–and for decades after his death he was put on display without dignity.

HERCULES OF THE PLAINS

When Edoard J. Beaupré was born in Willow Bunch, Saskatchewan, on January 9, 1881, he was by all appearances a normal baby. The son of a father who measured 173 centimeters (5 feet and 8 inches) and a mother who was 163 centimeters (5 feet and 4 inches), Beaupré was a slightly heavy baby at 6 kilograms (14 pounds). But at age 3, a growth spurt started–and it never stopped. At age 9, he measured 183 centimeters (6 feet) tall. By age 12, he gained another 15 centimeters (half a foot). At 17, he was a towering 216 centimeters (7 feet and 1 inch) tall. Beaupré would not stop growing taller, and the cause of this ceaseless growing would not be found until after his death.

Along with his increasing height, Beaupré gained great strength. When he was 17, he could lift a 360-kilogram (800-pound) horse. When he was 20, he tried lifting a 400-kilogram (900-pound) horse and apparently fractured his leg doing so. He didn't lift anything heavier than 400 kilograms after that.

AN ENORMOUS TALENT

He dreamed of being a cowboy. He was an excellent horseman and showed great talent with a lasso. For a short stretch as a young man, he traveled to the United States, where he worked as a ranch hand in Montana. But his unstoppable growth held him back from his dreams. Legend says he was forced to quit riding horses because his legs would drag on the ground. Although it's unlikely that he had legs that long, his weight of over 130 kilograms (300 pounds) could have easily taxed some of the strongest horses.

Beaupré was described as a sensitive and intelligent young man. Supposedly, he had a knack for learning languages; he could speak English, Sioux, Cree, and French. Although he could have tried to pursue other careers, he eventually decided to embrace his fate as a man of unusual height to earn money for his poor family. His parents wound up having 19 other children. Beaupré joined the freak show circuit and traveled around Canada and the States. At age 21, he measured 241 centimeters (7 feet and 11 inches) and weighed 166 kilograms (365 pounds). His neck was as big as a boy's waist at 53 centimeters (21 inches) around. His hands were over 30 centimeters (a foot) long from the bottom of his wrist to the top of his fingertips. His feet were at least double the size of the average man's. His size 22 shoes had to be made by special order. In his circus travels, the beds were never long enough. Some hotel staff reportedly set a second mattress atop trunks lined up at the foot of his bed so he could stretch out his amazingly long body. Thrill seekers who came to the sideshows marveled at his height and feats of strength. Lifting a 360-kilogram (800-pound) horse to shoulder height was a regular part of his act. As a traveling side show attraction, the quiet giant couldn't escape the gawkers, even when he wasn't performing.

THE GIANT BECOMES SICK

In 1902, he participated in a competitive fight with his acquaintance, the strong man Horse Barre, and the famous Louis Cyr, who was known as one of the strongest men in the world. Baeaupré lost the short competition—he had such a gentle nature that he wouldn't touch his opponents in the ring.

He didn't have much of a love life, unlike many young men. Some tried to arrange a marriage between Beaupré and the giantess Elle Ewing, who was an equally impressive 229 centimeters (7 feet and 6 inches) tall, but he wasn't interested in the least.

At age 21, Beaupré, who was now 249 centimeters (8 feet and 2 inches) tall and weighed just under 180 kilograms (400 pounds), was diagnosed with tuberculosis. Still, he insisted on working. He developed a persistent cough and grew more and more tired. Two years later, after his performance with the Barnum and Bailey Circus at the St. Louis World's Fair, Beaupré drank a cup of tea at about a quarter to midnight. He was extremely tired and felt a sharp chest pain. He began coughing and spitting up blood. He feared he would die and said, "'I will die; it's so sad to die so young and so far away from dear parents." He fell unconscious and was rushed to the hospital, where he died a few minutes later.

The Hotel New Hampshire was filmed in Quebec.

ON DISPLAY EVEN AFTER DEATH

At the St. Louis Morgue, Dr. R. B. H. Gradwohl performed the autopsy and found that Beaupré had a tumor on his pituitary gland, which was the likely cause of his unending growth. At the time of his death, he measured 251 centimeters (8 feet and 3 inches).

The corpse was then embalmed and to be prepared for a funeral. Beaupré's father, however, was poor and could not afford to transport his son home for burial. The circus manager promised to bury Beaupré in St. Louis, and his father believed that at least his son would receive proper last rights. The undertakers kept Beaupré's body, and they displayed it for a profit in a store window in St. Louis. Authorities ordered that the body be removed.

In 1905, Beaupré's body was delivered to the Eden Museum in Montreal, and curiosity-seekers packed in to see the tallest man in the world. Another traveling circus show supposedly got possession of the body after its museum exhibition. Apparently, the circus went bankrupt and the corpse was forgotten in a hangar at the Bellerive Park on Notre-Dame Street, across from Dufresne Street in Montreal. In 1907, children stumbled across the giant while playing in the shed; you can just imagine their faces when they inadvertently uncovered the famous goliath.

THE TALL BUT TRUE TALE COMES TO AN END

The corpse was transported to the University of Montreal's department of anatomy for study. His body was immediately put through a special mummification procedure, and the school kept Beaupré in a glass shrine where he would rest for the next 82 years.

One of Beaupré's nephews, Ovila Lesperance, located his uncle at the University of Montreal. His secretary had read about him in a medical journal. In 1975, Lesperance and a niece of his went to the university, where he found his long-lost uncle.

"They had him in a glass case," Lesperance said. "He was naked. My niece told them 'that's no way to leave a person.' He might have been a giant, but he was human."

Lesperance argued with the university about giving his uncle a proper burial, but the university felt it owned the body and would not let it go for many years.

Finally, on September 29, 1989, more than eight-and-a-half decades after his death, Beaupré was put to rest. His body was cremated, and his ashes were returned home to Willow Bunch, Saskatchewan, his final resting place.

Five percent of Canadians don't know the first seven words of the Canadian anthem.

UNCANNY CANADIAN CREATURES

The fabulous fauna of Canada attest to the nation's vastness and diversity.

BEARLY LEGAL

In the spring and summer in the far northern reaches of Manitoba, the ice starts to melt and the polar bears head into Churchill. The town calls itself the "Polar Bear Capital of the World," and tourists travel there to view bears as they roam the nearby tundra. When their usual food supply of seal starts running low, some hungry bears search for a meal in town. Some break into homes and cars. "In 2011, they were all over the place like rats," said one local. Because the townspeople don't really want bears roaming the streets, wildlife conservation officers try to capture the bears and put them in the "polar bear pokey". If someone spots a bear causing trouble, they just call 675-BEAR. The furry giants—some weighing 700 pounds—are locked in tiny cells in a warehouse with nothing but water for months. A worker at the holding facility says that they try to make the bears' stay there as unpleasant as possible so they won't want to come back. Officials say that the treatment isn't cruel—polar bears usually fast during the summer months. When the bay freezes up, these bears are released and go back out on the ice.

CHARMING CHIRPERS

Churchill also gets overrun with whales. One of the largest populations of beluga whales in the Arctic summers in the Churchill River estuary. About 3,000 of these relatively small white whales socialize there. Measuring about 3 to 4 meters (10 to 13 feet) and weighing from 300 to 500 kilograms (657 to 1,095 pounds), these big dolphin-esque creatures with globular heads are often called the "canaries of the sea." They are the most vocal of all whales—chirping, whistling, clicking, and clanging. These whales have a few other distinct traits—they can change the shape of their melon-like foreheads by blowing air around their sinuses, and they can even swim backwards.

Leslie McFarlane of Ontario wrote the first 20 Hardy Boy books as Franklin W. Dixon...

URSINE ART

If you're a true polar bear fanatic, you might want to pay a visit to the Polar Bear Habitat and Heritage Village in Cochrane Ontario, where you can swim with the polar bears. How do you do that without getting attacked? The Village has a human wading pool next to a polar bear pool separated by a thick protective glass divider. You are able to not only swim with him but buy some of his artwork as well. Ganuk enjoys sticking his paws in paint and making original paw prints. They sell for $50 to $130.

FISH OIL

The early British Columbian pioneers did not always use candles to see at night. Sometimes they lit a fish. The eulachon is a smelt found off the Pacific coast. This fish also goes by the names oolichan, hooligan, ooligan, and candlefish. The small fry (15–25 centimeters, or 6–10 inches, long) got the nickname candlefish because it is so fatty that it can be dried, strung on a wick, and burned like a candle. Lewis and Clark encountered the fish in the early 1800s, and they noted in their journal, "By inserting a wick into the mouth of these oil-rich fish, the dried fish could be used as candles."

SNOW CAMELS

Within the Canadian Arctic Archipelago on Ellesmere Island, Canadian paleontologists in 2013 found the bone of an animal that would seem to have strayed quite far from his home—a camel. But according to researchers, the humped quadrupeds roamed the area about 3.5 million years ago. This ancient version of the camel was covered in thick hair, stood about a third taller than today's modern dromedaries, and weighed about 1,000 kliograms (over a ton). In the Pilocene epoch, the Arctic was a very different place, covered in forests and having a much higher temperature. Vertebrate paleontologist Natalia Rybczynski from the Canadian Museum of Nature has posed that camels look the way they do today because of the time they spent in the Arctic. She theorizes that the wide flat feet, large eyes, and humps for fat may be adaptations derived from living in a polar environment.

BUSY BEAVERS

In 2010, Jean Thie, a member of the Google Earth Community, spotted a massive beaver dam that stretches 850 meters (2,790 feet)—almost a kilometer (more than half a mile). It's estimated to be twice the size of the Hoover Dam. Average beaver dams in Canada are 10 to 100 meters (33 to 330 feet) long, and only rarely do they reach 500 meters (1,640 feet). Located in Northern Alberta in Canada's Wood Buffalo National Park, it holds the record for being the biggest beaver dam ever. A 652-meter (2,139-foot) structure in Three Forks, Montana, previously held the record for world's largest beaver dam. Scientists now say that it has existed for more than 25 years and that several generations have worked on the major project. Apparently, researchers have known about the dam since 2007, but Thie was the first to spy the structure from outer space images. The dam is located in a nearly inaccessible part of the park, and park rangers had to fly over the heavily forested marshlands to have a look.

SLITHERING LUNGLESS CREATURES

Fundy National Park is one of the world's great havens for salamanders. Seven species reside there, including the yellow-spotted, red-backed, and two-lined. The red-backed, two-lined, dusky, and four-toed are all considered "lungless." These amphibians undergo a process called cutaneous respiration. They take oxygen in through their skin, which acts like gills; their skin then releases carbon dioxide.

*　　*　　*

LAST WORDS OF FAMOUS CANADIANS

"C'est fini."

—Wilfrid Laurier

"Did I behave well? Was I a good boy?"

—Stephen Leacock

"No."

—Alexander Graham Bell, in sign language, to his deaf wife, who pleaded, "Don't leave me."

"CALLING OCCUPANTS OF INTERPLANETARY CRAFT"

Here's the strange story of a strange man who inspired a strange band to write a strange song that later became a minor hit for the Carpenters.

SPACEY MEN

In the early 1970s, three young musicians from Toronto—John Woloschuk, Dee Long, and Terry Draper—formed the "space rock" band Klaatu. The name was inspired by the peaceful alien ambassador from the 1951 film, *The Day the Earth Stood Still*, who warned mankind about its warring ways: "Your choice is simple—join us and live in peace, or pursue your present course and face obliteration."

While working on their first album, Klaatu's fascination with aliens brought them in contact with a 1967 book called *The Flying Saucer Reader.* That's where they learned about an odd man named Alfred K. Bender, a scissors salesman at the Acme Shearing Company in Bridgeport, Connecticut.

HELLO UP THERE!

In 1952, the year after *The Day the Earth Stood Still* hit theaters, humans didn't yet know that Mars, Venus, and other nearby planets were unable to support life. The chances of an alien landing—Klaatu style—still seemed very real. With reports of "flying saucers" coming in from all over the planet, Bender wanted to send the E.T.s a message that humans are friendly. But he knew he couldn't do it alone, so he formed the International Flying Saucer Bureau (IFSB).

After recruiting thousands of members from all over Earth, Bender sent out a newsletter announcing "World Contact Day." The instructions: At 6 p.m. on March 15, 1953, every IFSB member to simultaneously "send out a message to visitors from space." How? *Telepathically*. Here's the message:

> Calling occupants of interplanetary craft! Calling occupants of interplanetary craft that have been observing our planet EARTH. We of IFSB wish to make contact with you. We are your friends, and would

> like you to make an appearance here on EARTH. Your presence before us will be welcomed with the utmost friendship. We will do all in our power to promote mutual understanding between your people and the people of EARTH. Please come in peace and help us in our EARTHLY problems. Give us some sign that you have received our message. Be responsible for creating a miracle here on our planet to wake up the ignorant ones to reality. Let us hear from you. We are your friends.

World Contact Day came and went...and the aliens didn't land. Shortly afterward, however, Bender claims to have been visited by "Men in Black" who told him to stop looking for aliens...or else. So he retired from the E.T. business and disbanded the IFSB. But ever since then, members have been trying to keep the message of World Contact Day alive and well. The movement might have faded completely into obscurity had it not been for Klaatu.

ULTRA-EMMISARIES

In 1976, after reading about Bender and the IFSB, Klaatu drummer Terry Draper asked his bandmates, "What if we turned the Message into a hit song with mucho airplay? Maybe the radio waves would reach the aliens. Mankind's puny brains didn't do much." (At least that's how Draper recalls his pitch.) So the band started working on "Calling Occupants of Interplanetary Craft (Recognized Anthem Of World Contact Day)." That's the actual title.

It begins with the sounds of crickets, birds, and other forest creatures, and soon footsteps can be heard walking through the brush. Then a needle is dropped on a record and the spacey music begins, followed shortly by an angelic voice singing:

In your mind you have abilities you know

To telepath messages through the vast unknown

Please close your eyes and concentrate

With every thought you think

Upon the recitation we're about to sing:

Calling occupants of interplanetary craft

Calling occupants of interplanetary, quite extraordinary craft!

The "Fog Bowl" Grey Cup football game of 1962 was played over two days because of weather.

BUSY SIGNAL

The song opened Klaatu's debut album, *3:47 EST* (the time of day in *The Day the Earth Stood Still* that Klaatu landed on Earth). It was a minor hit in Canada and the U.S., and not enough to convince the aliens to land.

It did, however, reach the ears of one the most famous groups of the day, the Carpenters. In the summer of 1977, as another space movie, *Star Wars*, was breaking box office records, the Carpenters' cover version of "Calling Occupants of Interplanetary Craft (Recognized Anthem Of World Contact Day)" reached #32 on the pop chart. It even spawned a 1978 TV special: *The Carpenters...Space Encounters.*

But still, the aliens didn't respond.

Don't give up hope, though—the movement is still active. In March 2013, on the 60th anniversary of the first World Contact Day, the event was stretched out to an entire week. Still no aliens, though. Perhaps it's time for another cover version of "Calling All Occupants" to be sent out into the vast unknown...

* * *

THE BEATLES/KLAATU SNAFU

When Klaatu released *3:47 EST*, they wanted to "let the music speak for itself," so they didn't include any personal information in the liner notes. It only said, "All words and music by Klaatu." While the boys were in England promoting the album, something interesting took place back in the U.S. and Canada: Rumors began circulating that "Klaatu" was a ruse—that this was actually a lost Beatles album recorded in 1967 between *Revolver* and *Sgt. Pepper.*

The rumor, started by an American radio station, goes that the tapes were lost because Paul McCartney had faked his death and the songs were recorded in secret. When the tapes were "found" ten years later, the Fab Four didn't want to deal with the inevitable hype, so they convinced Capitol Records (their North American label) to release the album without any reference to the Beatles. The fact that the songs "Calling All Occupants" and "Sub-Rosa Subway" sound like they could be Lennon-McCartney songs only fueled the rumors. There was no truth to them, obviously, but it must have been flattering for Klaatu to be mistaken for the most successful rock act of all time.

Eighty percent of the world's mustard seed is grown in Canada.

23(ISH) SHORT STORIES ABOUT GLENN GOULD

Amazing true tales about one of Canada's most important–and eccentric–composers.

• His recording of Bach's *Goldberg Variations* in 1955, when Gould was just 23, continues to be the best-selling solo-instrumental classical album ever made.

• The Toronto native had many eccentricities related to his playing. Although he played with great precision, Gould's home was often a mess. He couldn't leave for a recording or performance unless he was wearing the perfect shirt.

• He insisted that there were certain shirts that facilitate playing the piano because of the position of cuffs and feel of the fabric. He would often go through a dozen shirts before finding the right one and leaving his room for the day.

• Anytime he played, he brought a special rug and a chair that his father built for him. Called his "pygmy chair," the seat put Gould just 36 centimeters (14 inches) off the floor, which is exceedingly low. The position kept his face very close to the keys. Fans claimed that the peculiar position created by his pygmy chair gave his touch a purity compared to the shoulder-heavy approaches of most pianists. He refused to ever have his chair reupholstered. In time, the cushion wore away and he was left to sit on a narrow beam that ran from the front to the back of the seat.

• Before he would play, he would often limber up his hands by soaking them in the sink. He would begin with lukewarm water and gradually raise the temperature to almost scalding.

• Gould liked things hot in general. In the sweltering summer heat, he would wear heavy overcoats, a wool beret, and mittens.

• Whether performing for a live audience or at a recording session, Gould maintained a curious humming and grunting as he played. His mother had taught him to sing the notes as he performed–a habit that he could never quite shake.

• Recording engineers struggled to mask his vocal outbursts, and Gould at one point offered to wear a gas mask to muffle his noises.

• At times, he would wave a free hand in the air as if conducting himself.

• His face was also highly expressive, contorting as he got swept up in the emotion of the music.

• He hated to be touched and he hated shaking hands. This aversion for handshaking may have come from being a germaphobe. He wouldn't even visit his dying mother in the hospital because of his fear of germs.

• By 1964, at age 32, Gould was disenchanted with playing live. He called concerts "a blood sport," and he made the decision never to perform in a live concert again. This decision was not entirely a surprise; he had said that he hated being watched and the sound of clapping—plus, he didn't really like humans. He would only play for recordings, radio, television, and film.

• In the 1979 documentary *Cities: Glenn Gould's Toronto*, Gould said, "By the time I was six, I made an important discovery that I get along much better with animals than humans."

• He had a succession of canine companions, whom he loved dearly. He even sent his dog Banquo a postcard from the Soviet Union when he played a famous concert there in 1957.

• At his family's family cottage on Lake Simcoe in southern Ontario, the young Gould befriended a wayward skunk and he serenaded cows with his unique vocal renditions of Gustav Mahler compositions.

• Gould would not play the music of certain classical composers. He considered many of the works by Chopin, Schumann, Liszt, and Debussy to be "empty theatrical gestures."

• "I'm a Streisand freak, make no bones about it," Gould said in an interview with *Rolling Stone*. He wanted to record a classical album with Streisand, but it never came to be.

• He was critical of the Beatles, calling their music "a happy, cocky, belligerently resourceless brand of harmonic primitivism." He also said, "If what you want is an extended exercise in how to mangle three chords, then obviously the Beatles are for you."

The X-Files was filmed in Vancouver but moved to L.A.—David Duchovny didn't like rain.

• Who did he think was the greatest composer of all time? An obscure, 17th-century Englishman named Orlando Gibbons.

• He had a small but devoted group of friends, whom he would call at all hours of the night. One of his closest confidants was his cousin Jessie Grieg. He spoke to her daily. She eventually had to enforce a policy of no calls after 11 p.m.

• He loved to travel by car, boat, or train but had a horrible fear of flying.

• Just about every morning that he was in his Toronto apartment, he would go to Fran's, a 24-hour diner a block away and order the same dish:scrambled eggs.

• Despite all his quirks, Gould did find love. He had a passionate five-year affair with the wife of the composer Lukas Foss. In a letter, Gould said he loved Cornelia Foss "more than anything in the world and every minute I can spend with her is pure heaven." He even asked her to marry him, but she turned him down. At the height of their affair, Cornelia left her husband and moved to Toronto with her two children to be with Gould.

*   *   *

SPOOKY CANADIAN PLACES

- Bone Town (Alberta)
- Gore Bay (Ontario)
- Coffin Cove (Newfoundland and Labrador)
- Burnt Arm (Newfoundland and Labrador)
- Skull Creek (Saskatchewan)
- Hatchet Cove (Newfoundland and Labrador)
- Bloodvein River (Manitoba)
- Poison Creek (British Columbia)
- Destruction Bay (Yukon)
- Goblin (Newfoundland and Labrador)

THE GREAT PRETENDER

A woman's valor crosses national (and gender) lines.

FIGHTING FOR THE UNION, JACK!
Although she was Canadian, Sarah Emma Edmonds enlisted in the Union Army during the Civil War. She joined the Michigan Volunteer Infantry Company. It may have seemed odd for a woman to be accepted into the ranks of the Union Army, but her fellow soldiers has no clue she was a woman. She signed up while disguised as a man and maintained secret identities throughout her service in the military. She sneaked behind enemy lines while pretending to be a black man or an Irish peddler woman.

IT'S A GIRL!

Sarah Emma Edmondson was born in 1841 in Magaguadavic, New Brunswick, to a hot-tempered father, a farmer who had always wanted a boy who would help him with the crops. The father was so overcome with disappointment that he treated Sarah horribly. To win the approval of her father Sarah did all she could to prove that she was as worthy as a boy. Some accounts say that she hid all traces of femininity and dressed as a boy. Despite her efforts, her father continued to abuse her. So at age 16, Sarah left home and changed her name to Edmonds. Although she worked a short time in Moncton, New Brunswick, she feared that her father would find her, so she took off for the United States.

To protect herself from being discovered, Edmonds cropped her hair, bought a man's suit, and traveled disguised as a man under the name Franklin Thompson. Dressed as Franklin, she landed a job as a traveling Bible salesman with a firm in Hartford, Connecticut.

NOT EXACTLY AN OPEN BOOK

Edmonds proved herself to be a successful salesman. Leading up to the Civil War, she passionately defended Union beliefs and objectives. When the war broke out in 1861, Edmonds—who was then living in Flint, Michigan—wanted to help the Union cause. She thought she could contribute most by enlisting as a male soldier under her assumed identity of Franklin Thompson. Fortunately, at the time, the physical required only that the enlistee answer questions, and not have a full medical examination.

Wasaga Beach on Georgian Bay is the world's longest freshwater beach: 14 km, or 8.6 miles.

As Thompson, Edmonds served as a hospital attendant, helping wounded soldiers. In March 1862, she accepted a post as a mail carrier and later was transferred to Virginia to fight as part of General McClellan's Peninsula Campaign. Her regiment played a vital role in the siege of Yorktown in the spring of 1862.

During this time, Edmonds decided to become a spy. A Union agent working under McClellan had been captured and reportedly faced a firing squad. McClellan was now in need of a new spy. Edmonds heard of the position and decided to apply. Her preparation—intensely studying all she could about military tactics, local geography, and weaponry—paid off, and she officially became an agent for the Union forces.

WITH A LITTLE HELP FROM HER FRIEND

Historians say that there is no official record of Edmond's activities as a spy, which makes sense, but her memoirs give detailed accounts. For her first mission, she decided to disguise herself as a black man. She had become close to a local chaplain's wife and revealed her true identity to this friend. Edmonds gained her confidence, and the woman helped her with her first disguise. She used silver nitrate to blacken her skin, donned a black minstrel wig, and assumed the name Cuff. Behind enemy lines, she worked with local slaves to build defensive barricades. Not accustomed to the rigors of manual labor, Edmonds's hands became severely blistered. Exhausted from this hard work, Edmonds convinced a fellow slave to swap positions with her so she could work in a kitchen instead. Keeping her eyes and ears open about all military matters, she learned about troop morale, troop size, and weapons. She discovered that the Confederates were going to use "Quaker guns"—logs painted black—at the battle at Yorktown.

After two days, she was able to escape back into Union territory with the information. Two months later, she was sent back into Confederate territory. This time, she assumed the identity of a heavy female Irish peddler with the name of Bridget O'Shea. She sold some of her wares to Confederate soldiers, again keeping her ears open to all military matters that she might hear being discussed. She returned to the Union camp with details on military plans as well as a beautiful horse that she rode to escape from Confederate soldiers who pursued her.

The Château Frontenac in Quebec City is the most photographed hotel in the world.

BLESSINGS IN DISGUISE

Apparently, she crossed back over enemy lines a few more times as Cuff. At one point she served as an African-American laundress for Confederate officers. During this spying expedition, she found important papers in an officer's coat. She also posed as a young male Confederate sympathizer in Louisville, where she assisted in setting up a spy network there.

Eventually, she became ill with malaria and knew she would require hospital care. Because she didn't want her true identity exposed to the military, she went to a private hospital and checked herself in as a woman. When she was well, she prepared to return to the Union forces as Franklin Thompson. But she happened to see a list posted in the window of a newspaper office near the private hospital in Illinois. The list gave all the names of soldiers who were sought for deserting the Union Army—including Franklin Thompson.

A TRULY REVEALING MEMOIR

At this point, Edmonds gave up her male identity and signed up to help the Union as a female nurse, a job she carried out until the war ended.

After the war, she wrote a booked titled *Nurse and Spy in the Union Army*, which became a top seller. She gave all her profits to the war relief fund. In 1864, after completing the book, she decided to return to her beloved Canada. Three years later she married Linus Seelye, and together they had three children.

With her book published and true identity revealed to the world, Edmonds returned to Michigan in 1876 for a reunion of her infantry unit. Her Civil War comrades helped remove her dishonorable discharge and aided her quest to get a military pension, which Congress granted her in 1884. One soldier, Summer Howard, wrote: "More than one member of the company can attest to the care, kindness and self-sacrificing devotion of 'Frank' to the sick soldiers of the regiment." Edmonds was so moved by the help of her fellow soldiers, she said, "My dear comrades, my heart is so full I cannot say what I would to you. Tears are in my eyes, but I shall never, never forget your love and kindness to Frank Thompson. All that I can say is that I am deeply grateful, and may God bless you."

Near the end of her life, Edmonds moved to Texas. She died at her home in La Porte on September 5, 1898—an inspiration and heroine ahead of her time. "I am naturally fond of adventure, a little ambitious, and a good deal romantic—but patriotism was the true secret of my success," she said

The narrowest house in North America is in Quebec City—3.7 meters (12 feet) wide.

IT'S A GIRL, GIRL, GIRL, GIRL, GIRL!

The amazing saga of the Dionne quintuplets.

BATTLING HARD ODDS FROM START

At the height of the Great Depression on May 28, 1934, in Corbeil, Ontario, the first quintuplets who would survive past infancy were born. When Yvonne, Cecille, Annette, Emilie, and Marie were born, their survival was in question. Collectively, the Dionne girls weighed only 6 kilograms (13 pounds, 5 ounces). An adult could hold one in the palm of his hand. They were kept warm near the family stove, and they lived the first month of their lives in incubators. Local women donated their breast milk to help feed them. Doctors fed the girls diluted rum to help their tiny lungs so they could breathe more easily. Scientists gave the quints a less than 1 in 57 million chance of surviving. But when it was clear that the five would make it, people began calling them "the miracle babies." The five identical girls lifted the spirits of many who were struggling through the difficult economic time of the Depression, and the Dionne girls became a worldwide media sensation—a symbol of joy, hope, and strength.

A COMPLCIATED CUSTODY BATTLE

The Dionne parents (Olivia and Elzire) were poor, and days after the birth of the girls, the parents were made a financial offer by Chicago's Century of Progress exhibition. The parents agreed, but the contract was revoked. The Ontario government called into question the parents' ability to care for their children. So four months after their birth, the quintuplets were taken away from their parents by the Ontario government. The parents were declared unfit to care for their children, who became wards of the provincial Crown. Olivia, the mother, remained part of their guardianship, but the girls were put under the protection of Dr. Allan Roy Dafoe, who successfully delivered the girls, and two other guardians.

The government insisted that they were taking the children away from the parents in the interest of the children's well-being. However, many suspect that they had ulterior motives. The Canadian government was fully aware of the growing public interest in the quintuplets, and it

LG2, the world's largest underground hydroelectric power plant is in the Baie-James region of Quebec.

didn't take long for them to build a tourist industry centered around the girls. The girls lived in a hospital especially built for them near their home. That hospital became a tourist trap called Quintland.

THE BIRTH OF AN INDUSTRY

Between 1934 and 1943, about three million people queued up at Quintland to get a peek at the quints and see where they lived. When they were babies, nurses would stand on a balcony and hold up the babies so the gawkers could have a glimpse. Although some saw their upbringing as privileged because they had round-the-clock nursing, a swimming pool, and a playground to themselves, their world was surrounded with glass that allowed visitors to view them three times a day. The girls couldn't see the visitors because the glass was covered with fine-mesh screens on the inside. It was as if they were growing up in a human zoo.

The girls, always in their matching outfits, became a bigger attraction than Niagara Falls, and it's estimated that local businesses earned an estimated half-billion dollars from visitors. The parents, however, were made unwelcome, and they were rarely allowed to visit their own children.

LUCRATIVE LITTLE GIRLS

The quintuplets kept Ontario from going bankrupt. The government didn't charge tourists for parking or admission to Quintland hospital, but a store there raked in an estimated $350 million for the province. Souvenirs such as postcards, dishes, and Dionne dolls brought in a steady revenue stream. People gathered stones from the family farm and opened souvenir stands where the rocks were sold as fertility stones for 50 cents each. Even the quintuplet's father sold fertility stones to make a buck. The Ontario government sold photos of the quintuplets to publications at every major holiday—carving pumpkins for Halloween or sitting on Santa's lap.

Dr. W. E. Blat headed the team from St. George's School for Child Study at the University of Toronto who studied the girls. They X-rayed them and recorded their episodes of "anger and fear," tantrums, naps, and squabbles. They even catalogued what the girls ate.

In an interview with London's *The Independent*, Cecille Dionne said, "It wasn't human. It was a circus." She said she knew the word *doctor* before she knew the word *mother*. The nurses became their mothers, and the attending physician, Allan Roy Dafoe, their father. They made three movies for Twentieth Century Fox, and they made profitable endorsements for products from cod liver oil to typewriters

Canadian tattoo artist, Vivian "Sailor Joe" Simmons, had 4,831 tattoos on his body.

to automobiles. The Alexander Company manufactured dolls that looked like the girls. The quints were used to hawk Quaker Oats, Palmolive liquid detergent, Bee Hive golden syrup, toothpaste, and war bonds. The money apparently went to the parents, but the girls themselves weren't seeing much of it. When the girls were 7, only $1 million had been put in their trust fund. By the time they turned 21 and became eligible to receive the funds, only $800,000 remained.

THE GRASS ISN'T ALWAYS GREEENER...

After nine years of a bitter custody fight, the daughters were allowed to move back in with their parents and their other nine siblings. But apparently life back home was no picnic. They later wrote that life with their parents was "the saddest home we ever knew." As crazy as Quintland was, it was more pleasant than their real home. They declared that their mother was unloving and their father was a controlling tyrant. Later in life, the three sisters said their father abused them in the car. Later, each of the girls confessed that they longed to have been born separately.

They wrote, "Who could ever count the times we heard, 'We were better off before you were born, and we'd be better off without you now?'" The sisters said that they were asked to do more chores than the couple's other children and served the rest of the family their meals. At age 18, the girls all left home and struck out on their own as adults. But the girls said their sheltered life made it difficult for them to adjust to the real world.

CALLED TO TRIAL

Emilie became a nun and died of a seizure in 1954, and Marie died of a blood clot in 1970. When the three surviving sisters, Annette, Cecile, and Yvonne, reached their sixties, they were living together outside Montreal on a combined income of $746 a month. In 1998 the sisters successfully sued the government for separating them from their parents. The women asked to be compensated for the trust fund money that had been lost or taken. The government's first offer was to give the sisters $4,200 a month, but after public outcry, the sisters and the Canadian government reached a settlement of $2.8 million. Ontario Premier Mike Harris traveled to the three remaining sisters to make a formal apology and deliver the monetary settlement. Yvonne died in 2001, leaving behind Cecile and Annette.

ICE WONDERS

Canadian ice lore runs deep.

PLANES ON THE ROCKS

During World War II, German U-boats (submarines) trolled the Atlantic and sank many Allied ships. By the winter of 1942, Hitler's Navy had sent about 600 vessels to a watery grave. If the British could somehow construct an indestructible fleet, they might be able to gain an upper hand in the battle against the Nazis. Steel and aluminum were in short supply during the war, but Geoffrey Pyke thought he might have a solution. The journalist-turned-scientist, who was once an inmate at a mental hospital, envisioned making vessels of ice. They could be manufactured using only 1 percent of the energy needed to make an equivalent mass of steel. He suggested that an iceberg—natural or artificial—could be leveled to be an aircraft carrier. It could provide a runway and be hollowed out to shelter aircraft. The construction of "berg ships" would also be incredibly affordable . . . in theory.

COLD WARSHIPS

Pyke presented his idea to Lord Louis Mountbatten, who was Chief of Combined Operations and in charge of the development of equipment and special craft for offensive operations. Mountbatten proposed the idea to Prime Minister of Great Britain Winston Churchill. Rumor was that Lord Mountbatten demonstrated the advantages of the idea using ice cubes in a bathtub at the prime minister's office. Churchill was sold on the idea. He envisioned launching an invasion of Europe from a fleet of iceberg aircraft carriers. He also saw the potential to use the ships as floating refueling stations in the Pacific Ocean that could deploy fighter aircraft and B-29 bombers against Japanese forces. Churchill gave the green light to go ahead with research.

The British military commissioned Pyke to draw up plans for building an ice ship, and a prototype was to be built in Patricia Lake in Alberta's Jasper National Park, surrounded by Canada's Rocky Mountains.

The highly secret program was code-named Habbakuk after the Biblical prophet who promised "a work in your days which ye will not believe." With Pyke's idea as a starting point, the Habbakuk researchers, including Nobel Prize winner Max Perutz, combined water with wood pulp to create a substance that was stronger than mere ice. Called Pykrete, the material had strength both from the crystalline structure of ice and the wood cellulose fibers running through it. In its frozen state, the mixture was 14 times stronger than mere ice, and tougher than concrete.

AN IDEA THAT'S WORTH A SHOT

In seeking support for the Pykrete project, Lord Mountbatten took a sample of the substance to a meeting with a group of Americans. To demonstrate how tough the Pykrete was compared to ice, he shot a revolver into a block of ice, which immediately shattered. Then he shot his gun into a similarly sized block of Pykrete, which was so strong that the bullet ricocheted off and nearly hit an official in the room.

On Lake Patricia, workmen began constructing a vessel that was 18 meters (60 feet) long by 9 meters (30 feet) wide by 6 meters (19.5 feet) high to test how well ice in a ship would stay frozen. After all, a fleet of Pykrete or ice would gradually melt and sink into the sea. Adding wood pulp to the water slowed melting because it lowered overall thermal conductivity. The team needed to come up with equipment that could be kept on the ship to keep the entire structure at a freezing temperature. Scientists experimented with Freon compressors driven by electric motors. For two months, the workers toiled to build a 1-to-50-scale prototype of the planned Pykrete boat.

A CHILLING DEFEAT

Along the way in their research, members of project Habbakuk realized that Pykrete was not effectively buoyant, and they were concerned about how a Pykrete vessel might stay afloat when loaded with all the cooling equipment, crew, and aircraft. Ever the visionary, Pyke suggested that the ice could be filled with air, before construction, to make it lighter.

In addition, those analyzing costs for the project discovered that it would have taken more steel to build the housing required to store the ice for constructing a Pykrete ship than it would to build an entire battleship from steel.

Although these problems may have been addressed in due time, the battle for the Atlantic had been virtually won by the Allies by

Babe Ruth hit his first professional home run in Toronto on September 15, 1914.

August 1943. The war wouldn't officially end until 1945, but the Allies were again in control of the Atlantic Ocean. As a result, the Habbakuk plan was discontinued. The team took the machinery from the structure they had built, and they let the remaining shell sink into Lake Patricia. In the 1970s, scuba divers found the remains, which were later studied by the Archaeology Department of the University of Calgary. Along the way, some thought the idea of Pykrete ships should be reconsidered for use in the fishing industry. After this brief moment in World War II, however, Pykrete pretty much melted into history.

* * *

TWO WEIRD SPORTS

• **Wok on the wild side.** You've probably heard of race walking. Well, now there's wok racing. Although it was started in Germany by Stefan Raab in 2003, wok racing has gained in popularity on the mountains of Canada. The sport is exactly what it sounds like–you grab a wok (a large, deep pan used for stir-frying), go to the top of a ski slope, and then, with a flying leap, jump in the wok and shoot down the slopes, holding the handles for dear life. Some wok riders prefer bulleting down a bobsled track. As the sport has developed, competitors have created four-person woks where four woks are attached to one unified sled. The highest speed recorded for a one-person wok is 91.70 kph (56.98 mph), a record set by Georg Hackl in 2007. The four-person wok team, reached a speed of 114.30 kph (71.02 mph) in 2009.

• **Let's go skijoring!** This isn't a downhill sport so to speak, but competitors do wear skis. Instead of hurtling down the side of a mountain, skijorers are pulled by a team of dogs or supposedly Canadian arctic foxes. Admittedly, finding dogs is easier. Some say you can skijor being pulled by a horse or even a motor vehicle. There are skijoring tours through the Canadian Rockies. One such tour company is called Mad Dogs and Englishmen.

Simeon Perkins of Nova Scotia was the first to see a UFO in North American in 1786.

THE MONEY PIT

Many of us dream of finding hidden treasure. Well, the search for treasure on Oak Island off the coast of Nova Scotia has been going on since 1795.

BEING OBSERVANT PAYS

Although there are variations on how the pit was discovered, the basic story is as follows. One night in 1795, 16-year-old Daniel McGinnis saw lights coming from Oak Island, which is mostly covered in dense forest. His curiosity was sparked. He thought he'd explore and find out what activity might have been going on in such an unpopulated place. During his exploration, McGinnis found a circular depression in the ground that was 13 feet in diameter. On a tree branch overhanging the depression, McGinnis noticed that it had been cut in such a way to hold a pulley and tackle—as if something could be hoisted out of the ground or lowered into the ground.

McGinnis had heard tales of pirates in this area, so he decided to bring two of his friends back to the site to dig a little deeper and maybe uncover a pirate's chest of jewels and money. So McGinnis, along with his pals Anthony Vaughan and John Smith, returned to site and started to dig. Just two feet down, they were surprised when they hit a layer of flagstones, which are used for building. After removing about eight feet of these stones, the teenagers hit a new layer—oak logs that spanned the pit.

The trio were now very excited—it seemed certain to them that something must be hidden below. They dug beyond the logs, through dirt and then at about 20 feet, they hit another layer of logs. Down they went, and at 30 feet, they hit yet another layer of logs.

GOOD THINGS COME TO THOSE WHO WAIT

The boys couldn't go any further without help, so they vowed to come back. They kept their discovery a secret for eight years. Now in their twenties, they formed the Onslow Company to continue the dig. They discovered a layer of oak logs that every ten feet down. But they also found other layers as they descended deep into the ground. At 40 feet, they hit charcoal. At 50, it was putty. At 60, they found coconut fibers. Then at 90 feet a dramatic discovery was

"The Alex P. Keaton," a London, Ontario, pub, honors Michael J. Fox's character on *Family Ties*.

uncovered. The excavators found a mysterious stone, inscribed with mysterious symbols. With the help of a professor from Halifax, the trio decoded the message, which supposedly said: "Forty feet below here two million pounds are buried."

MATERIAL CONCERNS

But soon as they removed the stone, water started filling the hole and kept rising all the way back to the 33 foot level. They tried pumping the water out, but back in it came. The Onslow Company then decided to dig down parallel to the original hole. This may have been a bigger mistake. Digging the new hole made matters worse. The new digging unplugged a tunnel that fed into nearby Smith Cove and the ocean water rushed in. Again, they tried pumping out the water, but the sea refilled the hole immediately. The Onslow Company abandoned their search for the treasure.

In 1849, the Truro Company returned to the project. After encountering flooding like the Onslow Company, the new team decided to drill core samples beyond the water. The drill hit oak at 98 feet, and then almost two feet of metal pieces. They thought they may have actually drilled through hidden chests that were storing the alleged treasure. Although one account says that three gold links from a chain were found, no treasure was brought up.

GETTING TO THE SOURCE

The Truro Company still needed to get down deep to see what was actually there. They made the discovery that the channel feeding water into the pit was man-made, and if they could block the channel, they would stop the water and be able to proceed down to the treasure. They started work on a dam, but a storm destroyed their work before they could finish. They made other attempts to plug the water, but they all failed. The Truro Company gave up too.

Others were to come and attempt the same but they all met similar frustrating results. In 1897, the Oak Island Treasure Company made a new discovery. At just beyond 160 feet, the team drilled and found what they guessed was a cement vault. They estimated the vault was seven feet high and seven inches thick. They drilled through the vault and into wood, metal and various other materials. When the drill was brought back up to the surface, a new clue and mystery was found. On the tip of the drill, they discovered a small piece of sheepskin

Native legend: Kitchi-Kiwana fell holding a mountain. It shattered into the Thirty Thousand Islands.

parchment with two letters on it—they were either a *vi*, *ui*, *or wi*. They were now convinced that treasure was within grasp. They sank more shaft to retrieve the vault, but these efforts all failed. The Oak Island Treasure Company gave up.

SEEKERS COME AND GO

Other treasure-seekers came and went, but in 1936, a team did unbury a new piece to the puzzle. Gilbert Hadden and Fred Blair were cleaning out some of the shafts that were already constructed when they found a stone fragment bearing a similar inscription as the original stone. Still, no treasure was found.

More came, more dug, more gave up.

In 1959, Bob Restall and his family had a go at it. He found a rock with 1704 inscribed on it, although some think it may have been placed as a joke. His attempt ended in tragedy when in 1965 he passed out and fell into a shaft with water in the bottom. His son, Bobbie and two workers tried to save him but they were apparently overcome by some gas that must have also knocked out Bob. All four drowned.

MYSTERY ENDURES

In 1965, Daniel Blankenship took over the quest. He formed the Triton Alliance in 1970 to keep the dig going. He and his team have found some artifacts along the way, including iron-wrought scissors that were about 300 years old and probably Spanish. They also found several logs that were up to 65 feet long and had Roman numerals carved into them at four-foot intervals.

In 1976, Triton sunk a steel tube about 230 feet into the earth near the pit. They lowered a camera to a bedrock cavity at the bottom and saw some amazing images. They were shocked to see a severed hand floating in the water. Three chests and various tools were then spied and finally, a human body was seen. They attempted to send divers down to investigate, but the strong current and poor visibility stopped them. Soon the hole collapsed and has not been reopened since.

Still the riches that may be securely hidden far underground have not yet been found. Many have speculated on what the riches may be—a pirate's loot from the likes of Captain Kidd or Blackbeard, French naval treasure, Marie Antoinette's stolen jewels, or even a lost Freemason vault. Curious to find out? Head over to Oak Island . . . bring your shovel.

THE TAGISH ELVIS

There are Elvis impersonators, and then there's this guy. He seems so convinced that he actually is the King... that we're not going to rule out that possibility.

ALL SHOOK UP

"The UFO came over my head," said Elvis Aaron Presley. "And it zapped me with its light. I had this vision that I was wearing a maroon-coloured outfit, and the rhinestones on it were glowing. And I said, 'Holy sh*t, what's going on here? That's Elvis! But it's me, too!'" He said he could actually *feel* Elvis' DNA supplanting his own. Memories of the real Presley flooded his mind, as did the reason for his bizarre transformation: The U.S. government had hypnotized Elvis Presley in 1977 and sent him to the Yukon to live in obscurity as "Gilbert Nelles." Thirteen years later, he was "reactivated." The aliens told him so.

After the encounter, "Nelles" dyed his reddish-blond hair black and legally changed his name to Elvis Aaron Presley. Now he wears a sequined jumpsuit, oversized sunglasses, has jet-black sideburns, and speaks in the same Southern cadence as the King.

SUSPICIOUS MINDS

But it's not like Nelles was "normal" up until his alien encounter. He'd been known in the small Yukon town of Tagish to be a bit... eccentric. He'd tell people to watch what they say, because the CIA was monitoring him. He spent his evenings at bingo and karaoke, and made a modest living painting landscapes onto gold pans and selling them to tourists.

Locals say their Elvis really started losing it in the cold winter of 1990. That's when he built himself a cabin in the woods out of old, discarded telephone poles. The chemicals used to preserve the poles emitted noxious fumes—which may be to blame for his visions and belief that he's Elvis.

But to hear the man tell his odd tale, he doesn't come off like a loony. He sounds more like...Elvis (the latter, drug-addled Vegas version). And he's got lots of faithful fans: "People actually kiss my feet and say, 'Elvis, the Lord has brought you back to us!'"

The peregrine falcon, which lives in the Yukon, is able to fly at 200 km/124 mph.

VIVA LAS VEGAS

In the three decades since his transformation, the Tagish Elvis has become something of a celebrity. One of his proudest moments was when he performed with (the real) Chubby Checker in Las Vegas. One of his lowest points also happened in Sin City: He was assaulted at a party by a group of men, who left him with two black eyes.

Back in the Yukon, you might see Elvis tooling around in his old pink Cadillac (decorated with plaster cherubs). And if you head up there to do some gold panning, you might be lucky enough to be serenaded by the King himself—he has a kiosk set up at a mining site. Bonus: He really does sound a lot like Elvis Presley!

And he doesn't just sing covers. He's written and recorded three albums of Elvis-style music: *Still Living* (1996), *Armageddon Angel* (2003), and *A King's Ransom* (2007). He was even the subject of a 2008 independent documentary film called *The Elvis Project*.

JAILHOUSE ROCK

Aside from singing, one of Elvis' favorite things to do is sue people. His legal adventures began in 1996 when his wife, fed up with her husband's paranoid visions, told him she was moving out of the cabin. Enraged, Elvis accused her of being yet another pawn in the U.S. government's attempts to control him and then shot his gun toward her, but missed. When Mounties showed up and arrested him, one of them mentioned that he should seek "professional help." Elvis filed a $1-million lawsuit against the RCMP for defamation. The judge dismissed the case and charged him $10 for "wasting everybody's time."

But that was just beginning. According to CBC News, "Elvis has sued just about every legal authority in the country, including police officers, lawyers, judges, the RCMP Complaints Commissioner, and even the Solicitor General of Canada." He even once sued adult magazine magnate Larry Flynt for featuring the Tagish Elvis as the "a****** of the Month" in *Hustler*. Elvis wanted millions, but said he would be satisfied with a simple apology. So Flynt, not wanting to go to court, printed a short "sorry for calling you a crazy a******" note in the next issue.

Elvis would always represent himself in court. Dressed in full Elvis regalia, he was known to break out in song during his depositions. His rambling affidavits consisted of hundreds of pages of alien abduction and mind control stories.

Rumble in the Bronx was filmed at locations in Ontario and B.C.

Finally, in 2003 a judge in Whitehorse called Elvis a "vexatious litigant" whose suits were all "gibberish." He was fined $10,000 and banned from filing lawsuits. Elvis left the building...but not before threatening to sue the judge for $120 million.

DON'T BE CRUEL

Where do troubled individuals eventually wind up? Politics, of course. In 2005 Elvis ran for the leadership position of the Yukon Liberal Party, but garnered only five votes. He fared somewhat better the following year, when he got 40 votes while running as an Independent for the Yukon legislature, promising to fix the corrupt court system. He lost, but tried again in 2011, using the slogan, "Be A Hound Dog, Vote Elvis Presley, Make Yukon Graceland." He lost again.

Those defeats, however, were nothing compared to the drubbing he took on national television. The Tagish Elvis performed before his largest audience ever in 2010 when, at age 54, he appeared on the game show *Dragon's Den*, in which contestants pitch their business proposals to a panel of grumpy rich people. Wearing a white jumpsuit, Elvis burst on stage singing an "Elvis original" (that he wrote) called "Country Child."

Then he told the Dragons about the aliens. Not surprisingly, the Dragons mocked him, but Elvis stood his ground and pitched his pitch: For only $58,000, he'd sell them a 15-percent stake in his next two albums. He also offered up his memorabilia for sale. The answer: No. And not just no, but Dragon Kevin O'Leary called him a "nutbar." Elvis responded, "I'm making a chocolate bar called the Nutbar. We should go into business together." The answer: still no. Inspired by the insult, Elvis has since released the "Elvis Presley Nut Bar Experience Chocolate Bar" (which contains no nuts).

RETURN TO SENDER

Currently residing in Ross River, Yukon, he's still doing what he does best: being Elvis Presley. As he says on his website, "I have an affinity for writing smooth lyrics set to upbeat dancing music containing a country, pop, rock, easy-listening style flavored with a First Nation cultural musical styling, creating a new unique musical genre with a spiritual depth easily absorbed by all."

PUNKYDOODLES

The stories and/or legends behind some actual names of some actual places you can actually find in...Canada.

WITLESS BAY

This is the name of a body of water, as well as a small town, in southern Newfoundland. According to local lore, the name was originally "Whittle's Bay," so named after one of its early inhabitants, a Captain Whittle of Dorsetshire, England. When he died, his wife packed up the kids and belongings and went back to England—and Whittle's Bay became "Whittle-less Bay" . . . because there were no Whittles there anymore. That was eventually shortened to the name it bears today, Witless Bay.

PUNKEYDOODLES CORNERS

This is a tiny hamlet located north of Lake Erie in Ontario. According to the local Waterloo Region Museum, a German blacksmith who lived in the town in the late 1800s had a (possibly annoying) habit of regularly singing the song "Yankee Doodle"—except his thick accent made it come out more like "Punkey Doodle"—and that's how the town got its name.

One notable Punkeydoodles Corners' moment of fame: On June 26, 1982, former prime minister Joe Clark kicked off a week of Canada Day ceremonies in the hamlet. To celebrate the occasion, an official Canadian post office was opened in Punkeydoodles Corners—for six hours—so they could issue commemorative stamps.

BLOW ME DOWN

Blow Me Down was a tiny fishing village on the west coast of Newfoundland. Today the village is gone, but in its place is Blow Me Down Provincial Park. Local legend says Blow Me Down was named by legendary explorer James Cook. Further research says this is almost certainly wrong.

Cook was indeed a member of the British expeditions that charted Newfoundland between 1765 and 1767, but maps drawn some years earlier by Joseph Gilbert, a surveyor who sailed with similar British exploration teams, and who himself would later sail with Cook on his Pacific voyages, showed a nearby mountain as "Blow Me Down Mountain." Whether or not Gilbert, who is known to have named other nearby locations, named Blow Me Down Mountain himself is unknown, but the mountain was almost certainly the source of the name of the settlement, and through it the modern provincial park. (The mountain—probably got the name simply because it's a windy place.)

SAINT-LOUIS-DU-HA! HA!

Yep—that's a real town name. It's a very small town (technically a "parish municipality"), in southern Quebec. Now that we have that out of the way: Ha ha! What a funny town name! Actually, it's not that funny, according to the experts.

The exact origin of the name is unknown, but the "Louis" part is almost certainly an homage to 13th century French King Louis IX, the only king of France ever canonized into sainthood by the Catholic Church, and who, for this reason, became a popular namesake for French explorers. (St. Louis, Missouri, for example, is named for Louis IX.) The "Ha! Ha!," according to the Geographical Names Board of Canada, comes from the archaic French term *haha*, meaning the same thing as a "dead end" or "cul-de-sac." The haha here is Lake Témiscouata, which was deemed by early French explorers unpassable by canoe, forcing them to carry their canoes and gear on an 80 km detour around the haha that was the lake. (Which isn't funny at all.) Bonus: It's the only town in North America with two exclamation points in its name.

DILDO

Yes, it really is Dildo. The first known reference to this one goes all the way back to 1711, although then it was spelled Dildoe, and referred to nearby Dildoe Island. The name was subsequently used for the body of water there, Dildo Arm, a section of Trinity Bay, and the town of Dildo itself.

As for the origin of the name...nobody quite knows. The word "dildo" itself, with its well known adult meaning, has been around for a long time—since at least the late 1500s—and the fact is that Dildo Island (that's how it's spelled today), Dildo Arm, and the town of Dildo, may all have gotten their names simply because someone back in the early 1700s had a naughty sense of humor.

HEAD-SMASHED-IN BUFFALO JUMP

Located near the Rocky Mountain foothills town of Fort Macleod, Alberta, this is the site of an ancient aboriginal "buffalo jump"—a cliff used by native buffalo hunters. How it worked: Hunters would induce a bison herd to stampede toward the cliff, which is roughly 1,000 feet long and 35 feet high. Bison aren't stupid—they won't simply jump off a cliff, but the hunters would do their jobs so deftly that they'd cause some of the bison to go over simply by being pushed by the panicked herd behind them.

The fall would break the legs of the unlucky front-runners, allowing the hunters to get close enough to kill them. Archaeological evidence, including bison remains, as well as the stone tools used to butcher them, shows that Canadian First Nations peoples have been using this buffalo jump in this fashion—for at least 6,000 years. But that's not the source of the full name, "Head-Smashed-In Buffalo Jump."

Blackfoot Indians, who have inhabited the region perhaps for millennia, say the name comes from an old Blackfoot legend about a young man who positioned himself at the bottom of the cliff—so he could watch the bison plummet to their deaths. When his hunting mates later found him—under the bodies of the fallen bison—his head was smashed in. (The Blackfoot name for the site, Estipah-skikikini-kots, literally translates to, "Where we got our heads smashed in.") In 1981 UNESCO made Head-Smashed-In Buffalo Jump a World Heritage Site, a status shared with sites like the Egyptian pyramids and Stonehenge.

Some more interesting Canadian place names:

- Asbestos, Quebec
- Ochiichagwe'babigo'ining, Ontario
- Finger, Manitoba
- Shag Harbour, Nova Scotia
- Eyebrow, Saskatchewan
- Pekwachnamaykoskwaskwaypinwanik Lake. This is a lake in Manitoba and Nunavut. The name is a Cree word meaning "where the wild trout are caught by fishing with hooks," and it's the longest place-name in Canada.
- Adanac, Saskatchewan—that's "Canada" spelled backwards.

THE GREAT WHITE WEIRD

Weird, strange, odd, shocking, funny, hilarious, silly, and giggle-inducing news—all of it from Uzbekistan. No, Canada. We meant Canada. Sorry.

ROYAL CANADIAN NAUGHTY POLICE

In July 2012 Corporal Jim Brown of the Royal Canadian Mounted Police's Coquitlam, British Columbia, division was suspended after hundreds of photos of Brown were found online. They showed Brown in a variety of staged situations, including one where he is shown wearing only his high, leather RCMP boots and a kilt, while holding a large knife. On her knees beneath him is a smiling naked woman wrapped in cellophane.

Other photos show Brown using the knife to cut the cellophane from the smiling woman. The ensuing investigation found that Brown had an active life as a member of an adults-only internet club, under the name "the Kilted Knight." "I am personally embarrassed and very disappointed that the RCMP would be, in any way, linked to photos of that nature," British Columbia's RCMP commander Randy Beck said, but he also acknowledged that the photos had been taken on Brown's own time, so Brown was able to keep his job.

NO, REALLY—BLAME CANADA!

In 2003 the Canadian Tourism Commission released the inaugural issue of *PureCanada*, a 185-page magazine that was to come out twice a year, with the intention of enticing Americans to visit the country. Unfortunately, there were a few errors. Okay—more than a few. Maps in the magazine spelled place names incorrectly (Nunavut, for example, was spelled "Nunavit"); some provinces were mislabeled; and on some of the maps, Prince Edward Island and the Yukon weren't labeled at all. "It's unfortunate," Commission spokeswoman Isabelle Des Chenes said, "that there were a few things that slipped through."

When news of the gaffes made headlines all over Canada, the Commission blamed Fodor's Travel Guides for the mistakes, as the U.S.-based company had been contracted to create the magazine. The Commission later admitted that they had made the mistakes themselves, and were forced to issue apologies to both Fodor's and the Canadian public. ("For once," one newspaper report said, "the Americans are not the villains here.")

YOU HAVE A RIGHT TO (ANOTHER) LAWYER

Donald Johnson, a defense attorney in Cornwall, Ontario, was awoken by noises in his home one night in 2005. He had his wife call police while he investigated—and found a strange man in his house. He tackled the stranger, was able to take a knife from him, and then realized he recognized the guy: 34-year-old Scott Best—one of Johnson's clients. Police arrived, and Best was arrested. He apparently had no idea he was burgling his own lawyer's home. Bonus: At the police station Best was advised he could call a lawyer—and he asked if he could call Johnson. Police convinced him that that probably wasn't a very good idea.

UP GOES THE PLANE AND DOWN COMES THE...

In June 2013 Emma Gilfillan-Giannakos of Mississauga, Ontario, was in her backyard with her kids when something fell from the sky. "All of a sudden we heard this big bomb!" Gilfillan-Giannakos said. She and her kids investigated, and found brown splashes on her pool and around the yard. "I stuck my finger in it and I smelt it," Gilfillan-Giannakos went on, "and it smelled like poo." Just days later another Mississauga family reported a similar incident. Both families homes are in the flight path of Toronto's Pearson International Airport and they suspected that they had been the victims of "sky-poo" falling from passing airliners. Pearson officials said that toilets on planes are never evacuated during flight, and that whatever it was that fell from the sky must have come from something else—perhaps a large bird. "There's no way one bird could have done it," George Sullivan replied, "unless it was a pterodactyl."

PRISON BRAKE

Jorden Morin was arrested in July 2013 when he was caught driving a stolen car. What made that especially dumb was that Morin was on his way to jail: He had earlier pleaded guilty to an assault charge and had been sentenced to 60 days in jail, to be served on weekends. At his subsequent court hearing, Morin, who had a lengthy police record, told the judge he had only stolen the car so he could get to jail on time.

The judge added 10 months to Morin's 60-day sentence.

PUT YOUR HANDS IN THE AIR!

Steve Simonar of Saskatoon, Alberta, was given a ticket by police in May 2013 for not wearing a seatbelt. But he had a good reason: Simonar cannot put on a seatbelt by himself, because he has no arms—they were amputated at the shoulder after he was shocked by electricity in a boating accident in the early 1980s. Nevertheless, he is a legal driver. Simonar has a retrofitted truck that allows him to control the gas, brakes, and steering—as well as other things, such as indicator lights and windshield wipers—with this feet, and he has been driving this way for nearly 30 years. He cannot put on his seatbelt without assistance, so he sometimes drives without one. "I've had tickets before and police have stopped me," Simonar told reporters, "but nobody's ever given me a ticket because they figured out right away that I can't put one on."

Despite a public outcry over the ticketing of the armless man, and the fact that Simonar had a note from his doctor excusing him from wearing a seatbelt, the Saskatoon RCMP refused to rescind the ticket. As for Simonar, he said he'd take the case to the Canadian Supreme Court—and even go to jail if he had to. "I'm not ever gonna pay this ticket," he said.

IT'S ALL IN YOUR HEAD

In May 2013, Billy McNeely of Fort Good Hope, Northwest Territories, was scratching at a sore spot on his back when, as he later told reporters, it "made a little sound, so that worried me." He asked his girlfriend, Stephanie Sayine, to took a look. "I told Billy, 'There's a knife sticking out of your back'" she said. The pair went to the hospital, where doctors removed a three-inch-long knife blade from McNeely's back. It had been there for a while: McNeely had been stabbed in the back several times, he said, during a fight...three years earlier. Doctors had not done X-rays at the time, but had simply stitched him up and sent him on his way. McNeely had since then gone to doctors several times complaining of a "burning" sensation in his back, but each time the doctors had said it was just nerve damage from the stabbings. "I'm kind of upset with the health system," McNeely said.

In Yellowknife, you can see the Aurora Borealis (Northern Lights) an average of 243 days a year.

SWASTIKA, ONTARIO

The interesting story of an (eventually) unfortunately named town.

GOLD!

In the late summer of 1907, silver prospector James Dusty was inspecting a recent claim he'd made in the rugged, sparsley populated wilderness in western Ontario, about 360 miles north of Toronto, along the western edge of Otto Lake. The Temiskaming and Northern Ontario railroad had just been built through the area in 1904, and geologists working for the rail company reported that the area looked promising for mining. So far little had come of it. But on September 2, 1907, everything changed: Dusty didn't find silver—but he did find gold, and what appeared to be a healthy vein of it. According to company legend, a small crowd of miners and their families soon gathered around the opening to Dusty's pit—summoned by his cries of "Gold! Gold!—and a young girl asked the prospector what he was going to name his mine. Dusty looked at the girl, the legend says, and, spying the good luck charm on her necklace, proclaimed, "Swastika Mine!"

The young girl was wearing a swastika charm on her necklace. The symbol, which has been around for thousands of years, was at the time in the midst of a popular resurgence.

WHAT'S IN A NAME?

The exact origins of the swastika are unknown. Earliest records show it originating in Asia, most likely in ancient India. The name itself comes from the Sanskrit *svastika* more than 5,000 years ago, and the symbol was for centuries a sacred symbol to many Asian cultures. In the late 19th century the ancient symbol had an unexpected return to popularity: The birth of modern archaeology, and subsequent discoveries of ancient settlements in the Middle East and Asia, brought with it a craze of sorts, wherein ancient things became "in." One of those things was the swastika, and in the late 1800s it became popular in Europe and North America as a harmless "good luck" symbol.

All of which supports the idea of a young girl wearing a swastika charm on a necklace in Canada in 1907. And even if the legend isn't

The Ski-Doo was first called the Ski-Dog but a typo in the brochure forever changed its name.

true, the idea that the name of a popular good luck symbol might be chosen by someone who just discovered gold makes pretty good sense.

James Dusty and his brother William officially founded the Swastika Mining Company in 1908. A full-on mining operation commenced, meaning, at the time, steam-driven mining drills and mine elevators, along with logging operations both for construction and to acquire fuel for the steam engines. Over the next few years operations expanded to a few other sites in the area—and a small town sprang up around it all. In 1911 that town was recognized by the province of Ontario, earning it a post office, and the town of Swastika was officially born. By 1912 it held a population of more than 400 people, and was home to a hotel, railway station, general store, barber, baker, church, school—and four saloons.

THE NAME GAME

Unfortunately, the area was not as rich with gold as was originally hoped, and within a few years mining operations were just limping along. But the town persevered, if not flourished, over the following decades. Then, in the 1930s, the people of Swastika found themselves in an unexpected controversy—which you almost certainly have already guessed: Adolf Hitler's Nazi Party had taken power in Germany, and the swastika, the official symbol of the Nazi Party, came to represent something very different than "good luck" to much of the world.

When Canada entered World War II, the idea of a town called Swastika became, to say the least, awkward. So, the Ontario provincial government changed the name of the town to Winston, after British prime minister Winston Churchill. However, the people of Swastika—who had not been consulted about the name change—became angry. When road crews replaced the "Swastika" signs leading into the town with "Winston" signs—angry Swastikans tore the new signs down, and replaced them with their own homemade "Swastika" signs. And at least once, townspeople put up signs that read, "To hell with Hitler, we came up with our name first!"

SWASTIKA, ETC.

• To celebrate the official founding of the new town in 1911, the first two children born there after incorporation (both in October 1911) were granted free property lots in Swastika. The kids: Cecile Chaput, and her brother, Charles Swastika Chaput.

• Unity Mitford, born in London in 1914, was one of the famous "Mitford Sisters," five upper-class British sisters who all became famous for various reasons in the first half of the 20th century. (Two, for example, became well known writers.) Unity was the best known of all, for less than wonderful reasons: In the early-1930s she moved to Germany, and shortly thereafter publicly announced that she supported the Nazis and their anti-Jewish views. She even became a close confidant of Hitler, and for five years was a member of his innermost circle of friends and advisors.

When the war began in 1939, Mitford, torn between her allegiance to Hitler and her own family and country, attempted to commit suicide, shooting herself in the head with a small, pearl-handed pistol Hitler had given her. She survived—barely—and in January 1940, Hitler allowed her to return to England, where she was, for reasons that are not entirely clear, spared prison. She died in 1948 due to illness related to the bullet from the suicide attempt, which had never been removed from her brain. And while Mitford was born in London, England...she was not conceived there. In 1913 her parents, the Lord and Lady Redesdale, had visited Canada to prospect for gold. Unity Mitford, notorious British Nazi-sympathizer, and close and personal friend of Adolf Hitler himself...was conceived, ironically enough, in Swastika, Ontario.

* * *

JURASSIC PARK MADE REAL

Scientists have regularly conducted experiments on samples from long-extinct wooly mammoths. They say that there is enough genetic material available to one day clone the beasts, especially because they have preserved frozen meat from the animals. "Re-creating extinct organisms is definitely within reason," researcher Hendrik Poinar, an evolutionary geneticist at McMaster University in Hamilton, Canada, told LiveScience. "It will be possible."

But why try to bring these enormous elephant-like creatures back to life? "There is no good scientific reason to bring back an extinct species," Poinar said. "Why would one bring them back? To put them in a theme park? Doesn't seem like a good use of taxpayer dollars to me. Simply studying their evolution, which can be done from old fossil bones, seems far more satisfying to me—but that's just me."

The opossum is the only marsupial in Canada.

APRIL FOOL'S !

Canadians enjoy a bit of tomfoolery, and the often-staid CBC is no exception, playing April Fool's jokes on its listeners, viewers, and, at times, even its own presenters and reporters.

BIG FISH TALE (1978)

Dr. David Suzuki, a CBC radio reporter and award-winning Canadian geneticist with multiple degrees, was fed the ultimate big fish story. Giving him no time to prepare, CBC asked the unsuspecting scientist to interview a "shark expert" named Joshua Herman. Mr. Herman was a delightful guest who specialized in the study of a prehistoric, 80-foot long, and *totally made up* shark called a *Carcaridon*.

Most fascinating was his claim that while many believed this creature to be extinct, he believed it might still be alive. In fact, he told Dr. Suzuki that very day he had attempted to catch this monstrosity using a 495 pound Mako shark as bait and pinning "a row of the meanest looking biggest hooks you ever did see" to the Mako's dorsal fin and along his back.

POLLY WANT A CRACKER? (1979)

From 1978 to 1990, CBC radio aired *The Food Show* with Jim Wright, a former circus ringmaster. The entertaining program delved into topics as diverse as camel milking and microwave cooking. The show got in on the April Fool's Day fun when Jim interviewed Fiona Curtis, an Ontario woman who bought a slew of inexpensive budgies, not to keep as sweet songbirds, but to cook and sell to gourmet food shops as little edible delicacies. It was her husband's idea, she shared, saying that one day he looked over at her pet parakeets and remarked that those "little nippers would be neat to eat!"

So, how did Fiona prepare them? Jim wanted to know. Why, she made a rather involved three-part stuffing consisting of chestnuts, onions, and squid mashed together with bread and paprika. "Cook them slowly," Fiona advised those at home who might want to try for themselves—15 minutes, then baste with butter, turn, and 15 more. For their part, the "gourmets" who bought them in the specialty shops in Vancouver and Toronto admitted that the birds

Porky's may be a "Canadian" production, but it was filmed entirely in Florida.

didn't offer much meat, but "the incredible thing about them is you can eat the bones as well—they just crunch. They are juicy, but they need a lot of spice."

ROMANCING THE GRIDIRON (1980)

Although at times seeming skeptical, Vancouver radio reporter Karin Wells was clearly bamboozled during her interview with two men from Eastview Publications who claimed to be introducing romance novels just for men—Harlequin-style paperbacks that featured traditional male activities like gambling, hunting, fishing, and sports. The idea, they said, was that after a football game, men "will want to see a little romance, a little lyricism, a little sensitivity in the locker room instead of the shouting and yelling." While admitting the books would be "garbage" and would be written in Taiwan and then translated (cheaper that way, of course), these serious pranksters planted their tongues firmly in cheek while expressing the hope that someday construction workers all over Canada would keep these little romances tucked away in their lunchboxes next to their baloney sandwiches. Perhaps they would even be moved to read them out aloud to their blue collar brethren.

COLOR ME FOOLED (1988)

During a national radio broadcast, one Dr. Frederick Farben (a real CBC radio employee) shared his "research" on color allergies—physical reactions that people have when they see a certain color, causing them to break out in hives, sneeze, or coughing fits. When asked about what one could do to stave off a color allergy, Dr. Farben suggested avoiding the offending color altogether, or if that's impossible, they could sometimes fit people with tinted lenses to "serve as a temporary alleviation to that problem." The good doctor claimed that two percent of all Canadians may be affected by color allergies, and that they are not at all related to standard allergies: "You may have no reaction to pollen or ragweed, but you may come in contact with something which is ochre or puce and it may throw you off completely." While there is no cure, "Frederick" also shared that there is a low incidence of color allergies among the Inuit. They seemed to have immunity, he said, possibly from living so much of the year in monochromatic, white surroundings (a.k.a. snow).

For 25 years, *Porky's* was the highest-grossing Canadian film of all time...

SO LONG AS THEY'RE ORGANIC! (1990)

A CBC television broadcast covered—with all the conventions of a breaking news story—a new experiment in a Canadian school's kindergarten classroom: "Last week Tanya did something in school that most of us were told never to do when we were children: She ate worms." Included in the story were interviews with school officials and Tanya's slightly traumatized mom and dad. According to mom, Tanya had not been sleeping well since the worm meal, she had had bad dreams, and had been yelling a lot.

Later in the broadcast a man identified as Tanya's teacher stated, matter-of-factly, there was nothing wrong with eating the worms. After all, he said, we eat snails. Finally, this "news" feature included helpful information from the Ontario Science Center: "The worms were grown organically, boiled in lemon juice, then baked for 10 minutes" at 175°C (340°F).

DON'T TAKE THIS TALE LYING DOWN (1996)

The CBC aired Canadian humorist Barbara Nichol's mock documentary *The Lying Down: The Story of Sarner's Disease in Upper Canada.* Sarner's Disease, listeners learned, was a cholera-like epidemic that caused temporary paralysis and a death-mimicking sleep that led to being buried alive. It was said to be most common in the 1820s and '30s and was attributed to a veritable smorgasbord of possible causes, including bear consumption before winter hibernation, meteor showers, and possibly even the afflicted's religious beliefs! That the native population did not contract the disease, that it was exclusively suffered by settlers on newly cleared lands, lent credence to the theory that settlers brought it over from Europe. So believable was this radio show that some intrigued medical experts thought it was real and later contacted Ms. Nichol to get more information.

*   *   *

LIVING IN A CUBIST WORLD

Habitat 67 apartments in Montreal look like a crazy maze of Lego blocks. Some have said the 146-residence complex looks like a random pile of blocks, but it's a very livable space with gardens, fresh air, and privacy. Designed by Moshe Sadfie and built in 1967, the stacked modular units each have their own patio.

...*Bon Cop,* Bad Cop took the title in 2006.

THE BLACK DONNELLYS OF BIDDULPH

Land dispute raises ire.

THE GOOD EARTH

In 1880, southern Ontario was the scene of a mass murder, the bloody culmination of a feud that had spanned years and continents. Though there were numerous witnesses, no one was ever punished for the massacre. Yet, for almost 150 years, the dark legend of an ill-fated family has haunted what is now Biddulph, Ontario.

AN OLD COUNTRY FEUD IN THE NEW WORLD

James and Johannah Donnelly were born and married in County Tipperary, Ireland. In the nineteenth century, Ireland was ruled by Great Britain—or, more properly, absentee British landlords—and there were deep divides between the Protestant British and the Catholic Irish. James and Johannah immigrated to Canada to escape the crushing poverty of rural Irish life. In 1847, five years after their arrival in the New World, they and their infant sons James and William settled in what was then known as Canada West on 100 acres in the southeastern corner of Lot 18, Concession 6—or, as it was called because of the Irish Catholics living there, the Roman Line. Over the next 10 years, five more sons—John, Patrick, Michael, Robert, and Thomas—and a daughter, Jenny, were born. Life was hard: In order to eke out a living from the land, James and his boys had to clear acres of dense forest. But the land they were improving wasn't their own: Much as had been the case in Ireland, Concession 6 was owned by an absentee landlord—in this case, a man named John Grace. The Donnellys were squatters, hoping that by farming and holding the land, they would be able to claim ownership rights by common law and the long-standing custom of the frontier.

The Donnellys' semi-illegal occupation of their land was only the first ingredient in the volatile mix that would explode on February 3, 1880. The second was the fact that the nearby Biddulph Township was settled by just the right combination of Irish Catholics and Protestants to reignite the feuds of the Old World. Though Biddulph had originally been settled by Protestant Irish as well as Catholics, and with them the secret society known as Whiteboys—after the white smocks they wore during their nighttime guerilla raids against the British occupation—had come soon thereafter. The Donnellys, though Catholic, were considered unacceptably friendly to the Protestants. This earned them many enemies.

LIGHTING THE POWDER KEG

The spark that lit the fuse was when John Grace sold the land the Donnellys were squatting on to an Irishman named Patrick Farrell in about 1856 or '57. The Donnellys, of course, had a problem with this—after all, they'd been clearing and improving the land for almost 10 years. The case wound up in court, and the Donnellys wound up receiving just 25 acres of the land they'd cleared. Still, Farrell didn't let the matter go, and lambasted James Donnelly, Sr. in public. Bad feelings grew between the two men.

Farming on the frontier required self-reliance, but the goodwill of your neighbors was also important. For tasks too big for a single family to perform, like raising barns or harvesting timber, the entire community got together to help. It was at one of these events that the Donnelly/Farrell quarrel came to a head—literally. The two men got into a drunken brawl that ended with a spike used to split logs being used to split Farrell's head instead. He died two days later, and James Donnelly became an outlaw. Still, justice was slow to be served. James hid out for two years, living in the barn and working his fields while disguised in his wife's clothes. (Johannah claimed she didn't know his whereabouts, but their daughter's birth in 1858 indicated otherwise.) Finally, he turned himself in to a magistrate. After a trial where many neighbors testified to his bad nature, James was sentenced to be hanged, but Johannah began a petition for clemency and he was instead sentenced to seven years in prison. He was released in 1865, but a reputation for violence would follow the Donnellys all of their days.

SETTING THE STAGE

Just how much public opinion had swung against the Donnellys was shown by the fact that every petty crime in Biddulph was—right or wrong—blamed on them. William and James Jr. were both accused of theft, and Johannah was even charged with swearing at a constable.

The discrimination also took more insidious forms: The Donnelly barn burned down, perhaps by arson, and fathers wouldn't allow their daughters to marry Donnelly boys. Of course, the Donnellys were not entirely innocent. For instance, when Michael, James Jr., and Robert were evicted from a lot they had been living on, the man who took over the property, Joseph Carswell not surprisingly suffered unexplained fires and deaths of his animals.

The Donnellys' reputation also affected business. William Donnelly began a stagecoach line in the early 1870s that employed several of his brothers. They faced serious harassment from the rival Flanagan line whose owner, Patrick Flanagan, was determined to drive the Donnellys out of business by any means necessary. Stages were sabotaged and run off the road, and a mysterious barn fire killed some of their horses. The sabotage and physical altercations continued until 1878, when all the rival stagecoach lines were put out of business by a newly-built railroad.

Even the law and the church took sides in the growing violence between the Donnellys, their allies, and their enemies. The Donnellys were frequently accused of breaking the law, but hardly ever convicted. When Father John Connolly came to St. Patrick's church in 1879 and heard bad reports about the Donnellys, he sought to stop the violence by forming a Peace Association. Part of this association split off, calling itself the Vigilance Society. The Vigilance Society might have well been called the anti-Donnelly Society, doing such things as accusing them of stealing a cow—which was later found safely back at its home. Notable amongst the members of the Vigilance Society was James Carroll, a man who had tangled with the Donnellys on several previous occasions and who, after being made a constable, had vowed to rid the township of them.

A BLOODY MASSACRE

On the night of February 4, 1880, Constable Carroll came to arrest James Sr. and Tom Donnelly for barn-burning. According to Johnny O'Connor, a 13-year-old farmhand who was the sole survivor of what followed, Carroll was being taunted by a handcuffed Tom when a mob of about 30 men from the Vigilance Society broke into the Donnelly house and beat James Sr., Johannah, and their niece Bridget to death with sticks and farm tools. Johnny, who had hidden under the bed, escaped when the mob set the house on fire, passing

James, Johannah, and Bridget's bodies. Tom was still alive, but died in the fire.

The mob proceeded to William Donnelly's house, where they got John Donnelly to open the door by shouting "Fire!" John was shot dead. William, his wife Nora, and a friend remained hiding inside the house. The fact that Nora's brother John Kennedy, who had been outraged at her marrying into the Donnelly clan, was part of the mob shows just how internally divided the community was. Of the five Donnelly sons who were alive at the time, only William, Patrick, and Robert survived. Jenny also survived, and was the last of the clan to die, in 1917.

THE AFTERMATH

Despite two trials, James Carroll and the five other men William Donnelly and Johnny O'Connor accused of the crime were never convicted. In fact, the community conspired to ensure that justice could not be done: The bodies of the Donnellys had been burned and tampered with, and O'Connor's house was burned to the ground in retribution for his testimony. Finally, prosecutors decided that convictions could tear Biddulph apart and further inflame the feud, as well as harm the careers of local politicians who did not want to appear anti-Catholic. Thus, the first trial ended with a hung jury, and the second with an acquittal.

But this isn't to say that justice wasn't done. Thirteen years after the massacre, William Donnelly published a letter claiming that 32 of the killers had met gruesome fates. According to William, "several were killed by the London, Huron & Bruce train. More were found [dead] in bed without any apparent cause. More fell into a well. More dropped dead. More died suffering the agonies of a mad dog, and a few are in the asylum." The Donnellys had their vengeance from beyond the grave.

*   *   *

A RARE CONDITION

Canadian actress Catherine O'Hara has a medical condition called *situs inversus*. The organs in her chest and abdomen sit in a perfect mirror-image reversal of how they are normally positioned. Most people with the condition have no symptoms or complications. How many people have it? About one in 10,000.

THE "MAD," BRAVE PIPER OF NORMANDY BEACH

A little music can be essential to survival.

HIGHLANDS HERO

Born in Regina, Saskatchewan, Bill Millin learned to play bagpipes as a young man. During World War II, Millin served in Britain's First Special Service Brigade and he was there with his unit on June 6, 1944—D-Day—as the Allies prepared to invade the beaches of Normandy and begin a major push to liberate Western Europe from Nazi control.

As Bill Millin and his brigade approached their landing, code named Sword Beach, near the French City of Caen, Millin's commanding officer, Brigadier Simon Fraser, asked him if he would play his bagpipes to help raise morale. The playing of the pipes was an old Scottish and Irish battle tradition, and Fraser was a true Scotsman, the hereditary chief of the Clan Fraser. Private Millin had played the pipes as the soldier waited to board their landing craft, but he told Fraser that he would rather not play on the battlefield because it went against military code from World War I. It was forbidden to play in a war zone because it would do more harm than good—attracting enemy fire rather than raising morale. Fraser would hear none of it. He said, "Ah, but that's the English War Office. You and I are both Scottish, and that doesn't apply."

Millin wrote later that he felt seasick all night as they crossed the channel but as he waded into the cold water he was ready:

> "My kilt to the surface and the shock of the freezing cold water knocked all feelings of sickness from me and I felt great. I was so relieved of getting off that boat after all night being violently sick. I struck up the Pipes and paddled through the surf playing "Hieland Laddie", and Lord Lovat (Fraser's Scottish title) turned round and looked at me and [gestured approvingly].
>
> When I finished, Lovat asked for another tune. Well, when I looked round—the noise and people lying about shouting and the smoke, the crump of mortars, I said to myself, "Well, you must be joking surely."

He said, "What was that?" and he said, "Would you mind giving us a tune?"

"Well, what tune would you like, Sir?"

"How about The Road to the Isles?"

"Now, would you want me to walk up and down, Sir?"

"Yes. That would be nice. Yes, walk up and down."

So, following the orders of his commanding officer, the 21-year-old walked up and down the battlefield playing "Hielan' Laddie" and "The Road to the Isles" as German snipers shot around him. He saw many lying face down in the water going back and forwards with the surf, while others were able to move forward and dig in just off the beach. Although many of his fellow soldiers died that day, none of the German soldiers shot at Millins who was an easy target. When he spoke with Germans later, he found out that they didn't shoot him because they thought he was crazy.

THE MAGIC FLUTE

Millin did not regard himself as heroic—he was just following orders. He felt bad walking among his wounded comrades, but many of his fellow soldiers appreciated his playing on the battlefield. One commando, Tom Duncan, said, "I shall never forget hearing the skirl of Bill Millin's pipes. As well as the pride we felt, it reminded us of home, and why we were fighting there for our lives and those of our loved ones." From Sword Beach, the Allies were able to move successfully inland. As they headed toward a bridge near the village of Ouistreham, Fraser again asked Millin to play the pipes. As he played along one stretch of road, German snipers began taking out his fellow soldiers again. He looked around to the many of his comrades lying face down on the road and Lovat (Fraser) was down on one knee. They spotted a sniper scrambling down from a tree and he headed off through a cornfield. As he ran, Lovat shot at him and he fell. After Lovat had killed him, he commanded Millin to again start piping. As they crossed the Pegasus Bridge near Ouistreham, Lovat asked Millin to play. Again Germans fired around him as he and his fellow soldiers crossed. While none shot at him, many of his comrades were felled by sniper fire. "It was the longest bridge I ever Piped across," wrote Millin, "but I got safely over and shook hands with the two Airborne chaps in the slit trench."

A Canadian couple invented the game Yahtzee to pass time on their yacht.

Some gave the brave Canadian the nickname of the "mad piper," although Millin had said that it wasn't he who was mad—Lord Lovat was the one who was called "mad" by his troops. Millin was portrayed in the 1962 movie *The Longest Day*, starring John Wayne, Peter Lawford, Sean Connery, Michael Caine, and many others. Millin died on August 17, 2010. With the help of son John Millin and the Dawlish Royal British Legion, a bronze life-size statue of Piper Bill Millin was unveiled on June 8, 2013 at Colleville-Montgomery, near Sword Beach, in France.

* * *

YOU CAN'T KEEP A GOOD MAN DOWN

During the War of 1812, Canadian Isaac Brock was shot and killed at the Battle of Queenston Heights on Oct. 13, 1812. For three days, his body lay in state at the Government House in Niagara-on-the-Lake, Ontario. Then he and his aide-de-camp (field lieutenant), Lieutenant Colonel John Macdonnell, who was also killed in the skirmish, were laid to rest at nearby Fort George.

In 1814, the government of Upper Canada wanted to honor the heroes Brock and Macdonnell, so they voted to build a monument in Queenston where the brave warriors met their demise. Although the monument was not quite completed, Brock and Macdonnell were dug up and moved there, about 10 km away, on October 13, 1824.

Sixteen years later, the Irish Canadian Benjamin Lett led a movement to get revenge on the British and an explosion related to his rebellion damaged the monument. In 1842, Canadian officials decided a new monument must be erected. As building began in 1853, Brock and Macdonnell had to be moved to temporary graves. It can be hard to rest in peace when you're moving around so much, but finally, on October 13, 1853, the pair of soldiers were placed in what we think is their final resting place.

Quebec teen Xavier Menard couldn't use Wellarc for his business name because it's "too English."

SAUCERS IN THE SKY

Canada is popular with more than just the denizens of the home planet...

THE BLASTED AMATEUR PROSPECTOR

Where: Falcon Lake, Manitoba (May 20, 1967)

What happened: Stephen Michalak, a mechanic and amateur geologist, decided one day in 1967 to do some prospecting for quartz and silver in a small stream by Falcon Lake. At a little after noon, he heard the sounds of geese flying overhead and glanced up to the sky. Right then and there Stephen was astonished to see two bright crimson disk-shaped objects rotating and glowing in the sky. They came closer and closer until one landed on a nearby rock. A curious Michalak slowly approached, calling out to whoever—or whatever—might be inside.

Suddenly, the disk moved, then a strange exhaust vent appeared and without warning blasted him with a horrific hot gas, burning a grid-like pattern through his shirt and onto his chest. Michalak yelled out in pain, knowing that he needed to find medical help. He ran to the road and was able to wave down a Mountie, but then wouldn't let the officer get close (for fear of contaminating him) and declined a ride.

The aftermath: The officer's written report said that Michalak appeared to be drunk, refused to let the Mountie look closely at his shirt and hat, and seemed to have rubbed ash on his chest. No concrete evidence was ever found to support Michalak's claims of a close encounter, save some radiation detected in the rock where he said the craft landed.

RED CHARLIE PLAYS PEEK-A-BOO IN THE SKY

Where: Carman, Manitoba (May 1975)

What **happened:** In 1975, the town of Carman in Manitoba became a hotbed of UFO sightings, especially one involving a red light that looked like a star darting and weaving through the sky. People who saw it, including an RCMP constable, were amused by its hide-and-seek movements.

The constable reported seeing the strange "star" about 1,000 feet in the air—an oval red light, encircled by a white halo. Someone dubbed this curious red object "Charlie Redstar," and the name stuck. Later when similar objects were sighted in the same area, they were often referred to as Charlie's "friends" or "cousins." By May of 1975, locals Elaine and Bob Diemert began to have near-daily "Charlie" sightings while walking on their private airstrip. When the news got out, people from all over came to walk the Diemerts' land with hopes of seeing the fireball. One day, the Diemerts allegedly got close enough to see its shape, describing it as flat and disklike, with windowed domes on the top and bottom.

The aftermath: Charlie Redstar made appearances over the next year and a half and developed quite a cult following. In the early 2000s there was even a Canadian Band that adopted the name. But Charlie left nothing that could be scientifically substantiated. No official government investigation was launched.

GOING AGAINST THE GRAIN

Where: Many agricultural areas of Canada (1980s to the present)

What happened: During the 1980s, people from all over the world started to buy into a belief that aliens were bedeviling earthling farmers by flattening their crops into designs. Exhibiting an assortment of motifs and ability levels, the space travelers largely confined their work to England, for reasons unknown. Finally, though, "they" got around to practicing their craft in Canada, designing fields of wheat, hay grass, corn, sorghum, barley. Over the years, they had even given peas a chance.

In the early 1990s, the CBC's Valeria Pringle interviewed Manitoba farmer Joe Thomaschewski who had awoken one morning to discover a huge crop circle in his wheat field. Joined by Chris Rutkowski of Ufology Research, Pringle asked what he thought had caused this circle. Thomaschewski was clearly not a believer in UFOs and just wanted to farm. He had no idea, he answered, but he would leave the simple design for a few more days because crowds of people had already formed to see this strange occurrence. He then added that he planned to mow down the circle pretty soon. After all, "It's just a regular wheat field with a circle in it," Thomaschewski deadpanned. Ufologist Chris, however, provided some theories that he said had been considered recently to explain the appearance of these designs over the years. These included wind vortexes, human pranksters, and even one theory that the circles were the result of hedgehogs running around in frenzied circles while mating.

The aftermath: In recent years, a few crop circles have been discovered to be hoaxes meticulously orchestrated by tricksters...but not all of them. On the surface at least, some of the stories behind the crop designs defy explanation.

CLOSE AND QUIET ENCOUNTER OVER LITTLE FOX LAKE

Where: Little Fox Lake, Yukon (March 30, 2000)

What happened: One early morning, Leah Isaac took a drive around Little Fox Lake with a friend. As she came around a bend, a large, disk-shaped craft hovered in the air ahead of her—lights shone from two windows in a dome at the top of the craft. "It was silver and transparent," she told the Yukon Whitehorse Star. "It was like a mirror. It was almost like you could see right through the craft."

The silent UFO darted, turned, and zoomed away, but before it did Leah's watch stopped running, the truck's tape deck died, and her lights dimmed. Nothing ran normally again until about five minutes after the craft had whizzed away. While Isaac related that she was still scared to drive alone, she was now a believer, concluding, "Our universe is so big, there must be something out there."

The aftermath: Unfortunately for Isaac, local authorities no longer investigate UFO sightings.

* * *

CELINE DION ISLAND

Just 15 minutes from Montreal, Celine Dion has owned and occasionally lived in a castle on her very own island—Ile Gagnon, located in Quebec's Mille Iles River. Her home is an enormous French-style chateau with a wine cellar tasting room, game room, wood-paneled library, and outdoor swimming pool. The estate is accessible by a private bridge and surrounded by a fence to keep out prying fans.

The castle is not very far from where Dion grew up, although her life as a child was a far cry from her life today as one of the richest women in entertainment. She was the youngest of 14 children and lived in poverty in Charlemagne, Quebec.

Furry, magical Ice Hogs are the mascots for Ottawa's Winterlude festival.

THE GREAT STORK DERBY

A wealthy Toronto lawyer left a clause in his will that led to more births than V-Day and the Great Blackout combined.

HE WHO LAUGHS LAST...

The greatest practical joker in the history of Canada was, beyond a doubt, Charles Vance Millar. A wealthy Toronto Lawyer and Financier, Millar was born in the small Ontario town of Aylmar in 1853. He attended the University of Toronto and graduated near the top of his class before attending law school and opening a practice in Toronto in 1881.

Millar was a successful lawyer and an even more successful businessman. Among his early coups was to recognize how important the expansion of British Columbia was to be. In 1897 Millar purchased the B.C. Express Company, which gave him a monopoly on government mail deliveries in the Carriboo region of British Columbia. Through the acquisition of land around Prince George and of boats to carry the mail, Millar became one of the most prominent investors in Western Canada.

Problem was, Millar had no children. A life-long bachelor, he had never procreated, and this left him with a dilemma: to whom to leave his vast fortune? Fortunately for Millar, he never took life too seriously and also had a bit of a cynical streak. Millar believed that everybody had his price, and he reveled in corrupting the seemingly incorruptible. Among his favorite jokes was to leave money in the street and watch the furtive way that people would pick it up and scurry away.

THE WILL

Millar left his greatest practical jokes for his will. With no heirs he was able to use his estate for his own amusement. He is one of the few men who was ever able to enjoy his own death—which he managed by enjoying it ahead of time.

> *This Will is necessarily uncommon and capricious because I have no dependents or near relations and no duty rests upon me to leave any property at my death and what I do leave is proof of my folly in gathering and retaining more than I required in my lifetime.*

Boomer the Lightning Bolt is the mascot at Algoma University in Ontario.

Being a lawyer, and a good one, he wrote an iron-clad document that would be able to withstand what he must have known would be a series of vigorous legal challenges. One of the meanest clauses in Millar's will was the disposition of his vacation house in Jamaica. Millar left use of the house, jointly, to three rival lawyers who were known to hate one another. At the death of the last of them, the house was to be sold and the proceeds given to the poor of Jamaica, so even if they killed each other (likely a possibility Millar pondered) they would get no money out of it. Luckily for all involved, Millar sold the house before he died.

Millar left a sum of money to a priest he knew, but only for the purpose of saying masses and burning candles for the "soul of a certain prominent citizen," described in the will as someone "who will need [the prayers], wherever he is..." Millar never named the person specifically. Since he was a trickster who liked to stick it to those he considered powerful and greedy, we assume this left a small circle of prominent men in Toronto each wondering if he meant him.

THE JOKER

Millar bequeathed about $700,000 worth of stock in the Catholic owned O'Keefe Brewing Company to be divided among every practicing Protestant minister and Orange Lodge in Toronto. The strident prohibitionists and anti-Catholics were now faced with a huge problem. Do they profit from the sale of booze? Do they take money from the hated Catholics? Or do they stand on principle and turn the money down? In the end it turned out that Millar didn't actually own any O'Keefe stock, rendering the whole thing moot.

To every minister in three surrounding towns, Millar bequeathed one share each of something he actually did own, stock in the Kenilworth Jockey Club. After weeks of very public agonizing over whether or not they should accept the wages of sin, the ministers learned that each share was only worth about half a cent, and all their angst had been over something almost worthless.

Something Millar actually owned, $25,000 worth of stock in the Ontario Jockey Club, was left to three very vocal opponents of horse racing: W. E. Raney, onetime attorney general of Ontario; Newton Wesley Rowell, a member of the board of governors of the University of Toronto; and Ben Spence, head of the Prohibition Union. The will stipulated that, in order to receive the shares, the three men had to keep the stock and collect the dividends for a number of years. Once again, Millar was setting up a moral quandary for a group of proud moralists.

THE GREAT BABY RACE

But those clauses were just the warm-up. It was the ninth clause of his will that made Charles Vance Millar one of the most famous Canadians of all time:

> 9. All the rest and residue of my property wheresoever situate, I give, devise and bequeath unto my Executors and Trustees named below in Trust to convert into money as they deem advisable and invest all the money until the expiration of nine years from my death and then call in and convert it all into money and at the expiration of ten years from my death to give it and its accumulations to the mother who has since my death given birth in Toronto to the greatest number of children as shown by the registrations under the Vital Statistics Act. If one or more mothers have equal highest number of registrations under the said Act to divide the said moneys and accumulation equally between them.

In other words, Millar had created a baby race. The poor woman who bore the most children in ten years got the bulk of Millar's estate. Rapid Procreation could reap someone a nice healthy sum of money—enough to support all those kids. The press dubbed it "The Great Stork Derby," and as news spread so did the, uh, competitiveness.

Charles Vance Millar died on Halloween 1926. He was 73 years old and collapsed of a heart attack after running up a flight of stairs. Millar was a fan of long-shot, pie-in-the-sky stock investments, and at the time of his death he held 100,000 shares of stock in a cockamamie project to drill a tunnel beneath the Detroit River linking Detroit, Michigan, with Windsor, Ontario. The current tunnel, which on the Detroit side starts right below General Motors headquarters and, on the Windsor side opens up beneath a casino, is one of the most heavily travelled border crossings in the world. At the time of Millar's death the tunnel stock was valued at a paltry $2, but by the time the Stork Derby was over it had a value of right around $600,000 (that's a little over $10 million in today's money).

On average, thieves break into a Canadian home every three minutes.

PHOTO FINISH

As the Great Depression wore on and up to 30% of the Ontario workforce was unemployed, the baby race became a cause célèbre. Newspapers published regular updates. *Time* magazine profiled the frontrunners. It was a welcome diversion for a struggling city and, at the same time, gave a lot of Toronto couples a good reason to get close. As the clock ticked down the race was neck and neck. In its September 28, 1936 issue, *Time* noted that there were five finalists:

> Of these, three would be out of the money if anyone bettered their record of ten children in ten years. A fourth, now pregnant, needs twins before Oct. 31 to win. A fifth, with ten offspring sure and possibly two more off the record, is also expecting to deliver again before the deadline.

At the same time the will was facing several challenges in court. It became one of the most important legal precedents in Canadian probate history. The state tried to have it invalidated on public policy grounds, claiming that it would lead to immoral behavior, needlessly increase the population, and prompt people to have children that they couldn't afford, merely for the purpose of competing in the race. At the same time a distant relative of Millar's appeared out of the Yukon to argue that the will was so preposterous that it should not be enforced. The cases made it all the way to the Canadian Supreme Court, where the final appeals were all denied and the will declared enforceable. The Stork Derby was legitimate. In the end, 30 lawyers, nine judges, 125 hours of hearings, and forests of papers were spent trying to determine the fate of Charles Millar's joke. In 1938, after all the legal wrangling was over and the estate liquidated, four women were determined to have each borne nine children in the ten years following Millar's death. The families of the heroic mothers Annie Smith, Kathleen Nagle, Lucy Timleck, and Isabel Maclean each received $125,000. Two other claimants, who were shown to have had children either stillborn or illegitimately, were given $12,500 each as a settlement.

The press hounded the winning families mercilessly over the next few years. The McClean family eventually dropped out of site completely to avoid the publicity. Nonetheless, the money was spent on houses, cars, and on the children's education. Nobody knows for sure how many children were conceived by parents hoping to win a big cash prize. However, it was noted that more children than usual were given up for adoption in the years surrounding the baby race.

Canadian Alexander Graham Bell thought people should answer the phone with "Ahoy!"

THE MURDER OF JULIEN LATOUCHE

Even before the days of tabloid journalism, the public heard the grisly details of bizarre crimes of the day. One such crime occurred in the 1670s.

CHILD BRIDE—OR NO?

Although the legal age for marriage at the time was 12, most families didn't encourage their children to marry at such a young age. One person who seemed to have a different opinion on the subject was Jacques Bertault, who had four daughters he was apparently anxious to rid himself of. Two of his older daughters were both married young, at age 12 and 14, and he wasted no time in arranging a marriage for one of his other young daughters, Elisabeth "Isabelle" Therese. He promised her to a man named Charles Denart dit Laplume when she was just 10 years old. But it seems the man returned to France before he could fulfill his marital obligation. The engagement was annulled and Bertault began searching for another husband for his daughter.

He settled on 29-year old Julien Latouche, a man who seemed to have a bright future. Julien had arranged to work for five years on a farm, which would give him time to save money to buy a good-sized farm of his own. When Bertault told Isabelle about her engagement, she was very unhappy, telling her father she did not like the man. Isabelle's mother, Gillette, also had concerns and let her husband know she was opposed to the marriage. But Bertault claimed his right as "master" of the house to make the decision and the marriage took place when Isabelle was 12.

NOT A MATCH MADE IN HEAVEN

It soon became apparent after the marriage that it had been a dreadful mistake. Julien turned out to be a lazy, uncaring, and abusive man that couldn't provide the basic necessities for himself or his bride, and also often beat her. Her parents tried to provide them both with food and resources, but it's not hard to imagine that both Gillette and Bertault felt guilty about the situation. If Bertault's goal in marrying off his daughter was to have one less mouth to feed, ironically he now had gained one instead.

But this is when the story becomes bizarre. At the time, there were some legal actions that a woman could take to separate from a husband who abused her. But Isabelle didn't do this, and her parents didn't advise her to. After seeing their daughter so beaten and abused, and hearing Isabelle say that she wished Julien were dead, they decided to make that wish come true.

THE MAN WHO WOULDN'T DIE

Perhaps Gillette saw some resemblance between the pigs on the Bertault farm and Isabelle's husband, but something inspired her to try and poison Julien with a plant that had killed some of their pigs. She took four or five leaves from the plant and added it to a flavorful soup she had cooked. The family watched anxiously as Julien ate all of his soup to the last drop...without a single ill effect.

The next day, Isabelle's parents visited Isabelle and Julien and Gillette entered the barn where Julien was doing something it seemed he rarely did: working. Gillette supposedly remarked, "Well there's a nice son-in-law," sarcastically, and Julien replied equally sarcastically. In a burst of anger, Gillette picked up a hoe and struck Julien in the head with it. It did little damage to him, but caused him to respond in kind, and he attacked Gillette. Gillette screamed for her husband and daughter to help her. Bertault entered the barn and grabbed the hoe from Gillette and repeatedly struck Julien with it while Gillette screamed "Kill him! Kill him!"

SELF-DEFENSE OR RETRIBUTION?

The perpetrators of Julien's murder didn't conceal their crime very well. They dragged out Julien's body and threw it in a nearby river. Neighbors had heard the commotion and traveled to the barn where they saw the horrific sight of blood everywhere, and even some teeth. They had also recognized the voices of Isabelle's parents. After a brief investigation, Isabelle and her parents were arrested for Julien's murder.

During the trial, Gillette and Bertault confessed their role in the crime. They both claimed that Isabelle was only a bystander. Isabelle claimed that Gillette was defending herself against Julien's attack. Unfortunately, the court decided that all three were guilty of murder.

Rooms at the Gladstone Hotel (Toronto) include a Teen Queen Room with photos of teen idols.

Gillette and Bertault were executed and just as she had watched the death of her husband, she was forced to watch her parents' execution. At the time, execution involved breaking the person's arms and legs prior to strangulation on a wooden cross. Fortunately for the Bertaults, members of the court were compassionate, and the couple was strangled before their limbs were broken.

What happened to Isabelle afterward isn't clear. Some historical accounts say she remarried twice, others just once. Some say she had children by Julien, others that she was childless. One thing is clear: she lived with the notoriety of the murder for the rest of her life.

* * *

ANOTHER URBAN LEGEND

LEGEND: Late one night in 2004, RCMP Constable Bill Wisen responded to a report of a motorist stuck in the snow near Medicine Hat, Alberta. With his cruiser's lights flashing, Wisen parked behind the running car, got out, and approached it. Peering in the window, he saw an older gentleman passed out at the wheel next to an empty bottle of vodka. Wisen knocked on the window, waking up the man, whose name was Robert Duport. Seeing the flashing lights in his rear view mirror, Duport hit the gas pedal and tried to get away. The wheels were spinning, but the car wasn't going anywhere. Duport didn't realize that, though. All his drunken eyes could see was his speedometer htting 30 kph and rising. Amused, Constable Wisen started running in place right next to the car. When Duport looked out at him, he panicked and accelerated to "50," but the Mountie was *still there* running beside him! "Pull over!" yelled Wisen. The drunk man skidded to a "stop," flopped out of the car, and gave himself up, saying, "Man, you guys are in good shape!"

HOW IT SPREAD: Variations of this tale go back to the late 1970s. This particular version supposedly came from an article in Toronto's *Globe and Mail* (which we couldn't locate). It shows up a lot on police blogs.

TRUTH: According to the Urban Legends website Snopes.com, there's no evidence that this incident took place. As with the best urban legends, each retelling adds new details.

THE MAD TRAPPER OF RAT RIVER

In 1931, the greatest manhunt in Canadian history unfolded in the dead of winter 65 miles above the Arctic Circle.

THE FROZEN NORTH

As the great depression wore on into the 1930s, many people—U.S. Citizens, Canadians, and others, drifted north into Alaska and the North West Territories hoping to live as trappers and mountain men, self reliant and independent, not in need of any factory job or clerk's wages. The man calling himself Albert Johnson arrived in Fort McPherson, North West Territories, in July 1931. When he got there he was questioned by Constable Edgar Millen of the Royal Canadian Mounted Police. He was not very forthcoming. He had lots of money, marking him not as someone trying to escape the Depression but something else.

He did not, however, have a trapping license. He left Ft. McPherson and travelled to the banks of the Rat River, where he built himself an 8×10 log cabin.

As the refugees drifted north they were coming into conflict with native trappers in the region, and this probably led to the conflict that erupted that winter. In December, a native trapper accused Johnson of pulling up his trap lines. Two Mounties went out to investigate and that is when things got weird.

CABIN BOY

On Boxing Day 1931, Millen sent constables Joe Bernard and Alfred King to visit Johnson and question him about the traps. When they got there, Johnson behaved very oddly—he completely ignored them. He pretended they were not there. When they asked him a question, he looked right past them. They were at a loss. Was this guy crazy? Unable to see into Johnson's cabin they left to get a search warrant.

On New Year's Eve they returned to Rat River with a warrant and two other constables. Once again, Albert Johnson simply ignored the Mounties. But when Constable King tried to break down Johnson's door, he fired through the door, severely wounding King. After some shooting, the Mounties dragged King away, and he survived.

A nine man posse returned to arrest Johnson and they brought along 20 pounds of dynamite, which they kept warm by keeping it inside their coats. When Johnson refused to come out of his cabin they lobbed the dynamite onto it and blew it to pieces.

Amazingly, as the Mounties approached the shattered cabin, Johnson opened fire on them. He had dug a trench into the floor of his cabin. It had saved him from the explosion and gave him a spot from which to fire at the Mounties (it has been argued that Johnson had the opportunity to kill most if not all of the Mounties at this time, but he let them go). The firefight and standoff lasted into the early frozen hours of the morning.

THE BIG MANHUNT AND THE KILLING

Because of the brave new world of radio, word of the manhunt began to spread, and it became a sensational news story throughout North America. The press dubbed Johnson "The Mad Trapper of Rat River." A bigger posse returned on January 16, 1932, but, in the middle of winter, under the midnight sun, with temperatures at -40, Albert Johnson had flown the coop. He had taken off across the snow on foot. Search parties on dog sleds scoured the countryside until, on January 30, Constable Millen's party cornered Johnson in a grove of trees. The Mounties opened fire (according to Mark Fremmerlid, author of "What Became of Sigvald Anyway?", the Mounties fired first) and when Johnson returned fire he shot and killed Constable Millen.

After Millen's death the Mounties backed off to compose themselves for a drawn-out effort. They realized that Johnson was a more skilled woodsman than they were prepared to deal with. The posse kept getting bigger and bigger. Native trackers joined in, and the Mounties called in Wilfred "Wop" May, a WWI ace who had been involved in the death of the Red Baron. In addition to snowshoes and dog sleds, this was the first time Canadian police used two-way radios and aerial surveillance in a manhunt.

THE DEATH OF ALBERT JOHNSON

By now dozens of Mounties and scores of local trappers were out chasing Albert Johnson. A blizzard slowed them down awhile, and grounded the plane, but it didn't stop Albert. Johnson was obviously

Hurry Hard condoms are named after a curling term.

headed for the Yukon Territory, but the Mounties were determined to stop him. They blocked the only two passes through the Richardson Mountains and believed they had Johnson cornered, but the intrepid trapper scaled a 7,000 foot peak, including a sheer ice face, and then hid his tracks among a herd of caribou in order to cross the mountains. It was only after he had reached the Yukon that tracker May spotted his tracks leaving the caribou herd and heading for the woods. He radioed in the position.

Three days later a group of Mounties, creeping along on the frozen Eagle River, rounded a bend and spotted Johnson standing on the ice. Johnson ran for the riverbank but, not wearing his snowshoes, he couldn't make it. In the gunfight that ensued another Mountie, named Hershey, was wounded and Albert Johnson was shot dead.

When they searched his body they found a compass, a knife, a razor, $2,400 in cash, some gold, five pearls, and—in a glass jar—seven teeth with gold fillings (believed to be his own). During the entire encounter, from December 26 till his death on February 17, although they had hailed him and tried to talk to him several times, Albert Johnson had not uttered a word.

WHO WAS THIS GUY?

Nobody is completely sure who Albert Johnson was. Some claim he was John Johnson from North Dakota, a former inmate of San Quentin and Folsom Prison. Others claim he was named Arthur Nelson. The Johnson family of Nova Scotia claims that he is their long lost cousin Owen Albert. Or he might have been Sigvald Pedersen of Norway.

In 2007 Johnson's body was exhumed so that DNA testing could be conducted, all of which was chronicled in a Discovery Channel documentary, *The Hunt for The Mad Trapper*. It was discovered that Johnson came from a well-to-do family (from his diet and teeth), that in spite of his incredible physical abilities he had a twisted spine and one foot was longer than the other. He most likely grew up in the United States grain-belt region and had Scandinavian heritage. Nonetheless, all of the people tested as possible familial matches for Johnson were ruled out. The identity of the Mad Trapper remains unknown.

Norman Breakley of Toronto revolutionized painting when he invented the roller in 1930.

NOT PROVINCIAL

Provinces that never came to pass. Throughout Canadian history, there have been several movements to redraw borders and reorganize provinces for cultural, political, economic, and other reasons. Such plans rarely gain enough support to be realistically considered. Here area a few provinces that never came to pass.

Province: Maritime Union

Year: 1960s and '70s

Story: The Maritime Union is an oft-proposed plan to join the three Maritime provinces: New Brunswick, Nova Scotia, and Prince Edward Island. (Another version this plan, called the Atlantic Union, includes these three plus Newfoundland and Labrador.) While there is already a great deal of cooperation between the Maritimes, the proposed union would consolidate the population of 1.8 million, hypothetically making it the fifth-largest province.

Support for the plan peaked in the 1960s and '70s, when an economic downturn forced the Maritimes to reconsider how they would acquire and distribute governmental resources. While the idea was publicly debated in all three provinces, the end result was a call for greater efficiency in regional cooperation. Standardization of educational curricula across the Maritimes was a notable outgrowth of these discussions. The concept of the Maritime Union resurfaced in 2012 when three Conservative members of the Senate suggested it as a means of acquiring greater political and economic authority.

Province: Cape Breton Island

Year: 1820s to Present

Story: Currently a part of Nova Scotia, many residents of Cape Breton Island would love to declare their independence and form their own province. Such big ideas are nothing new: They date back to the 1820s, when Britain first added the island to Nova Scotia after a prolonged period of self-rule.

In the year 2000 the movement was reinvigorated after the closing of a major coal mine on the island caused a major economic downturn. With the threat of a second coal mine closing, as well as a large steel mill, residents believed their hardship was caused in large part by Nova Scotia's fiscal irresponsibility. A group met on November 11, 2000

(Remembrance Day across the Commonwealth of Nations), to discuss the logistics of separation. While they managed to gain the support of two local senators who brought the issue to the Senate, no definitive steps were taken to secure Cape Breton's independence.

Province: Northern Ontario

Year: 1970s

Story: In the 1970s, the Northern Ontario Heritage Party (NOHP) was formed expressly for the purpose of lobbying to separate Northern from Southern Ontario, the most densely populated region in Canada. The movement had its unofficial beginning when the government of Ontario voted for a 7 percent sales tax on heating and electricity, a budgetary idea that didn't sit well with the residents of the (much colder) north. Upset with what they perceived as Southern Ontario's dominance over financial and political affairs, the NOHP gathered over 24,000 signatures for a petition demanding the overturn of the tax.

While the government rejected the petition, the party soldiered on, expanding and refining their statement of secession. Their central goal involved the creation of an independent economic state, establishing systems of production utilizing the area's abundant natural resources. This, they felt, would stem the tide of young Northern Ontario residents moving south in search of work. They hoped to implement this system using environmentally friendly methods and in a sustainable fashion.

Though idealistic in nature, these goals were ultimately a bit beyond the NOHP's grasp, and the party gradually faded away. In 2010, however, it resurfaced with a more moderate platform.

Province: Province of Montreal

Year: 1960s to Present

Story: Since the mid-twentieth century, there have been several movements to make the non-Francophone regions of the city of Montreal a separate province from Quebec. At points this has dovetailed with the Quebec separatist movement, so that Montreal reserves the right to secede from Quebec if Quebec indeed secedes from Canada.

As with the case of most secessionist movements, the central motive from the outset was financial in nature. In the 1960s many residents felt that Montreal's mayor, Jean Drapeau, was allocating too

It takes eight to 12 birch trees to make a single canoe.

many funds generated by the city of Montreal to other parts of the province. Some at the time even suggested joining with the United States as the fifty-first state. The movement has since quieted, though its popularity surges every so often.

Province: Turks and Caicos Islands

Year: 1917 to 2004

Story: Movements to alter Canada's political boundaries are not confined to the mainland itself. In 1917 Canadian Prime Minister Robert Borden first suggested the idea of annexing the Turks and Caicos Islands, a British territory in the Caribbean. Interest in the plan waxed and waned for many years, with reassessments in 1974, 1986, and 2004.

Citing the fact that the bulk of international visitors to the islands are Canadian, as well as a long history of trade links between the two countries, supporters from both places say a union could be mutually beneficial. In 2004, in an effort to simplify the process of annexation, the people of Nova Scotia extended an invitation to the Turks and Caicos Islands to join their province should the islands ever join Canada. Other Canadian politicians have suggested building a state-of-the-art port in the Turks and Caicos. While providing a lift to Canada's international trade, they say such a port would also improve the safety and quality of life for the residents of the islands.

While support for the merger was a remarkably high—90 percent among islanders in the 1990s—today it has fallen to around 60 percent. Still efforts continue to integrate, mostly in the areas of commerce and security.

*   *   *

JUST LIKE HARRY POTTER

Hyperstealth Biotechnology in Maple Ridge, British Columbia, claimed in 2012 to have created the first real invisibility fabric. The material is a type of camouflage that bends light around the wearer or an object to create the illusion of invisibility. The biotech firm says that the material is lightweight, inexpensive, and uses no batteries, cameras, or projections. President and CEO Bob Cramer has been pitching the product to U.S. and Canadian military. While the company does show mock-ups of the invention on its website, skeptics point out that Hyperstealth has not yet shown its super-secret invention to the public, so there is no actual proof that it exists.

St. Joseph's Oratory in Montreal displays the preserved heart of Brother Andre in a glass jar.

CHASED BY A WOLF

In June 2013, Mac Hollan, a 35-year-old school teacher from Sandpoint, Idaho, set out with two friends on a 2,750-mile charity bicycle ride from Idaho to Prudhoe Bay, Alaska. On July 6, while passing through a remote part of the Yukon Territory, Hollan had an encounter...that he will never forget. Here's the whole story, from Hollan himself.

THE ATTACK

It was around 2:30, about 60 miles west of Watson Lake. I was a bit ahead of the guys when I heard something to my right. Thinking Gabe or Gordo had caught up without me noticing, I looked over my shoulder and was shocked at what I saw. The first thought that ran through my head was, "That is the biggest damn dog I have ever seen!" This surreal moment of shock and confusion passed immediately—as the "dog" lunged for my right foot and snapped its jaws, just missing my pedal.

WOLF!

At this point I received the biggest jolt of adrenaline I have ever had in my life. Without so much as a thought I shifted my bike to the highest gear possible, started to mash the pedals like never before, and reached for the bear spray in the handlebar bag. I threw off the safety and gave the wolf a quick blast in the face, which served to slow him down so that he was now twenty feet behind me but still not stopping. He hung back for maybe 20 seconds and then raced forward and attacked my panniers [baskets], in the process ripping my tent bag and spilling my poles onto the highway.

I gave him another shot of pepper spray, which again backed him off to about 20 feet behind. Despite pedaling like I have never pedaled before, the wolf kept pace with me easily. It was at this point that I saw an 18-wheeler round a corner, and began to wave, shout, and point to the wolf frantically. As the truckdriver slowed I began to breathe a sigh of relief, thinking if I could just get off my bike and into the truck fast enough I would be safe. After taking a good look at the scene...the driver resumed his speed and drove on.

At Humber College in Ontario you can earn a four-year degree in Comedy Writing and Performance.

DESPERATION

This same scenario would happen to me four separate times, with my desperation growing with each car that passed me by. Every time the wolf would begin to close on me again, I would shoot a quick blast of bear spray behind me to slow him down.

As I came around yet another corner, to my horror I saw a quick incline, and knew that I would not be able to stay in front of this wolf for much longer. I just kept thinking about all the shows I have seen where wolves simply run their prey until they tire and then finish them. It was a surreal moment to realize that I was that prey, and this hill was that moment. The only plan I could think of was to get off my bike, get behind it, and hope that I had enough bear spray to deter him once and for all when he got close enough.

HOPE

It was also at this point that I realized I might not be going home, and I began to panic at the thought of how much it was going to hurt. About 0.2 mile before the hill I saw an RV approaching from behind me, and I knew this was it. I placed myself squarely in the center of the road and began screaming at the top of my lungs, "Help me, there's a wolf, please help me!" while waving frantically. Seeing the situation the driver quickly passed me and stopped on a dime right in front of my bike. I don't know how I got unclipped or off my bike, but I swear I hurdled the handlebars without missing a beat or letting go of my can of bear spray. When I got to the back door of the RV still screaming, the door was locked. In an absolute panic I began to climb in the passenger window, but the driver reached across and threw the door open to let me in. By the time I shut the door the wolf was already on my bike pulling at the shredded remains of my tent bag. I began to shake, and cuss.

POST-TRAUMATIC RELIEF

More cars began to pull up and honk at the wolf, but he would not leave my bike, as though he thought it was his kill. It took someone finally beaning him in the head with a rock to get him to leave. At this point Gabe and Gordo showed up, looking confused and concerned with a set of shattered tent poles in hand. While I know I got the names of the man and woman who saved me, for the life of me I can't remember them now. I do remember the woman giving me a hug that felt like the greatest hug of my life.

A thief in Guelph in 2012 returned the stolen items with a $50 check to repair a broken door.

Still jacked on adrenaline, all I wanted to do was get out of that place, and get out fast. The folks in the RV were nice enough to watch our backs as we got a ways down the road before leaving, and gave one final wave as they passed by. I hope they are reading this so that they know how much I am in their debt and how grateful I am that they stopped to save me. Otherwise I honestly don't think this story would have ended well.

CONCLUSION

We made it about ten miles down the road before the full adrenalin rush wore off, and then everything seemed to go into slow motion, and I just felt dizzy and tired. We pulled over to a roadside creek, where I stumbled down to splash water on my face and basically sat in the creek and lost my s%$t. The full implication of what had just happened to me sank in, and I just lost it for a good fifteen minutes.

We have spent a lot of time talking about the incident since, and the only conclusion we can come up with is that the wolf was old, sick, or injured, to be chasing something down on the highway. I would not doubt I am the first cyclist ever to have this happen to them on the Alaska-Canadian Highway. That being said I have tried to not let this experience change my positive feelings about being out here—but I do look over my shoulder more, and am a bit jumpy.

We're in Whitehorse, Yukon now, having pulled off a century before 2:30. We're planning on doing some bike work here and relaxing for the afternoon. That's all for now.

EPILOGUE

As of press time, Mac and his buddies were still on the road. We are very happy Mac made it through his ordeal safely, and we are very thankful for his permission to share his story here. The charity the guys were raising money for was the Sandpoint Backpack Program, which provides weekend meals for kids in low-income homes. You can find them at:
http://foodbank83864.com/the-backpack-program.html.

*   *   *

A CANADIAN JOKE

Q: What are Canada's four seasons?

A: Winter, Still Winter, Almost Winter, and Construction

In 2012, Pizza Hut Canada produced its own perfume, Eau de Pizza Hut.

TRUNK FOOD

When Jumbo the circus elephant died, many cried and were upset, but still through their sorrow, somehow, Canadians who were near Jumbo at the time of his demise managed to find their appetite.

WORLD TRAVELER

Jumbo got his start in the French Sudan in 1861. His mother was hunted and killed. Taher Sheriff, a Sudanese elephant hunter, took the captured orphan Jumbo and sold him to Lorenzo Casanova, and he made his way to France two years after his birth and wowed the crowds at the Jardin Des Plantes in Paris—one of the top zoos in Paris.

But Paris already had a popular pair of pachyderms—Castor and Pollux. The London Zoological Gardens, on the other hand, were eager to get an African elephant. In 1865, an exchange was agreed upon. The four-year-old Jumbo was traded to England for a rhinoceros, two dingoes, a possum, a kangaroo, and a pair of eagles.

The French had treated Jumbo poorly, and he was overly thin, dirty, and sick. In London, Jumbo met his devoted trainer, Matthew Scott, who nursed him back to health and gave the elephant his name, which comes from the Swahili word, "jumbe" for "chief." Little did Jumbo know, as he gave rides to many of the zoo visitors, that stardom awaited in North America.

A STAR IS BORN

When Jumbo was 21, the Barnum & Bailey Circus made an offer to purchase him. Queen Victoria received about 100,000 letters from schoolchildren begging her not to sell their beloved Jumbo. The animal, with his howdah (traditional elephant saddle) on his back, had given rides to the Prince of Wales and the other offspring of Queen Victoria, as well as a young Winston Churchill. But the pleadings of children were drowned out by hard cold cash. Jumbo was sold for $10,000 (the equivalent of about $220,000 today). Many English citizens were sent into a tizzy over the sale and a fund was set up to purchase the elephant back from Barnum. The public outcry was so great that the zoo tried to revoke the sale. But Barnum would hear none of it. "I would not sell him for $100,000. America is waiting for Jumbo, said Barnum."

At Reversing Falls, NB, tides force water to flow in the reverse direction.

And it literally was true that America was waiting When Jumbo arrived by ship in New York to become part of "The Greatest Show on Earth." Promotional posters advertised the 12-foot tall, six-ton as a "monster," but the thousands of curiosity seekers who turned out for his arrival encountered a very mild-tempered creature.

For three years, Jumbo traveled through the U.S and Canada in his own special train car, "Jumbo's Palace Car." During 31 weeks after Jumbo has joined the circus, Barnum raked in $1.75 million, which Barnum mostly attributed to Jumbo.

TRAGEDY IN ONTARIO

On September 15, 1885, the circus played St. Thomas, Ontario, a booming railroad town. The town's location near the railway tracks made it a convenient stop for the big top, which traveled by train. Jumbo was in the prime in life—a robust 25 years old, which is young, considering that an African elephant can live until age 60. The 29 elephants had finished their performance for the evening a little early that night. They were usually loaded into their car after 9:55, but on this night their handler was escorting them at about 9:30 back to their train cars along designated stretch of track. The final two elephants—Jumbo and Tom Thumb—were reaching their cars when an unscheduled freight train barreled down the tracks.

Its engineer did all he could to stop the train. He saw the elephant and sounded his warning horn. He thrust the train into reverse but was unable to stop. The train first hit Tom Thumb. Tom was scooped up in the cowcatcher and knocked down an embankment, and he tumbled into the ravine. Jumbo, however, was trapped between the oncoming train and circus train and was crushed. The impact derailed the train. Jumbo's skull was broken in a hundred places, though it took poor Jumbo a few minutes to die in the company of Scott, his longtime caretaker. Jumbo reached out his long trunk and drew Scott toward his large head. Scott cried and cried until Jumbo slipped away.

A SIX-TON SPILL

Once Jumbo passed, the most immediate problem was how to get him off the tracks. It took 100 spectators to move the enormous body. Barnum & Bailey wished to have Jumbo stuffed so the circus got local butchers to cut up his carcass in order to preserve the hide and

Skookumchuk! The BC town means "big rapids" in Chinook (and it's fun to say).

skeleton. In a letter in the *Ottawa Sun*, a woman recounted her great grandfather's tales about the days following the horrific accident. He had told her that the butchers were given no instructions on what to do with the meat from the elephant so they tossed in on a huge fire to burn it so the meat would not rot. The smell of roasting elephant was supposedly so appealing that many of the residents of St. Thomas stopped by the pyre with utensils and helped themselves to a plate of pachyderm.

PERSONALITY SURVIVES

The stuffed version of Jumbo traveled with the circus until 1889. Then Barnum donated the elephant to Tufts University. The school kept it on display until 1975 when it was destroyed in a fire. Jumbo's tail was the only part left after the blaze. University officials keep it preserved in its archives, and Jumbo's ashes are stored in a 14-ounce Peter Pan Crunchy Peanut Butter jar in the office of the Tufts athletic director.

St. Thomas built a life-size statue in tribute to Jumbo 100 years after the elephant's death. The town's Railway City Brewing also keeps the memory of Jumbo alive by making Dead Elephant Ale, which has the slogan: "When you raise your glass of Dead Elephant Ale, you will enjoy everything that Jumbo was and became." San Jose Sharks NHL star Joe Thornton is known as "Jumbo Joe" in part because he hails from St. Thomas. Jumbo's legacy also lives on in our language. The word "jumbo" has come to mean "huge" and its used often in for such things as a jumbo jet or jumbo-sized hot dog. So next time you order something that's jumbo-sized, take a moment to remember the majestic mammoth circus entertainer who may have wound up as lunchmeat for the townsfolk in St. Thomas.

* * *

"There has been testing done that has shown that picking your nose while driving is even more dangerous than using a cell phone because of the high occurrences of physical injury while conducting this type of behavior. I would like to see all types of distractions lead to a hefty fine, my advice for this particular offense would be an $850 fine."

—Ontario Transportation Minister Jim Bradley

LIKE A VERIGIN

Pacifist Russians meet discord in the plains.

ON THEIR OWN

The Doukhobors were a spiritualist sect founded in 18th-century Russia. They denounced all forms of organized authority, both of the church and the state. The group believed that the divinity of God is in all people and that formal religious rituals are unnecessary. They were devout pacifists and committed to leading lives of humble toil, often working communally to grow their own food.

After years of persecution and forced removal at the hands of the Russian Empire, the Doukhobors were finally granted permission to leave the country and pursue an independent life elsewhere at the end of the 19th century. The conditions were that the migrants never return; that they finance the cost of migration themselves; and that any Doukhobor currently serving time in prison (a common penalty for what were seen as their subversive activities) must carry out his or her sentence before leaving.

SWEET HOME CANADA

Some Doukhobors chose to migrate to Cyprus, but the majority opted for Canada due to its expansive open spaces and welcoming attitude. Six thousand made the move in the first half of 1899, followed by about 1,500 more later in the year. Writer Leo Tolstoy and the prominent anarchist Peter Kropotkin assisted the migrants both financially and logistically.

Born into a Doukhobor settlement in the Russian village of Slavyanka (present-day Azerbaijan) in 1859, Peter Vasilevich Verigin was groomed from very young to be the leader of the group. Along with two of his brothers, he was home-schooled and learned to read and write. He married in 1882 and soon was appointed secretary to the leader of his group, Lukerya Gubanova.

When Gubanova died in 1886, there was a disagreement as to who would take her place. While Verigin was the clear frontrunner, other candidates were suggested. During the meeting when a vote was to occur, the authorities came in and arrested Verigin. He was given a sentence of 16 years in governmental custody. During his time of exile in the Russian north, the Doukhobors made their Canadian migration. Verigin joined them in 1902, meeting the group in Yorkton in present-day Saskatchewan.

PROBLEMS BEHIND THE SCENES

After moving from Yorkton to Poterpevshie (which the community renamed "Otradnoye," meaning "place of rejoicing"), the group began to splinter over concerns about land management. The Dominion Lands Act, a series of Canadian laws designed to encourage the settlement of the prairie provinces and through which the Doukhobors received their land, required all settlers to register property under individual names. Some of the group, especially the younger members, could be persuaded; other members, and those who had fewer resources to draw from, wanted to preserve collective ownership and live in multi-family villages in which everything was shared.

Verigin came up with a compromise: members should register their land individually (and thus meet the prerequisite of the Dominion Lands Act) while keeping all of their holdings in common. The majority of the community disagreed with him, and when the Canadian government began to enforce the Act with greater force, the group found itself at a crossroads.

In 1908 Verigin led 6,000 of the group to British Columbia. Here he purchased land under his own name so that the Doukhobors could continue to live in a collective fashion. Those more amenable to the demands of the government stayed behind. Now renamed the Christian Community of Universal Brotherhood (CCUB), the group had a stable period of commercial success with their self-owned agricultural, forestry, and industrial pursuits.

Still, problems remained. The fact that many of the group had chosen to stay in Saskatchewan meant that Verigin had to travel great distances to oversee the affairs of the community. To help with this he appointed local managers, many of whom abused their power. They became interested in material gain, and were suspected of wanting to usurp their leader to better serve their own interests. More traditionalist members disliked Verigin's movements toward modernization (i.e., using machinery as opposed to old-fashioned farming methods).

NAKED HATRED

The surrounding population in British Columbia began to resent the community for its economic power as well as the fact that it imported many supplies from outside the region. They also resented the fact that the Doukhobors had their own schools: many natives wanted to establish a stronger sense of Canadian identity, and saw a common public school system as the best means of doing so. For their refusal to participate the Doukhobors were given excessive fines and jail sentences; they retaliated with nude demonstrations at schools and even by burning a few of them. Verigin was caught between the group and the government, forced to play difficult games of diplomacy to keep both sides content.

One of Verigin's most pressing problems did not come from the Doukhobors or the government, but from within his own family. His son by his first wife visited his estranged father in Canada in 1905 and derided him openly as a liar and a cheat. When the group forced him to leave the country for his slanderous remarks, he reportedly threatened to kill the older man.

A STANGE AND SUDDEN DEATH

On October 28, 1924, Verigin boarded a train in Brilliant, British Columbia, where his main residence was located. He was headed to Grand Forks on the Kettle Valley Line. Accompanying him on the journey was his companion, the twenty-year-old Marie Strelaeff. Just past one in the morning on October 29, an explosion occurred in Verigin's car. The roof and sides were blown out immediately. All but two of the twenty-one passengers were killed or injured. Among the deceased were Verigin and Strelaeff. Verigin's body—minus a leg—was eventually found fifteen meters away.

Since the location of the blast was in such a remote site, police and government officials had difficulty getting there. They arrived on special trains or even hand-powered cars. The first major piece of evidence was a part of an Italian clock wired to a battery discovered 75 meters from the site. Based on this, police suspected a time bomb was involved. They initially felt the Doukhobors were the culprits, though as the investigation continued it became apparent Verigin had many enemies: the resentful native population, the Canadian government, the Russian government (upset at Verigin's snubbing their invitation for him to return with the Doukhobors after the Bolshevik Revolution), and even his own son. Some authorities discounted all of this and believed the explosion was simply an accident caused by the gas used to heat and light the train car.

Why has a conclusive answer never arisen? Historians have accused the Canadian government of rushing the inquiry in haste to blame the Doukhobors, an argument that still stands. The rudimentary tactics of 1920s frontier police work have also been blamed, as well as investigators' fatigue and burnout by the early 1930s. Whatever the case, the strange and sudden death of Peter Verigin remains a mystery to this day.

* * *

ACUPUNCTURE FOR FISH

Antonio Park, executive chef and co-owner of Kaizen Sushi Bar in Montreal, is a firm believer in giving acupuncture to fish. He's in the business of selling high-end fresh seafood. Park endorses a technique used on some of his fish called Kaimin Katsugyo, or "sleeping technique." It roughly translates to "live fish sleeping soundly." The technique was first used by a family in Okinawa around 2005.

These acupuncturists strategically insert needles into the fish, sending them into a trance-like state. Their nervous systems are arrested so they are breathing but not moving. Park and a handful of chefs in British Columbia now import these paralyzed fish from Japan. With any dead fish, the color, flavor, and freshness begin to fade immediately. This approach keeps the fish alive and easy to transport, and there is no decomposition.

A commonly used method for importing fish is to put them in salt-water soaked padded envelopes. As oxygen runs low, the fish typically die in 12 hours. With needles inserted, these fish enter a state of limbo between life and death. Those who sing the praises of acupunctured fish say that their deaths are more peaceful as well, which improves the taste. When the fish flesh is served as sushi, it's the absolute freshest. Naturally, acupunctured fish comes with a cost. A tiny slice of snapper costs at least $7. Park says you're also paying for the fish's dignified death because the fish feel no pain with the technique. In addition to that Park says, "It's going to be the freshest snapper you've eaten."

EARLY CANADIAN FILM

Hooray for Hollywood...of the north!

FARM-FILM FLIM-FLAM

Film was a brand new, even novel technology at the turn of the 20th century. While French director Georges Méliès wowed audiences across Europe with his innovative science-fiction films such as *A Trip to the Moon*, Hollywood was just getting started. As far as entertainment was concerned, vaudeville was still tops.

Things were even quieter in Canada. In 1898, the Canadian film industry began to take root. That's when the Toronto-based Massey-Harris company decided to dabble in "moving pictures." They contacted Thomas Edison (one of the developers of the technology) to help them make short films for a very important purpose. Massey-Harris was a manufacturer of farm equipment, and they wanted to advertise their tractors via filmed advertisements across Canada and the U.K.

Oddly enough, at the around the same time in Brandon, Manitoba, another farmer was interested in the nascent world of film. James S. Freer bought a movie camera and projector and became Canada's first film "producer" and the first man to shoot moving pictures in Canada. Freer shot short movies about life around Manitoba and footage of Canadian Pacific Railway trains. The CPR caught wind of Freer's work and paid him to screen his films around the U.K. in late 1898. His tour, titled "Ten Years in Manitoba," was a hit, which perked up the ears of officials in Ottawa.

LIKE MOTHS TO A FLAME

Some bureaucrats thought film might make a powerful tool of persuasion and advertisement—they were worried that Canada was losing its distinctive English character in favor of an American influence, in part due to an influx of American immigrants.

The government teamed up with the CPR, who shared a similar mass persuasion goal in getting as many people as possible to ride the train. In 1902, the CPR agreed to film sections of Canada, coast-to-coast, which would then be screened in the U.K. to promote immigration to Canada. The government and the CPR recruited a few filmmakers and formed them into a group called The Bioscope Company. Their instructions–film the majestic natural beauty of Canada...but absolutely no winter scenes. (At the time, the average British notion of Canada was that it was a frosty, desolate backwater populated only by polar bears and igloos.)

OUR HOME AND NATIVE LAND

The crew spent nine months touring the country from Quebec to Vancouver Island and filmed everything from lumberjacks to lush meadows and happy immigrants arriving in Quebec City. They called their film series *Living Canada*. It debuted at a gala London premiere in 1903 and received rave reviews from critics and audiences alike.

In the decades that followed, much of the almost entirely non-existent Canadian film industry was dominated by such corporate-sponsored promotions and productions funded by the CPR and government designed to further bolster British immigration. (And it worked–millions moved to Canada from England in the early 20th century.)

Meanwhile, uptight film exchange and censorship groups in each province filtered the flow of much more entertaining international movies into Canada. In what was a predecessor to the "Canadian Content" distinction, at one point, Ontario's board banned American films that contained "excessive" amounts of pro-American sentiment, up to an including scenes of American flags literally waving. Curiously, after the U.S. joined the U.K. and Canada in World War I, the ban was lifted.

COURTING CONTROVERSY

That's not to say that a few fictional movies weren't made in Canada back then. The first known drama produced in Canada was *Hiawatha, The Messiah of the Ojibway*, a film about the famous Native American leader. It was filmed in 1903 by *Living Canada* filmmaker Joseph Rosenthal.

After the conclusion of World War 1, Nell and Ernest Shipman, a husband and wife production team, also shot silent films around Canada. Their most notable effort was 1919's *Back to God's Country*, a movie based on American author James Oliver Curwood's short story about a schooner travelling through the perilous waters of the Arctic

Ocean. It's also the first Canadian film to feature female nudity. Nell, who wrote the screenplay, shifted the story's focus to Dolores, a young woman who flees the ship on dog sled and avenges her father's death. Nell also starred in the 73-minute film and is the one who stripped down.

The incredibly controversial scene helped *Back to God's Country* to become both an international hit and the most successful Canadian silent film of all time. The bold production, which was one of the first in cinematic history to feature a woman as a courageous hero instead of a helpless damsel in distress, posted an astounding 300% profit.

Nell divorced Ernest shortly thereafter, moved to the U.S., and formed Nell Shipman Productions, her own film company (with her new lover). She produced, wrote, co-directed and starred in a successful sequel called *The Girl From God's Country* in 1921. Nell created several more films throughout the '20s before her company went bankrupt.

SILVER STREAK

Unfortunately, most all prints of both *Hiawatha, The Messiah of the Ojibway* and *Back to God's Country* are lost, and in all likliehood were destroyed long ago. Desperate for cash during the Great Depression, the Ontario Motion Picture Bureau melted down most of the movies in its archive to salvage and sell all of the silver nitrate contained in the film stock. Decades later, however, a copy of *Back to God's Country* was discovered in Europe. It was restored and re-released in 2000.

The film is still considered one of the finest early achievements in Canadian cinema. Its contentious nude scene also served as an unwitting precursor to another Canadian blockbuster—the teenage sex romp *Porky's*, released in 1982.

* * *

QUIRKY COMICS

Mike Myers. Myers collects model soldiers, which he enjoys painting while watching old war footage.

Dan Aykroyd. The former criminology student was born with webbed toes and two different-colored eyes—one green, one brown.

WEIRD CANADA

Crystal lakes, snow-capped mountains, hockey, Mounties, bilingual traffic signs...and some really, really weird news stories.

AN "A+" FOR CREATIVE THINKING

In January 2006, history professor David Weale of the University of Prince Edward Island had a severely overcrowded class, with 95 students. His solution: He offered a work-free B-minus to any student who agreed not to show up for the rest of the semester. Twenty accepted. When administrators found out, Weale, who had come out of retirement to teach the class, was asked to re-retire.

NAME GAME

James Clifford Hanna, a resident of the Yukon Territory, argued before a court that he didn't have to pay his taxes. Reason: "James Clifford Hanna" was a name given to him involuntarily. Since he never asked for nor accepted the name, he wasn't legally responsible for paying the taxes of anyone named James Clifford Hanna. Whatever his name is, he lost the case.

A BIRD IN THE HEAD

Shawn Hacking, 13, of Winnipeg, suffered scraped knees, a sprained wrist, and a bruise on his face when a Canada goose landed on the boy's head and slapped a wing into his face at the same time. The force knocked Hacking off his skateboard. Hacking's friend Brent Bruchanski, who witnessed the event, said, "It was so funny...but I felt sorry for him at the same time."

HOW MUCH FOR NOT ROBBING SOMEONE?

Over the 2000 holiday season, officials in Edmonton tried to encourage motorists to obey the rules of the road by having police officers in unmarked cars find and reward the safest drivers in town. Traffic officers tailed drivers for as long as half an hour to determine if they were truly law-abiding, then pulled the puzzled motorists over and offered them a free steak dinner for two at "Tom Goodchild's Moose Factory."

It's illegal to threaten a bird in Canada.

MORE! MORE! MORE!

After winning a $1.2 million lottery jackpot in 1989, Barbara Bailey of Montreal enjoyed her windfall modestly, buying a house for about $200,000 and loaning money to friends and relatives. Then she started blowing it on extravagances, and within two years she was broke and living on welfare. Desperate to recapture her millionaire lifestyle, Bailey got her niece, a bank teller, to divert $500,000 from other peoples' accounts into Bailey's. The bank quickly caught on. She was sentenced to a two-year jail term.

THE REAL POOP

Bill Sewepagaham, a leader of the Cree tribe in northern Alberta, offered a good luck charm to the Edmonton Oilers during the 2006 National Hockey League playoffs: a necklace made of lacquered deer and moose feces. Sewepagaham claimed it was based on an ancient Cree tradition in which hunters who'd had a fruitless day would smear their weapons in animal droppings and the next day they'd have better luck. Unfortunately, the charm didn't work—the Oilers lost in the Stanley Cup finals.

TOKEN OF OUR APPRECIATION

Over a period of 13 years, Edmonton transit worker Salim Kara patiently built a fortune of $2.3 million (Canadian) by stealing coins from fare machines using a rod with a magnetized tip. No one suspected the 44-year-old delinquent until he purchased an $800,000 house on a yearly salary of $38,000. He was sentenced to four years in prison in 1996.

STICKS AND STONES

In 1991, a GM assembly line foreman in Ontario, reprimanded a worker for having bad body odor. The worker complained to the Workers Compensation Tribunal about loss of appetite, lack of sleep, and sexual dysfunctions brought on by the foreman's insensitive remarks. The Tribunal awarded him $3,000 for "job stress."

A QUICK STOP

In October 2012, a city bus driver stopped the bus and gave the shoes off his feet to a homeless man who had no shoes on that freezing morning.

Vancouver is tied with Zurich, Switzerland for highest quality of life of any city in the world.

THE CRUSADES OF LOUIS RIEL

While the use of the "insanity defense" has been a legal tactic for ages, one curious instance of its use—and the story behind it—continues to fascinate.

THE EARLY YEARS

Louis Riel was born on the Red River Settlement, in what is today the borderland between the province of Manitoba and the United States, in the year 1844. The Red River Settlement was then occupied by First Nations tribes and Métis families, a group of both First Nations and European ancestry. A Métis of seven-eighths European ancestry, Riel showed precociousness in his studies and was recommended for coursework at a seminary in Montreal. While he did well, the untimely death of his father in 1864 caused him great emotional pain; he became prone to bouts of depression, and left the seminary in 1865. He tried formal study again, this time at a convent school run by nuns, but was asked to leave due to his dissolute attitude.

A period of waywardness and itinerant labor followed. Riel worked as a law clerk in Montreal, had a love affair and thwarted marriage proposal with a young woman, took clerking jobs in Chicago and St. Paul, tried his hand at poetry, and ultimately returned to the Red River Settlement in 1868. His future was uncertain, but he had the life experience of a man more than twice his age.

THE MAKINGS OF A LEADER

The Settlement was in the midst of great changes. New migrants from America and other Canadian cities such as Ontario were openly hostile to the Métis and to Roman Catholicism, the predominant religion of the area. What was more pressing, however, was the fact that the area on which the Red River Settlement stood—a wide swath of property known as Rupert's Land—was in negotiations to be sold. The Hudson's Bay Company owned it at the time, but the Canadian government had strong interest in purchasing it. The new American settlers, naturally, wanted the United States to annex it.

News of a Canadian-sponsored governmental survey of the Red River Settlement in August 1869 unsettled Riel and the Métis community. They feared displacement, the loss of their language and way of life, and suppression of their religious beliefs. As few held deeds to their property, there was no way of proving what was theirs. The community quickly began organizing resistance efforts. Riel emerged as a natural leader when he gave an incendiary speech against the survey in late August. That October, he and several other Métis tried to blockade progress of the survey; the group formally collectivized into the Métis National Committee and began fighting for Métis rights.

SQUARING OFF

Throughout the autumn of 1869, the Métis National Committee did all it could to stymie the efforts of the government. This included denying entrance of survey participants into Métis territory—including the lieutenant governor of the Northwest Territories, William McDougall. They also captured a major Hudson's Bay Company trading post, Fort Garry.

In November, the Métis National Committee met with new settlers of the Red River Territory to discuss how to best deal with the infiltration of the Canadian government. That month the government demanded the Métis cease their disruptive activities. The Committee responded by drafting a list of grievances and desired rights.

On December 1, Rupert's Land was formally transferred to the Canadian government. This did not stop the activity of the Committee. Riel and his men met with other settlers of the Red River Territory and presented the list of rights and conditions for accepting the new political boundaries. Most of the settlers agreed with these conditions, though several staunch pro-Canadians did not. They splintered off into the "Canadian Party" and found support with governmental officials. When it was discovered that the leader of the Canadian Party, Dr. John Christian Schultz, was recruiting men to fight against the Métis, Riel ordered Schultz's home surrounded. Those who went forward with his instructions were arrested and imprisoned, adding further divisiveness to the already agitated area.

SUCCESS AND EXILE

The Métis National Committee announced itself a provisional government on December 8, 1869. Hearing of all the unrest, the

Canadian government sent delegates from Ottawa to try and negotiate with the Métis. Formal talks began in January 1870 and went through the month. In the beginning of February the Canadian delegation accepted a new set of terms from Riel and agreed to let him send his own delegates to Ottawa to discuss the matter officially.

Things seemed to be going well for the Committee when an error in judgment nearly derailed its momentum—and Riel's reputation. In an altercation with the Canadian Party in mid-February, Riel and his band captured 46 insurgents bent on bringing down the provisional government. One of the captured men, Thomas Scott, was tried for insubordination and sentenced to death by the provisional government. Riel refused to commute the sentence, despite pleas from his political allies, and Scott was executed on March 4.

Ottawa officially accepted many of the Métis' demands for religious and language rights later that month. They were adapted into the Manitoba Act in May, which created the province of Manitoba. For this Riel is still called "The Father of Manitoba" and looked upon as a Canadian folk hero.

Still, at the time the Scott execution was still fresh in people's minds, and the Canadian government used it as propaganda against Riel. When a military brigade was dispatched to the Red River Settlement to quash the final vestiges of the Red River Rebellion, Riel was forced to flee his beloved homeland.

TRIAL AND DEATH

In forced exile (to various Canadian cities and eventually the United States), Riel began to exhibit signs of mental illness. He was said to believe he was the divinely chosen leader of the Métis people. He was committed to two different mental institutions between 1876 and 1878, where he began writing lengthy pseudo-religious tracts and referring to himself as a prophet. Gradually his mental health was restored, and he relocated to Montana upon his release. Here he married, had children, and taught school.

In June 1884 his political fervor returned. Hearing that Métis settlers to the Saskatchewan territory were being denied land rights by the Canadian government, he traveled north to help their cause. The duration of his stay extended into the following year, when tensions between the Métis and the government triggered the North-West

Rebellion. Riel and his forces surrendered following the Battle of Batoche in May of 1885.

With his long history of antigovernment activity, Canadian officials wasted no time in trying Riel for treason. In July he was brought before a jury in Regina, Saskatchewan. In the case's most curious moment, Riel argued *against* his own lawyers when they tried to claim insanity as the cause of his actions. He maintained that all of his political involvement was justified and done for love of the Métis and his homeland. Despite his impassioned defense, the jury found him guilty. The judge, the very pro-Canadian Hugh Richardson, sentenced him to death by hanging. Riel was executed on November 16, 1885, a man with a complex personal history who nevertheless helped shape a fair and free modern Canada.

*   *   *

MORE LOONY LAWS

• In Petrolia, Ontario, a law says that anyone who whistles, sings, shouts, yells, or "hoots" will be arrested.

• In Sudbury, Ontario, it's illegal to mount anything that makes noise to your bike, except a bell or a horn.

• In Quebec, it is considered illegal to impersonate a foreigner.

• In Halifax, Nova Scotia, it's illegal for taxi drivers to wear T-shirts, and socks must be worn at all times.

• It's against the law there to swear in French in Montreal.

• Snowmen taller than 30 inches are illegal in Souris, Prince Edward Island.

• The dairy industry was so opposed to margarine in Ontario between 1886 and 1948, margarine was banned in Ontario. After 1948, it became was legal to sell it, as long as it wasn't the same color as butter.

• There is a much smaller selection of comic books in Canada: Any comic books that depict a crime are illegal in Canadaa

ALERT!

This much is certain: you can't find a decent taco anywhere in Alert.

LIFE IN A NORTHERN TOWN

Alert is a community that sits almost literally at the top of the world. It's a research facility on the northern tip of Ellesmere Island in Nunavut, and it's just a hop, skip and jump away from the North Pole. (Okay, it's 508 miles.) Alert's main claim to fame is that its the northernmost permanent settlement in the world.

After the end of World War II, both the United States and Canada developed an interest in funding a network of stations in the Arctic that could serve as transportation and communications hubs while also facilitating scientific research projects. As part of their efforts, construction began on a joint U.S./Canada weather station named "Alert," which opened on Easter Sunday in 1950.

A crew had hoped to break ground, er, tundra a year prior but a harsh spring and unfavorable ice conditions kept ships from sailing any further north than Resolute Bay. Alert's first weather report was finally sent out on July 1st. (The facility's namesake: The HMS *Alert*, a British navy schooner that wintered in nearby Cape Sheridan in 1875.) Sadly, that same year, nine members of the Royal Canadian Air Force died in a plane crash while attempting to drop supplies nearby. It was just the first of two major tragedies that have befallen the facility.

THE REALLY, REALLY COLD WAR

In 1958, as Cold War tensions festered, the army took an interest in Alert. They were also eager to maintain the country's sovereignty over the region. Alert quickly expanded into a military outpost, but, no doubt due to its extremely isolated location, it was never a focal point for espionage or any international intrigue involving the Soviet Union.

The most exciting things that happened in Alert during the remainder of the Cold War:

• In 1964, a Norwegian daredevil named Bjorn Staib tried to reach the North Pole, using Alert as his staging area. His expedition failed.

• This wouldn't be an Uncle John book if we didn't note that, in 1965, Alert got its first flush toilets.

• A year-round team arrived in 1971 to monitor seismological readings and operate something called a "super-neutron monitor" for Atomic Energy of Canada, the nuclear science and tech company.

• In the early '70s, Italian businessman and adventurer Guido Mozino led 27 hearty souls out of Alert and towards the top of world to recreate Robert E. Peary's fabled Arctic campaign.

• Japan's Naomi Uemura passed through Alert before becoming the first person to reach the pole alone in 1978.

• On October 30th, 1991, a Canadian transport plane headed for the Alert research station crashed 19 miles short of the facility's runway. Four people on board were killed instantly. It took rescue teams 30 hours to reach the survivors in the middle of a fierce blizzard. Of the 14 remaining souls that endured the storm only one of them, the pilot, perished. The disaster was later chronicled in the 1993 TV film *Ordeal in the Arctic,* starring Richard Chamberlain.

ON TOP OF THE WORLD

So what's it like up there? Global warming be damned, snow covers the ground ten or more months out of the year and temperatures can reach as low as -40 degrees Fahrenheit in the wintertime. And the wind chill? It could freeze your skin in seconds. Going outside during the winter without heavy thermal gear and a lifeline is considered madness. However, the Arctic's midnight sun keeps everything well lit from April through early September. Local wildlife, including wild foxes, hares, and wolves routinely pass through on their way to drink water at Dumbell Lake.

At its peak in the '80s, over 200 people lived in Alert. Over the years, the population has steadily declined as the facility becomes increasingly automated and as cutbacks take their toll. The Canadian government has outsourced many of the remaining positions to outside contractors in recent years. The facility itself is pretty drab, consisting entirely of unremarkable, warehouse-like buildings designed to endure all that frigid weather.

IT'S A LIVING

As boring as life up there might sound, those who venture to Alert keep themselves entertained. Employees traditionally add signs pointing to their hometowns, complete with the mileage, to a growing collection that greets visitors. A radio station and the occasional live concert also help keep things lively. "Ladies eat free," according to a sign posted outside The Igloo Restaurant, Alert's cafeteria. What's on the menu? Pea soup, scallops, and "wild cod steaks."

In 2006, Prime Minister Stephen Harper visited Alert during his campaign tour to promote continued Canadian sovereignty over its northernmost regions. On November 9th, 2009, the Olympic Torch also reached the facility during the relay for the 2010 Winter Olympics in Vancouver.

* * *

CRAZY FOOTBALL LEAGUE

Football has been a part of Canadian sporting life since 1861. The Canadian Football League or CFL (sometimes called the Crazy Football League) is the oldest professional sport league in North America. Football has a long and interesting history in Canada, and by some accounts it is the second most popular sport after hockey.

Some facts:

• The championship Grey Cup trophy was stolen from Lansdowne Park in Ottawa and held for ransom for two months before being returned safely.

• The 1950 Grey Cup was called the Mud Bowl because the field was so wet—at one point fans literally thought a player was drowning on the field.

• The week before the 1939 Grey Cup in Toronto, the weather turned wet and then cold. To soften the rock-hard turf, the grounds crew decided to pour over 1,700 liters (400 gallons) of gasoline on the field and set it ablaze the day before the game.

After 20 years of promising, John Marillo of Windsor swam to Detroit after chugging eight beers (2013).

DEFYING GRAVITY

Ontario native Frederick Banting is best known for discovering insulin, saving the lives of millions of diabetics. Here's a story of another of Banting's scientific pursuits.

THE AIR UP THERE

Prior to World War II, fighter pilots had to contend not only with the inherent dangers of dogfighting, but with the possibility of fainting in the cockpit. When they hit high-enough speeds—in a dive or while pulling out of a steep turn—high gravity force (G-force) could cause their blood to be drawn from the eyes and the brain. The centrifugal force was pushing blood into the legs and abdomens, with sometimes-lethal physiological repercussions. Blinded, they would crash.

(A quick primer on G-force: It's measured in units called "Gs." At sea level, our bodies are at one G. A roller coaster, depending on how extreme it is, delivers G forces between four and six. Without protection, pilots can withstand no more than about 6 Gs.)

As World War II began, Canadian physician Frederick Banting took an interest in the health problems surrounding flying, particularly the blackouts. Banting was well suited to military medicine—he was a decorated World War I soldier and in 1923 was awarded the Nobel Prize for discovering insulin. Finding a solution would give Allied pilots a great advantage over the enemy. In 1939, the Royal Canadian Airforce established the Institute of Aviation Medicine on the site of the Eglinton Hunt Club in Toronto. Here Banting directed secret research on the physiological effects of combat flying.

OF MICE AND MEN

At the Institute, Banting constructed the first decompression chamber in North America. Completed in 1941, it allowed atmospheric pressure to be gradually raised or lowered. Banting explored the effects of high altitudes, where the atmospheric pressure is lower because the air is less dense.

Eager to understand the effects of high altitude on his the body, Banting would sometimes forge recklessly ahead to find answers, and experiment with his own body. Shortly after testing the effects of mustard gas on himself, Banting wanted to experience the effects of intense decompression. Fortunately, his team of fellow scientists kept him from taking such a risk.

At the Institute, Banting also built an accelerator to test the effects of high speeds on the human body. A colleague working in cancer research, Wilbur Franks of Weston, Ontario, had observed that test tubes would break under high centrifugal force. To prevent their shattering, Franks figured out to insert them into bigger and stronger liquid-filled bottles before subjecting them to centrifugal force.

NOTHIN' BUT A G THANG

Following on his success with the test tubes, Franks thought that water-filled suits might provide a similar type of protection for pilots. To test if water-filled suits might help counter the effects of the G force, Dr. Franks and fellow scientists fashioned tiny water-filled suits out of condoms and put them on lab mice. Franks placed the mice in a centrifuge and found that they could withstand at least 150 Gs. Even at that great force, the mice came out of the experiment with unharmed hearts and all bodily functions intact. Without the glove, the water-filled condom suit, the little rodents would have been crushed.

Encouraged by the results, Franks and Banting had a tailor make an anti-G suit for humans, constructed of cotton and rubber with sewn-in water bladders. In May 1940, Franks himself slipped on the newly created suit, which was filled with water to the level of the heart. Wearing the prototype, the doctor boarded an aircraft at Camp Borden near Barrie, Ontario, and remained conscious at about 7 Gs while pulling out of a steep dive. The pressure from the water in the suit pushed against the legs and abdomen and kept his blood where he needed it—in the heart and head.

The suit was a success but needed some tweaks. Franks had tailored the suit to fit him standing up. Sitting down it put more pressure on him than he had suspected. "The suit had been cut to fit me perfectly, standing up...In the airplane I was sitting down, and when the pressure hit I thought it was going to cut me in two. The idea became practical only when we realized that great areas of the body could be left outside the fluid system."

CLOTHES MAKE THE MAN

To test and perfect his suit, Franks invented a "human centrifuge." The machine ran on the same power grid that supplied electricity to Toronto's electric streetcars. And it ran on a *lot* of electricity. Whenever Franks conducted a test, the streetcars nearby came to a stop.

After several modifications, the Franks Flying Suit was tested in the spring of 1941 when Royal Canadian Air Force Squadron Leader and Canadian pilot F.E.R. Briggs wore the outfit in flight. The suit had its first battle test in November 1942, in the invasion of North Africa at Oran, Algeria. Pilots were able to make dangerous maneuvers without blacking out. It was the world's first anti-gravity suit worn in combat.

However, some pilots complained that the suit was uncomfortable to wear, specifically because the weight of the water made it extremely heavy. In 1944, the U.S. Air Force and Navy, working with the Mayo Clinic and Berger Brothers Company, designed a new model G-suit using compressed air. It had the same results as the Franks suit except it was much more comfortable to wear, and much lighter. The suits with compressed air weighed just three pounds, compared to 18 pounds for the Franks suit.

THE WAR HEROES

While Banting saw the development of suit, he did not get to see its success in battle. Ironically, he died in an airplane accident. As Banting flew on a mission to the U.K. to discuss the transfer of certain research projects to Canada, an engine in his plane failed. The pilot turned the plane around, but the second engine failed as well, causing the bomber to crash near Musgrave Harbor, Newfoundland, on February 21, 1941. Always determined to serve his fellow man, Banting managed to wrap the wounds of the injured pilot before dying from his own injuries at age 49.

In 1944, Franks received an Order of the British Empire for giving "the Allied forces a tremendous tactical advantage" and "saving the lives of thousands of Allied fighter pilots."

Street hockey in Canada is often called Shinny because of the shin pads worn.

WEIRD HISTORY

There is nowhere stranger than Canada, present or past.

BACK TO THE FUTURE

In 1941, the South Forks Bridge in Gold Bridge, B.C., had a grand reopening. A black-and-white photo captured the moment. While everyone in the throng looks straight from the World War II era, one fellow sticks out. With his modern-looking printed T-shirt, a sweater, and his sunglasses, the man appears to have stepped back in time from the future. The photo went viral due to the "time-travelling hipster." But the young man is actually wearing items that were available in the early 1940s. A close look at the t-shirt suggest that it may have hand-sewn emblem on it, which was common practice for sports teams at the time. Some say it may even be for the Montreal Maroons. So the time traveler, in all likelihood, is just a young man who dressed casually...and maybe ahead of his time.

HILLS, THAT IS

In the mid-1960s, one of the biggest voices on the Canadian pop music scene was Lucille Starr from St. Boniface, Manitoba. In 1964, she released "The French Song," which sold seven million copies. Like many Canadian entertainers, Starr (real name Savoie) moved to California. She landed a job on *The Beverly Hillbillies*—supplying Cousin Pearl's (Bea Benaderet's) yodeling voice.

ALL CLOGGED UP

Probably one of the quietest times at Niagara Falls was during a freezing spell in 1848. The mighty flow was reduced to a mere trickle for 30 to 40 hours because of an ice jam at the mouth of Lake Erie. The riverbed at the base of the fall dried up enough so that people could walk out into it. Those who did found all sorts of interesting items including bayonets, muskets, and tomahawks from the War of 1812. Reports say that eventually people heard a huge crack and the falls returned to their normal, ferocious state.

St. John's is the foggiest Canadian city, with about 124 days of fog a year.

A SUPER-FREAKY MUSIC STORY

In 1964, Rick James was planning his career as a musician...and he certainly didn't want to go fight for the U.S. in the Vietnam War. So, he did what many young American men did, and he fled his naval reserve post and escaped to Canada. He bummed around Toronto for a while, and joined a garage band called the Mynah Birds. The band eventually got a deal with Motown, but they only ever recorded one single, "It's My Time," but it was never released. However, every member of the Mynah Birds would go on to huge success in popular music. James became a funk superstar with hits like "Give it To Me Baby" and "Super Freak." Goldie McJohn and Bruce Palmer went on to join Steppenwolf. The other member of the band? Some guy named Neil Young.

READY, AIM.....FAINT!

In August 1873, two men, Mr. Dooley and Mr. Healey (their first names are strangely lost to history), fought the last duel in Canada in a field near St. John's, Newfoundland (although it was not Canadian territory at the time). The two friends had fallen in love with the same young woman, and they fought bitterly over her. They decided that the only honorable way to decide who should be with the maiden was a duel. After quickly setting up the time and place, they met one morning with no one else present except the two men's seconds. In classic dueling fashion, the friends stood back to back with their pistols raised and proceeded to take their paces away from each other. Each was having second thoughts and growing terrified at the prospect of dying in a duel and killing a friend. At 9 meters (10 yards), they turned and fired. Dooley collapsed to the ground instantly. Healey was convulsed with horror that he had somehow killed Dooley. But Dooley had merely fainted. Fortunately, their seconds had so dreaded the outcome that they loaded the pistols with blanks. Although this was a serious breach in dueling etiquette, Healey and Dooley, so thankful that they hadn't killed each other, settled their differences and went on as friends.

GOES TO 11

There's loud, and then there's ear-splitting. In the world of rock 'n' roll, being the loudest is something to strive for. The Who held the title for years, hitting a max of 126 decibels, but Manowar turned it up a notch. They pushed the levels of loudness to new extremes at

The TV show *Smallville,* which is set in Kansas, was filmed in British Columbia.

one of their shows in 1994, during which they hit 129 decibels. Many say that KISS deserves the title now. On July 15, 2009, at the Cisco Ottawa Bluesfest in Ottawa, Canada, KISS achieved 136 decibels, as measured by City of Ottawa Bylaw officers. Although there is no definitive record holder, the KISS show in Ottawa is among the loudest ever.

THE NARROWEST BUILDING IN THE WORLD

In 1912, Chang Toy owned a plot of land in Vancouver's Chinatown that was reduced to a very narrow size when part of it was appropriated to build a road. Many thought Toy, the owner of the Sam Kee Company, couldn't do much with such a narrow lot, but he constructed a building that was just 6 feet deep (1.8 meters). He added bay windows and public baths under the sidewalk to maximize the oddly shaped site. Visitors can see what Ripley has officially called the narrowest building in the world at the corner of Carall and Pender Streets, which is just about a 10-minute walk from Vancouver's Gastown.

* * *

REAL CANADIAN JOBS

According to Ancenstry.ca, these were real jobs in the late 19th century.

- Lunatic Keeper
- Criminal
- Idiot
- Beggar
- Witch
- Monster
- Pig Nurse

WEIRD CANADA

Crystal lakes, snow-capped mountains, hockey, Mounties, bilingual traffic signs...and some really, really weird news stories.

SHARING DINNER WITH MUM

It was only days since their mother had passed away in 2009, and the seven Blair sisters were gathered to celebrate Thanksgiving in her honor. Each of them wore a locket with a small bit of their mother's ashes sealed within. But now as they dined in their Hamilton, Ontario home, they began to see bits of gray in the mashed potatoes, in the gravy, and on the turkey. Then, to her horror, Lisa Blair saw gray dribbling down the front of her white sweater. The lockets, supposedly sealed by the funeral home, were leaking. "Not only was it in my food," said Lisa, "it was all down my sweater."

BEACHED CAMPAIGN

In 2009, Premier Ed Stelmach's $25 million campaign to promote Alberta and "get the correct information out" fell on its face after some false advertising. An ad showing two cute kids romping on a seaside beach promoted the new provincial motto, "Freedom to Create, Spirit to Achieve." One local, Peter Baily, liked that shoreline so much he contacted provincial officials for the exact location. Turns out the featured beach was in Northumberland, UK. Even the children in the ad weren't Canadian. The official response from Alberta spokesperson Tom Olsen was that the British beach showed that "Albertans are a worldly people." Today, Alberta's motto is "Fortis et Liber," aka "Strong and Free." And it's written on the Alberta Coat of Arms, which features a stag, a beaver, a mountain lion, flowers and mountains—all native to Alberta.

ULTIMATE BELIEVERS

Though University of Saskatchewan graduate Hulda Clark was a "doctor" because she had a PhD, she claimed to have found the cause of cancer and offered an alternative, naturopathic remedy. In her 1993 book, The Cure for All Cancers, Clark writes: "All cancers are alike. They are all caused by a parasite. A single parasite! It is the human intestinal fluke." Clark claimed to cure cancer with a combination of herbs (black walnut hulls, wormwood and cloves plus amino acids ornithine and arginine) and treatment with her two special devices: the Syncrometer (a galvanometer) and her Zapper (a low voltage device).

IF THE CLICHÉ FITS...

In January 2013, two police officers in Calgary, Alberta, were investigated after a video was posted on YouTube of the officers in their police cars racing down a Calgary street...to a doughnut shop. An investigation was launched and the two officers came forward, admitting that they were the ones who had staged a short car race to the doughnut shop. They were not named, and, as they had not appeared to exceed the speed limit, they were not disciplined. "They didn't break any laws," police spokesman Kevin Brookwell said, but admitted that "the optics looked bad."

CREDIT CARDS WITHOUT LIMITS

If you've ever had trouble getting credit, don't read this. Kelly Sloan of Sarnia, Ontario, received a letter in the mail from Capital One not long ago offering up to $30,000 in credit and a credit card. The letter wasn't to her, though. It was addressed to her dog. The announcement, addressed to "Spark Sloan," explained, "We're not offering our low long-term rate to just anyone." Spark had been dead for 10 years.

FOUR FACTOR

We all know that the number 13 is considered an unlucky number, but what is there to fear about the number 4? The Toronto suburb of Richmond Hill dislikes the number so much it has officially declared that the number 4 should not be used in new addresses. The fear of four—or tetraphobia—rises from the Asian community in the area. In Mandarin and Cantonese, the word for "death" happens to sound like the word "four." Town councilman Castro Liu has said that those shopping for a new home don't want to buy a place with that number in it. Town councillors have expressed concerns that the change could be confusing and possibly cause trouble for emergency responders, as many have rewritten their addresses to remove the 4s. One realtor in the area has said that getting rid of the 4 in an address can raise the home value by $25,000 to $35,000.

The country's largest producer of french fries is McCain Foods in Florenceville, New Brunswick.

PROUD CANUDIANS

It may be colder in Vancouver, but that doesn't stop some locals from stripping down. In addition to the nude sunbathing at Wreck Beach, the city plays host to a World Naked Bike Ride. On June 15, 2013, hundreds of naked cyclists pedaled their way through the city in protest of oil dependency and car culture. The ride began at Sunset Beach with two hours of body painting and performances before the bare-bottomed bicyclists took off into the streets of Vancouver.

FILE UNDER IRONIC

In 2012, Canadian officials said Avmor Ltd. is voluntarily recalling one lot of its antimicrobial foaming hand soap because it is contaminated with microbes. Health inspectors detected the bacteria *Pseudomonas aeruginosa*, which can pose serious health risks, especially for those with weakened immune systems. The soap is commonly used in hospitals, offices, and schools.

THE THIEF WHO SWALLOWED 20 GRAND

A thief with an appetite for expensive jewelry walked into Precision Jewellers in Windsor, Ontario, and swallowed a 1.7-carat diamond ring worth $20,000. A store clerk nabbed him, and the police put him in a cell where they could wait for the evidence to emerge.

*　　*　　*

CANADIAN IN NAME ONLY

The band Cross Canadian Ragweed formed in Yukon...*Oklahoma*, which happens to be in *Canadian* County. Furthermore, its singer and guitarist is named Cody Canada. But despite all these Canada connections, the band's name is actually a fractured amalgam of the three founding members' names: Grady Cross, Cody Canada, and Randy Ragsdale, with a little "weed" thrown in for good luck.

EVERYTHING'S GONE "GREEN"

No book with the words "weird" and "Canada" in its title would be complete without a look at Tom Green.

ORGANIZED NONSENSE

Born in Pembroke, Ontario, Green spent a few years as a stand-up comedian and college DJ before pursuing a career as a rapper named M.C. Bones—as a joke. Nevertheless, Green's group Organized Rhyme scored a hit with "Check the O.R.," which was nominated for a Juno Award in 1993.

Organized Rhyme had disbanded by 1994, when 23-year-old Green premiered his TV series, *The Tom Green Show*. A bizarre amalgam of talk show, variety show, and hidden-camera series, *The Tom Green Show* was so popular on cable access that it got picked up by The Comedy Network, and then MTV.

RAZZED

Some highlights: mocking his uneasy sidekick Glenn Humplik, riding a horse into a grocery store, and painting an X-rated scene on his parents' car. Green even used the show to return to music, releasing a hit novelty single called "Lonely Swedish (The Bum Bum Song)"—so named because the lyrics consist mostly of Green talking about putting his "bum bum" on things.

The series went on hiatus in 2000 when Green was diagnosed with testicular cancer—for which he underwent surgery, and filmed for an MTV special. He rarely left the public eye, thanks to his short-lived marriage to Drew Barrymore and a jump to films, such films as *Road Trip*, *Stealing Harvard*...and *Freddy Got Fingered*. More performance art and a series of ironic, gross-out sketches than a movie, it was Roger Ebert's most hated movie and won Green a Razzie Award for Worst Actor—for which he accepted in person, a Hollywood first.

Although Green's career has suffered numerous ups and downs over the years, he continues to be a pop culture innovator. He hosted a long running web series *Tom Green's House Tonight!*, which became Tom Green Radio, one of the first podcasts.

In Fredericton, New Brunswick, it's against the law to wear a snake.

LOONY LAWS

Believe it or not, all of these are real.

• If you own pigeons and live in Toronto, it's illegal to allow them to perch on any property that you don't own.

• If your parrot talks too loudly in Oak Bay, B.C., you could be fined $100.

• Selling artificially colored chicks is illegal in Nova Scotia.

• Public spitting is against the law in Kanata, Ontario—including baseball players attempting to throw a spitball.

• Also illegal in Kanata: purple garage doors.

• Washing your car in the street is illegal in Montreal.

• Nationwide, it's against the law to let a perfectly edible fish you caught in national park waters go rotten.

• Trash bags in St. John's, Newfoundland, must be at least 1.5 mm thick and hold between 25 and 90 litres.

• Removing your feet from the pedals when bicycling is illegal in Ottawa.

• Hunting by flashlight is against the law in Alberta.

• Chipped or cracked bathtubs are forbidden in Dartmouth, Nova Scotia.

• In Canada, it's illegal to enter a plane...mid-flight.

• Still on the books in Alberta: Once you're released from prison, the government is required to give you a handgun, bullets, and a horse...so you can get the heck out of town.

• You can take the bark off of a tree in Halifax...provided you've gotten written permission from the city government.

• Unhinging somebody else's front gate is a crime in Wolfville, Nova Scotia.

• Living inside a streetcar is illegal in Thompson, Manitoba.

The Leopard's Lounge, a strip club in Ontario, offers college tuition to its dancers.

IT'S A RECORD!

Enterprising Canadians, setting world records.

Playing *Diablo III*: In 2012, a man known only by the online handle "Kripparrian" became the first person in the world to complete the computer game on the insanely hard "Inferno" difficulty level.

Juggling chainsaws: In Sept. 2011, Ian Stewart of Windsor, Nova Scotia, juggled—and caught—94 chainsaws.

Largest parking lot: The lot at the West Edmonton Mall can accomodate 20,000 vehicles.

Most expensive hot dog: DougieDog in Vancouver offers the Dragon Dog. It costs $100, because it's made with 100-year-old cognac, Kobe beef, truffle oil, and lobster.

Needles in the head: Mohanathas Sivanyagam of Toronto stuck 2,025 needles in his head in 2001 (we don't know why).

Largest collection of Santa Claus memorabilia: Jean-Guy Laquerre of Boucherville, Quebec, possesses 25,189 different Santa items (as of press time).

Simultaneous head shaving: At the 2010 Terry Fox Run in Port Colborne, Ontario, 57 people shorn their locks all at the same time.

Heaviest triplets: Upon their birth in November 2009, the Kupresak triplets of Toronto weighed a combined 7.78 kg (17.2 pounds).

Longest drumming marathon: Over five days in August 2011, Burlington, Ontario, man Steve Gaul drummed for 121 hours.

Rapid onion eating: Peter Czerwinski of Mississauga, Ontario ate a complete raw onion in 43.53 seconds. (Ew!)

Fastest marathon in a mascot costume: "Jefferson the Dog" (David Hiddleston) ran the 13 miles in four hours, 16 minutes, in the 2010 Toronto Waterfront Marathon.

Most bone tattoos: Which is to say tattoos of bones. Canadian artist Rick Genest has 139 of them (and he looks like a skeleton).

Winnipeg produces over 25,000 pounds of Golden Caviar a year.

"CREATIVE" CANADIAN TEACHERS

Some (not) excellent examples of how (not) to be an excellent teacher.

TEACHING IS A (FE)BREEZE!

In February 2012, a teacher at Twillingate Island Elementary School, in Newfoundland, Canada, took a ten-year-old boy out of her classroom and into the hallway…and sprayed him down with Febreze odor eliminator. She told the student she was doing it because his fried fish lunch made him smell bad. She then made the boy spend the entire period in the hallway because of his fishy smell. The student's very angry mother—who had made the boy's fried fish lunch—and who said the incident caused other students to mock her son, demanded, and received, an apology from the school's principal, and the anti-odorizing teacher as well. The teacher received a short suspension for the incident, and the school promised that similar spraying incidents would "never ever happen again."

WE'RE GOING TO…NOWHERE!

In February 2013, all the eighth-grade students at Roseland Public School in Windsor, Ontario, were called into an assembly, and were told some amazing news: for their graduation celebration, they were all going to Disney World in Florida for their graduation celebration. A PowerPoint presentation was shown to the kids, showing them all the wonderful things they would be seeing on their trip, and travel and hotel brochures were passed around, along with permission slips. As the excitement in the room reached a peak, the teachers told the kids to yell out together, "We're going to Disney World!" At the end of the assembly, one final PowerPoint slide was presented…which revealed that they weren't really going to Disney World, they were going to a local bowling alley. It had all been a joke. Worse: one of the teachers took a video of the kids getting all excited…and then their heartbroken reactions when they found out they weren't really going…and showed it to the rest of the school. The reaction from the kids' parents, and from the community—and from just about everyone who heard about the bizarre prank—was pretty much the same: shock and disgust. "I have a lot of respect for teachers and what they do," said Peter Topolovec, whose son was one of the pranked students, "but this was really stupid judgment." A local psychologist, Noreen Chevalier, added that the prank amounted to "bullying." The local school board released a public apology, but said the teachers would not be disciplined.

SCHOOL OF DEATH

In June 2013, a high school teacher outside of Montreal, Quebec, told her students that a stray cat had recently given birth to a litter of kittens on her property. She said she had tried to drown the kittens with a hose. That didn't work, she said, so she put the kittens—all eight of them—into a plastic bag and filled it with water. That worked, she said, and all the kittens died. Except for one of the kittens, which had inexplicably survived being in a plastic bag filled with water. She killed that one, she told the kids, by beating it to death with a piece of wood. When the horrified students told their parents what the teacher had told them, dozens of complaints were lodged, and the school launched an investigation into the incident. The local SPCA, in the meantime, said that if what the teacher had told the kids was actually true (let's hope it wasn't!), the teacher would be guilty of animal cruelty, and could be fined as much as $25,000. As of press time, the incident was still being investigated.

YOU CAN'T BLAME HIM

Ryan Hazelton is a teacher at Mount Douglas Secondary School in Saanich, British Columbia. In June 2012, Hazelton requested three days off so he could take "an emergency trip to Vancouver to be with a terminally ill family member." Hazelton was granted the leave...but the school later found out that he did not actually go to Vancouver "to be with a terminally ill family member." He went to Los Angeles, California...to be with a Stanley Cup Finals hockey game. (It was Game 4, between the L.A. Kings and the New Jersey Devils. The Kings went on win in six games.) Hazelton admitted to what he'd done when confronted, and was put in the penalty box... er...suspended...for five days without pay.

Winnipeg was the first city in the world to develop the 9-1-1 emergency phone number.

THE LAST LAUGH

Some unusual epitaphs and tombstone rhymes from Canada, sent in by our crew of wandering BRI tombstone-ologists.

Weep not for me,
Weep for me never
For I'm going to do
Nothing for ever & ever
(Okotoks, AB)

Here lies the body of Jonathan Blake. Stepped on the gas instead of the brake.
(Niagra Falls, ON)

It's not that I am always right
It's just that I am never wrong
(Barryvale, ON)

He did his bit.
(Moose Jaw, SK)

Died February 31, 1860
(Picton, ON)

To be continued.
(Red Deer, AB)

Here lies all that remains of Charlotte. Born a virgin, died a harlot. For 16 years she kept her virginity, a marvelous thing for this vicinity
(Welland, ON)

This wasn't my idea
(Salmon Arm, BC)

I told you I was sick.
(Pleasant Home, MB)

Here lies
Petter D. Brodair
In his last and best bedroom
(Pictou, NS)

She loved, was loved, and died.
(Vernon, B.C.)

A victim of fast women and slow horses.
(Kirkland Lake, ON)

Here lies
Ezekial Aikle
Age 102
The good die young.
(East Dalhousie, NS)

Here lies the body of Ephraim Wise. Safely tucked between his two wives. One was Tillie and the other Sue. Both were faithful, loyal, and true. By his request in ground that's hilly, his coffin is set tilted toward Tillie.
(Niagra Falls, ON)

Let 'er rip.
—Leslie Nielsen's tombstone

CANADIAN JOKES

Lighten up, eh.

Q: What do you call a sophisticated American?

A: A Canadian

Q: What's the difference between an American and a Canadian?

A: A Canadian not only has a sense of humour, but they can spell "humour."

Q: Who would win in a fight between Celine Dion and Shania Twain?

A: Everybody.

Q: What do urine samples and American beer have in common?

A: The taste.

Q: What does Canada produce that no other country produces?

A: Canadians.

An Albertan went to France and visited the Eiffel Tower. The first question he asked the tour guide was, "How many barrels a day does it produce?"

Q: What does a Canadian say when you step on his foot?

A: "Sorry"

There are two seasons in Canada: winter, and poor snowmobiling season.

Q: How many Canadians does it take to change a light bulb?

A: None. Canadians don't change light bulbs, we accept them as they are.

Q: What's the difference between Canadians, Australians, and Americans?

A: Canadians say, "eh." Australians say, "eh, mate!" Americans say, "Hey, wanna mate?"

Q: Why are most Canadian jokes so short?

A: So Americans can understand them.

Q: What's the best thing about America?

A: It borders on the magnificent.

ROCKIN' IN THE FREE WORLD

Neil Young has successfully recorded rock, folk, folk-rock, country, techno, and blues over his five-decade career. He has also made some consummate weird news.

• In 1965, Young first rolled into Los Angeles from Toronto in a black 1953 Pontiac—a hearse, *Mort II*. He slept in it for a week before meeting up with his friend and future collaborator Steven Stills.

• One of Young's current projects is building an electric car he hopes to drive to the White House. This is not his first attempt at eco-friendly cars. In 2010, in an attempt to turn his (5,000- 5,000-pound) 1959 Lincoln Continental into a biodiesel-electric hybrid, a malfunction occurred while the car was charging, setting off a fire and causing $1 million in damage, including the destruction of a building filled with Young's memorabilia.

• Young loves model trains and is listed on seven U.S. model train–related patents as a coinventor.

• In 1989, MTV banned his video "This Note's For You," which brutally satirized both product placement and MTV. What won the MTV Video Music Award for Video of the Year in 1989? Neil Young's "This Note's For You."

• Young directed the 1982 film *Human Highway* described as a "surreal nuclear comedy" set in a gas station diner next to a nuclear power plant. Its customers' last day alive on earth, and these unknowing customers include actors Young, Dennis Hopper, and Devo.

• During the late '60s Young met and played guitar with future mass murderer Charles Manson. Young describes Manson as, "kind of like Dylan. The songs were fascinating."

• In the liner notes to the 1977 anthology *Decade* Young reveals that he wrote three songs on *Everybody Knows This Is Nowhere* while sick with a 103 degree fever—in one afternoon.

...She was born in Kemouraska, Quebec, in 1880 and died in 1998 at age 117.

WILL POWER

Will Ferguson is a humorist and novelist who writes a lot about what it means to be Canadian. Here are some choice bon mots.

"Many Canadian nationalists harbour the bizarre fear that should we ever reject royalty, we would instantly mutate into Americans, as though the Canadian sense of self is so frail and delicate a bud, that the only thing stopping it from being swallowed whole by the U.S. is an English lady in a funny hat."

"It is considered bad manners to point out to Canadians that, although their country is indeed very large, more than 50% of it is permanently frozen. This is the 'We burned your fries so we gave you extra' school of customer satisfaction."

"More polar bears live in Canada than in the rest of the world combined, which raises the question, why did we choose the beaver as our national emblem? We got stuck with Squirrelly McTeeth."

"It sure is great being a Canadian. You get to share the material benefits of living next door to the United States, yet at the same time you get to act smug and haughty and morally superior. You just can't beat that kind of irresponsibility."

"It is never cold enough for Canadians. Hence the question: 'Cold enough for ya?' The inevitable answer being, "Are you kidding? It's only –50 out. This is nothing. When I was up in Timmins, it was minus 800 jillion, at least.' Self-deluded regarding their endurance, self-congratulatory in their masochism, Canadians are a breed apart. When it comes to winter, they are legends in their own minds."

"I read and learned and fretted more about Canada after I left than I ever did while I was home. I ranted and raved and seethed about things beyond my control. In short, I acted like a Canadian."

"You ever want to negotiate a hostage situation in Quebec, I'm your man. Send me in for a little *parley* and the francophone miscreants will flee, hands over bleeding ears."

UNCLE JOHN'S PAGE OF LISTS

Bundles of trivia from our bottomless files/

FAR AWAY, INDEED

In 2011, *B.C. Business* published a retrospective on Canadian pop music, including the "10 Best Classic Canadian Albums" and the "10 Best Modern Canadian Albums." Of far more interest are the "10 Worst Canadian Songs Ever.":

1. Nickelback, "Far Away"
2. Celine Dion, "My Heart Will Go On"
3. Bryan Adams, "Everything I Do (I Do It For You)"
4. Kon Kan, "Harry Houdini"
5. Alanis (Morissette), "Too Hot"
6. Snow, "Informer."
7. Roch Voisni, "Helene"
8. Trooper, "Boys in the Bright White Sports Cars"
9. Corey Hart, "Never Surrender"
10. William Shatner, "Rocketman"

PRIORITIES

In 2008, the CBC asked viewers to rank the most important Canadian inventions. Some highlights of the final "top 50":

1. Insulin (Frederick Banting and Charles Best, 1921)
4. Five-pin bowling (Thomas Ryan, 1874)
5. The Wonderbra (Louise Poirier, 1964)
10. Poutine (Fernand Lachance, 1957)
12. The Caesar cocktail (Walter Chell, 1969)
15. Ski-Doo (Armand Bombardier, 1922)
20. Retractable beer carton handle (Steve Pasjack, 1957)
22. Instant replay (Hockey Night in Canada, 1955)
39. Instant mashed potatoes (Edward Asselbergs, 1962)

GETTING ICED

Maclean's held a poll in 2012 to determine the most-hated hockey team nationwide. The results:

1. Toronto Maple Leafs (19%)
2. Montreal Canadiens (15%)
3. Vancouver Canucks (4%)
3. (tie) Ottawa Senators (4%)
5. Calgary Flames (3%)
5. (tie) Edmonton Oilers (3%)
7. Winnipeg Jets (1%)

The most common response, by 51% of respondants: "none."

BLAME CANADA

Ask Men Canada ran a list of "The Top 10 Canada Hating Countries." Here are the countries you should stay out of, and why:

1. The U.S., because conservative polticians think Canada is too liberal.

2. Russia, because of property disputes in the Arctic.

3. Spain, due to lingering ill will over the 1995 incident in which Canadian ships fired at a Spanish fishing boat.

4. Mexico, because a string of Canadian tourists have mysteriously been murdered at Mexican resorts.

5. Iran, due to the "Canadian Caper" hostage extraction drama, as depicted in the movie Argo

6. Denmark, because of continued bad feelings over the Hans Island dispute.

7. Chile. After losing a 2007 soccer tournament game in Toronto to an Argentine team, the Chilean team got rowdy and were roughed up by Toronto police.

8. Brazil, because Canada banned imported Brazilian beef in 2001 over Mad Cow Disease concerns.

9. The African Union, which resents Canada, because Canada mines its own diamonds, and doesn't need their business.

10. China, because of the Canadian government's calls for human rights improvements there.

NORTHERN NOVELTIES

Here's a look at a few of the funny Canadian songs that have inspired equal parts laughter and toe-tapping over the years.

Song: "Don't Play Bingo Tonight, Mother"
Artist: The Happy Gang (1945)
Story: There are plenty of warning songs out there, that warn listeners about the perils of everything from drinking to gambling to bad hygiene. This 1945 single advises all the moms out there to avoid Bingo Night—while it seems like good clean fun at the local church or community center, it's actually a sinful lure. The song is actually satirical. It reflects and mocks a mid-'40s craze of temperance advocates were actually convinced that the game was brainwashing Canadian women into becoming negligent mothers. It didn't quite work…but the song was a hit.

Song: "Gilly Gilly Ossenfeffer Katzenellen Bogen by the Sea"
Artist: The Four Lads (1954)
Story: Lots of artists performed this silly song, but the best known version was by the Canadian all-male singing quarter the Four Lads ("Istanbul," "Moments to Remember"). This impossible-to-remember-the-name-of song is about a lovestruck girl who lives in a small coastal town, and probably always will because of her unpronounceable name. During the recording session in February 1954, however, the Four Lads thought the song needed a more youthful, and feminine vibe. So they invited the two teenage members of their fan club visiting the studio at the time to jump in on the mic. Good move—the song peaked at #18 on pop chart later that year.

Song: "Honky the Christmas Goose"
Artist: Johnny Bower (1965)
Story: This song tells the tale of an overweight goose with powerful honking skills that helps Santa Claus escape from an interstellar traffic jam on Christmas Eve—he saves Christmas! It was recorded by Johnny Bower, the famous NHL goaltender, along with his son John and a group of young vocalists called "The Rinky Dinks." The song hit #29 on the charts, which led Bower to pursue

music more. He recorded a few more singles, but none were as successful as this holiday oddity.

Song: "The Hockey Song"

Artist: Stompin' Tom Connors (1973)

Story: Folksinger Connors recorded this ode to the "best game you can name" in the '70s, but it didn't become a hit until years later. In 1992, it was selected to be used as a fight song at home games for the Ottawa Senators. It took off like a wildfire from there and has since become a staple at hockey games all over Canada and even in the U.S. The song has been used to promote video games and also served as a protest anthem during the 2012–2013 NHL lockout. Connors passed away on March 6, 2013, and on that day Newfoundland folk act Great Big Sea performed "The Hockey Song" in tribute at a concert in San Francisco.

Song: "The Safety Dance"

Artist: Men Without Hats (1983)

Story: Ivan Doroschuk, the lead singer of new wave group Men Without Hats wrote this song after he got thrown out of a rock club for "pogoing"—a minor dance craze at the time that involved participants standing in one place and bouncing up and down like they were on pogo sticks. (Bouncers had no tolerance for it, apparently.) While spectulation has ran wild for 30 years that the song's lyrics are actually about avoiding nuclear warfare (a big subject of '80s pop songs) or the importance of safe sex (also a big subject of '80s pop songs), Doroshuk has steadfastly admitted that they're reading too much into them, and that it's about pogoing, or "the safety dance." Further adding to confusion, the music video for The Safety Dance features the singer cavorting his way through a medieval village along with a pint-sized jester and various townsfolk dressed as farm animals. The song peaked at # 11 on the Canadian Top 50, and was a smash hit all over the world, on its way to becoming one of the most definitive songs of the '80s. (Uncle John would like to point out your friends don't dance, and if they don't dance, well, they're no friends of his.)

OOPS!

You think you're gaffe-prone? Sit back and enjoy some boners made by other people for a change!

MISSED UNIVERSE

In May 2013, beauty queen Denise Garrido, 26, of Bradford, Ontario, was crowned Miss Universe Canada in Toronto. The win meant Garrido would be representing Canada at the international Miss Universe pageant later that year in Moscow, Russia...but she didn't make the trip. The day after winning the crown, Garrido was called to a meeting with pageant officials, and was told that a mistake had been made: an employee transferring judges' scores into a computer, they said, had made a typo. She was not actually the winner—the real winner was Calgary's Riza Santos. Adding insult to injury: Garrido hadn't even been the runner-up—she had actually come in third. "I thought that I was dreaming and it wasn't real," Garrido said in an interview the next day. "Unfortunately it was real." Pageant organizers apologized profusely for the gaffe, and promised to bring in safeguards so that such a mistake would never happen again. Garrido, for her part, said she would try to at least enjoy being crowned Miss Universe Canada..."even if it lasted only 24 hours."

OH SAY CAN YOU...UM...UM...

In May 2013, Saskatoon jazz singer Alexis Normand was invited to sing the national anthem before an internationally broadcast hockey game between Canadian and American teams in Saskatoon's Credit Union Center. Because the game included an America team, Normand would be required to sing both the Canadian and American national anthems. She jumped at the chance, as the game was part of the Memorial Cup tournament, one of the country's most widely-watched sporting events. At the game, Normand stood in the center of the rink, began to sing "The Star-Spangled Banner," and, just a few lines in—forgot the words. Then she just kind of made mumbly sounds where the words were supposed to be. Then she stopped singing altogether for about ten seconds. Then she started singing again, making more mumbly sounds. The crowd gasped, jeered, guffawed, and finally just started singing the song—really loud—to help the poor singer out. A very embarrassed Normand apologized the next day, via her Twitter account, and in interviews with television stations, said she simply hadn't had enough time to learn the lyrics. By that time video of her anthem debacle had become a YouTube sensation—and has since been viewed by more than 740,000 people.

Bonus: Here's an approximate transcript of the "Star-Spangled Banner," as sung by Alexis Normand—mistakes and mumbly sounds included—at the game:

> Oh, say can you see by the dawn's early light
> What so proudly we hailed at the twilight's last.....first...gleaming?
> Whose broad stripes and bright stars through the...paralay night...
> [ten second pause; crowd jeers; hockey players on rink try to hide their laughing behind their gloves]
> Whose broad stripes and bright stars...at zuh lawn's early light
> What so ahh ver zwee svade and the jarlight still leaving
> And the raas arr fil frehhh the bombs bursting in air
> aiiii...and the gland was still there
> Oh, say does that star-spangled banner yet wave
> O'er the land of the free and the home of the brave?

Bonus II: A few days later Normand was invited to sing before another Memorial Cup game, only this time organizers made sure it was between two Canadian teams...so she wouldn't have to sing the American anthem.

YOU'RE (NOT) HIRED

In July 2012, Vanessa Hojda of Toronto, sent an email to the city's York University to inquire about an administrative assistant position she had heard about. She wrote that she had seen an ad for the job, was interested in it, and finished with, "I've attached my resume and cover letter for your consideration." Except she hadn't actually attached her resume and cover letter—she had accidently attached a photo of actor Nicolas Cage making a wide-eyed, teeth-bared, maniacal-looking face instead. Hojda realized her mistake almost immediately; she had simply clicked on the wrong file. She posted a screen-pic of the email to her Tumblr blog, asking "is there a way to take back an email?" (There's not.) From there, the Nicolas Cage-scary email story went viral. So much so that the it was covered by newspapers and television shows all over Canada, and Hojda was even interviewed by *Time* and the *Washington Post* in the U.S. She told the *Post* she had changed the name of her resume file to "ThisIsYourResumeThisIsNotAPictureOfNicolasCage.doc," and that she had deleted the photo of Cage from her computer. Why did she have the photo of the maniacal-looking Nicolas Cage on her computer in the first place? She had found in online, she said, and simply thought it was funny.

Bonus: Hojda did not get the job—the person who got the email was not as amused as everyone else—but the fame generated by the gaffe worked out for her: In the days that followed she received several job offers via her Facebook page.

*   *   *

THINGS TO DO IN SASKATCHEWAN

Shaunavon, Saskatchewan, farmer Joe Murray has been excavating the basement under his farmhouse since 2005. Why is it taking so long? Because he's doing it with remotely controlled miniature machinery. Farming season only lasts seven or eight months in Saskatchewan, so the project gives Murray something to do, in the warmth of his basement…alone…for hours every day …during the long winter. He has several different pieces of machinery: steam-shovels; front-end loaders; several dump trucks; and even semi-like trucks for transporting large amounts of dirt. Murray has even built a system of ramps, so the loaded trucks can be (remotely) driven outside to dump the dirt in his yard. How slow is the going? This slow: Murray manages to remove just two to three cubic yards of dirt—or about two large pickup truckloads—each year. Bonus: Murray videos his remote control machinery digging out his basement—and he has posted more than 150 of the videos on his YouTube channel. He has more than 3,000 subscribers, and the videos have been viewed more than four million times. "It's not important that it ever gets done," Murray said in 2012 of his interesting hobby. "It's just something to do."

Copiers and printers in Canada use the U.S. letter size, rather than the metric A4.

NATURALLY WEIRD

Come to Canada, where things are weird—just the way Mother Nature intended.

ICE TO SEE YOU

Cold weather is certainly no big deal in Canada, and even horrible ice storms are fairly common. Until 1998 that is. An ice storm in January of that year was so severe that it caused widespread power outages in Ontario and Quebec. Ultimately, a state of emergency was declared, and the Canadian armed forces had to be deployed to distribute supplies.

SINGING SANDS

The sands at Basin Head on Prince Edward Island don't exactly belt out "Tom Sawyer," but they do "sing." When you walk on the golden beaches there, the sand gives off a distinctive "squeak." The sound is similar to that of rubbing a balloon. Scientists attribute the mysterious noise to quartz grains in the sand that are abnormally extremely spherical.

A DELUGE OF DIAMONDS

There's precious "ice" beneath the ice at the Diavik Diamond Mine in the Northwest Territories. Just a few degrees south of the Arctic Circle in an area that's considered barely inhabitable, shimmering diamonds sparkle beneath the surface of the earth. Workers at the Diavik Diamond Mine extract about 1,600 kilograms (3,500 pounds) of diamonds annually—that's eight million carats valued at about $100 million. One of the complicated aspects of the operation is accessing the huge hole during the frigid winter months, when high temperatures stay below zero. For about ten weeks, from late January through early April, a road made of ice connects the mine to Yellowknife. At that time of year, the weather is cold enough to maintain a frozen road. The icy highway can withstand the weight of trucks transporting materials, machinery, and fuel. For truckers, it's a long haul requiring 19 hours of travel time between Yellowknife and Diavik. Vehicles with heavy loads travel at carefully controlled speeds to protect the ice. If a truck travels too fast, it creates waves underneath that have the potential to break the ice at the shoreline.

Largest lake on an island: Manitou Lake on Manitoulin Island in Lake Huron (103 sq km).

FEARLESS LEADERS

At least our politicians are mostly normal. Oh, wait...

"If this thing starts to snowball, it will catch fire right across the country."

–Social Credit Party leader Robert Thompson

"Canada is the greatest nation in this country."

–Toronto mayor Allan Lamport

"Anybody may support me when I am right. What I want is someone that will support me when I am wrong."

–John A. Macdonald

"I'm not going to play politics on the floor of the House of Commons."

–Liberal leader John Turner

"Your majesty, I thank you from the bottom of my heart, and Madame Houde here thanks you from her bottom, too."

–Montreal mayor Camillien Houde, to King George VI

"Dalton McGuinty. He's an evil reptilian kitten-eater from another planet."

–Ontario PC news release

"Canada is like an old cow. The West feeds it. Ontario and Quebec milk it. And you can well imagine what it's doing in the Maritimes."

–Tommy Douglas

"A proof is a proof. What kind of a proof? It's a proof. A proof is a proof, and when you have a good proof, it's because it's proven."

–Jean Chrétien

"The election is not a time to discuss serious issues."

–Kim Campbell

"My conduct had nothing to do with me."

–Ontario MPP Al McLean, defending his conduct during a sexual harassment case

"Paul Martin commits to positions like Britney Spears commits to marriage."

–Stephen Harper

"You cannot name a Canadian prime minister who has done as many significant things as I did, because there are none."

–Brian Mulroney

Per capita, more Guinness records are broken in Canada than in any other country.

WAYNE & SHUSTER

Before Lorne Michaels, before SCTV, *before* The Kids in the Hall, *there was Wayne and Shuster, the original Canadian comedy team.*

PRESERVING CAREERS

Johnny Wayne and Frank Shuster met in high school at Toronto's Harbord Collegiate Institute. Even as teenagers, they found a rapport and began writing and performing short comic sketches together for the school's Drama Guild. The partnership continued at the University of Toronto, and in 1941, when both were barely in their twenties, they got their own show on CFRB, a local radio station. It was a daytime show called *The Wife Preservers*, in which the two would demonstrate cleaning and cooking tips… but punched up with lots of banter and comic nonsense.

Their nightclub/variety show act didn't quite work on daytime, and the duo were fired. But the national CBC knew they were something special, and snatched them up to do a nighttime comedy show called *The Shuster and Wayne Comedy Show*. It was a huge hit, but went off the air just a year later in 1941. Reason: Like most young men in North America, Wayne and Shuster (or Shuster and Wayne) enlisted in the military to fight in World War II. They didn't see much combat, however—the Canadian Army enlisted them in "troop entertainment duty."

RADIO, RADIO

After the war ended, Wayne and Shuster returned to Canada…and mega-stardom. Many of their performances for the troops had been broadcast back home, and they were in high demand. The CBC put them back on the air in 1946 with *The Wayne and Shuster Show*. The competition: popular imported American radio shows. *Wayne and Shuster* beat them all—a radio first.

When the CBC debuted television service in 1952, Wayne and Shuster were an obvious fit, and *The Wayne and Shuster Hour* became one of the network's first shows and biggest-ever hits. That began a nearly uninterrupted four-decade streak of TV presence from the comedy duo.

In 1998 1,000 University of Guelph students formed the longest human conveyor belt...

JULIE, DON'T GO!

Wayne and Shuster called their style "literate comedy," but it also involved a great deal of gentle parody, slapstick, and pantomime. They had a lot in common with other comedy duos, then and now—such as joke rhythm, the straight man/jokester setup, a love of puns and ethnic jokes. The one huge difference was that the duo loved to use literary references. That kind of thing probably wouldn't fly today, but in the mid-20th century, mainstream audiences would understand Wayne and Shuster's many Shakespeare-based premises and jokes, because back then more people read Shakespeare (particularly in England-influenced Canada).

And it took off. In 1958, the duo was booked on *The Ed Sullivan Show*, the most popular and influential variety show on American television. They performed a sketch called "Rinse the Blood Off My Toga," which was Shakespeare's *Julius Caesar* performed in the style of the TV cop show *Dragnet*. (It also spawned the catchphrase, "Julie, don't go!"

Sullivan publicly stated that Wayne and Shuster were one of two of his favorite all-time acts (the other: ventriloquist Topo Gigio). He paid them more than any other act (including Elvis Presley and the Beatles) and signed them up to make regular appearances. In fact, they appeared on the show 67 times between 1958 and 1969—that's once every seven episodes.

Also in 1958, the duo opened Canada's Stratford Festival. They performed a scene called "The Shakespearean Baseball Game."

STARS' SCHTICK

Wayne and Shuster were so busy with TV and live shows (and recording a string of hit comedy albums) that by 1965, they asked the CBC to reduce *The Wayne and Shuster Hour* from a weekly series to a monthly one. The network complied, and the show ran this way into the early '80s. Some memorable sketches from the show:

• "All in the Royal Family": a reimagining of *Hamlet* with characters from All in the Family. The king even calls Hamlet "Meathead" and Gertrude "Dingbat."

• "The Six Hundred Dollar Man," an obvious goof on *The Six Million Dollar Man*, in which a cyborg is created with body parts purchased on the cheap "at Loblaws."

• "Star Schtick," a parody of *Star Trek: The Motion Picture*.

• When the Prince Edward Island-set TV movie *Anne of Green Gables* aired in 1985, Wayne and Shuster responded with "Sam of Green Gables," in with the pastoral community is met with the arrival of not a spirited young girl, but an old codger.

• "The Brown Pumpernickel," a parody of *The Scarlet Pimpernel*.

• "Frontier Psychiatrist" was about a therapist trying to analyze the denizens of the wild, wild west. (The audio of the sketch later became the basis of the hit song "Frontier Psychiatrist" by Australian electronic act the Avalanches.)

END OF THE ROAD

The duo's relevance started to fade in the late 1970s. It was a tough era, and comedy reflected that in edgy voices like Richard Pryor, George Carlin, and *Saturday Night Live* (created by Lorne Michaels, Shuster's son-in-law). Wayne and Shuster's comedy seemed dated and slight by comparison, and ratings for the monthly specials gradually but steeply dropped. By 1980, *The Wayne and Shuster Hour* was airing just two episodes a year. The last episode aired in 1988.

But oddly, reruns of the show were doing great. The CBC repackaged old sketches into half-hour episodes and sold them into syndicated in Canada, Australia, and the U.S. The network earned millions.

In 1990, just two years after the series stopped airing original episodes, Johnny Wayne died. Frank Shuster continued to make public appearances, and filmed introductions for Wayne and Shuster compilation videos. He passed away in 2002.

EVERYONE'S A CRITIC

Not everybody was a fan of Wayne and Shuster. In *Right Here on Our Stage Tonight*, Gerald Nachman's oral history of *The Ed Sullivan Show*, Wayne & Shuster merit only three mentions. And two of them are mean remarks by erudite talk show host Dick Cavett:

• "Wayne and Shuster are the only comedy team in which you couldn't say either one is the funny one."

• "Ed Sullivan was partially deaf, according to some, which is the only thing that would explain why Wayne & Shuster were on so many times."

Four hundred mothers in Vancouver broke the record for mass breast feeding in 2002.

ODD EATERIES

Beyond Tim Hortons and beaver tails, Canada has a few truly specialized eateries to accommodate, uh, different tastes.

THE FLYING SAUCER

Location: Niagara Falls, Ontario

The Hook: Shaped like two 1950s spaceships, the Flying Saucer is a throwback to a time when folks first became fascinated with outer space and sci-fi. This novelty restaurant is basically a diner with a spacey décor—and as they say: "out-of-this-world food at down-to-Earth prices." Their classic dishes include the Jupiter Burger and the Star Dust Medley Stir Fries. The owner, Henry Di Cienzo, offers a $1 million reward to anyone who can bring him an actual UFO or UFO pieces.

GARLIC'S

Location: London, Ontario

The Hook: This upscale institution is dedicated to the stinky bulb. Try some garlic martinis, cream of garlic soup, garlic ice cream, or even garlic cloves dipped in chocolate.

O.NOIR

Location: Montreal

The Hook: You can't see a thing when you dine at O.Noir. The idea is to focus on the tastes and smells of your food to heighten the eating experience. The wait staff is blind. You may want to wear a bib—finding your own mouth can take some work. It takes great care to eat here.

THE OLD COUNTRY MARKET

Location: Coombs, British Columbia

The Hook: It's "goats on a hot sod roof. For 30 years, live goats have grazed on the sod roof" of this market that includes an Italian restaurant.

DOGGY STYLE DELI

Location: Edmonton

The Hook: This restaurant's specialties include Shih Tzu Stew, Houndburger Helper, and liver brownies. Because it's a restaurant

During WWII, Britain's wealth was secretly packed in crates and shipped across the Atlantic Ocean.

for dogs. There is also a Kibble Buffet, a modified steam tray full of various kinds of dry dog food. Other specials include Rottweiler Rice, Meat Mania, and Pooch Pockets, which are like pizza pockets. The restaurant doesn't serve food to people, but pet owners are welcome to bring in a bagged lunch and eat with their pets.

RESTO MÜVBOX

Location: Montreal

The Hook: This eatery, made from a shipping container, is known for its lobster rolls. Müvbox is developing more of these restaurants constructed from reused shipping containers. The eateries are designed to be environmentally friendly; solar panels provide up to 40 percent of their power, and the floors are made from recycled tires.

LEIFSBURDIR

Location: Fishing Point, Newfoundland

The Hook: You can eat like a Viking at this sod-covered restaurant, which replicates the 1,000-year-old home of Leif Erickson at nearby L'Anse aux Meadows National Historic Site. The restaurant hosts the Great Viking Feast of moose stew, cod casserole, cod tongues, roast capelin (similar to smelt), baked Atlantic salmon, roast beef, and squid fried rice. (Bring your own horned helmet.)

* * *

THE "LOST VILLAGES"

Ten communities in the Canadian province of Ontario were permanently submerged by the creation of the St. Lawrence Seaway in 1958. The seaway was created to allow massive ocean-going ships passage from the Great Lakes to the Atlantic Ocean. The flooding was planned, and all families and businesses were moved to the new, planned communities of Long Sault and Ingleside. On July 1, 1958, a dam was destroyed and the flooding began. Some remnants from sidewalks and building foundations can still be seen underwater.

HANS ISLAND

For years, Canada and Denmark have waged a low-key power struggle over a tiny rock island that from the air looks like a flattened cow patty.

LOOK MA, NO HANS!

It's unfit for human habitation and is pretty bare of vegetation and land-dwelling animals. It doesn't have a Tim Hortons, Internet access, or a cell phone tower. It's sandwiched in the thin, ice-filled passage between Nunavut's Ellesmere Island and the semiautonomous Danish territory of Greenland, and there has been little reason to take note of Hans Island except as a potential navigational hazard. In fact, for most of its history almost nobody has. What is it about this icy rock?

It's possible that indigenous people encountered the island while hunting walrus on the ice. We know it got its present-day name between 1871 and 1873 during American explorer Charles Francis Hall's ill-fated third North Pole expedition. Someone decided to name the lump of rock after an Inuit guide the explorers called Hans Hendrik...even though his name was really Suersaq.

Yet, during the 2000s, Hans Island became the center of a bizarre sovereignty dispute between Canada and Denmark. As global warming melts long-frozen ice, opening sea routes that have been impassable for centuries, the ownership of this barely existent island of 1.3 square kilometers (0.5 square mile), could provide benefits in terms of navigation, fishing rights, and natural resources like oil.

Denmark claims that maps point to Hans Island being part of Greenland since 1933. Canada, on the other hand, showed Hans Island as Canadian territory on a map for the first time only in 1967. There have never been any known permanent inhabitants.

KEEP YOUR ILLEGAL DRILLING TO YOURSELF

Canadian oil company Dome Petroleum has been scouting oil on and around Hans Island since the 1980s...without the knowledge of Denmark or the acknowledgment of the Canadian government. In fact, it was a chance encounter that uncovered this, gave it international attention, and sparked the struggle over Hans Island. In 1984, Nunavut historian Kenn Harper wrote an article about

Hans Island for a tiny newspaper in the palindrome-named town of Qaanaaq, Greenland (population 620). In the article, Harper mentioned meeting a man on the ice near Resolute, Nunavut, who was wearing a hat boldly reading "HANS ISLAND." After striking up a conversation, Harper learned that the man had spent the summer on the island doing research for Dome Petroleum. Harper mentioned this in his story.

The article, published in a tiny, isolated town, made its way to the Danish newspapers, which played it up as an affront to Danish sovereignty. They were half-kidding...but they were also half-serious.

OF COURSE, YOU REALIZE...

The Danish government, though, wasn't messing around. The country's minister for Greenland, Tom Høyem, chartered a helicopter and flew to Hans Island in order to plant a Danish flag, a bottle of cognac, and a message saying, "Velkommen til den danske ø" ("Welcome to the Danish island"). That was the beginning of a series of visits by Canadian and Danish officials and fishing crews, both bearing flags and drinking whatever alcohol had been left by the previous group.

Meanwhile, in cyberspace, satirical Web sites waged a battle for the island. One promoted the Hans Island Liberation Front, which claimed that the island's nonexistent inhabitants wanted to cast off the yoke of both Canadian and Danish imperialism. Another "represented" Radio Free Hans Island, a fictional radio station supposedly broadcasting from the frozen wastes. A Swedish radio station even entered the fray, satirically claiming Swedish ownership of the island.

...THIS MEANS WAR!

The governments of Canada and Denmark, though, didn't think the issue was a joke, and tensions boiled again in 2005. In an escaltion of the conflict, the Canadian defense minister landed on Hans Island in a helicopter to reassert Canadian claims. That led to outrage in Greenland, where people called the action a foreign invasion and occupation. This was followed by the visit of a Danish warship to the island. In fact, over the years, both nations have made the effort and taken the expense of sending warships to the

The first Canadian of European ancestry was named Snorri...

area—fortunately, at different times—with no shots fired.

The dispute has quieted down recently. Perhaps both parties are in the process of coming to a mature resolution and a recognition of the fact that the island is probably more trouble than it's worth. As Canada's chief of defense staff, General Walter Natynczyk, noted, "The Arctic is a very harsh environment. If someone were to invade the Canadian Arctic, my first task would be to rescue them."

SPLITTING THE BABY IN HALF

In July 2007, based on satellite imagery, Canadian authorities finally admitted that Hans Island is not completely inside Canadian territory, but that the international border runs roughly through the middle of the island. Although that offers a solution to the Hans Island problem, it also ruins Canada's status as being the largest country with a land border on only one other country. Instead, Canada now can boast of having a 5,061-kilometer-long (3,145-mile) land border with the United States and a 1.3-kilometer-long (0.8-mile) border with Denmark.

* * *

"AMAZING" ANAGRAMS

PAMELA ANDERSON *becomes...*
ROMAN ESPLANADE

CELINE DION *becomes...*
CONNIE LIED

WILLIAM SHATNER *becomes...*
LAMINATES WHIRL

LESLIE NIELSEN *becomes...*
SELL SIN, EILEEN

KIEFER SUTHERLAND *becomes...*
INTERFERED AS HULK

ALANIS MORISSETTE *becomes...*
SNOT MATERIALISES

SKIRTING AROUND THE CORNER

In St. Andrews-by-the-Sea, New Brunswick, a curious tradition as emerged in the past few years among outdoor enthusiasts: kilt cycling.

A TAILOR-MADE GOOD TIME

When artist and mountain-bike enthusiast Geoff Slater relocated to St. Andrews in the early 2000s, he immediately worked to build mountain-bike trails and introduce local residents to the sport. The town now boasts 50 miles of trails. Soon after, he met resident Kurt Gumushel, a trainer, and the two began riding together. When Slater found out that Gumushel's father, Fuat, was a master kilt-maker, he had one tailored for a cyclist's specifications: lightweight, and with a hemline that wouldn't get tangled in the wheels (or flash too many people). Slater immediately took to riding in his kilt, and he, Kurt, and Fuat came up with the idea of having guided "kilt rides" as a way to boost Gumushel's personal-training business.

PEDDLING TO THE CUSTOMER

The trend soon took off. Fuat made a series of "loaner kilts" for riders to borrow for their tours around St. Andrews. More enthusiastic customers opted to have their own kilts tailor-made. The loaner kilts have Velcro straps for easy fitting adjustments. Riders say they help one keep warm while pedaling through the often breezy, cool Maritime weather. Also, what better way to honor the town's Scottish heritage than having a line of tartan-clad riders weaving through the streets?

Today the kilt rides are the calling card of Kurt's training business. A local group called "Off Kilter" also coordinates rides with Kurt, often going well outside of city limits into more rugged terrain. Athletes of many other sports, such as distance running, have taken to the kilt rides as a fun way to diversify their training regimens. One tip: if you do decide to try a kilt ride, you may want to wear a pair of compression shorts beneath—leggings or tights are strongly recommended for the cooler months.

BIRD IS THE WORD

Dead birds, lost birds, camera-fishing birds—if you're looking for weird bird stories, step right up—because we've got 'em!

HE HAS CEASED TO BE!

One morning in January 2011, Sylvain Turmel, who owns a farm outside of Quebec City, Quebec, walked out of his home...to find a bunch of dead pigeons in his yard. "I was stunned," he told CTV News. In the time it took to pick up the more than 20 dead pigeons, he said, five more fell out of the sky into his yard, and, after flapping around for a while, they were soon dead, too. Turmel called the local wildlife agency, and tests were performed on the birds. Result: They couldn't figure out why the birds had died. Over the next three weeks, Turmel said, he found more than 80 dead pigeons in his yard. (And nobody still knows why.)

SOMETHING TO CROW ABOUT

In between May and August 2013, more than 30 crows and ravens were dropped off at an animal rehabilitation clinic in Dawson Creek, British Columbia. They were all paralyzed, and had broken bones in either their wings or legs. Veterinarians at first thought the birds had the West Nile virus, but that was ruled out after testing. Just like the pigeons on the farm yard of Sylvain Turmel—what had happened to the birds remains a mystery.

A GAGGLE OF GRACKLES

In yet another bizarre Canadian mass bird death incident, in August 2013, dozens of grackles—large, dark-colored songbirds—plummeted from the sky and landed on the ground in a small section of downtown Winnipeg. Many were dead. Others were alive, and seemed alert, but could not stand or fly. Wildlife officials had to euthanize the living birds. Witnesses said they had seen thousands of the grackles massing in the area in the hours before the incident, perching in trees, and even on top of cars—and said they were acting "dizzy," before they started "falling like raindrops" out of the sky. One resident told reporters "it was like a Hitchcock movie." Once again...tests could find no cause for the bizarre bird behavior.

...They all wore big swastikas on their uniforms.

MUST HAVE MISSED HIS FLIGHT

In early April 2013, birdwatchers from all over Canada flocked to blustery Lawrencetown Beach on the Atlantic coast of Nova Scotia. Why? Because someone had spotted a crested caracara hanging out there. What's a crested caracara? The national bird of Mexico. The majestic-looking bird of prey, with a distinctive red face, an impressive, bald eagle-like curved beak—and a wingspan of more than four feet—is normally found only in southern Mexico and Central and South America. And it's not migratory. Local ornithologists could not explain why the bird was in the very un-tropical Nova Scotia—more than 2,500 miles north of its tropical native territory—nor why it seemed perfectly comfortable there. (The temperature was rhovering around freezing at the time.) The bird was seen in the area for several days before it finally disappeared. It remains the only time a crested caracara has ever been seen in Nova Scotia.

SHUTTERBIRD

Karen Gwillim was driving through the village of Craven, Saskatchewan, in September, 2012, when she came across a large black bird in the road. It was a cormorant, a type of diving bird. Gwillim pulled over, and noticed the bird "had something silver on its back," she told reporters later. As she got closer still, she saw the silver thing was a digital camera—the bird had somehow become entangled in the camera's strap. The weary bird let Gwillim approach it, but she was able to untangle the strap from its neck—and the bird flew off. Gwillim took the waterlogged camera home, and was surprised to find that the flash card still worked: there were hundreds of photos on it—mostly of guys on a boat holding fish they had caught. Gwillim contacted local news organizations, and—long bird/fish story short—two months later the owner of the camera had his camera back. He had dropped it while fishing in nearby Shell Lake…eight months earlier. The cormorant had apparently become entangled in the camera's strap while fishing at the floor of the lake, and had somehow made it to the road…to give to a friendly human. "I think it's interesting," Gwillim said as an afterthought, "that a fisherman's camera was retrieved by a fisher bird."

WEIRD CANADA

Crystal lakes, snow-capped mountains, hockey, Mounties, bilingual traffic signs...and some really, really weird news stories.

BEAVER FEVER!

In June 2003, two disc jockeys in Toronto caused a SARS panic– in the Dominican Republic. Z103.5 Morning Show hosts Scott Fox and Dave Blezard thought it would be funny to call the resort where their co-worker, Melanie Martin, was vacationing. They told the desk clerk that Martin had smuggled a "rare Canadian beaver" into their country. But the desk clerk, who didn't speak much English, thought he'd heard the word "fever." With SARS (Severe Acute Respiratory Syndrome) being big news at the time and Toronto being one of the cities where the disease had spread, the clerk panicked—and locked the woman in her room. The entire hotel wasn't quarantined, according to the station's news manager, but staff were at the point of contacting medical authorities when the disc jockeys finally convinced them that it was all a misunderstanding. Martin was released from her room that afternoon.

COMING IN FOR A LANDING

Lucette St. Louis, a 66-year-old woman from Corbeil, Ontario, was rounding up three runaway pigs owned by her son, Marc, when she became the victim of a bizarre accident. One of the 180-pound pigs had wandered into the road and a passing car hit it. The impact sent the pig airborne, landing on top of Mrs. St. Louis and breaking her leg in two places. "Well, at least," she said, "I can tell my grandchildren that pigs really do fly."

LEGAL BRIEFS

The Canadian Defence Department has 17 pages of guidelines for manufacturers who want to supply underwear to the Canadian military. According to the document, the underwear must be durable enough to be worn for up to six months without being changed. (It must also be invisible to the enemy's night-vision goggles.)

Canadian Criminal Code prohibits "causing a stink in public."

POOPUS INTERRUPTUS

In May 2006, Guy Fournier, chairman of the state-run Canadian Broadcasting Corporation, appeared on the TV talk show *Tout le Monde en Parle* ("Everyone's Talking About It"). Fournier commented on the air that at his age (74) he enjoyed defecation more than lovemaking. The remark created such a public outcry that he had to resign his job.

ANIMAL ACT

In 2007 Mike Lake, a Member of Parliament from Edmonton, Alberta, presented a petition from 500 of his constituents to the House of Commons to "establish legislation to effect immediate protection" of Bigfoot. Lake essentially asked the Canadian government to put Bigfoot—nearly universally believed to be a myth or a hoax—on the endangered species list. The House of Commons declined.

WAITING FOR MOMMY

Roxanne Toussaint, a single mother of three, felt unappreciated for the hard work she does cooking, cleaning, and raising her kids. So in 2006, she went on strike. She moved into a tent on her front lawn and spends the day holding up a sign that reads "Mom on Strike." Toussaint's demands: that her kids sign a pledge to clean up their rooms, contribute to the housework, and be quieter.

WEATHERING CHANGE

Dexter Manley played defensive end in the NFL for 10 seasons until he failed his fourth drug test in 1991. The following year, he resumed his career by playing for the Ottawa Rough Riders of the Canadian Football League. That appears to be when he got in touch with his "inner Canadian." In 1994 Manley claimed he was visited by the ghost of deceased Canadian prime minister William Lyon Mackenzie King. "We talked about thunder and lightning," Manley said.

BOOKED

While serving a prison sentence in Winnipeg, James Skinner asked the warden's office for a copy of Funk and Wagnall's Canadian College Dictionary to keep in his cell. The officials turned him down, saying that the book was so large it could be used as a weapon.

A traveler on a Canadian plane wrenched open the door at more than 10,000 meters (33,000 ft)...

IS THIS PERSON CANADIAN?

Think you know Canada? Think you know Canadians? Then take our quiz and see if you can pick out the true Canucks from the rest. *(Answers on page 406.)*

1. Wayne Gretzky
2. Tommy Douglas
3. William Lyon Mackenzie King
4. Don Cherry
5. Stockwell Day
6. Margaret Atwood
7. Bryan Adams
8. John Candy
9. Sheila Fraser
10. Cirque du Soleil
11. Celine Dion
12. Alanis Morissette
13. William Shatner
14. Steve Nash
15. Alex Trebek
16. Gordie Howe
17. Brian Mulroney
18. John Molson
19. Lord Stanley
20. Mr. Dressup
21. Tim Horton
22. Rick Hansen
23. Dan Aykroyd
24. Sandford Fleming
25. Louis Riel
26. John A. MacDonald
27. Pierre Trudeau
28. Geddy Lee
29. Jean Chrétien
30. Bobby Orr
31. Frederick Banting
32. Shania Twain

...and fell to his death in 2009.

CANADIANS ON CANADA

It's perfectly fine for Canadians to make fun of Canada.

"Canada is the only country founded on the relentless pursuit of the rodent."

—Preston Manning

"Canada was built on dead beavers."

—Margaret Atwood

"Canada was my whole world and my whole reality, and now I meet people who've never been there, and it's like, 'You've never been to my whole world?'"

—Carly Rae Jepsen

"I see Canada as a country torn between a very northern, rather extraordinary, mystical spirit which it fears and its desire to present itself to the world as a Scotch banker."

—Robertson Davies

"Outside Canada I carry the flag. Canadian nationalism isn't as insidious as American nationalism, though. It's good natured. It's all about maple syrup, not war."

—Feist

"If some countries have too much history, we have too much geography."

—William Lyon Mackenzie King

"Canada is not a country for the cold of heart or the cold of feet."

—Pierre Trudeau

"We sing about the North, but live as far south as possible."

—J.B. McGeachy

"Canada is an interesting place; the rest of the world thinks so, even if Canadians don't."

—Terence M. Green

"There are few, if any, Canadian men that have never spelled their name in a snow bank."

—Douglas Coupland

"A Canadian is someone who keeps asking the question, 'What is a Canadian?'"

—Irving Layton

The first flag in the British Empire was granted to Nova Scotia in 1625 by King Charles I.

More UNCLE JOHN than you can shake a stick at!

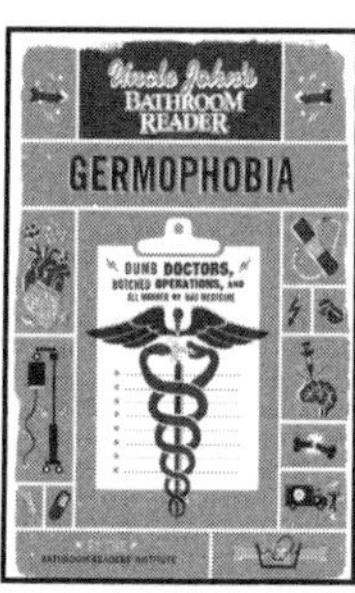

Log onto our online store at www.bathroomreader.com for dozens more great titles in the Bathroom Reader line: You'll find puzzle books, regional-interest books, big books, little books, and introducing—e-books! Great reading no matter where you are!

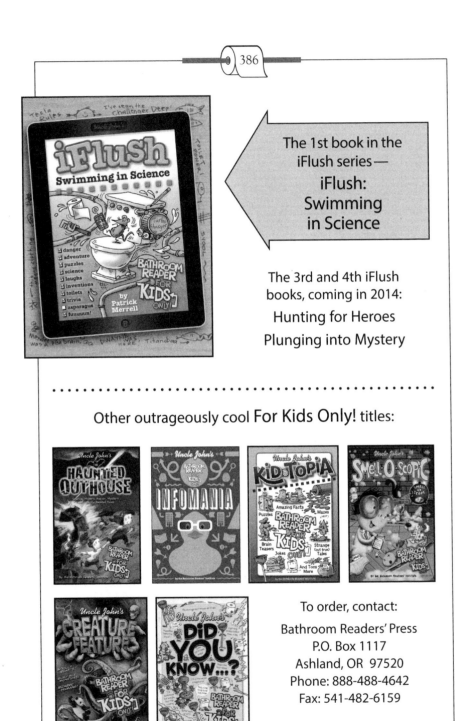